Salmon Ranching

Salmon Ranching

edited by

J. E. Thorpe

Department of Agriculture and Fisheries for Scotland
Freshwater Fisheries Laboratory
Faskally, Pitlochry
Perthshire, U.K.

1980

ACADEMIC PRESS

A Subsidiary of Harcourt Brace Jovanovich, Publishers

LONDON   NEW YORK   TORONTO   SYDNEY   SAN FRANCISCO

ACADEMIC PRESS INC. (LONDON) LTD.
24/28 Oval Road
London NW1

United States Edition published by
ACADEMIC PRESS INC.
111 Fifth Avenue
New York, New York 10003

British Library Cataloguing in Publication Data

Salmon ranching.
1. Salmon   2. Fish-culture
I. Thorpe, John
639'. 375'5   SH167.S17   80-41017

ISBN 0-12-690660-2

Printed in Great Britain by
The Lavenham Press Limited, Lavenham, Suffolk

Contributors

E. L. BAKSHTANSKY   *All-Union Research Institute of Marine Fisheries and Oceanography (VNIRO), 17 V. Krasnoselskaya, Moscow B-140, 107140, U.S.S.R.*

H. T. BILTON   *Fisheries and Marine Service, Pacific Biological Station, Nanaimo, British Columbia V9R 5K6, Canada.*

T. G. CAREY   *Fisheries and Oceans, 240 Sparks Street, Ottawa, Ontario, Canada.*

L. R. DONALDSON   *University of Washington, College of Fisheries, WH-10, Seattle, Washington 98195, U.S.A.*

Á. ÍSAKSSON   *Institute of Freshwater Fisheries, P.O. Box 754, 101 Reykjavik, Iceland.*

T. JOYNER   *1515, 4th Avenue North, Seattle, Washington 98109, U.S.A.*

T. KOBAYASHI   *Hokkaido Salmon Hatchery, Nakanoshima, Sapporo, Hokkaido, Japan.*

S. M. KONOVALOV   *Pacific Research Institute of Fisheries and Oceanography (TINRO), 4 Shevchenko Alley, 690600, Vladivostok, U.S.S.R.*

J. E. LANNAN   *Department of Fisheries and Wildlife, Oregon State University, Marine Science Center, Newport, Oregon 97365, U.S.A.*

P.-O. LARSSON   *Salmon Research Institute, S-810 70 Älvkarleby 1, Sweden.*

W. H. LEAR   *Department of Fisheries and Environment, Fisheries and Marine Service, Research and Resource Services, P.O. Box 5667, St. John's, Newfoundland A1C 5X1, Canada.*

W. J. MCNEIL   *Oregon Aquafoods Inc., 88700 Marcola Road, Springfield, Oregon 97477, U.S.A.*

J. H. MUNDIE   *Fisheries and Marine Service, Pacific Biological Station, Nanaimo, British Columbia V9R 5K6, Canada.*

A. J. NOVOTNY   *National Marine Fisheries Service, Northwest and Alaska Fisheries Center, 2725 Montlake Boulevard East, Seattle, Washington 98112, U.S.A.*

D. J. PIGGINS   *Salmon Research Trust of Ireland Inc., Farran Laboratory, Newport, Co. Mayo, Eire.*

J. A. RITTER   *Fisheries and Oceans, P. O. Box 550, Halifax, Nova Scotia, Canada*

J. E. THORPE   *Department of Agriculture and Fisheries for Scotland, Freshwater Fisheries Laboratory, Pitlochry PH16 5LB, Scotland, U.K.*

G. D. WAUGH   *Ministry of Agriculture and Fisheries, Fisheries Research Division, P. O. Box 19062, Wellington, New Zealand.*

Preface

All salmon species are dependent to a greater or lesser degree on the freshwater environment for reproduction and early development. Progressive modification of that environment by man, especially since the Industrial Revolution, through obstructions, pollution, water abstraction, and hydroelectric development, has had detrimental influence on salmon. Various approaches have been taken to compensate for the loss of salmonid production as a result of these changes, notably programmes of enhancement of natural stocks by cultivation of juveniles for release to sea at the time of natural seaward migration. Such programmes, started in the nineteenth century, have increased dramatically since the Second World War. Almost the entire Baltic salmon fishery is maintained by hatchery production of smolts, a necessary consequence of power generation on most of Sweden's rivers, 70-80% of the Japanese chum salmon industry (over 30 000 tons annually) depends on artificially reared juveniles, and currently Canada has a $300 million programme designed to boost the salmon output of British Columbia's rivers, to double the annual harvest which already has a landed value of over $1 billion annually. The U.S.A. and Japan have similar investments, and that of the U.S.S.R. is probably comparable. Recently both Japanese and American interests have built hatcheries in Chile, introducing salmon from the north Pacific in an attempt to use them as a means of harvesting the vast resources of Antarctic krill. Atlantic salmon have been planted in Argentina, and in the north Atlantic the Canadians, Icelanders, Irish and British are all enhancing the natural production of salmon from their rivers. In the Kola Peninsula the Russians have introduced Pacific Pink salmon to crop plankton in the Arctic, and various Pacific salmons have been introduced to the Laurentian Great Lakes in an attempt to rehabilitate salmonid fisheries there.

Cultivation of salmon has thus grown from an activity designed to maintain stocks into a ranching phase, where the potential of the animals is being exploited beyond the level achievable in the natural environment. This book attempts to describe the state of the art of salmon ranching through brief accounts from the various regions of the world in which it is practised. Species, rearing and exploitation methods, objectives and control measures all differ from region to region, but it will become clear that the practice is essentially the same although its state of development varies widely. These common elements lead to some overlap in the separate chapters. I have tried to reduce this repetition by limited cross-referencing between chapters.

The views expressed are those of individual authors and should not necessarily be construed as a common consensus.

Pitlochry, September 1980   *John Thorpe*

Contents

Contributors   v

Preface   vii

  1. The Development of Salmon Culture towards
      Ranching
      J. E. THORPE   1

  2. Salmon Ranching in Alaska
      W. J. MCNEIL   13

  3. Salmon Ranching in Washington State
      L. R. DONALDSON   29

  4. Salmon Ranching in Oregon
      J. E. LANNAN   47

  5. U.S.S.R.: Salmon Ranching in the Pacific
      S. M. KONOVALOV   63

  6. Salmon Propagation in Japan
      T. KOBAYASHI   91

  7. Salmon Ranching in the Atlantic Maritime
      Provinces of Canada
      J. A. RITTER and T. G. CAREY   109

  8. Salmon Ranching in Iceland
      Á. ÍSAKSSON   131

  9. Smolt Rearing and the Baltic Salmon Fishery
      P.-O. LARSSON   157

10. Salmon Ranching in Ireland
      D. J. PIGGINS   187

11. Salmon Ranching in Britain
      J. E. THORPE   199

12. The Pink Salmon Transplant Experiment in
      Newfoundland
      W. H. LEAR   213

13. Introduction of Pink Salmon into the Kola
      Peninsula
      E. L. BAKSHTANSKY   245

14. Salmon Ranching in South America
    T. JOYNER 261
15. Salmon in New Zealand
    G. D. WAUGH 277
16. Experimental Releases of Coho Salmon in British Columbia
    H. T. BILTON 305
17. Delayed Release of Salmon
    A. J. NOVOTNY 325
18. Intensive Use of Streams
    J. H. MUNDIE 371
19. Legal Aspects of Salmon Ranching in the Pacific
    W. J. MCNEIL 383
20. Salmon Ranching: Current Situation and Prospects
    J. E. THORPE 395
Index 407

Chapter 1

The Development of Salmon Culture towards Ranching

J. E. THORPE

Department of Agriculture and Fisheries for Scotland,
Freshwater Fisheries Laboratory, Pitlochry, Scotland

Salmon ranching is defined as an aquaculture system in which juvenile fish are released to grow, unprotected, on natural foods in marine waters from which they are harvested at marketable size (Thorpe, 1979). It is practised in slightly differing forms around the world, as will be evident from the following chapters. In its distinctive form the young fish are released to sea through ponds, enclosures or channels, to which they home on maturation and which thus become the harvesting devices. The success of the system depends on the high degree of homing accuracy of the salmon, which has been investigated in several species, notably in coho (*Oncorhynchus kisutch* Walbaum) and chinook (*O. tschawytscha* Walbaum) by Hasler and his co-workers at the University of Wisconsin (Cooper and Hasler, 1973, 1974, 1976; Cooper and Scholz, 1976; Cooper *et al.*, 1973, 1976).

The natural predators of salmon, including man, have taken advantage of their anadromous habits and have exploited them heavily as the mature adults aggregate in restricted estuarine and riverine environments after wide dispersal at sea. This habit has led to the development of a range of exploitation methods in the fishery which, as long as they concentrated on the individual river stocks and had inbuilt inefficiencies that allowed adequate escapement of breeding stock, permitted the maintenance of a valuable and sustainable high yield. A combination of human activities resulting in environmental degradation from the salmon's viewpoint, together with overfishing,

1

especially through the development of extensive open-sea fisheries, has resulted in a general decline of salmon stocks in both the North Atlantic and Pacific basins (Netboy, 1974). In an attempt to reverse this trend, heavy investment was made in hatcheries to maintain the output of juvenile migrants into the oceans and thus maintain the numerical strength of the exploitable stocks. This management activity, initially largely an act of faith, has become refined into a disciplined and rational practice as information has accumulated on the biology of salmonid fishes, in particular on their freshwater developmental phase, migratory behaviour and homing precision. The historical development of salmon conservation practices in various parts of the world is traced in this book. Methods developed in one continent have been copied in another, adapted to the specific needs of different species, and modified to suit local conditions. However, in essence they are aimed at the same goal: the maintenance of a plentiful supply of salmon which can support heavy human predation.

Total annual production of tissue by a population of animals depends on two factors: the number of individuals in the population and their growth rate. The upper limitation on numbers in a salmon population is most probably determined by the restricted availability of spawning substrate and nursery ground for juveniles in rivers. Over 95% of the increase in weight of individuals occurs during the ocean phase, in which limitations on growth are not well understood. The decrease in the size of the salmon harvest has occurred through reduction of the numerical element of production, both directly through removal of too many potential spawners and indirectly through environmental alterations which decreased the availability of spawning and nursery grounds. Conservation measures have aimed at mitigating the effects of both these major intrusions. Regulation of fishing methods, seasons, and areas, together with imposition of quotas, have all been designed to curb the deleterious effects of overfishing. Environmental improvements, such as anti-pollution measures, fishways, spawning channels, and compensation flows, have aimed at rectifying the major physical changes imposed on salmon habitat by the industrial use of rivers. The former controls can only work within the range of possibilities achieved by the latter, and these still impose severe numerical restrictions which are ultimately dependent on the biological productivity of rivers and their capacity to support populations of small predatory fish.

Hatcheries represent controlled environments in which energy inputs to the fish stocks can be maintained at levels above those normally available in the wild. High growth rates can thus be achieved, and through the minimising of disadvantageous features of the wild environment mortalities can be reduced to trivial levels and the numerical element of production kept at 10-100 times that achievable in nature. Hatcheries provide a way not only of compensating for loss of natural stocks but also of increasing production beyond the level possible in natural environments. This general proposition was seized on avidly in the late nineteenth and early twentieth centuries and applied throughout the range of salmon species. Hatcheries were set up well in advance of the biological knowledge required for their successful operation and use, in many areas bankruptcy and discredit followed, and enthusiasm for the practice waned (Bowen, 1972). Although inefficient and (where evaluated) uneconomic, some hatchery programmes persisted for public relations or social amenity reasons, and accumulating knowledge of the biological needs of the salmon species permitted refinements of design, husbandry, and breeding programmes ultimately leading to the efficient and economic production systems in use today. These systems have developed in two ways: when ready to move to sea, the fish can either be released into the wild or be transferred to seawater enclosures (tanks, pens or impoundments) for on-growing in captivity to market size. This book is concerned only with the first method, but it is pertinent at the start to contrast the two approaches.

Total culture in enclosures has the advantage of control over the stock throughout life, so there is a reasonable hope of retention to marketable size of the total numbers transferred to seawater. Release of fish to sea involves the number harvestable ultimately being reduced to 1-15% of the number released, depending on species and locality. Both systems involve feeding the fish up to the seawater stage (about 1% of their total lifetime food requirement); from then on captive fish require feeding throughout life, whereas the released fish do not. Satisfactory diets are based on high-grade protein, primarily fish-meal, obtained through traditional fisheries which depend on the maintenance of increasingly expensive fleets of ships. With the increasing sophistication of detection and capture devices, these fleets threaten to deplete fish populations beyond the point at which they are self-sustaining. With increasing scarcity of fish the fleets move further afield, increasing logistic costs, social disruption, and human risk. Cage culture depends on the continuing supply of protein from such fisheries, so cultivated salmon become net consumers rather than producers of available protein. Ranching substitutes predatory fish for ships: the growing free-ranging salmon obtains its own protein by foraging, packages this in a form highly acceptable for human consumption, and returns to deliver itself to the harvester with only minimal use of boats in the whole production process. As they are likely to concentrate for much of their feeding on small life-forms, unexploited by or presently unavailable to man, they represent net producers of available protein.

Mathews *et al.* (1976) have made the comparison in energy terms (Table I): because the released fish are being used as harvesters of marine protein at no energy cost to the ultimate exploiter, the energy/efficiency ratio (i.e. energy value of the product divided by the energy cost of producing or obtaining it) of this production system was approximately twice that of the cage-cultivation system. That the difference between the two was not greater was largely because of the current dependence on production facilities of high energy cost at the freshwater stage. The authors pointed out that if substantial reductions in energy costs at this stage could be achieved, salmon ranching (as opposed to cage cultivation) could become more efficient than milk production, which was currently the most energy-efficient protein production system. Recent developments in rearing methods of the pre-release stages of some salmon in Alaska, using protected lenses of freshwater floating over seawater, promise well for such an achievement.

Whatever the precise details of the mechanisms by which salmon distinguish the characteristics of their natal streams and orientate into

Table I. Energy/efficiency ratios of U.S. animal protein-producing systems. (After Mathews *et al.*, 1976.)

System	Ratio (%)
Beef, grain-fed	10
Salmon, pen-reared	13
Bottom fish, otter-trawled	16
Salmon, ranched	25
Beef, grass-fed	35
Eggs	40
Milk, grass-fed	100

them, it seems likely that other mechanisms govern their orientation in the oceans. It is known that fish from widely separated geographical areas intermingle on feeding grounds sometimes thousands of miles from their natal streams, so these mechanisms of orientation must also differ in action (either in character or timing) between populations belonging to different areas and within areas to different rivers and streams. Maintenance of this distinction of action of orientation mechanisms is most easily considered as genetically determined but, as with most biological capacities, environmentally modifiable. Cooper and Hasler (1976) have shown that coho salmon and rainbow trout (*Salmo gairdneri* Richardson) have the capacity to distinguish specific chemical compounds present in water at high dilution. Scholz *et al.* (1976) have shown that they use this capacity to distinguish the home stream from other waters. However, this capacity was revealed and tested by training the fish through exposure to unnatural chemical cues, and it was found that the timing of imprinting with these cues was critical, implying that wild fish acquire home orientational information at a precise period of outmigration as smolts. It was assumed for a long time that freshwater played an indispensable role in this imprinting process, but it has now been demonstrated in America that various species can be imprinted to home to seawater sites, and several commercial salmon ranches have now been started using seawater release and recovery facilities (see Chapter 4).

In view of the high probability of genetic discreteness of individual stream and river stocks (Simon and Larkin, 1972; Saunders and Bailey, 1979), any rational system of salmon exploitation should attempt to treat each stock as a separate unit. In the absence of adequate knowledge of the degree of mixing of these stocks at sea, exploitation should be concentrated preferably on the stocks once they have segregated, i.e. at or within the river mouths (cf. *Fish Farming International,* 1978). Even this limitation on exploitation method is hardly adequate in large river systems, where there may be many discrete stocks. However, on the assumption of high homing precision and with the possibility of reinforcing this by decoying returning fish following imprinting them as smolts, ranching offers the opportunity of concentrating exploitation precisely on one artificially maintained stock, with minimal interference to the neighbouring wild populations. It has another major biological advantage. The survival of juvenile hatchery salmon to the smolt stage may be 10-100 times higher than that of equivalent wild juvenile fish, and production of large quantities of smolts for augmentation of river stocks is achieved through the use of relatively few brood fish with a restricted range of genetic diversity. Survival to spawning of these hatchery fish therefore threatens to reduce the genetic range of that river's population and thus its evolutionary adaptability to environmental change in the system (cf. Vida, 1978). To reduce this risk, very large numbers of brood fish are required for hatchery spawnings. Ranchers, however, can afford to select their stock and to narrow the range of genetic expression in their populations to suit the specific needs of their form of fishery, because it is axiomatic that high homing precision and low probability of escapement to participate in the wild reproducing population are required of these fish. "Artificial" stocks, distinct from the wild, can be developed, requiring a very low proportion of spawners for "escapement" and allowing a very high level of exploitation.

Taking into account the high mortality of these fish between release as smolts and recovery as mature adults, the return to the rancher is currently of the order of 2-50 kg of salmon per kg of smolts released (see Chapters 7 to 11). This yield varies with species and has recently reached almost 300 kg adults per kg of pink salmon fry (*O. gorbuscha* Walbaum) released at an Alaskan enterprise in 1978 (*Fish Farming International,* 1979a). In economic terms McNeil (1979) reported that $1 invested in hatchery production in the U.S.S.R. and Japan yielded $50 in produce (see also Chapter 6).

Moiseev (1977) and others have suggested that maricultural practices will ultimately replace traditional fisheries. However, this will not happen rapidly, and the ranching form of mariculture has developed in association and competition with conventional fisheries. For example, the greater part of the salmon catch in both the Pacific Ocean and the Baltic Sea is taken on the high seas, not in estuarine or river fisheries (see Chapters 2 and 10). To maintain such fisheries economically requires conservation and management measures, involving agreements by national bodies and funded from taxes, levies or licences on the fishery operators, from general public funds, or from revenue obtained through competing activities (*Fish Farming International,* 1979b; Crutchfield 1972). For example, Sweden sees the maintenance of the large Baltic salmon (*Salmo salar* L.) fishery as part of the cost of producing hydroelectricity and requires the power companies to maintain the output of salmon smolts from rivers modified and obstructed for power generation, by cultivation of these in hatcheries, and release at specified locations along the Baltic coast. The U.S.A., Canada, U.S.S.R. and Japan have all attempted to maintain the Pacific salmon harvest by augmenting the natural output of smolts from their rivers, especially where this has been severely reduced by river modifications, and by overfishing.

Overfishing has become the subject of international fishery regulation, with zoning of extraterritorial waters for fishing by specific nations, and more recently by control of the quantities of fish removed from such mixed stocks by limiting the entry of vessels and operators (Adasiak, 1977, 1979; Crutchfield, 1977, 1979; Fraser, 1979; Pearse and Wilen, 1979; Rogers, 1979; Young, 1977). Regulation of fishing by seasons and quotas is aimed primarily at conserving the total stock and ensuring an adequate escapement for reproduction and thus recruitment to future fisheries. Such regulations are essential with current methods of exploitation, but ultimately become less so in the practice of ranching. Since complete ranching involves the maintenance of a discrete stock of fishes returning to harvest points controlled by the rancher, the necessary regulatory measures to ensure the continuance of his business lie in the rancher's own hands. Hence current legislation designed to protect wild self-maintaining stocks is relevant to the practice of ranching only where open sea fisheries may affect the ranchers' stocks. New statutes become necessary to define the ownership of ranched fish and the conditions under which they may be reared, introduced into the wild, and harvested from it, to avoid conflict with existing traditional fisheries and measures designed to protect them. Several countries are considering these problems actively (Chapters, 2, 4, 5, 8, 9, 10, 11, 12, 16, 19), but for the foreseeable future it will be necessary for the rancher to regard the loss of a portion of his harvestable fish to the high-seas fishermen as a part of the unavoidable cost of doing business.

It is a small conceptual step, but a large practical one, from ranching a species within its native range to ranching it as an introduced species elsewhere. Most of the early attempts to transplant salmon species into new environments failed (Davidson and Hutchinson, 1938; McNeil, 1976), but some succeeded (e.g. chinook salmon in New Zealand, Chapter 15) and, more recently, sustained plantings of pink salmon in arctic European Russia have resulted in the establishment of reproducing stocks (see Chapter 13). Coho and chinook salmon have been introduced to the American Great Lakes (Scott, 1976), originally to aid in the restoration of these environments as suitable habitats for the native salmonids, but, with success, demand for their retention and more widescale use has built up there. As well as inherent problems in matching exotic species with appropriate environments (see Chapter 14), there are also problems of biological interference with native species. The full implications of these may never be completely understood, but immediate effects upon native species of importance to man must be considered. Within the temperate northern hemisphere, salmonids have evolved all around the Atlantic and Pacific shores, specific radiation being greater in the Pacific, but the plasticity and adaptability of the fewer Atlantic species may be comparatively greater. With high salmon diversity in the Pacific there seems little virtue in introducing exotic salmons there. With relatively low diversity in the Atlantic the idea of introductions is tempting but must be viewed with extreme caution. The pink salmon introductions in the Kola peninsula (Chapter 13) led to widespread occurrence of stray fishes in Norway and casual fishes in Iceland and Scotland. Norway now has a fishery for them, and there may be established stocks reproducing in its northern rivers. It is not clear what interactions occur between this species and the native Atlantic salmon (*Salmo salar* L.) sea-trout (*Salmo trutta* L.) and arctic char (*Salvelinus alpinus* L.), but since they live sympatrically at times it would be surprising if conflicts did not arise. Since the introduced fish has spread, the interactions must by implication be in its favour and therefore at the expense of the native species. The benefit of introducing such a salmonid of relatively low value becomes doubtful if it results in the restriction of more valuable native ones.

Introductions outside the temperate northern hemisphere have other implications, particularly for the biological needs of the species being introduced, as is clear from the account of introductions into New Zealand (Chapter 15); it is considered further in Chapter 20. However, all such introductions for ranching depend on the assumption that the homing behaviour of the species can work adequately in environments alien to those in which the species evolved. The successful establishment of salmon in New Zealand and of sea-trout in southern South America confirms the validity of this assumption for the species concerned in these specific localities, but their mechanisms of oceanic orientation are almost totally unknown. When more is discovered, it may be possible to manipulate these mechanisms to the rancher's advantage, and leads in this direction have been provided through delayed-release studies in the U.S.A. (see Chapter 17; Saunders 1977). As more becomes known of the biology of the fish, the greater become the possibilities of manipulation and control and thus of harnessing the productivity of salmon species for human advantage. This volume surveys the current state of the practice of ranching salmon world wide and discusses some of the promising developments and potentially valuable manipulations that are becoming available.

REFERENCES

Adasiak, A. (1977). Limited entry in Alaska. In Ellis, D. V. (ed.) *Pacific Salmon Management for People.* pp. 187-225. Western Geogr. Ser. 13, 320 pp. Univ. Brit. Columbia.

Adasiak, A. (1979). Alaska's experience with limited entry. *J. Fish. Res. Bd Can.,* **36**, 770-782.

Berg, M. (1977). Pink salmon, *Oncorhynchus gorbuscha* (Walbaum) in Norway. *Rep. Inst. Freshwat. Res. Drottningholm,* **56**, 12-17.

Bowen, J. T. (1970). A history of fish culture as related to the development of fishery programs. pp. 71-93. *In* "A Century of Fisheries in North America" (ed. N. G. Benson). Amer. Fish. Soc. Spec. Publ. 7. Washington.

Cooper, J. C. and Hasler, A. D. (1973). An electrophysiological approach to salmon homing. *Fish. Res. Bd Can., Tech. Rep.* **415**, 44.

Cooper, J. C. and Hasler, A. D. (1974). Electroencephalographic evidence for retention of olfactory cues in homing coho salmon. *Science* **183**, 336-338.

Cooper, J. C. and Hasler, A. D. (1976). Electrophysiological studies of morpholine-imprinted coho salmon *(Oncorhynchus kisutch)* and rainbow trout *(Salmo gairdneri). J. Fish. Res. Bd. Can.* **33**, 688-694.

Cooper, J. C. and Scholz, A. T. (1976). Homing of artificially imprinted steelhead (rainbow) trout, *Salmo gairdneri. J. Fish. Res. Bd. Can.* **33**, 826-829.

Cooper, J. C., Scholz, A. T., Horrall, R. M., Hasler, A. D. and Madison, D. M. (1976). Experimental confirmation of the olfactory hypothesis with homing, artificially imprinted coho salmon *(Oncorhynchus kisutch). J. Fish. Res. Bd. Can.* **33**, 703-710.

Crutchfield, J. A. (1972). Economic and political objectives in fishery management. pp. 74-89. *In* "World Fisheries Policy" (Ed. B. J. Rothschild). Seattle.

Crutchfield, J. A. (1977). The Fishery—economic maximization. pp. 1-30. *In* "Pacific Salmon Management for People" (Ed. D. V. Ellis). Western Geogr. Ser. 13, 320 pp. Univ. Brit. Columbia.

Crutchfield, J. A. (1979). Economic and social implications of the main policy alternatives for controlling fishing effort. *J. Fish Res. Bd. Can.* **36**, 742-752.

Davidson, F. A. and Hutchinson, S. J. (1938). The geographic distribution and environmental limitations of the Pacific salmon (genus *Oncorhynchus*). *U.S. Bur. Fish. Bull.* **48**, 667-692.

Fish Farming International (1978). Should salmon be grown for fishermen? **5** (4), 3.

Fish Farming International (1979a). Remarkable one in five return of salmon. **5** (5), 3.

Fish Farming International (1979b). Fishermen pay to boost chinook run. **5** (5), 3.

Fraser, G. A. (1979). Limited entry: experience of the British Columbia salmon fishery. *J. Fish. Res. Bd. Can.* **36**, 754-763.

Mathews, S. B., Mock, J. B., Willson, K. and Senn, H. (1976). Energy efficiency of Pacific salmon aquaculture. *Progve. Fish. Cult.* **38**, 102-106.

McNeil, W. J., (1976). Review of transplantation and artificial recruitment of anadromous species. *FAO Tech. Conf. on Aquaculture, Kyoto:* Paper R24, 10 pp.

McNeil, W. J. (1979). Reported in *Aquaculture Digest* **4** (6), 28.

Moiseev, P. A. (1977). Living resources of the world ocean: prospects of utilization and augmentation. *Proc. 5th Japan—Soviet Joint Symp. Aquaculture, Tokyo and Sapporo:* 14-18.

Netboy, A. (1974). "The Salmon, their fight for survival". Houghton Mifflin Co., Boston. 613 pp.

Pearse, P. H. and Wilen, J. E. (1979). Impact of Canada's Pacific salmon fleet control program. *J. Fish. Res. Bd. Can.* **36**, 764-769.

Rogers, G. W. (1979). Alaska's limited entry program: another view. *J. Fish. Res. Bd. Can.* **36**, 783-788.

Saunders, R. L. (1977). Sea ranching—a promising way to enhance populations of Atlantic salmon for angling and commercial fisheries. *Int. Atl. Salmon Foundation,* Spec. Publ. 7, 17-24.

Saunders, R. L. and Bailey, J. K. (1979). The role of genetics in Atlantic salmon management. *In* "Atlantic Salmon: its future" (Ed. A. E. J. Went). Fishing News Books, Farnham.

Scholz, A. T., Cooper, J. C., Madison, D. M., Horrall, R. M., Hasler, A. D., Dizon, A. E. and Poff, R. J. (1973). Olfactory imprinting in coho salmon: behavioural and electrophysiological evidence. *Proc. 16th Conf. Great Lakes Res.* 143-153.

Scholz, A. T., Horrall, R. M., Cooper, J. C. and Hasler, A. D. (1976). Imprinting to chemical cues: the basis for home stream selection in salmon. *Science* **192**, 1247-1249.

Scott, J. A. (1976). History of introduction of coho and chinook salmon into waters of the Great Lakes. Abstract of paper given at *Amer. Fish. Soc. Ann. Meeting,* 1976.

Simon, R. C. and Larkin, P. A. (eds) (1972). *The Stock Concept in Pacific Salmon.* H. R. MacMillan Lectures in Fisheries, University of British Columbia. 231 pp.

Thorpe, J. E. (1979). Ocean ranching: general considerations. *In* "Atlantic Salmon: its future" (Ed. A. E. J. Went). Fishing News Books, Farnham.

Vida, G. (1978). Genetic diversity and environmental future. *Env. Conserv.* 127-132.

Young, O. (1977). *Resource Management at the International Level: the case of the North Pacific.* Pinter, London, and Nichols Publishing Co., New York. 252 pp.

Chapter 2

Salmon Ranching in Alaska

W. J. McNEIL

Oregon Aquafoods Inc., Springfield, Oregon, U.S.A.

INTRODUCTION

An ambitious programme to rehabilitate depleted salmon fisheries is emerging in Alaska. Public and private hatcheries are being phased into operation in western, central, and south-east Alaska as a result of joint planning by government, commercial fishermen, and other groups. The Alaska legislature has authorised low-interest loans administered by the state to finance private non-profit hatcheries. Public hatcheries are being financed through the sale of state bonds.

The programme has been gaining momentum since 1974, when the private sector was first authorised by the Alaska legislature to participate in salmon ranching. The first major bond issue for public hatcheries was also approved by Alaska voters in 1974. Numerous economic, social, biological, environmental, and engineering problems are recognised as obstacles to the future success of salmon ranching in Alaska. The ingredient most critical to success, however, could be the willingness of the Alaska salmon industry, particularly fishermen, and government to work together to achieve common objectives. A successful programme also requires a strong commitment from educational institutions as well as research laboratories to provide technically trained people and the knowledge necessary to implement it.

Salmon hatcheries have been constructed or are under construction in diverse geographic regions within Alaska (Fig. 1). It is somewhat premature to attempt an evaluation of contributions of these facilities to salmon fisheries, but there are indications that at least some projects

13

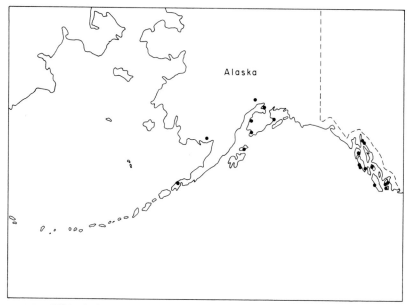

Fig. 1. Locations of salmon ranching facilities in Alaska.

will be successful. Research hatcheries have been operated successfully for several years at two locations in south-east Alaska and in the Kodiak Island area and have generated good returning runs of pink salmon *(Oncorhynchus gorbuscha)* and coho salmon *(O. kisutch)*. The first solid evidence of an economically successful private salmon ranching project occurred at Sitka, Alaska, in the summer of 1977. A hatchery operated by Sheldon Jackson College released 1·7 million juvenile pink salmon in spring 1976, and 125 000 adult pink salmon returned to the campus hatchery, located in downtown Sitka, in summer 1977 (Fig. 2). Earnings from the sale of surplus fish have been invested by Sheldon Jackson College in the education of aquaculture specialists for Alaska's emerging salmon ranching programme.

Alaska's second private hatchery, located in Prince William Sound and operated by a fishermen's association, also enjoyed a successful season in 1977. Despite handicaps imposed by a severe winter on a partially completed hatchery, Prince William Sound fishermen managed to release one million pink salmon fry which generated a return of 60 000 adults to the hatchery in 1977.

This chapter considers several questions relating to the emergence of salmon ranching in Alaska and likely to affect future directions of the

Fig. 2. Salmon hatchery on the campus of Sheldon Jackson College, Sitka, Alaska, 1976.

programme. The steady decline of salmon stocks has led to depressed salmon fisheries in many Alaska fishing areas. The depressed state of the salmon fisheries along with successful applications of technology for artificial propagation of salmon in other states and countries led to major policy decisions by Alaska law-makers in the 1970s. These policy decisions have provided a foundation for salmon ranching by private and public institutions. However, implementation of salmon ranching in Alaska has raised biological, social, and economic problems which can influence the future participation of private and public institutions. It is too early to decide whether the programme will trend more toward private enterprise or public agency involvement.

GROWTH AND DECLINE OF SALMON FISHERIES

Alaska's economic development has in the past been closely tied to salmon fisheries on wild stocks. There is much speculation about the continued dependence of the Alaska economy on salmon and the role of salmon ranching in it.

The United States government purchased Alaska from Russia in 1867, and commercial exploitation of Alaska's salmon resources began in 1878, when canneries began to operate in south-east Alaska. Exploitation continued to expand until salmon stocks began to decline in most areas of the state by the 1940s. Record low catches occurred in the early 1970s (Fig. 3), stimulating the Alaska legislature to authorise funds for construction of public hatcheries and for loan programmes to assist private hatcheries.

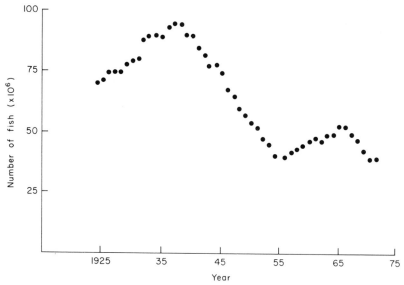

Fig. 3. Ten-year moving average of catch of Pacific salmon in Alaska.

HISTORY OF ARTIFICIAL PROPAGATION

Hatchery production of salmon in Alaska dates back to 1891, when private operators began to release juvenile salmon into the Karluk River, Kodiak Island. This was not the first attempt to propagate Pacific salmon by artificial means: the modern history of salmon ranching in the Pacific Ocean dates back at least to 1872, when the U.S. Fish Commission established a hatchery on the McCloud River,

California. The first private hatchery was established on the Rogue River, Oregon, in 1877. The emerging technology for artificial propagation of salmon was introduced to Japan in 1877 and to western Canada in 1884.

The first Alaska salmon hatchery in 1891 was soon followed by others: in 1892, the second private Alaska hatchery was constructed in south-east Alaska, and at least six private salmon hatcheries were established before the turn of the century. In 1900, the U.S. Congress enacted a law requiring salmon canneries to operate hatcheries. Congress revised the law in 1906 to provide tax incentives for canneries which complied voluntarily with regulations calling for artificial propagation of ten fry for each adult fish harvested by commercial fishermen. By the end of 1906, private hatcheries in Alaska had released approximately 450 million salmon fry, mostly sockeye *(O. nerka)* and some coho salmon.

Only private hatcheries existed in Alaska until 1905, when the U.S. Fish Commission constructed a hatchery in south-east Alaska. A second federal hatchery was constructed in the Kodiak Island area in 1917, by which time only four private hatcheries remained active. Also in 1917, the territorial legislature first appropriated funds for public hatcheries. Territorial hatcheries were operated at Cordova, Ketchikan, and Seward until 1927, when the programme was terminated. The Ketchikan hatchery was assigned to the Territorial Board of Road Commissioners and continued to operate after 1927, but the hatcheries at Cordova and Seward were closed. The two federal hatcheries closed in 1933, and the last of the early private hatcheries closed in 1936.

The early period of salmon hatcheries in Alaska lasted 45 years (1891-1936) (Roppel, 1978). Expectations of large returning runs of hatchery-produced salmon were never realised. Wild salmon remained abundant during this early period, and there was little incentive to perfect hatchery technology. Sockeye salmon fry were released by the hundreds of millions into streams which flowed directly into marine waters. Most of these hatchery fry must have been swept downstream to almost certain death in high salinity water. Sockeye require one to three years of freshwater growth in lakes before emigrating to sea, and the basic biological requirements of this species were generally ignored by hatchery operators, who were committed only to hatching eggs and dumping fry.

EVOLUTION OF TECHNOLOGY

Early hatcheries in North America raised mostly those species of salmon whose juveniles acquire freshwater growth before emigrating to sea. Sockeye was the principal species raised in Alaska and Canada. Chinook *(O. tshawytscha)* was favoured most in the Pacific Northwest states, along with coho. Little attention was paid to artificial propagation of pink and chum salmon *(O. keta)* in North America, but in Asia the Japanese applied hatchery technology primarily to chum and, to a lesser extent, pink salmon.

Neither pink nor chum salmon have a requirement for freshwater feeding, and the technology for their artificial propagation is therefore less complex than for other species, in which facilities are provided to grow juveniles in captivity much beyond fry and fingerling stages. The new hatchery programme in Alaska will concentrate on pink and chum salmon, and technology will be adapted in many instances from that used in Japan and the U.S.S.R.

Japan *(see also Chapter 6)*

Most Japanese hatcheries employ gravel-lined raceways to incubate larval salmon (alevins). Use of a substrate for incubation of salmon alevins is being applied extensively in new public and private hatcheries throughout Alaska. The practice of short-term feeding of newly emerged chum fry on artificial diets in Japanese hatcheries is also expected to find widespread application in Alaska. Chum salmon fry weigh about 0.4 grams when they begin to feed. The Japanese usually release them at a size of about one gram. Methods currently employed in Japanese salmon hatcheries are described in detail by Moberly and Lium (1977).

The Japanese hatchery programme has undergone rapid expansion in recent years. A five-year programme is under way to increase capacity of salmon hatcheries from 1·4 billion eggs to 2·0 billion eggs by 1980. A previous five-year programme resulted in egg capacity increasing from 0·7 billion in 1971 to 1·4 billion in 1976.

U.S.S.R. *(see also Chapter 5)*

In 1976, the Soviet programme included at least 24 hatcheries, mostly on Sakhalin Island. Pink and chum salmon are raised in about equal numbers in Soviet hatcheries, using technology similar to that used in Japan. Production of juvenile salmon from Soviet hatcheries compares favourably with that from Japanese hatcheries (Fig. 4) although the Soviets operate far fewer hatcheries. Individual Soviet hatcheries typically produce about 40 million juvenile salmon annually, with the

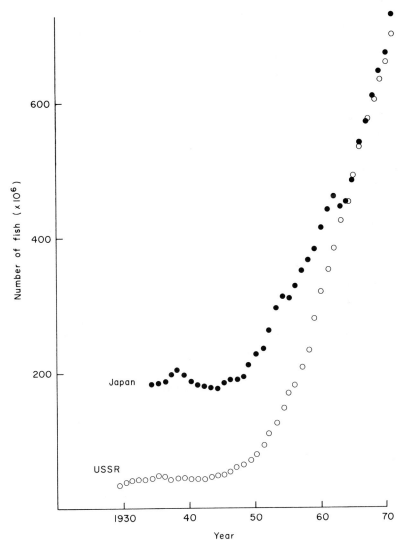

Fig. 4. Ten-year moving averages of production of pink and chum salmon juveniles from hatcheries in Japan and the U.S.S.R.

largest hatchery producing about 140 million. Many new hatcheries in Alaska will follow the Soviet example for large-scale production to achieve efficiency of scale.

Pacific Northwest *(see also Chapters 3-4)*

Raceways and ponds for feeding juvenile fish are prominent features of most salmon hatcheries in the Pacific Northwest (Fig. 5), because chinook and coho salmon are the species that are raised predominantly. Salmon hatchery programmes in the Pacific Northwest have generated technological innovations in the following areas which are likely to find application in Alaska:

Disease diagnosis, prevention, and control;
Nutritional requirements of salmon and artificial diets;
Water quality management;
Storage and transport of eggs and sperm;
Transport of juvenile fish;
Control of age, size, and time of smoltification;
Control of adult homing behaviour;
Tagging;
Genetic selection.

Canada

Canadian workers have pioneered development and application of spawning and egg incubation channels. Channels provide favourable environmental conditions for eggs and alevins and have been applied most successfully to sockeye, pink, and chum salmon. Difficult topographic and climatic conditions and other environmental constraints are likely to make construction of similar facilities too costly for practical application in many areas of Alaska.

Substrate incubators are among the most recent innovations to originate in Canada for salmon ranching. A variety of incubators using gravel and various artificial media for substrate materials are also being evaluated in Alaska (Fig. 6).

Alaska

Construction and operation of salmon hatcheries is made difficult in Alaska because of topography, climate, geography, and logistics.

Fig. 5. Raceways for growing juvenile salmon at a private hatchery operated by Oregon Aquafoods, Inc., near Springfield, Oregon.

Fig. 6. Substrate incubators for pink salmon in a hatchery near Juneau, Alaska. (Photo courtesy of NMFS-Alaska by J. M. Olson.)

Fig. 7. Floating raceways and netpens for salmon ranching, Baranof Island, Alaska. (Photograph courtesy of NMFS-Alaska.)

Application of existing technology in Alaska frequently requires modification to accommodate environmental constraints. Rough terrain, for example, may make it impractical to locate raceways for growing young salmon on land. An alternative is to locate floating structures in protected saltwater bays (Fig. 7). The floating raceway is but one example of innovative technology which will find application in Alaska with expansion of programmes for artificial propagation of salmon.

INSTITUTIONAL FRAMEWORK FOR SALMON RANCHING

Alaska law is designed to provide a framework for co-operative planning between public and private sectors for construction and operation of hatcheries to benefit common property salmon fisheries. This programme began in 1971 when the Alaska legislature created the Fisheries Rehabilitation and Enhancement Division (FRED) within the Alaska Department of Fish and Game. By 1977, FRED had assumed responsibility for operation of state hatcheries and regulation of private hatcheries. Creation of FRED in 1971 has been followed by additional legislation to provide an institutional framework for salmon ranching in Alaska:

1972. Alaska constitution amended by public referendum to permit legislation authorising limited entry to fisheries and aquaculture.

1973. Bill for limited entry to fisheries becomes law and is first applied to salmon fisheries.

1974. Bill authorising private non-profit salmon hatcheries becomes law.
First permits for private non-profit hatcheries issued.
State bonds approved for construction of public salmon hatcheries.

1975. Private non-profit hatcheries begin operations in south-east Alaska and Prince William Sound.
Bill authorising state loan programme to help finance private non-profit hatcheries becomes law.

1976. Legislation authorising private non-profit hatcheries (1974 law) amended to encourage formation of regional hatchery associations of fishermen and other user groups. Amended law also authorises formation of regional planning teams consisting of representatives from government and industry. Legislation authorising state loans for private non-profit hatcheries (1975 law) amended to provide more favourable conditions for hatchery operators to repay state.

1977. Legislation authorising private non-profit hatcheries (1974 law as amended in 1976) further amended to authorise formation of salmon enhancement authorities.

The advantages of an institutional framework for private non-profit hatcheries are mostly economic (Orth, 1978). By allowing the private sector to participate in salmon ranching, the state avoids total dependence on public institutions, which tend to be isolated from the discipline imposed by normal market forces. Furthermore, the incentive structure of private hatcheries should be more conducive to cost efficiency and productivity than public hatcheries. The production of salmon by the private sector relieves the state of the heavy annual financial burden of operating hatcheries, which can detract from resources available for managing fisheries on wild and hatchery stocks.

SOME UNANSWERED QUESTIONS

Restoration of Alaska salmon fisheries to historic levels would add about 75 million salmon annually to the catch. It is estimated that full restoration with artificial propagation would require a hatchery system capable of handling between 3·6 and 6·2 billion salmon eggs annually (McNeil, 1976a). Although the State of Alaska plans a somewhat more modest long-term production goal with hatcheries, a very large hatchery programme is in the making. Potential impacts on Alaska salmon fisheries are substantial, and there are a number of questions which require careful assessment:

Protection of Natural Populations from Over-fishing

Hatchery production of salmon raises questions vital to conservation of natural populations, especially where naturally and artificially propagated fish intermingle in a common property fishery. Hatchery fish can withstand a much higher rate of exploitation than wild fish. The fishery manager faces a dilemma: if the common property fishery is permitted to remove hatchery fish surplus to the needs of reproduction, any intermingled natural populations will be overfished and rapidly depleted; if exploitation is held down to conserve natural populations, surplus fish will return to hatcheries in substantial numbers.

The problem of managing fisheries on mixed stocks is fundamental to conservation of natural populations whether or not fish are produced in hatcheries. Inability to resolve this problem (often due more to social than biological problems) is possibly the key factor contributing to depletion of salmon in Alaska. Hatcheries have the potential of confounding or relieving the problem of managing fisheries on mixed populations, depending on how they are used. Comprehensive regional planning is essential to determine locations of hatcheries, species produced, levels of production, and methods and locations of harvesting surplus fish.

Genetic Adaptation

When salmon are removed from their natural environment, spawned artificially, and raised in the controlled environment of a hatchery, they become exposed to new sets of environmental experiences. The hatchery environment minimises many of the stresses that greatly reduce egg-to-fry survival rates in nature, but the hatchery can impose other stresses which are not experienced by wild fish to the same degree. The genetic question of greatest concern is whether the hatchery will contribute to loss of adaptive genetic variability which might affect the ability of fish to adapt to changing environmental conditions. Although this problem is somewhat speculative, it is prudent to take precautions which will minimise genetic risks associated with artificial propagation until more is known about the impact of hatcheries on the genetic adaptation of stocks.

Transplantation of Stocks

The record of successful transplantation of salmon stocks is mixed (McNeil, 1976b). Success of a hatchery is best assured by using a stock native to the hatchery stream. The next best alternative is to transplant stocks from nearby streams (or lakes) which have environmental characteristics similar to the hatchery water source.

Transplantations over long distances have proved successful in some instances, but more often transplanted stocks fail to adapt to a new environment. Transplantations also carry the risk of spreading disease to areas where it might not otherwise occur. Most countries and states, Alaska included, require testing and certification of transplanted stocks to be free of specified disease agents.

Capacity of Natural Waters to Grow Salmon

There is every indication that the number of salmon recruited to marine waters from hatcheries and spawning channels will increase steadily in the years ahead and could double in about ten years if recent rates of growth of hatchery programmes are sustained. It is not too soon to examine the danger of overstocking the ocean with juvenile salmon. This may seem an academic exercise in Alaska, where stocks are depleted, but experience in Japan and elsewhere suggests that improvements in technology combined with high economic value of salmon provide a foundation for rapid expansion of salmon production through artificial methods.

The Japanese release primarily chum salmon from private and public hatcheries. Approximately 30% of the total tonnage of Pacific salmon harvested by all nations consists of chum salmon. Japanese fishermen account for slightly more than 50% of the world catch of chum salmon, and about 50% of these are fish from their own hatcheries. Simple arithmetic ($0.3 \times 0.5 \times 0.5 = 0.075$) leads to the conclusion that chum salmon from Japanese hatcheries alone contribute 7-8% of the tonnage of salmon from all sources. Because the production of chum salmon from Japanese hatcheries represents about 40% of all artificially propagated salmon, it is possible that the present contribution of artificial propagation to the world supply of Pacific salmon is approaching 20%.

Implementation of the Alaska salmon fisheries plan (*Alaska Dept. Fish and Game*, 1977) would add approximately 2·5 billion juvenile salmon to the release of artificially propagated fish into the north Pacific by 1990. World production was estimated to total about 2·1 billion juveniles in the mid 1970s (McNeil, 1976b). Even partial implementation of planned production in Alaska and other states and countries will continue to generate rapid growth of artificial propagation. It seems entirely possible that artificial propagation of salmon will continue to expand at a rapid rate until the carrying capacity of marine waters for salmon is approached.

DISCUSSION

Public policy in Alaska allows the private sector to share responsibility for artificial propagation of salmon with public agencies. Policy has been established to encourage co-operative planning between public and private institutions. Progress of this programme will be closely followed by economists as well as by fishery managers.

A similar programme is being developed in the State of Oregon (Chapter 4). The major difference is that public policy in Oregon allows private hatcheries to engage in salmon ranching for profit; in Alaska, only non-profit corporations can raise salmon. Oregon private hatcheries are tax-paying businesses and receive no subsidy from government. The institutional framework for private hatcheries in Oregon should represent an even greater inducement for cost efficiency and productivity than in Alaska, where private non-profit hatcheries can qualify for subsidies from the state.

Further changes in institutional arrangements for salmon ranching in Alaska and elsewhere can be expected while society continues to encourage development of food production from marine waters through aquaculture. Recent emergence of salmon ranching in Alaska is further evidence that traditional hunting economies are in transition. Salmon ranching represents a significant economic opportunity for Alaska, and Alaska policy makers have wisely chosen to make it possible for private enterprise to participate with government in the realisation of this opportunity.

REFERENCES

Alaska Dept. Fish and Game (1977). 157.
McNeil, W. J. (1976a). *Univ. of Alaska Sea Grant Rpt.* **76-2**, 25-67.
McNeil, W. J. (1976b). *FAO Tech. Conf. on Aquaculture, Kyoto, Japan* R. 24, 13 p.
McNeil, W. J. (1977). *Northwest and Alaska Fish. Center Processed Rpt.* 13 p.
Moberly, S. A. and Lium, R. (1977). *Fisheries* **2**, 2-7.
Orth, F. L. and Kerns, C. L. (1978). *Alaska Seas and Coasts* **6**, 8-11.
Roppel, P. (1978). *Alaska Fisherman* **5**, 3-4.

Chapter 3

Salmon Ranching in Washington State

L. R. DONALDSON

College of Fisheries, University of Washington, Seattle, Washington, U.S.A.

The State of Washington extends along the eastern coast of the Pacific Ocean between latitudes 47° 15′ and 49° 0′N. The waters of the state all drain into the Pacific Ocean and are populated with representative stocks of all the major members of the family Salmonidae. On the south, Washington State is bounded for much of its border by the Columbia River, with its great spawning runs of anadromous salmon and steelhead trout *(Salmo gairdneri)*. On the north, the gigantic Fraser River enters Puget Sound just a few miles north of the border. The Fraser, especially the sockeye *(Oncorhynchus nerka)* run, is one of the world's great natural resources. The rivers and streams of Puget Sound and along the coast have migratory runs of coho *(O. kisutch)*, chinook *(O. tschawytscha)*, chum *(O. keta)*, pink *(O. gorbuscha)*, and sockeye salmon. Sea-run cutthroat trout *(S. clarki)*, migratory rainbow-steelhead, and Dolly Varden trout *(Salvelinus malma)* migrate from the freshwater incubation and early rearing places to the sea for their major feeding and growth periods. In addition to the native salmonids, Atlantic salmon *(Salmo salar)*, European brown trout *(S. truttà)*, and Eastern Brook trout *(Salvelinus fontinalis)* have been introduced into the waters of the state and are used in a variety of management programmes.

Historically and down to the present the native Indians have depended on the salmonid fisheries for food and trade. The fish originally were captured as they left the sea on their spawning migrations and along the rivers, especially where there is swift water, such as at Celilo Falls on the Columbia (Fig. 1).

Fig. 1. Indian dip net fishing at Celilo Falls on the Columbia. Historically the Indian fishery was estimated at 8 000 000 kg annually from the Columbia River system. Celilo Falls was inundated by the reservoir behind The Dalles Dam virtually eliminating the dip net fishery. (Photograph by L. R. Donaldson.)

The aboriginal people were skilled fishermen who used spears, gaffs, dip-nets, brush weirs, traps of basketry, fibre nets, rocks and sticks to catch the salmon. Part of the catch was used fresh, but a major portion was dried or smoked for winter use or used as an item of trade with more inland tribes. The extent of the historical Indian salmon fishery can only be estimated, but from all accounts it was very substantial. Craig and Hacker (1940), using information supplied by early explorers, calculated the annual catch of salmon for the Columbia River at 8 000 000 kg. Indians living along the Washington coast and in Puget Sound also used salmon as food, but probably in lesser amounts because of the ready availability of other sea foods.

The Indian fishing rights are protected by treaties signed in 1855 by the tribes and the Federal Government. For years the legal interpretation of the original treaties confined the exclusive Indian fishing rights to the reservations, and Indian fishermen fishing off the reservations were in competition with white fishermen. The legal decision of U.S. District Court Judge George Boldt in February 1974 greatly expanded the impact of the Indian fishery to include ''the right to half the fish returning to off-reservation traditional fishing areas''.

The management of Washington State's fisheries resources is divided between two state agencies. Berg (1968) traces the evolution of the state fisheries agencies from the first four-member Fish Commission, established by state law in 1890 to manage, protect, and conserve the state's food fish resources, to the present system, which grew from the 1932 initiative that separated food and game fish and created two departments: The Department of Fisheries, with a director appointed by the Governor of the State, and the Department of Game under a six-member Commission.

Sandison (1977) summarises the responsibilities of each of the departments:

> Washington's first fisheries management agency was a four-member Fish Commission established by state law in 1890 to manage, protect, and conserve the state's food fish resources. This commission underwent many changes over the next 40 years until the mid-thirties, when an initiative action established the Department of Fisheries as we know it today.
>
> The same initiative established the state's Game Department and made a clear jurisdictional distinction between the two departments: Fisheries is responsible for all food fish (species which may be harvested for both sport and commercial purposes) and all shellfish; Game is responsible for all game fish (which, by state law, may be harvested for sport only). In general, the species under the protection of the Game Department are freshwater, those under Fisheries marine; but there are some important exceptions. The Department of Fisheries is responsible for several species of anadromous fish (those which migrate from freshwater to saltwater and back again during the life-cycle) such as salmon, shad, sturgeon, and smelt, in both marine and fresh waters; while the Game Department has jurisdiction over all searun trout (including steelhead) even in saltwater.
>
> Washington's growing industrial economy and its increasing population continue to place heavy demands on both our supply of food fish and shellfish and the habitat and environment in which these animals live and propagate. It is the responsibility of the Department of Fisheries to achieve optimum annual harvest of these species without impairing their reproductive capacity or endangering the state's overall resource. The Department manages harvests to ensure fair distribution among three user-groups: licensed commerical fishermen, treaty-right (Indian) fishermen, and personal-use (sport) fishermen.

The salmon fisheries of the State of Washington are the most valuable of the states fisheries and receive most of the Fisheries Department's efforts and expenditures. The 1976 season, with a total catch of 6 852 372 salmon of all species, had a value of $122 235 099 (Table I). The sport-recreational catch of 1 749 560 salmon, mostly coho and chinook, was one of the largest recorded.

The management of the salmon resources of the State of Washington is a complex problem of balancing the harvest between the various user groups, maintaining the natural and hatchery stocks, constructing, operating and maintaining facilities, and carrying on a comprehensive research programme.

Table I. Fish food statistics in the State of Washington 1976 (from Sandison, 1977).

1976 Commercial catch

Chinook	513 619	Units of fishing gear	5 932
Chum	525 351	Number of processors	150
Coho	1 816 607	Number of employees	61 000
Pink	1 591	(vessels and shore)	
Sockeye	1 223 682	Cash accruals to Washington	
Total	4 080 050	residents and wholesale value	
		of Washington salmon products	$58 858 579

1976 Indian commercial and personal use catch

Chinook	267 936	Units of fishing gear	1 500
Chum	297 969	Number of employees	5 440
Coho	345 548	(vessel, gear and shore)	
Pink	42	Cash accrual to Indian fishermen	
Sockeye	110 467	and tribal enterprises	$10 727 820
Total	1 021 962		

1976 Sport and recreational catch

Chinook (marine)	477 911	No. of Fisherman trips	1 883 525
Coho (marine)	1 166 764	No. of marine boat access	
Pink (marine)	587	points	1 200
Other (marine)	3 697	No. of charter boats	427
Freshwater mixed	100601	Value of recreational	
Total	1 749 560	fishery at $28.00 per	
		fisherman trip	$52 738 700

Total number of salmon caught	6 852 372
Total value of catch	$122 235 099

In an effort to supplement the natural salmon reproduction, the State of Washington has developed a comprehensive programme of artificial propagation. Berg (1968) describes the early history of this development from the construction in 1895 of the first salmon hatchery on the Kalama River, a tributary of the Columbia River. Other hatcheries and rearing facilities followed this initial effort (Fig. 2). By 1977 the Department of Fisheries operated 33 major rearing facilities and 15 satellite stations, producing a total of 1 922 000 kg of young salmon for release to the sea in 1978 (Foster *et al.*, 1978) (Fig. 3).

Since 1890 the Department of Fisheries has published annual reports that record in detail the operations of the Department and information on the numbers of fish reared for release and numbers returning to the hatcheries. Foster *et al.* (1978) provided the latest information.

Fig. 2. Green River salmon hatchery built on Soos Creek in 1901. The station was completely rebuilt in 1907, 1926 and 1948. It has been one of the most successful salmon hatcheries in the state. (Photograph from W.S.D.F. files.)

Fig. 3. Present Green River salmon hatchery near Auburn, Washington. In 1976 this station produced and released 8 720 865 chinook and coho fry and fingerlings with a weight of 80 500 kg.

Most of the hatcheries and release sites maintain recapture facilities to which the salmon return from the sea and provide eggs for continuing the programmes. From the total of 327 608 salmon that returned during the fall of 1977 to the hatcheries, 293 586 586 eggs were harvested. In the adult returns were 72 666 chinook, 185 194 coho, 38 081 pink, and 31 667 chum salmon. The returning adults in 1977 provided 17 028 149 spring chinook eggs, 100 537 236 fall chinook, 120 537 375 coho, 15 428 038 pink, and 40 055 788 chum eggs. Table II records the annual egg take for the years 1960 to 1977. The 1977 egg harvest was the largest recorded to date, reflecting the Department of Fisheries efforts to increase their salmon enhancement programme.

The adult salmon, on arrival at the collecting sites, are retained until they reach sexual maturity and can be spawned. Spawning techniques are described by the Washington State Department of Fisheries (WSDF) (1977) as follows.

After fish are trapped at the hatchery, they are tested for "ripeness". The "green" salmon are returned to the water to ripen; those whose eggs are fully formed and fall from the egg skein are selected for spawning. Because all Pacific salmon die after spawning, fish selected for hatchery spawning are first killed. Better spawn can be obtained from killed females, as the abdominal wall can be split upwards while the fish is held tail down, allowing clean spawn to spill into the spawning pan. After the required eggs have been accumulated, milt is extruded from the male by "stripping" and stirred among the eggs. Inside the hatchery, these are measured by weight into lots and placed in troughs or trays.

Table II. Comparative salmon egg take at Department of Fisheries hatcheries, 1960-1977.

Year	Chinook[a]	Coho	Chum	Pink	Total
1960	51 286 404	37 751 295	7 979 844	—	97 017 543
1961	65 710 925	32 582 566	2 346 660	2 369 216	103 009 367
1962	57 139 496	33 084 758	6 230 481	—	96 454 735
1963	67 704 428	24 948 044	3 778 620	6 064 938	102 496 030
1964	81 186 464	40 033 826	3 551 024	—	124 771 314
1965	59 013 818	41 651 140	1 556 540	472 328	102 693 826
1966	60 564 216	41 549 266	1 714 683	—	103 828 165
1967	70 951 672	47 593 625	1 726 773	615 000	120 887 070
1968	80 096 125	58 333 346	3 408 074	1 250	141 838 795
1969	88 295 008	65 100 038	4 393 294	2 407 094	160 195 434
1970	114 887 210	86 930 901	4 479 300	—	206 297 411
1971	110 580 678	71 855 731	5 599 660	2 000 975	190 037 044
1972	116 091 142	91 395 510	8 985 928	—	216 472 580
1973	105 389 942	90 022 385	10 084 559	1 551 160	207 048 046
1974	90 457 408	93 652 014	19 032 916	—	203 142 338
1975	93 177 536	89 911 914	11 280 625	6 473 340	200 843 415
1976	103 324 080	102 028 840	60 961 351	—	266 314 271
1977	117 565 385	120 537 375	40 055 788	15 428 038	293 586 586

[a]Fall and spring chinook combined.

Most salmon hatcheries in the State of Washington use water directly from streams with no preliminary treatment except for trash racks in the entrances to screen out the larger debris. Bell (1973) describes in detail the hatchery specifications for water quality, amounts and the equipment used in the hatcheries and rearing ponds (Figs 4-8).

Fig. 4. Cowlitz River trout hatchery constructed by the City of Tacoma to compensate for the steelhead lost to Mayfield and Mossy Rock dams on the Cowlitz River, one of the tributaries of the Columbia River in southwestern Washington. (Photograph by J. O. Sneddon.)

Fig. 5. Ponds used for holding spring chinook brood stock at the Cowlitz River salmon hatchery. The spray on the ponds helps to prevent the adult fish from jumping. (Photograph by L. R. Donaldson.)

Fig. 6. Each fall 5-6 thousand chinook and coho salmon return from the ocean to a man-made pond (dark pool, centre) on the edge of the University of Washington campus. (Photograph by J. O. Sneddon.)

Fig. 7. Adult chinook salmon returning up the small ladder that leads into the salmon "home" pond on the University of Washington campus. (Photograph by J. O. Sneddon.)

Fig. 8. Partial view of the interior of the experimental hatchery at the University of Washington. The Heath incubation trays, left centre, are especially useful for isolating individual egg lots for selective breeding studies. The troughs are of concrete, a design extensively used by Washington State Fisheries and Game Department hatcheries. (Photograph by S. Olson.)

The early salmon hatcheries harvested large numbers of eggs from the wild runs and, after incubation of the eggs, released the unfed fry. Such procedures did little to enhance the salmon runs; in fact, they depleted many. The present practice is to rear the young salmon to a size and time that they normally migrate to the sea.

Chum and pink salmon normally migrate to the sea at small size in the early spring of their first year. Most are released from the hatcheries as unfed fry, while other lots are fed for a few days or weeks in an effort to increase their survival. The spring stocks of chinook salmon are reared for a year or more and released at a large size, 18 to 80 grams in weight. Fall chinook stocks are fed for 90 days and released at a much smaller size, 3 to 12 grams in weight. Coho salmon spawn in the late fall. The eggs incubate during the winter months with the young fish spending a year or more feeding in freshwater before migrating to sea. The hatchery-reared coho follow this pattern: they spend about 18 months in freshwater and are released in late spring at a weight of 12 to 30 grams.

During 1977 the Washington Department of Fisheries planted a total of 178 864 335 young salmon (Table III). The releases consisted of 20 763 926 fry, fish that had been reared 0 to 14 days; 112 371 734 fingerlings, fish that had been reared 15 to 269 days; and 45 728 675 yearlings, fish that had been reared 270 or more days.

Table III. Summary of Department of Fisheries Hatchery Plàntings of Salmon 1960-1977. (From Foster, Flecher and Coleman, 1978.)

Year	Fry	Fingerlings	Yearlings	Total fish planted	Total kg planted
1960	5 684 384	62 969 498	9 173 028	77 862 910	186 200
1961	13 192 908	51 107 950	15 214 611	79 515 469	257 900
1962	22 110 411	53 165 448	14 907 302	90 183 161	287 500
1963	19 301 932	55 776 991	14 116 873	89 195 796	297 100
1964	14 190 982	60 119 401	16 694 966	91 005 349	440 600
1965	16 993 989	63 537 365	18 558 430	99 089 784	495 900
1966	6 817 202	56 452 366	21 097 300	84 366 868	634 300
1967	13 233 854	50 484 207	22 267 346	85 985 407	696 800
1968	7 666 076	63 694 268	21 342 809	92 703 153	814 800
1969	16 644 805	68 122 374	32 317 741	117 084 920	1 155 900
1970	11 788 005	80 031 244	43 678 985	126 498 234	1 313 800
1971	33 673 189	106 069 542	36 902 929	176 645 660	1 543 700
1972	33 020 043	84 332 765	42 427 557	159 780 365	1 766 800
1973	12 793 627	95 930 508	39 612 774	148 336 909	1 755 700
1974	16 496 003	95 391 177	42 473 822	154 361 002	1 907 700
1975	12 769 569	92 960 935	44 751 513	150 482 017	1 871 600
1976	14 538 320	90 596 390	43 454 500	148 589 210	1 856 000
1977	20 763 926	112 371 734	45 728 675	178 864 335	1 922 000

The total 1 922 000 kg of young salmon released consumed about 3 630 000 kg of food. The Department of Fisheries contracts with commercial processors who prepare a mixture of dry and wet ingredients that are pelleted, frozen and bagged for delivery to the hatcheries. The composition varies from time to time, but generally 60% of the mixed food is a meal mixture of cottonseed, herring, shrimp or crab, wheat germ, kelp, and dried corn solubles and 40% is a wet mixture of such fish products as tuna viscera, turbot, pasteurised salmon viscera, dogfish, or pasteurised herring. The moist meal-fish mixture is fortified with a vitamin package containing ascorbic acid, biotin, B_{12}, E, folic acid, inositol, niacin, pantothenic acid, thiamin, and riboflavin. The efficiency of the food varies from place to place, with most hatcheries using 1·5 to 2·0 kg of the moist pelleted food to produce a 1 kg of young salmon.

U.S. Federal Hatcheries

In addition to the efforts of the Washington State Department of Fisheries in salmon propagation, the U.S. Bureau of Sport fisheries and Wildlife, Division of Fish Hatcheries operate nine hatcheries, which release 62 000 000 young salmon into the waters of the state and recapture adults as they return from the sea to the release sites to provide eggs to continue the programmes. Seven of the hatcheries are located along the Columbia River and release their salmon fry and smolts directly into the Columbia River or tributaries to the river (Fig. 9). One hatchery, on the Quilcene River, empties into Hood Canal, one of the major arms of Puget Sound, and one hatchery is on the Quinault River on the Washington coast.

The production of salmon from the nine federal hatcheries for the 1977-1978 fiscal year was 61 000 000 fish, weighing 634 400 kg (Dunn, 1977). The release was made up of 7 350 000 coho weighing 189 000 kg, 45 280 000 chinook weighing 422 400 kg, and 8 450 000 chum salmon weighing 22 900 kg. The young salmon in the federal hatcheries are fed a number of commercial fish foods, Oregon Moist Pellet and Abernathy dry pellets being the most popular. An estimated 1 141 700 kg of food were given during the year.

Indian Aquaculture

Several treaty Indian tribes in the State of Washington have greatly expanded their aquacultural activities in the past decade. This expansion includes all phases of aquaculture: rearing and releasing, pen-culture of pan-sized fish, and ocean ranching with fish returning

Fig. 9. Spring Creek Hatchery of the U.S. Fish and Wildlife Service produces chinook salmon smolts for release into the Columbia River a short distance above Bonneville Dam. The hatchery's annual production is about 21 000 000 fall chinook salmon smolts weighing 135 000 kg. The station operates on about 4000 g.p.m. of 46°F spring water using a water reconditioning-reuse system. (Photograph by Fish and Wildlife Service.)

for harvest to fresh- and saltwater sites. The salmon from the Indian-operated facilities are subjected to commercial, sport and Indian fishery while in the sea, but on return to the recapture site the fish are the property of the Indian tribes that released them. Under present regulations only Treaty Indians can legally carry out private commercial ocean ranching in the State of Washington.

The state expects the Washington Indian tribes, with financial help of the Federal Government, to release about 32 100 000 chum salmon smolts and 5 800 000 salmon of other species between July 1977 and June 1978. This production is presently divided among thirteen tribes,

Fig. 10. The Lummi Indians constructed a 3-mile long dike around 750 acres of tide flat creating a pond for salt water rearing of salmon and a site to which salmon return as adults. (Photograph from Lummi Aquaculture.)

Fig. 11. Floating net pens in Lake Quinault are used by the Quinault Indians to rear coho, chinook, chum and sockeye salmon and steelhead trout smolts for release. The annual production is about 1 300 000 fish weighing 47 250 kg. (Photograph by Larry Gilbertson.)

with two of the tribes, the Quinaults and the Lummis, having the most advanced programmes (Fig. 10). The Quinault tribal salmon programme is unique, with a sockeye run that the Quinaults have managed for many years. In addition to the normal natural spawning and rearing of the naturally spawned fry in Lake Quinault, the tribe has developed a floating pen system in the lake where each year a million young sockeye are protected from predation and fed pelleted food until they reach migratory stage and are released to go to sea (Fig. 11).

Fig. 12. Coho salmon reared in warmed water in the University of Washington Experimental Hatchery to accelerate growth. The two small fish at the bottom of the photo are one-year-old cohos from non-accelerated stock, average weight 4 grams. The medium-sized fish is from the same stock, and same age, but reared in warmed water for six months and released in June to migrate to sea. The fish returned in November as a "jack" weighing about 500 g. The two large fish went to sea after six months rearing and returned after 18 months in the sea as 2-year-old adult salmon. (Photograph by R. Whitney.)

Private Salmon Aquaculture

In recent years several unsuccessful attempts have been made in the Washington State Legislature to legalise private salmon ranching. The state has, however, passed legislation enabling private growers to purchase surplus salmon eggs from the state-operated hatcheries for use in commercial sea farms. Following the pioneering work by personnel of the Northwest Fisheries Center of the National Marine Fisheries Service, who reared salmon in floating net pens near Manchester, a commercial culture system has evolved that is producing in excess of 450 000 kg of pan-size salmon a year.

Coho salmon are used almost exclusively in net-pen culture in Puget Sound. In the wild or in state hatcheries coho normally spend about 18 months in freshwater growing to smolt size and an additional 18

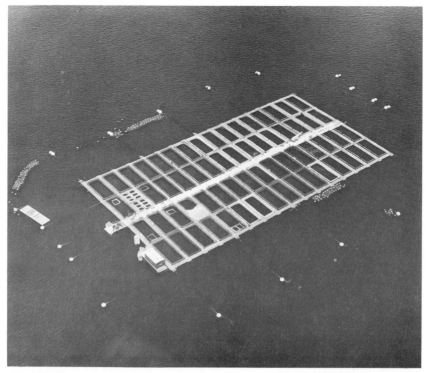

Fig. 13. Floating net pens used by Domsea Farms for rearing pan-sized coho. (Photograph by National Marine Fisheries Service.)

months feeding in the sea before returning as adults to spawn. In an effort to speed up the growth and reduce costs commercial salmon farmers follow the methods described by Donaldson and Brannon (1976), using warm water to accelerate the growth of the young coho salmon so they will reach 15-20 gram smolt size in 8 months and thus saving almost a year of rearing expense (Fig. 12). In the net pens floating in protected Puget Sound, the fish are fed high-protein diets that produce pan-sized fish in 12-14 months after hatching. Cost of the food and available supplies of eggs from the state are important limiting factors in expanding the commercial net-pen culture of salmon in Washington State (Fig. 13).

REFERENCES

Bell, M. C. (1973). Fisheries Handbook of Engineering Requirements and Biological Criteria. U.S. Army Corp of Engineers.

Berg, Iola I. (1968). History of the Washington State Department of Fisheries, 1890-1967. State of Wash. Dept. of Fish.

Craig, J. A. and Hacker, R. L. (1940). The history and development of the fisheries of the Columbia River. *U.S. Bur. of Fish.* **49** (32), 133-216.

Donaldson, L. R. and Brannon, E. L. (1976). The use of warmed water to accelerate the production of coho salmon. *Fisheries* **4**, 12-16.

Dunn, C. (1977). State of Washington Salmon Cultural Program, 1977-1978. State of Wash. Dept of Fish.

Foster, B, Flecher, V. and Coleman, P. (1978). 1977 Hatcheries Statistical Report of Production and Plantings. Progress Report No. 75, State of Washington Dept. of Fish.

Sandison, Gordon. Department of Fisheries Natural Resources and Recreation Agencies. 1977 Annual Report, State of Wash., Olympia.

Washington State Dept. of Fisheries (1977). Salmon and the Salmon Hatcheries. Dept. of Fish., Olympia.

Chapter 4

Salmon Ranching in Oregon

J. E. LANNAN

*Department of Fisheries and Wildlife, Oregon State University,
Marine Science Center, Newport, Oregon, U.S.A.*

INTRODUCTION

In Oregon, the term "salmon ranching" is used in the broadest sense.
It denotes the production of juvenile salmonid fishes in hatcheries, the
subsequent release of these fish to harvest energy from natural
production in the marine environment, and finally, harvest of the fish
in commercial and recreational fisheries. The distinction between
harvesting in near-shore and terminal fisheries is not made. Production
activities are directed towards chinook salmon *(Oncorhynchus
tschawytscha)*, coho or silver salmon *(O. kisutch)*, chum salmon *(O. keta)*,
and steelhead (anadromous rainbow trout, *Salmo gairdneri*). Salmon
ranching in Oregon is practised by both public agencies and the private
sector. Their combined activities are an integral part of the State's
management programme for the enhancement of its anadromous
salmonid resources.

THE ECONOMIC IMPORTANCE OF SALMON RANCHING TO OREGON

The products of salmon ranching in Oregon contribute to common
property resources and thus are shared by commercial and recreational
fishing interests. Commercially, salmon ranks as Oregon's principal

47

fishery in terms of estimated dollar value of the catch, and during the five-year period from 1971 to 1975, salmon averaged 34% of the total value of Oregon's commercial fisheries (Rompa *et al.*, 1978). The 1976 catch of 6 370 000 kg was worth an estimated $20 100 000 to the fishermen. When one considers the additional revenues from whole-saling, processing, distribution and retailing, one can appreciate the importance of Oregon's commercial salmon fisheries to the State's economy.

Recreational fishing also contributes substantially to the State's economy. The Oregon Department of Fish and Wildlife Anglers Survey for 1975, for example, indicates that 1 700 000 angler days resulted in a harvest of over 480 000 salmon and 250 000 steelhead. In addition to the value of the fish landed, recreational fishing has a substantial economic impact through expenditures on travel, accom-modation, and purchase of equipment and services. An economically important component of the recreational salmon fishery is the Oregon charter boat industry. According to Giles *et al.* (1976), 375 vessels participated in the charter boat fishery during the 1975 salmon season. The industry employed 384 persons. Charter vessels carried over 105 000 passengers and landed in excess of 121 000 salmon for an average of 1·2 fish caught per passenger day. Gross revenues from fares were in excess of $2 300 000.

Oregon's salmon and steelhead fisheries are important to the state, and salmon ranching is important to Oregon's fisheries. Although the true proportions are difficult to determine, management biologists are largely in agreement that over one-half of the Pacific salmon landed in Oregon originated in hatcheries and that the hatchery contribution to the steelhead fishery is substantial.

OREGON HATCHERY PROGRAMMES

Public Hatcheries

The Oregon Department of Fish and Wildlife was formed by the merger of the Fish Commission of Oregon and the Oregon Wildlife Commission in 1975 and operates 32 public hatcheries. The Federal Government also operates two hatcheries in the State of Oregon. Some were developed solely for enhancement purposes; others have been developed to mitigate various environmental perturbations (hydro-electric installations, flood-control projects). Most are multi-purpose multi-species hatcheries producing two or more species and utilising the products for a variety of purposes. Of those presently producing salmon, ten produce fall chinook, twelve produce spring chinook, one produces summer chinook, fifteen produce coho and one releases chum salmon. Sixteen State hatcheries produce steelhead. Pink salmon *(O. gorbuscha)* and sockeye salmon *(O. nerka)* are not produced in State hatcheries, with the exception of kokanee, a landlocked variety of the latter which is stocked in certain lakes for recreational fishing.

The State hatchery system has an annual budget of approximately $6 500 000, representing a substantial public commitment. State hatcheries employ some 160 full-time employees, supplemented by part-time and seasonal employees as situations dictate. Annual releases of coho and chinook salmon from Oregon hatcheries are summarised in Fig. 1 for the period from 1958 through 1973. The dramatic increase in hatchery production commencing in 1960 corresponds with the development of improved husbandry techniques, especially with the adoption of the Oregon Moist Pellet as the standard state hatchery ration.

While the State's commitment to salmon enhancement is manifest in Fig. 1, the crucial question is to what extent these releases have contributed to the State's salmon fisheries. Oregon landings of coho

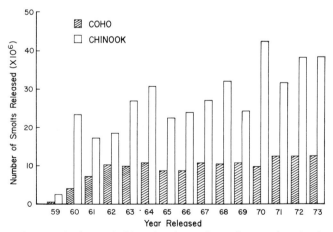

Fig. 1. Releases of coho and chinook salmon from Oregon hatcheries, 1959-73 (Wahle *et al.*, 1975).

and chinook salmon are presented graphically in Fig. 2 and demonstrate that the hatchery programme has been effective in sustaining the State's salmon fisheries as natural production has declined. However, only part of the total landings of salmon produced in Oregon hatcheries are reflected in Fig. 2: salmon released from Oregon hatcheries are also harvested in offshore fisheries in California, Washington, British Columbia, and to a lesser degree, south-east Alaska. For example, of the total recreational and commercial ocean harvest of coho salmon from Columbia River hatcheries from the 1965 brood, 8·7% were caught in British Columbia, 39·9% in Washington, 39·5% off Oregon, and 11·9% off California (Wahle *et al.* 1974). Similarly, the landings of fall chinook from 1961 through 1964 broods from 13 Columbia River hatcheries were distributed as follows: 0·2% were caught in south-east Alaska, 33·7% in British Columbia, 38·1% in Washington, 4·6% off Oregon, and 0·4% off California (Wahle and Vreeland, 1978). The remaining 23·1% were taken in terminal fisheries in the Columbia River. These statistics underscore the importance of salmon ranching activities in the eastern Pacific ocean, not only to Oregon but to the regional economy as well.

Releases and catches of steelhead are summarised in Tables I and II. The proportions of the annual catches resulting from hatchery releases

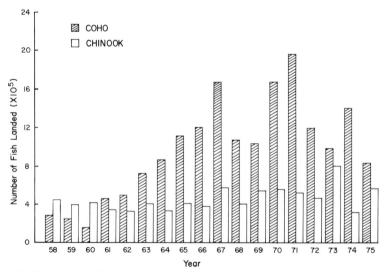

Fig. 2. Oregon landings (recreational and commercial) of coho and chinook salmon, 1958-75 (Aro and McDonald, 1974).

Table I. Releases of steelhead from Oregon hatcheries.[a]

Year Released	Coastal Drainages	Columbia River Drainage	Total
1960	295 429	477 057	772 486
1961	436 826	370 741	807 567
1962	662 434	1 096 848	1 759 282
1963	591 891	816 501	1 408 392
1964	855 488	790 986	1 646 474
1965	831 878	817 371	1 649 249
1966	839 037	692 514	1 531 551
1967	889 585	1 119 615	2 009 200
1968	1 206 463	1 006 090	2 212 553
1969	1 412 743	1 413 565	2 826 308
1970	1 742 532	1 168 843	2 911 375
1971	1 750 151	1 190 083	2 940 234
1972	1 839 107	1 646 662	3 485 769
1973	1 731 210	1 655 057	3 386 267

[a]Wahle *et al.* (1975). Includes releases from Eagle Creek National Hatchery.

are not well documented, although they are considered to be substantial. In this sense it is important to recognise that the State's programme has established important summer runs in drainages where they did not previously exist (e.g. Nestucca and Wilson Rivers). Other systems (e.g. Siletz and Alsea Rivers) have been enhanced to a degree which approaches or exceeds historical levels.

Table II. Oregon steelhead landings 1966-67 to 1974-75.[a]

Year	Coastal Drainages	Columbia River Drainage	Total
1966-67	93 264	61 297	154 561
1967-68	113 858	51 586	165 444
1968-69	109 489	56 518	166 007
1969-70	98 019	43 543	141 562
1970-71	154 751	51 028	205 779
1971-72	135 980	64 732	200 712
1972-73	112 264	54 453	166 717
1973-74	99 324	37 610	136 934
1974-75	144 798	51 839	196 637

[a]Source: Oregon Department of Fish and Wildlife 1975 Annual Report.

Present-day hatchery methods for coho and chinook salmon and steelhead evolved rapidly during the 1950s and 1960s. The Oregon programme contributed substantially in this development, especially in the area of improved hatchery rations. The Oregon Moist Pellet ration (Hublou *et al.*, 1959) remains the standard of the industry. Production methods have been streamlined and standardised but otherwise have not changed dramatically in recent years. Present emphasis in the State's programme has shifted to assessment intended to optimise existing technology.

More recently developed methods are used for chum salmon propagation. The Netarts Bay hatchery, operated by Oregon State University under a co-operative agreement with the Oregon Department of Fish and Wildlife, utilises shallow gravel streamside incubators which satisfy the developmental requirements of the species, a production system which is low in labour and capital intensity. Chum salmon eggs are incubated on screens in shallow gravel-lined raceways. The raceways are covered so that the eggs are incubated in nearly total darkness. As the eggs hatch, the emerging alevins find their way on to the gravel in the bottom of the pond where they remain until their supply of yolk is utilised. When the fry emerge from the gravel, they may be released unfed or fed in the same ponds until they reach the size at which they are to be released. This system is also used for chum salmon by Oregon private hatcheries.

Private Hatcheries

Historical Perspective
During the late nineteenth century, a private salmon hatchery was operated by R. D. Hume on the Rogue River and another operated by the Oregon-Washington Propagation Company on the Clackamas River. Apparently neither of these endeavours proved financially feasible, and by the early twentieth century all of Oregon's salmon hatcheries were operated by governmental agencies. During the 1960s a rebirth of interest in private salmon propagation resulted from the development of improved hatchery technology. In 1971 legislation was enacted which authorised the State to license private salmon hatcheries to produce chum salmon, and the 1973 Legislature revised the law to include coho and chinook salmon. State laws do not permit private

sector involvement in steelhead production: Oregon statutes of 1969 designate steelhead as game fish, and a 1974 Initiative bars the commercial sale of steelhead and stipulates that any incidental commercial catch of this species must be surrendered to the State for institutional use.

Nature of the Oregon Private Hatchery Law

The crux of the Oregon laws pertaining to private salmon hatchery permits is the explicit statement that ''all fish released [under such a permit] during the time they are in the wild will be the property of the State and may be taken under angling or commercial fishing laws of this State until they return to the private hatchery'' (Oregon Revised Statutes, Chapter 508.725). This means that the fish are the property of the producer during the time that they are confined within a designated production facility, but from the time they are released until the time they return to that facility they are part of the common property resource and subject to capture in the State's commercial and recreational salmon fisheries.

Other aspects of the law provide conditions for granting or denying permits, place certain conditions on the permits that are granted, and require the State to ensure that the activities of the private sector are not detrimental to natural stocks or to the State's public hatchery programme.

Rationale for Private Hatcheries

The 1971 legislation was enacted in response to interest within the private sector, and the State did not strongly oppose it or the revision of 1973. Oregon's salmon enhancement activities represent a substantial investment of public funds, and as pressure continues to mount on the State's salmon resources, it is questionable whether public funding increases will meet increasing demands for salmon enhancement. The State could increase the input of public funds or, alternatively, financial incentives might be provided to attract private investment. Oregon's private salmon hatchery programme represents an attempt to integrate the activities of the private sector into the State's salmon enhancement programme.

The activities of the private sector have met with some opposition, including an element of adverse public opinion, although the public has largely supported the concept. The opposition takes several forms.

There is some valid concern as to what the biological impact of salmon ranching will be on existing resources and also some relating to the potential impact of additional fish on existing salmon markets. The most vocal opposition expresses a fear that the private salmon hatchery industry, which includes large corporate interests, may develop into a political force powerful enough to dictate State fishery policies. Thus, the decision to allow private salmon ranching in Oregon is the subject of some controversy.

The relative merit of the private hatchery concept may be placed in perspective by comparing the salmon enhancement activities of the States of Oregon and Washington (see Chapter 3). Washington has recently embarked on a publicly funded, large-scale salmon enhancement programme intended to contribute 41 000 000 adult salmon to Washington fisheries. It will require a capital outlay of $29 000 000 of public funds, and the continuing annual cost will be about $5 000 000 derived from taxes, licences, etc. In the private hatchery programme in Oregon, however, when the present licence holders have reached full production capacity they will contribute an equivalent number of adult salmon to Oregon's fisheries with no expenditure of public monies, either for capital outlay or for annual operating costs, and assuming the private sector can produce salmon, the State of Oregon stands to derive substantial benefits from private salmon ranching.

Status of Private Hatcheries
At present, 20 private salmon hatchery licences have been authorised in Oregon to 12 firms or individuals: four for coho, five for chinook, and eleven for chum salmon. In addition to the licences authorised to date, several applications are pending review. The total numbers of salmon authorised for release by private hatcheries is presently 37 800 000 coho, 42 000 000 chinook and 100 000 000 chum. The private sector does not actually have the capabilities to release these numbers at the present time: the total number authorised includes permits to firms who have not as yet developed production facilities. These authorised releases contrast with present State production of 14 100 000 coho, 52 200 000 chinook and 2 000 000 chum. Additionally, hatcheries operated by the Federal Government release 1 300 000 coho and 1 100 000 chinook.

Although private hatchery development is proceeding in an orderly fashion, production has not yet approached projected levels. The industry is presently in the process of developing proprietary broodstocks. Releases of salmon from private hatcheries are summarised in Table III. Since the numbers of fish released to date have been relatively small, the numbers returning have also been small. The actual numbers are considered proprietary information and are not available for publication, but the returns are encouraging and suggest that if present trends continue, private hatcheries will make a substantial contribution in the foreseeable future.

Table III. Releases of Pacific salmon from Oregon private hatcheries.[a]

Brood year	Coho	Chinook	Chum[c]	Totals
1971	—	—	276 150	276 150
1972	—	1 025	846 375	847 400
1973	103 782	40 000	1 336 082	1 479 864
1974	812 511	1 014 407	3 746 730	5 573 648
1975	2 019 000	650 000	602 400	3 271 400
1976	1 400 000	110 000	716 050	2 226 050
1977[b]	12 000 000	400 000	1 362 300	13 762 300
Totals	16 335 293	2 215 432	8 886 087	27 436 812

[a]Cummings, 1977, and personal communication.
[b]Estimated—actual 1977 release data not available at time of writing.
[c]Includes releases from Oregon State University experimental hatchery.

Hatchery practices and production concepts employed in private hatcheries are similar to those used by public agencies, but the private sector has instituted some innovative production strategies. One innovation effectively shortens the life cycle of coho salmon by one year. Coho are normally ready to migrate to sea in the spring or summer of their second year. By employing thermal enhancement during the freshwater rearing phase, private hatcheries produce coho smolts that can be released into the marine environment during their first summer of life. The practice results in a substantial reduction of production costs (see also Chapter 3). Thermal enhancement of rearing ponds is achieved in two ways. Some growers use water taken from springs or deep wells at a temperature which will produce the desired acceleration of growth. Another mixes hot water from a paper-making plant with cooler surface water to achieve the desired rearing temperature.

A second innovation made by private salmon hatcheries is the seawater release and recapture concept. Salmon smolts are produced in inland freshwater hatcheries and transported to coastal release sites where they are imprinted in seawater ponds for one to three weeks. Fish are released directly into the marine environment at a stage at which they are ready to migrate to sea in order to bypass the estuarine period during which they are susceptible to predation and infectious disease. This element of the strategy is at present presumptive in that it has not yet been determined how long smolts released into the marine environment remain in estuaries and near-shore waters. The recapture of returning adults in seawater facilities yields a product of high market quality. The flesh quality of adult salmon deteriorates rapidly once they enter freshwater, but fish captured in seawater facilities are comparable in quality to those taken in offshore fisheries, and this strategy may substantially improve the economic outlook for commercial salmon ranching.

THE RELATIONSHIP OF PUBLIC AND PRIVATE HATCHERIES

Under Oregon law, the Department of Fish and Wildlife has a statutory responsibility for the conservation and utilisation of the State's food fish resources. According to the law, "conservation means providing for the utilization and management of the food fish of Oregon to protect the ultimate supply for present and future generations, preventing waste and implementing a sound management program for sustained economic, recreation and esthetic benefits" (Oregon Revised Statutes, Chapter 506.028). Consistent with this responsibility, the aim of State hatcheries is to stock the river systems for purposes of mitigation and enhancement and provide recruitment to the marine environment. The aim of private hatcheries is profit: fish are produced to be sold and any fish contributed to common property resources are considered to be a cost of doing business. While these aims may appear inconsistent, they are in fact complementary.

To fulfil its responsibilities, the State must employ a variety of strategies concurrently. For restoration and enhancement purposes, fish must be released in stream systems where suitable spawning habitat exists. Recreational fishing objectives require that fish are available throughout the drainages as well as in the near-shore region. Finally, since fishing exploits adult and sub-adult fish, the releases must provide a substantial recruitment to marine stocks. These goals present certain conflicts in production strategies. Releasing fish upstream in various drainages, while consistent with mitigation and enhancement objectives, probably does not contribute as great a recruitment to offshore stocks as would releases made in the lower portions of the drainage systems. This is where public and private hatcheries are linked: most State hatcheries are located fairly well up the river systems, but private hatcheries are required by law to be close to the ocean, thus supplementing recruitment to marine stocks and reducing the need for the development of additional State hatcheries at coastal locations.

The relationship between public and private hatcheries also facilitates the degree to which the various species can be included in the State management programme. Coho, chinook, and steelhead all make relatively extended freshwater migrations and are therefore amenable to production in the State's facilities, but chum salmon reproduce in the lower portions of coastal rivers. The private producers are well situated to propagate this species and therefore assume a major role in the enhancement of chum salmon.

The proportions of the various species which private enterprise might release in Oregon has been the subject of some controversy. Recreational and commerical fishing interests argue that the production of coho and chinook salmon should be emphasised, since these species are their primary target, and that since chum salmon are not routinely sought in troll or sport fisheries, their production should not be emphasised.

Chum salmon were once the object of important commercial fisheries in Oregon. In 1942, for example, commercial landings exceeded 2 700 000 kg. Stocks have declined rapidly since then. The last remaining coastal fishery was closed in 1962 and Oregon's Columbia River landings totalled only 1350 kg in 1974. A loss of spawning habitat has hindered the recovery of Oregon chum salmon stocks since the termination of the commercial fisheries. Artificial propagation by the State has not received the same priority as other species. Obviously, the private hatchery programme provides a potential means to enhance this once important resource.

From the private grower's point of view, a mix of species is a matter of economic concern. It is difficult to demonstrate economic feasibility for the production of a single species, but when two or more species are produced, each serves to drive the other in an economic sense. The combination increases the efficiency of utilisation of manpower and facilities and allows staging production over an entire calendar year. Additionally, ocean production trends for each species are to some degree independent of other species. Thus, when the producer is confronted with poor seasonal production of a particular species, production of others may preclude a financial disaster.

There are also biological arguments for including a good species mix in salmon ranching activities in Oregon. Each species of Pacific salmon has characteristic migratory patterns during the marine phase. Although the migratory routes of all the species overlap, each probably utilises distinct regions of the ocean range at times. Therefore a good species mix makes the best use of the range and provides for the most efficient harvest of energy from natural production.

THE FUTURE OF SALMON RANCHING IN OREGON

A review of salmon ranching in Oregon would not be complete without some discussion of the future. Needless to say, this involves a high degree of conjecture. Shifting patterns of public opinion, unpredictable climatic and oceanographic circumstances, fickle international markets, and evolving fisheries regulation at the state, national, and international levels all contribute to the uncertainty of the future. There are current considerations which will influence the immediate future of salmon ranching in Oregon and these merit discussion.

Oregon is in the midst of an era during which its releases of artificially propagated salmon will increase approximately fivefold. This expansion raises questions which will not be answered for some time; until they are answered and the impacts assessed, the State has little choice but to approach further expansion very cautiously, and it seems likely that salmon-ranching activities in Oregon will not expand much beyond the presently authorised levels of production in the immediate future. One area of concern to management biologists is how many fish can be released without overstocking the ocean range. The carrying capacity of the ocean is a question of some controversy. Present out-migration of salmon smolts probably does not approach that which must have occurred to maintain stocks at historical levels, but evaluation of hatchery releases in recent years reflects a trend which is consistent with the notion that a density asymptote may already be exceeded. While hatchery releases have been maintained at high levels or increased, the return to various fisheries and hatcheries does not reflect a proportional increase. This observation alone does not constitute proof, and additional research will be required before generalisations about optimum stocking levels can be made.

There are alternative explanations of the trend toward decreasing productivity. For example, stocks have been transplanted from one drainage system or hatchery to another with little regard for the adaptations which exist in the donor and recipient stocks. Also, subtle modifications have been made to hatchery rations as a result of escalating prices of various ration components. It is possible that salmon smolts released in recent years are of inferior quality to those released previously.

A third consideration is that the returns to commercial and rec- reational fisheries consist of wild fish as well as fish from hatcheries. The apparent decrease in returns may merely be a consequence of diminishing production from the natural stocks, and the returns from hatchery production may not actually be decreasing. When wild and hatchery stocks are harvested in common fisheries, as is the case with salmon, the wild stocks may be over-exploited. The problem results because hatchery stocks can withstand higher rates of exploitation than naturally reproducing stocks, since fewer hatchery spawners are needed to produce equivalent recruitment. As hatchery production increases, the availability of fish increases, and exploitation usually increases. This poses a real dilemma for fisheries managers. If exploitation is managed to assure adequate escapement to the hatcheries, the escapement for natural reproduction is not adequate to sustain the stocks. On the other hand, if the fishery is managed to assure adequate escapement for natural reproduction, the surplus production of hatchery fish is not harvested. Since political and economic considerations tend to drive management decisions towards increasing harvests, artificial propagation indirectly places severe stress on wild populations and may result in their depletion.

Although there is some controversy about the current carrying capacity of the marine environment, there can be little doubt that the productivity of the major drainage systems and estuaries has become drastically reduced in recent decades. Forest exploitation, road construction, commercial and residential development of the river drainages, and industrialisation of the estuaries have combined to take their toll on the reproductive habitat of Pacific salmon. Many of the State's hatcheries are located relatively far up the drainage systems, and fish released from these hatcheries may be dependent on the productivity of the drainages and especially the estuaries for some period during the out-migrations. Although hatchery production has remained at high levels, the actual recruitment to the marine environment may in fact be diminishing because of this dependence. If this is the case, private hatcheries would be expected to contribute a greater proportion to marine recruitment because of their proximity to the ocean.

The expansion of hatchery production in Oregon has necessitated the development of new broodstocks, mainly by the private hatcheries. Consequently, there has been an increase in the transportation of fish and eggs between drainages within the state and importation from other states. These activities increase the danger of the introduction and spread of infectious disease.

The State has implemented restrictive disease certification policies in an attempt to preclude introduction of diseases which have not been reported in Oregon and to prevent the spread of existing pathogens into drainages in which they are not known to exist. Certification involves sampling fish to be transported or adult fish from which eggs are to be taken and holding the fish or eggs in quarantine until viral, bacterial, and parasite evaluations have been completed. These may take six to eight weeks and must be performed by a fish pathologist recognised as competent by the Oregon Department of Fish and Wildlife. Once certified, the fish or eggs may be approved for transportation. In the case of transportation requests by private hatcheries, the cost of obtaining the certification, including those associated with quarantine, is borne by the producer. These costs may be substantial.

In addition to these concerns, other constraints make extensive expansion seem unlikely. In State-operated hatcheries, additional public funds would be required to finance any substantial increase in production. Present State fiscal policy is such that these funds are probably not forthcoming. One of the primary constraints to the development of private hatcheries at the present is the non-availability of eggs to be used for the development of proprietary stocks. Coho and chinook eggs may be purchased from the State when there is a surplus to State hatchery needs, and some producers have been able to obtain eggs of these species from out of state. Neither source has proved reliable because eggs are only available when substantial surpluses exist, and the disease certification criteria, while absolutely essential, further limit the importation of salmon eggs.

Chum salmon eggs have been in critically short supply because of a scarcity of chum salmon in general and because other Pacific states and provinces have recently commenced substantial chum salmon enhancement programmes. The primary source of chum salmon eggs for Oregon growers has been the Oregon State University experimental chum salmon hatchery at Netarts Bay. Surplus eggs have only been available in occasional years, and this shortage has severely curtailed the growth of private chum salmon production in Oregon. Chum salmon eggs from out of state are also in short supply, although 1 500 000 eggs have been imported since 1974.

Until the biological, social, and economic impact of commercial salmon ranching has been more completely assessed and until the shortage of broodstocks has been resolved, the Oregon Fish and Wildlife Commission may be expected to continue its cautious approach to private salmon production. Although there is a vocal minority which claims that restrictive policies of the State have impeded the development of private salmon aquaculture, there is a consensus that the State's position is a responsible one and in the long term will be in the best interests of all concerned.

REFERENCES

Aro, K. V. and McDonald, J. (1974). Commercial and sport catches of chinook and coho salmon along the west coasts of Canada and the United States. *Fisheries Research Board of Canada,* Manuscript Report Series No. 1325.

Cummings, T. E. (1977). Private salmon hatcheries in Oregon. Oregon Department of Fish and Wildlife Processed Report. 11 pp.

Giles, D. E., Ball, J. and York, P. (1976). The ocean charter industry in Oregon, 1975. Draft report; Oregon State University Sea Grant College Program.

Hublou, W. F., Wallis, J., McKee, T. B., Law, D. K., Sinnhuber, R. O. and Yu, T. C. (1959). Development of the Oregon pellet diet. Research Briefs, Fish Commission of Oregon **7** (1), 28-56.

Rompa, W. J., Smith, F. J. and Miles, S. D. (1978). The seafood industry, its importance to Oregon's economy. Draft Report; Department of Agricultural and Resource Economics, Oregon State University. 24 pp.

Wahle, R. J. and Vreeland, R. R. (1978). Bioeconomic contribution of Columbia River hatchery fall chinook salmon, 1961 through 1964 broods, to the Pacific salmon fisheries. *Fishery Bulletin* **76** (1), 179-208.

Wahle, R. J., Vreeland, R. R. and Lander, R. H. (1974). Bioeconomic contribution of Columbia River hatchery coho salmon, 1965 and 1966 broods, to the Pacific salmon fisheries. *Fishery Bulletin* **72** (1), 139-169.

Wahle, R. J., Parente, W. D., Jurich, P. J. and Vreeland, R. R. (1975). Releases of anadromous salmon and trout from Pacific coast rearing facilities. U.S. Department of Commerce, National Marine Fisheries Service Data Report NMFS-DR-101.

Chapter 5

U.S.S.R.: Salmon Ranching in the Pacific

S. M. KONOVALOV

Pacific Research Institute of Fisheries and Oceanography (TINRO) and Population Biology Department, Institute of Marine Biology, the U.S.S.R. Academy of Sciences, Vladivostok

Revision of legal regulations for exploitation of biological resources of the World Ocean, and the introduction of the 200-mile economic zones will not settle all the problems that face mankind: salmon recognise neither borders nor economic zones and undertake feeding, wintering and spawning migrations through and beyond the 200-mile zones. Consequently they are accessible to the fishing fleet of any country and mankind must choose between alternative strategies for a salmon fishery. Offshore fishing could be developed, but this leads to the disappearance of salmon, because the countries that reserve rivers for their reproduction cannot exercise control over preservation of those stocks. Such was the case recently with Asiatic stocks of sockeye salmon *(Oncorhynchus nerka)* which were fished almost solely by Japan, whereas the U.S.S.R. prohibited the harvesting of main stocks within the country.

Alternatively, as salmon home to their native rivers to spawn, each stock could be harvested separately in strict relation to its abundance. Then, countries with spawning rivers become directly involved in their preservation and in maintenance of stocks at a high level, while keeping in check the industries that affect salmon. Concurrently this strategy fosters development of artificial propagation, and salmon-ranching projects may turn into the most profitable ventures in aquaculture (Calaprice, 1976). Only the latter strategy will allow maintenance of salmon stocks at a high level as well as maximal harvesting. In this context a summary of studies of artificial propagation of salmon in the Soviet Far East is opportune. Examination of promising trends in such research will aid in defining the most urgent problems, whose solution may improve the efficiency of artificial culture.

FAR EAST SALMONIDS

All six species of Pacific salmon inhabit the Far East. Pink and chum salmon (*Oncorhynchus gorbuscha* and *O. keta*) are widespread from the River Anadyr to South Primorye (Table I), while sockeye, coho (*O. kisutch*) and chinook (*O. tschawytscha*) inhabit mainly Kamchatka and the Bering sea along the Chukotka coast. Some coho are found in the Kuriles, Sea of Okhotsk, and on Sakhalin Island. Three species are known in the Amur—pink, chum and masu (*O. masou*). Masu inhabit the southern part of the habitat of genus *Oncorhynchus* in Asia only, and were formerly a game fish in North Primorye, the Amur and on Sakhalin Island (Fig. 1).

According to the time spent in fresh water and at sea, Pacific salmon can be divided into three groups (Table II). (1) Pink salmon migrate to sea as the yolk sac disappears; chum remain a while and also stay at sea longer than pink salmon. (2) Coho and masu spend 1-2 years in freshwater and 1-2 years at sea (Konovalov and Shcherbinin, 1973). (3) Sockeye and chinook spend 0-2 years in freshwater and have a comparatively long sea life, normally 3 and occasionally 4 years.

Chum and sockeye are the only Far Eastern Pacific salmon with seasonal strains. The greatest distinctions in major characteristics e.g. body weight, lifespan, sea feeding areas, are those of the summer and autumn chum of the Amur and Sakhalin Island. From the Amur summer chum migrate towards the southern Kuriles and Japan and remain there; autumn chum migrate in a year through the Sea of Okhotsk and then via the oceanic drift to the near Aleutian region of the Pacific and the Bering Sea (Hartt, 1962, 1966; Hanamura, 1966).

Not all large local sockeye stocks of the Asiatic coast show seasonal strains. Lake Azabachye, Kamchatka is a spawning ground for spring and summer sockeye. Spring sockeye start spawning in the river about July 15-30, a month after the breakup of the lake ice. Summer sockeye

Table I. Principal regions of Pacific salmonid reproduction in the Far East

Geographical regions	Pink (*Oncorhynchus gorbuscha*)	Chum (*O. keta*)	Coho (*O. kisutch*)	Masu (*O. masou*)	Sockeye (*O. nerka*)	Chinook (*O. tschawytscha*)
Chukotsk Peninsula	+	+	—	—	ssp	+
Kamchatka Peninsula	+	+	+	ssp	+	+
Okhotsk-Penzhinsk region	+	+	+	—	+	—
Sakhalin Island	+	+	ssp[a]	+	—	—
Kuriles	+	+	—	—	ssp	—
Amur River	+	+	—	ssp	—	—
Primorye	+	+	—	+	—	—

[a]Separate small populations

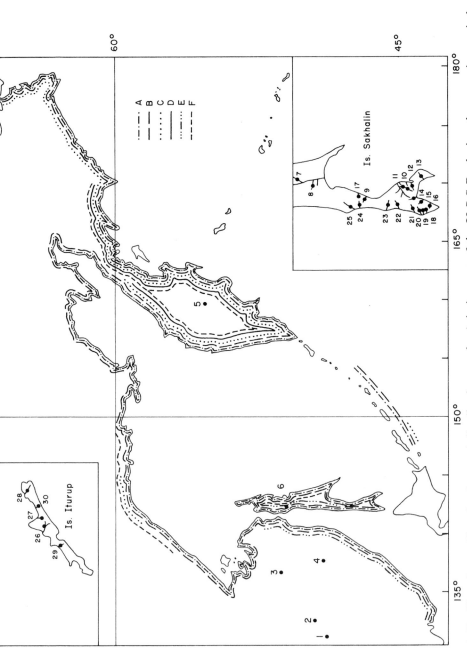

Fig. 1. Pacific salmon (*Oncorhynchus spp.*) distribution on the Asiatic coast of the U.S.S.R. during the spawning period. A: pink (*O. gorbuscha*). B: chum (*O. keta*). C: sockeye (*O. nerka*). D: chinook (*O. tschawytscha*). E: masu (*O. masou*). F: coho

Table II. Maximal frequency occurrence of age groups in the reproductive parts of isolates of *Oncorhynchus* spp.

Age Groups (years)	Group 1		Group 2		Group 3	
	Pink (*O. gorbuscha*)	Chum (*O. keta*)	Coho (*O. kisutch*)	Masu (*O. masou*)	Sockeye (*O. nerka*)	Chinook (*O. tschawytscha*)
0·1	100	6·9	2·6			1·9
0·2	+ ᵃ	90·7	+		+	9·7
0·3		98·2	+		14·6	51·6
0·4		85·4			8·1	32·9
0·5		19·8			+	+
0·6		+				
0·7		+				
1·0			6·3			
1·1			100	99	89	
1·2			5	67	99	90
1·3					95·4	76
1·4					29·7	62·6
1·5					+	3
2·0			+			
2·1			70·6	38	50	+
2·2			5	25	96·7	41
2·3					92	20·1
2·4					9	14·6
3·0					+	
3·1			5		4	
3·2					51·6	
3·3					71	
3·4					+	
4·1					+	
4·2					+	
4·3					+	

ᵃ + = 0·01-1·5% frequency.

prefer lacustrine spawning grounds and spawn from August 20-September 5 (Konovalov, 1972). The river sockeye of the upper reaches of the Kamchatka belong to the spring strain; Lake Kurilsky sockeye belong to the summer strain. From the distribution of sexually mature fishes in May-June, spring and summer sockeye of Lake Azabachye seem to differ in their wintering areas in the ocean. Usually the spring strain is found near the Komandorskie Islands and the summer strain in waters west of the Aleutian ridge.

All species except masu salmon spawn in the Kamchatka R., chinook being fished as early as May, and the main run is observed in the first half of June (Kuznetsov, 1923). Spring sockeye run up in June and summer sockeye in the second half of July. At the same time pink salmon ascend the river and in later July and early August they are followed by chum. From the second week of August coho enter the river, and fishing for them continues throughout September. A small number of coho may enter rivers as late as December. In the Amur, summer chum enter from the end of June until the second half of August (Levanidov, 1969; Pravdin, 1940), and autumn chum appear at the end of August and in September. Pink salmon migrate into spawning bayous from the second half of June till the beginning of August. Masu salmon approach the rivers Tumnin and Amur at the end of May, and migrate up river until mid-July (Vorobyev, 1926; Navozov-Lavrov, 1927; Smirnov, 1975). Pacific salmon usually spawn from several days to a month after entering the river depending on the remoteness of spawning grounds from the sea.

The different species spawn in different areas of a body of water. Masu dwelling together with pink and chum salmon spawn in the upper reaches of rivers with a rapid flow and no spring water. Pink salmon spawn in the river-bed of foothill sites with spring water (Smirnov, 1975). Summer chum reproduce in rivers with a marked underchannel stream mixed with spring water; autumn chum prefer spawning grounds with spring water. Sockeye spawn in the channels of mountain rivers and along the banks of lakes, choosing sites fed by springs. Coho may lay eggs in the main watercourse, preferring headwaters, and streams. Kuznetsov (1928) thought they were confined to sites with springs. Chinook spawn in the main watercourse of large rivers and in wide bayous in the upper reaches of the Kamchatka which are shallower and slower (Vronsky, 1972; Kuznetsov, 1928). In the Paratunka basin, sockeye salmon spawn in Lakes Dalny and Blizhny: coho spawn in the rivers flowing out of these lakes, and in mid-channel and foothill pools of the Paratunka; chinook spawn in deeper faster reaches and also further upstream. In the Nizhne Kamchatsk region sockeye spawn mainly in Lake Azabachye and other shallower lakes and in their inflowing streams. Chinook spawn in the upper reaches of the Raduga, discharging into the Kamchatka, while pink salmon spawn in the central part. Coho spawn in spring brooks linking L. Azabachye to the Kamchatka, and in some large rivers like the Bushiuka. Pink salmon spawn in the central part of the Lamutka Creek in places avoided by sockeye. Chum are not numerous in the

Table III. Average annual harvest of Pacific salmonids (after Levanidov *et al.*, 1970).[a]

Species	Asia (1925-1966) (Nos. × 10⁶)		America (1920-1966) (Nos. × 10⁶)	
	(Nos. × 10^6)	(%)	(Nos. × 10^6)	(%)
Chum *(Oncorhynchus keta)*	33·1	22	12·3	12·9
Pink *(O. gorbuscha)*	104·1	69·3	49	51·3
Sockeye *(O. nerka)*	10·4	6·9	24·5	25·6
Coho *(O. kisutch)*	2·6	1·7	6·7	7·0
Chinook *(O. tschawytscha)*	0·1	0·1	3·0	3·2

[a]Maximum annual harvest of masu *(O. masou)* in the Far East was 250 000 fish (Vorobyev, 1926).

lake but may be found occasionally with sockeye spawners, leading to some natural hybridisation.

Pacific salmon abundance is determined chiefly by conditions of reproduction. Thus the large numbers of lakes in Alaska and in N.W. America have permitted large natural sockeye populations, and the numerous large rivers abundant chinook populations. On the Asiatic coast pink salmon is the most numerous, spawning in the short, shallow rivers of Sakhalin Island, the Kuriles, and in large valley rivers of western Kamchatka. Chum is the next most abundant and the remainder are less important commercially (Alexin, 1923; Levanidov *et al.*, 1970) (Tables III and IV).

Table IV. Average salmon catches by U.S.S.R. and Japan in north-western Pacific (tonnes × 10^3)[a]

Year	U.S.S.R.	Japan	Total
1926-1929	63·7	116·9	180·6
1930-1934	133·0	155·1	288·1
1935-1939	131·4	300·7	432·1
1940-1944	157·4	167·9	325·3
1945-1949	182·5	2·6	185·1
1950-1954	159·1	34·6	193·7
1955-1959	129·9	175·9	305·8
1960-1964	67·1	133·9	201·1
1965-1969	66·9	125·1	192·0

[a]From 3 to 5% of total numbers of Pacific Salmon of Asiatic origin are reproduced in Japanese rivers.

EXPEDIENCY OF ARTIFICIAL CULTURE

The low cultural level of indigenous inhabitants and migrants in the
Far East, the total absence of legislation safeguarding biological
resources, the powerful and uncontrolled influence of foreign owners of
fisheries (Alexin, 1923; Brazhnikov, 1900; Kramarenko, 1898;
Netboy, 1974), and the complete ignorance of the biology of these fish
all contributed to irrational exploitation of Pacific salmon stocks.

Russia, like other developed countries, showed periods of serious
decline in abundance of salmon (Netboy, 1974). Urbanisation and
industrialisation, as elsewhere, necessitated attention to spawning
rivers to keep them habitable for salmon. Concern for salmon following
commercial tree-felling was even voiced in the 1920s. (*Bull. Fish. Ind.
Publ.*, 1926). From the end of the last century Russian naturalists
repeatedly visited the Far East to consider problems of biological
exploitation. It was found necessary to improve legislation to regulate
fisheries and conserve salmon (Brazhnikov, 1900; Bykov, 1898;
Kryukov, 1894; Soldatov, 1912, 1915). Soldatov (1910) carried out the
first experiments there on artificial fertilisation of salmon eggs and their
incubation. He also studied the salmon fisheries and concluded that
only artificial propagation might compensate for overharvesting of the
Amur stocks. This conclusion was preceded and accompanied by
extensive studies of natural spawning and salmon spawning grounds.
Kuznetsov noted that under natural conditions up to 70% of the eggs
were lost at spawning, and subsequently the redds might freeze or dry
up, leading to heavy losses of salmon larvae. He considered that having
brought these "bottle-necks" in salmon biology under control, it was
possible to increase the numbers of fish greatly.

The Tsarist Government decided to construct the first experimental
fish hatchery, using funds derived from licence fees. In 1909 K. L.
Lavrov, a fish industrialist, was encouraged to build an experimental
hatchery near a rich fishing ground, Bolshoi Chkhil, near the Amur
estuary. Kuznetsov's experiments were started there in the autumn of
that year (Kuznetsov, 1912, 1923, 1928; Soldatov, 1910, 1912). He was
faced with many hindrances. In the first year 69% of the maturing
brood fish did not survive the long stay in nurseries until complete
maturity. A regular supply of good water for incubation was lacking
and the water temperature depended chiefly on weather conditions,
but fish-rearing was pronounced promising and the hatchery would be

able to release up to 250 000 salmon fry. However, when kept in nurseries chum salmon were restless and tried to leave them, and the loss of parent fish was high. Consequently, Kuznetsov (1923) concluded that fish-rearing could be a success only in natural spawning locations, and not in the lower reaches of large rivers. At an early date, he started feeding the fry with grated eggs, fish brain and cottage cheese. The hatchery was transferred to the Praure River and operated from 1916 to 1919. Its capacity was 3 500 000 larvae, but it was only in 1918 that they succeeded in fertilising up to 3 000 000 eggs.

About the same time, two hatcheries were built on Kamchatka Peninsula, one in the Bolshaya basin by Grushetsky and the other in the basin of Lake Nerpichy (Ust-Kamchatsk) by Denbigh. Grushetsky's hatchery is illustrated in Kuznetsov (1923), where there is also a description of Denbigh's hatchery. Rearing experiments were carried out here with chum and sockeye salmon. Kuznetsov (1923) describes Denbigh's hatchery as the Japanese summer type, because at the approach of frosts the larvae and the remaining eggs were transferred from incubators into a specially heated nursery. In the difficult economic situation, these hatcheries were short-lived.

Kuznetsov also attempted to prove the expediencey of artificial fertilization of eggs and planting them in redds. He considered this imitative method would be the most effective (Kuznetsov 1923, 1928, 1937). However, his idea was criticised from the start and probably was finally condemned as labour-consuming (Navozov-Lavrov, 1927). It followed from the first research on artificial propagation that the studies should be extended and experimental fish hatcheries be built nearer to the spawning grounds.

EARLY YEARS OF THE SOVIETS

Despite the difficult economic situation large-scale construction of fish-rearing establishments was started in 1928. The Teplovsky hatchery in the Amur basin, for autumn chum, and the Ushkovsky in the Kamchatka basin for sockeye, coho and chum were the first to be built with capacities of 20 000 000 eggs each. These were followed in 1930 with the Adatymovsky hatchery on Sakhalin Island with a capacity of 15 000 000 chum eggs (Kuznetsov, 1937; Pravdin, 1940). These hatcheries differed from previous ones in their location near large spawning grounds. By 1934 39 000 000 fry were released annually from these three hatcheries. The Adatymovsky hatchery was heated and had a gravity-fed water supply through the incubators. The Teplovsky and Ushkovsky hatcheries were wooden buildings where eggs in Atkins frames were flushed by warm spring water on the nursery floor. The Bidzhansky hatchery was built in 1933, with a capacity of 20 000 000 autumn chum eggs, and the capacity of the Teplovsky hatchery was subsequently raised to 60 000 000 eggs a year.

On the basis of experience, the following basic hatchery requirements were formulated: a hatchery must: (1) have brood fish; (2) be located near natural spawning grounds; (3) not be flooded; (4) have warm springs for spawning; (5) have considerable storage of ground water; and (6) have sufficient head of water for construction of a gravity flow system (Kuznetsov, 1937). Spring water would secure temperature stability during the incubation period.

ECOLOGICAL   STUDIES

After World War II Japanese industrialists left twelve operating hatcheries on Sakhalin Island with a capacity of 130 000 000 eggs and one on Iturup Island with 30 000 000 eggs. Many of these hatcheries were badly in need of repair and reconstruction. From 1951-1954 five were restored, and water supply systems were reconstructed in five more. Construction of two hatcheries was begun on Iturup Island.

The capacity of hatcheries had increased steadily as their number declined slightly. The volume of construction in the post-war period is shown in Tables V and VI, which also show specialisation of hatcheries to chum and pink salmon only. Hatchery capacity increased at the expense of extension and reconstruction, and water supplies were typically gravity fed, some using spring water and others surface water also. In those with mixed water supplies the temperature was unstable, falling in winter to $0 \cdot 1$-$0 \cdot 3$°C; in warmwater hatcheries it did not fall below $1 \cdot 5$-$3 \cdot 0$°C (Kanidyev, 1965). Reduced efficiency due to high egg and larval mortality led to closure of four coldwater hatcheries out of six (Kanidyev, 1965). Water quantity limits the capacity of hatcheries, but increased capacity of hatcheries on Sakhalin Island was made possible by using underground water drainage, a suggestion of Koposov (1959, 1964). This made available high-quality silt-free water and permitted a high survival of eggs (Kanidyev and Zhuikova, 1970).

The large numbers of hatcheries have provided favourable conditions for scientific research. At Teplovsky, Levanidov (1954a, b, 1957, 1964, 1969) demonstrated that by eliminating predators in lakes like Teploe, they could be used as finishing reservoirs for autumn chum salmon. He suggested that special finishing channels for young fish be constructed suitable for propagating aquatic invertebrates, noting that chum larvae have a subterminal mouth, an adaptation to feeding on bottom fauna. Andreyeva (1953), Vasilyev (1954, 1957, 1960), Dvinin (1954), and Lazarev (1954) analysed the hatchery work, and Disler (1954) defined developmental stages of young fish on a nutritional basis.

Smirnov (1954) raised the question of broodstock selection, noting the wide variability of males and females in length, body weight and fecundity. Observations made during the spawning run showed that fish came up in various physiological conditions, differing in sex ratio and exterior indices between the beginning, middle and end of the run into Sakhalin rivers. Wide egg variability and occasional instances of small eggs in large females convinced him of the inexpediency of using such females in the rearing process. He favoured the heterospermic fertilisation of eggs, in which eggs of 10-12 females are fertilised with sperm of 10-12 males (Vasilyev, 1960). Smirnov observed that larvae feed before their yolk is finished, develop the surface vascular system, and need a lower oxygen supply than had been thought before. However, Vasilyev (1957) showed that embryos suffered at reduced oxygen levels: 6-8 mg per litre satisfied both chum and pink salmon. The incubation period in degree-days did not vary greatly with temperature being 530 or 425 respectively for autumn chum at 10·4°C and 3·4°C (Smirnov, 1954). Moreover, the duration of incubation is specific in salmonids (Smirnov, 1975).

Research on artificial feeding of hatchery fry is not yet extensive. Kanidyev (1966), Frolenko (1964), and Shershnev (1968) noted the value of extra feeding for chum and pink salmon fry, but more work is needed on this. The problem of predation was treated in theoretical works by Popov (1953), Girsa (1962), Gerasimov (1965), and Rekubratsky (1965), who showed that fry might develop a defence reflex. This idea was never developed (Kanidyev, 1966) and is not used in the rearing process.

In summary, marked progress has been made with egg fertilisation and improving the biotechniques of embryonal and larval development.

Table V. Far Eastern hatcheries.

No.	Hatchery name	Region	Year of construction	Capacity planned (eggs × 10^6)	present	Species	Change of water temperature during incubation
1	Teplovsky	Amur	1928	44	64	autumn chum	slight
2	Bidzhansky	Amur	1933	20	44	autumn chum	slight
3	Udinsky	Amur	1963	15	15	pink, chum	slight
4	Gursky	Amur	1967	20	20	autumn chum	slight
5	Ushkovsky	Kamchatka River	1928	20	5	sockeye, coho, chum	slight
6	Adatymovsky	Sakhalin Is.	1928	20	48	autumn chum	slight
7	Pobedinsky	Sakhalin Is.	1924	10	20	pink, chum	slight
8	Buyuklinksy	Sakhalin Is.	1924	10	34	pink, chum	moderate
9	Pugachevsky	Sakhalin Is.	1929	20	56	pink	great
10	Sokolovsky	Sakhalin Is.	1940	14	95	pink, chum	slight
11	Breznyakovsky	Sakhalin Is.	1924	20	55	pink, chum	slight
12	Lesnoy	Sakhalin Is.	1933	10	35	pink	great
13	Okhotsky	Sakhalin Is.	1941	5	35	chum	slight

14	Anivsky	Sakhalin Is.	1941	1·5	17	pink, chum	great
15	Taranaisky	Sakhalin Is.	1938	2	30	pink, chum	slight
16	Kirillovsky	Sakhalin Is.	1957	11	16[a]	pink, chum	great
17	Vatutunsky	Sakhalin Is.	1956	3	12	pink	great
18	Lovetsky	Sakhalin Is.	1956	3	12[a]	pink, chum	great
19	Yasnomorsky	Sakhalin Is.	1925	5	17	chum	slight
20	Sokolnikovsky	Sakhalin Is.	1926	5	24	chum	slight
21	Kalininsky	Sakhalin Is.	1925	20	89	chum	slight
22	Pionersky	Sakhalin Is.	1932	2	6	chum	slight
23	Urozhainy	Sakhalin Is.	1956	4	10	pink, chum	slight
24	Parusny	Sakhalin Is.	1956	5	5·5[a]	pink	great
25	Ainsky	Sakhalin Is.	1929	5	31	pink, chum	great
26	Kurilsky	Iturup. Is.	1919	20	60	pink, chum	slight
27	Reidovy	Iturup Is.	1927	?	56	pink, chum	slight
28	Aktivny	Iturup Is.	1928	8	14·5[a]	pink, chum	slight
29	Osenny	Iturup Is.	1922	10	13	pink, chum	slight
30	Sopochny	Iturup Is.	1922	8	8[a]	pink, chum	great

[a]Hatcheries that were closed

Table VI. Total capacity of Far Eastern hatcheries in different years.

Year	Number of hatcheries	Output (eggs × 10⁶)	Information source
1939	?	166?	Rukhlov (unpublished)
1946	13	150	Rukhlov (unpublished)
1958	25	320	Rukhlov (unpublished)
1965	25	500	Kanidyev (1965)
1970	21	600	Kanidyev et al. (1970)
1976	18	800	"Glavrybvoda" data

Despite the view of some authors that it is impossible to achieve in hatcheries results as good as those of natural propagation (Abramov, 1953; Vasilyev and Yurovitsky, 1954; Kuznetsov, 1928), progress in technology and increase in rearing efficiency testify to the correctness of the chosen direction (Vasilyev, 1960; Kanidyev, 1965; Kanidyev et al., 1970; Levanidov, 1954). High egg fertilisation (99%) has been attained, loss of eggs has dropped (2%), and total waste has been only 2·8-9% for pink and 3·3-8·5% for chum salmon (Kanidyev and Zhuikova, 1970).

Many problems have been left unsolved, such as the theoretical foundations of feeding with artificial nutrients, the interrelations between hatchery juvenile fish and biotic and abiotic factors outside the hatcheries, problems of intrapopulational variability and the consequent strategies for fish culturists.

POPULATION RESEARCH

The end of the 1960s and the 1970s has seen the accelerated decline of local Pacific salmon due to irrational intensive offshore fishing. Therefore scientists have focused on one important problem area, the marine phase of salmon, to learn to identify fish of local stocks and to assess the consequences of offshore fishing on stocks of Asiatic salmon. Lack of control over fisheries, diminishing stocks and direct evidence that hatcheries were in effect working for fishing companies harvesting salmon at sea, reduced the interest of scientists and the government in artificial propagation.

Extensive studies have been made of the migrations of different species of salmon and of individual local stocks (e.g. Konovalov,

1975a). Hydrological conditions in the habitats of chum and pink salmon in the first months of life are very important. High mortalities occur when smolts enter seawater at temperatures lower than 2°C, which may occur around Sakhalin Island. Releases of smolts from hatcheries into the sea should be co-ordinated with the hydrological forecast, thus providing the smolts with an optimal environment for their entry.

Extensive population studies of Pacific salmon began in 1968. Their great practical significance for fish hatcheries has become clear. Population biology explores the spatial structure of a species and biological structure of a population, as well as the functions of these structures. For artificial populations, science recommends the formation of natural-type spatial and biological structures. For example, when a biological structure is formed it should possess population homeostasis, i.e. should be capable of response to any environmental action.

In the field of population genetics Altukhov (1974) has described some biochemical polymorphisms of almost all species of Pacific salmon. Sockeye salmon from Lake Azabachye (Kamchatka) showed differences in the concentration of genes in the subisolates forming an isolate (local stock), but stability in the concentration of genes from year to year in one isolate. The change of the genetic structure in different years correlates with the number of generations. He pointed out the necessity in fish-rearing practice of maintaining the spatial structure of the isolate, its genetic polymorphism, and its level of heterozygosity. He noticed that mature chum salmon migrating for spawning at different times differ in sex ratio and genetic structure. Assuming that every isolate has a long evolutionary history in a given river, he suggested that rearing should try to sustain genetic hetero-geneity by artificial reproduction of early, late and "normally" maturing fish, allowing the natural population to serve as the matrix for artificial propagation.

Current studies of seasonal strains indicate genetic and occasionally chromosomic polymorphism. Therefore hatchery reproduction of only early and normally maturing fish might be selection for early maturation. Where only normally maturing fish are reproduced, we may assume stabilising selection. The weighted-average reproduction of early, middle and late spawning fish is essential (Fig. 2), and the reproduction of fish in only one of these periods should be avoided.

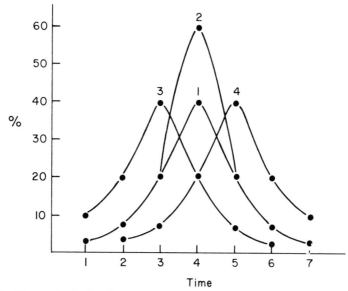

Fig. 2. Theoretical distributions of salmon during spawning time in (1) natural and artificial (2) stabilized (3) early (4) late reproduction.

This requires the ability to forecast the number of early, late and normally maturing fish in filial generations.

Since the late nineteenth century fertilised eggs have been sent to various remote regions of the globe. Experience has shown that salmon can be acclimatised in lakes, but few populations have established in rivers discharging into seas or oceans. One reason for failure is ignorance of the complexity and environmental dependence of Pacific salmon. Distant transport of eggs within the species habitat was also a failure. Altukhov (1974) showed that the survival of fry from eggs delivered to a new place is extremely low. Population genetics explains this by the fact that in ordering egg deliveries the fish culturists did not consider climatic analogues. Since introduction into a population of a large number of less viable genotypes in the given conditions leads to a reduction of adaptation of the population as a whole in subsequent generations, we should agree with Altukhov (1974) and abstain from experiments of this kind.

Population genetics recommends restoration of depressed populations by reciprocal crossing of males and females of the donor and recipient populations. The offspring inherit from the local parent the ability to adapt to the local environment. The fish of the donor stock should be selected so as not to lower the stamina of the local population. Bams (1976) reached analogous conclusions with British Columbia pink salmon populations.

The author's laboratory has kept 25 subisolates of the model sockeye salmon isolate from Lake Azabachye under observation for many years. Every isolate in the first place adapts to the conditions at the spawning sites. Thus, form, weight and body length depend primarily, not on the final conditions in fresh water or the sea, but on the depth of the spawning grounds and on accessibility for predators. This relationship holds true for the subisolates of geographically remote isolates as those of Lakes Alecnaguik and Nerka (Wood R.) in Alaska. On deep spawning grounds large sockeye of age 1·3 and 2·3 have a bulky form, while on shallow spawning grounds they are more slender (Fig. 3). Differences in body weight of fish of a given length from the shallowest and deepest spawning grounds may reach 1 kg, half the weight of small males and females. On shallow spawning grounds movement is difficult for large males which often fall prey to predators (Konovalov and Shevlyakov, 1978). On deep-water spawning grounds elimination by predators is reduced to a minimum, therefore there prevails a selection for large body size conditioned by assortative mating (Hanson and Smith, 1968).

We conclude that the two trends in selection caused by action of predators and assortative mating determine the size structure of the subisolate at any given moment. An important precept results for fish-cultural practice: it is possible to direct selection for body size of parent

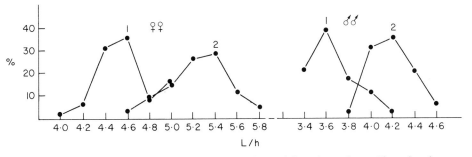

Fig. 3. Distribution of large spawning male and female sockeye *(Oncorhynchus nerka)* at the age of 1·3 and 2·3 by the body height index (L/h) in the deep Pick Creek (1) and shallow Hansen Creek (2) Wood R. Alaska.

fish since the fish will be propagated artificially. However, it is necessary in hatchery rearing that a variety of sizes be maintained so that a population could reclaim its initial state under any extreme conditions.

The role of age structure in environmental adaptation has not yet been fully elucidated. We have therefore undertaken comparative studies of the age structure of subisolates, which are formed through aggregates of age groups that characterise fish of all sizes. If conditions are changed, age structure permits regulation of interrelations between individuals of different age and size groups. Analysis of sex-age structure of parent fish and of the first generation in the subisolates of sockeye salmon of Lake Azabachye revealed a number of regularities. First, the duration of freshwater and sea periods of life is of a qualitative, discrete character, being sex-linked. Secondly, when crossing fish of 1·3 and 2·3 ages, average (1·2;2·2) and small (2·1) males are separated in the progeny. Thirdly, in the offspring of average males there are more small fast-maturing males and fewer large males. Fourthly, crossing a male of age 1·2 with a female 2·3 produces a considerable quota of females of age 2·2 (Table VII). Continuation of these observations suggests that we may ultimately be able to advance a theory of age regulation of Pacific salmon which will allow the prediction of the age structure of parent fish and should permit control of the age structure of artificially propagated populations. The next important and complex problem facing fish culturists is the deliberate imposition of the sex structure of every artificial population. Sexual reproduction reveals all its merits when a species is found in a markedly changeable environment. Complex life cycles as well as rigid requirements of extremely exact and speedy transmission of information on a population interaction with environment give advantage to sexual reproduction. Pacific salmon have a complex life cycle and have rigid requirements concerning exactness and speed of handing down information from generation to generation.

The 25 subisolates of Lake Azabachye sockeye salmon are distinguishable in the ratio of males to females in every age group. This suggests that local conditions in the reproduction area determine the degree of similarity of sexual structures of subisolates. A heightened heterogeneity of males dominated among extreme biological types of subisolates (Fig. 4). For example, the smallest and largest fish were males. The findings support this hypothesis of the role of sexes. It

Table VII. Ratio of age groups of the 1970 generation parent sockeye (*Oncorhynchus nerka*) and progeny, of several subisolates of Lake Azabachye, expressed in percentatges.

		Subisolate									
		Timofeyevskaya 2		Timofeyevskaya 3		Lotnayazemlyansk		Rybovodnaya-Lotnaya		Snovidovskaya-Arishkin	
Sex	Age	Parents	Progeny	Parents	Progeny	Parents	Progeny	Parents	Progeny	Parents	Progeny
Male	1:1	4·8	0	0	0	0	0	0	0	0	0
Male	2:1	3·6	36·6	0	19·6	0	0·4	0	1·9	0	10·9
Male	1:2	54·8	20·9	93·5	19·6	0	0·2	0	0·6	35·7	3·1
Male	2:2	16·7	23·8	2·2	32·1	0	1·2	0	0	7·1	14·3
Male	1:3	3·6	2·9	4·3	7·1	10	38·5	9·7	8·7	16·7	22·1
Male	2:3	16·7	15·7	0	21·4	90	59·8	90·3	88·8	40·5	49·5
Female	1:2	2·1	0	10·5	0	0	0	0	0	0	0
Female	2:2	2·1	13·6	3	14	0	0	0	0	0	0
Female	1:3	20·6	77·3	20·3	33·3	13·5	22·3	10·2	9·4	8·6	45
Female	2:3	75·2	9·1	66·2	52·6	86·5	77·3	89·9	90·6	91·4	55

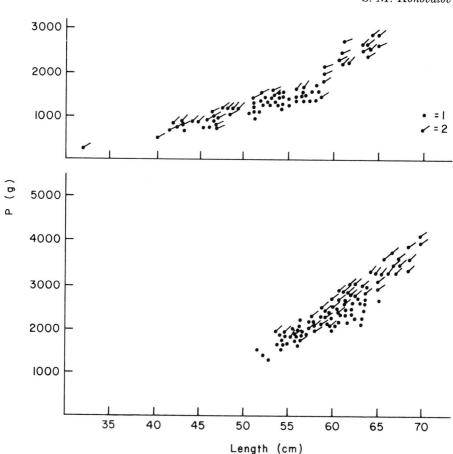

Fig. 4. Distribution by length (L) and weight without viscera (P) of sexually mature sockeye *(Oncorhynchus nerka)* of the subisolates: *(upper)* Olezhkin pond (Lake Azabachye, Kamchatka) and *(lower)* Pick Creek (Nerka L., Alaska). 1—females, 2—males.

implies that among bisexual species a division of functions takes place in handing down hereditary information to succeeding generations.

Geodakyan (1965a, b) considered that a division of species memory into constant and operational memories occurred at sex differentiation. The operational memory (variability tendency) is typical of males, and the constant memory (inheritance tendency) of females. The quantity of females determines the numbers of offspring; that of males the rate and variability value of median offspring genotype. Our data have confirmed this and showed that the sex ratio is an important population parameter related to habitat. Transition of a subisolate (subpopulation) from one state into another is performed with a strict observance of transition of each sex into a new state. The splitting of a new age group in the subisolate is always connected with an appearance of males (Table VII). Only when hereditary information is handed down through males will females of succeeding generations pass into these size, age, morphological and other groups.

Adaptation connected with an environmentally induced change in the sex structure is defined by us as homeostasis of control, enabling the subisolate to adapt to new conditions with minimal losses in number. Thus, a deliberate imposition of the sex structure may secure transition of a population into a new state. Assimilation of rivers previously uninhabited by salmon and restoration of populations impoverished by fishery or other factors should be accompanied by reproduction of the most diverse first generation males in predominating numbers. The quota of females should be considerably lower than that of males. In a protracted fish-rearing process, however, a controlled predominance of males is justified only if reproduction conditions are essentially changed.

Development of population biology concepts has greatly expanded our understanding of the biological structure of subisolates (subpopulations) of Pacific salmon, especially the role of variety, and has led us to apply it to artificial fish propagation. The spatial structure concept enables us to work out requirements for artificial populations that ensure minimal mortality in fresh waters and at sea due to the homing instinct.

PROSPECTS FOR ARTIFICIAL CULTURE

With 200-mile economic zones most North Pacific countries have recognised sovereign rights of the state of origin of anadromous fish. The U.S.S.R. and Canada have agreed that the migratory species should not be fished outside the bounds of national jurisdiction over fishing. If all countries support the U.S.S.R. and Canada in recognising that salmon will return to their native rivers, where they may be harvested, then interest in artificial propagation will increase as it will in all measures directed at a rapid increase in the numbers of these marvellous fish.

Table VIII. Predicted release of fry from hatcheries in different regions of the Far East ($\times 10^6$).

Province	Year	Pink (O. gorbuscha)	Chum (O. keta)	Coho (O. kisutch)	Masu (O. masou)	Sockeye (O. nerka)	Chinook (O. tschawytscha)	Total
Sakhalin Is. Kuriles	1980	690	295	5	5	5	—	1000
	1985	1000	440	15	30	15	—	1500
	1990	1360	540	30	40	30	—	2000
	2000	1970	860	60	60	50	—	3000
Amur River, Khabarovsk province	1980	—	100	—	—	—	—	100
	1985	5	150	—	—	—	—	155
	1990	40	235	—	—	—	—	275
	2000	130	555	—	—	—	—	685
Kamchatka Peninsula	1980	—	—	—	—	—	—	—
	1985	—	30	10	—	5	10	55
	1990	—	100	50	—	8	30	188
	2000	—	200	80	—	10	50	340
Magadan province	1980	19	19	—	—	—	—	38
	1985	53	76	—	—	—	—	129
	1990	110	266	23	—	—	—	399
	2000	163	346	23	—	19	—	551
Primorye	1980	—	—	—	—	—	—	—
	1985	75	75	—	50	—	—	200
	1990	110	110	—	75	—	—	295
	2000	150	150	—	100	—	—	400

In the U.S.S.R. interest is growing in Pacific salmon as a potentially valuable commercial species. In the peak years of abundance over 400 000 tons of salmon were harvested; the catch is now 150 000-200 000 tons. Over-harvesting is connected with development of a large-scale offshore fishery, unable to harvest each stock proportional to its numbers. This fishery, by its nature, selects for an early age of maturation, decrease of body size, increase in the proportion of small males etc., and disturbs the stock strucutures. If the offshore fishery is prohibited, the numbers of natural populations can be restored and conditions created for artificial salmon culture. With increasing salmon numbers entering the spawning grounds, it will be vital to expand ameliorative operations, to clear the logging rivers, and to reafforest spawning river basins.

Table IX. Total planned release of fry from Far Eastern hatcheries ($\times 10^6$).

Year	Pink (O. gorbuscha)	Chum (O. keta)	Coho (O. kisutch)	Masu (O. masou)	Sockeye (O. nerka)	Chinook (O. tschawytscha)	Total
1980	719	414	5	—	5	—	1143
1985	1133	771	48	80	20	10	2062
1990	1620	1251	103	115	38	30	3157
2000	2413	2111	163	160	79	50	4976

A great expansion of artificial propagation of Pacific salmon is then planned. Hatcheries will be developed on Sakhalin Island and the Kuriles, primarily for chum and pink salmon (Tables VIII, IX). Experimental hatcheries will be built in Primorsky and Khabarovsky districts, and in Magadan and Kamchatka provinces, to test new technological schemes of hatcheries for certain species and regional conditions. Besides reconstruction and increasing the capacity of hatcheries in operation 52 hatcheries will be built, one-third on Sakhalin Island and the Kuriles (Table X). By the year 2000 we plan to release five billion fry of all the six species of Pacific salmon, mainly chum and pink.

Scientific planning may heighten operational efficiency of hatcheries considerably, especially if directed at studying the critical periods when massive stock losses occur. As the rearing process will be combined

S. M. Konovalov

Table X. Planned construction of hatcheries in the Far East.

Location	Number of new hatcheries to be put in operation			
	1985	1990	2000	Total
Sakhalin Island	2	5	10	17
Kuriles				
Amur River, Khabarovsk				
Province	1	3	3	7
Kamchatka Peninsula	3	4	4	11
Magadan Province	5	3	4	12
Primorye	2	1	2	5
Total	13	16	23	52

with natural reproduction, care must be taken to strengthen the adaptive possibilities of every population. This is possible only if population biology research data are utilised. Thus, formation by the subisolate (subpopulation) of a very complex structure is of great biological significance, and the structure of artificial populations must be formed carefully. The primitive formation of panmictic, i.e. structureless, populations negates the functional meaning of such a community. Composite-structured populations like subisolates of salmon acquire a new functional property, population homeostasis, which allows a population to change various biological parameters rapidly and to uphold a high density even with abrupt changes of habitat conditions. Artificial propagation in future must be organised to meet this requirement (Konovalov, 1975b).

In some cases average values of some structures can be changed, especially when limiting factors are eliminated in the rearing process. Thus, selection for more large hatchery brood fish does not essentially influence population fitness as a whole, since it is the water level on spawning grounds and elimination by predators that limit the body size of sexually mature fish (Konovalov and Shevlyakov, 1978). Both these limiting factors are excluded in the rearing process. If the hatchery operation is discontinued, large brood fish will not be able to propagate successfully due to inaccessibility of spawning grounds for them and the high coefficient of selection. Therefore the natural portion of a population will be able to continue its existence.

Scientific research should be directed at construction of high-quality water-recirculation systems. In future all hatcheries should be scheduled for accelerated development of eggs, larvae and fry by using warmer water, thus shortening the life of salmon. The problem of rations and supplementary feed for rearing the salmon fry is a pressing one in the U.S.S.R., and this trend of research should be continued.

Floating fishpen rearing of Pacific salmon will not be developed: it is much more expensive than hatchery rearing and requires a number of deep, sheltered bays. It is expedient only near densely populated areas, particularly near resorts. Salmon abundance that originated from natural and artificial populations will also contribute very little to fishpen rearing. It is supposed that Peter the Great Bay and some regions of southern Sakhalin will become sites of more or less intensive Pacific salmon rearing, and the maximum harvest may reach 4000 tons by the end of the century.

REFERENCES

Abramov, V. V. (1953). Trudy Soveshch. po Vopr. Lososevogo Khoz. dal. Vostoka, 4, 49-69. Vladivostok.

Aleksin, M. S. (1923). *In* Fish & Fur Resources of Far East. Publ. 'Nauch-prombureau' 'Dalrybokhoty', 3-133. Vladivostok.

Altukhov, Yu. P. (1974). Population Genetics of Fish. Izd. Pishchevaya Promyshlennost, Moscow. 274 pp.

Andreeva, M. A. (1953). Trudy Soveshch. po Vopr. Lososevogo Khoz. dal. Vostoka, 4, 70-77. Vladivostok.

Bams, R. A. (1976). *J. Fish. Res. Bd. Canada* **33**, 2716-2725.

Brazhnikov, V. (1900). Agric. Dept Publ. 133 St. Petersburg.

Bykov, P. T. (1898). *In Proc. Fish Ind.* **13**, 113-122. (1897, Priamur. Ved. No. 204).

Calaprice, J. R. (1976). *J. Fish. Res. Bd. Canada* **33**, 1068-1087.

Dvinin, P. A. (1954). Trudy Soveshch. po Vopr. Lososevego Khoz. dal. Vostoka 4, 78-86.

Disler, N. N. (1954). Trudy Soveshch. po Vopr. Lososevogo Khoz. dal. Vostoka, 4, 129-143.

Frolenko, L. A. (1964). Lososevoe Khozyaistvo Dal'nego Vostoka, Nauka, Moscow. 184-185.

Geodakyan, V. A. (1965a). Problemy Peredachi I, 105-113.

Geodakyan, V. A. (1965b). Problemy Kibernetiki, 13, 187-195, Moscow.

Gerasimov, V. V. (1965). *In* Biologicheskoe znachenie i funktsionalnaya determinatsiya migratsionnogo povedeniya zhivotnykh. Publ. "Nauka", pp. 53-58. Moscow.

Girsa, I. I. (1962). *Vopr. Ikhtiol.* **2**, 747-749.
Hanamura, N. (1966). *INPFC Bull.* **18**, 1-28.
Hanson, A. J. and Smith, H. D. (1968). *J. Fish. Res. Bd. Canada* **21** (3), 1955-1977.
Hartt, A. C. (1962). *INPFC Bull.* **6**, 157.
Hartt, A. C. (1966). *INPFC Bull.* **19**, 141.
Kanidev, A. N. (1965). *Trudy Murmanskii morskoi biol. Inst.* **9**, 47-61.
Kanidev, A. N. (1966a). *Rybn. Promyshlennost* **6**, 18-19.
Kanidev, A. N. (1966b). *Trudy Murmanskii morskoi biol. Inst.* **12**, 101-111.
Kanidev, A. N. and Zhuikova, L. I. (1970). *Izv. TINRO.* **74**, 193-209.
Kanidev, A. N. Kostyunin, G. M. and Salmin, S. A. (1970). *Vopr. Ikhtiol.* **10**, 360-373.
Konovalov, S. M. (1972). *Zh. Obshch. Biol.*, **33**, 668-682.
Konovalov, S. M. (1975a). Differentiation of local populations of sockeye salmon *Oncorhynchus nerka* (Walbaum). 290 pp. Wash. Univ. Press, Seattle.
Konovalov, S. M. (1975b). *Zh. Obshch. Biol.* **36**, 731-743.
Konovalov, S. M. and Shcherbinin, G. Y. (1973). *Zh. Obshch. Biol.* **34**, 837-854.
Konovalov, S. M. and Shevlyakov, A. G. (1978). *Zh. Obshch. Biol.* **39**, 194-206.
Koposov, A. F. (1959). *Rybn. promyshlennost* **2**, 21-24.
Koposov, A. F. (1964). Lososovoe Khozyaistvo Dal'nego Vostoka. "Nauka" pp. 179-183, Moscow.
Kramarenko, G. A. (1898). *Proc. Fish Ind.* **13**, 468-475.
Kryukov, N. A. (1894). *Proc. Amur. Rus. Soc.* **1**, 87. St. Petersburg.
Kuznetsov, I. I. (1912). *Publ. Agric. Dept.* **1**, 31.
Kuznetsov, I. I. (1923). Fish & Fur Res. of Far East Publ. "Goskniga" pp. 134-214.
Kuznetsov, I. I. (1928). Some observations of the spawning of Amur and Kamchatka salmons. Publ. "Knizhnoe Delo", Vladivostok. 196 pp.
Kuznetsov, I. I. (1937). Keta i ee vosproizvodstvo. Publ. 'Dalgiz', Khabarovsk. 175 pp.
Lazarev, M. S. (1954). *Trudy Soveshch. po Vopr. Lososevego Khoz. dal. Vostoka* **4**, 87-93.
Levanidov, V. Ya. (1954a). *Rybn. Promyshlennost* **6**, 34-38.
Levanidov, V. Ya. (1954b). *Trudy Soveshch. po. Vopr. Lososevogo Khoz. dal. Vostoka* **4**, 120-128.
Levanidov, V. Ya. (1957). *Proc. Conf. Fish Culture. Publ. Acad. Sci. U.S.S.R. 219-226. Moscow.*
Levanidov, V. Ya. (1964). *Vopr. Ikhtiol.* **4**, 658-663.
Levanidov, V. Ya. (1969). *Izv. TINRO.* **67**, 243 pp.
Levanidov, V. Ya. *et al.* (1970). *Izv. TINRO* **73**, 3-24.
Navozov-Lavrov, N. P. (1927). *Proizvodetelnye sely Dalnego Vostoka* **4**, 75-177. Vladivostok.
Netboy, A. (1974). "The Salmon. Their Fight for Survival". Houghton Mifflin Co., Boston. 613 pp.

Popov, G. V. (1953). *Zh. Vysshei Nervnoi Deyatelnosti* **3**, 774-7787.

Pravdin, I. F. (1940). *Izv. TINRO* **18**, 5-105.

Rekubratskii, V. A. (1965). *In:* Biologicheskoe znachenie i funktsionalnaya determinatsiya migratsionnogo povedeniya zhivotnykh. Publ. "Nauka", pp. 29-91. Moscow.

Shershnev, A. P. (1968). *Izv. TINRO* **65**, 273-275.

Smirnov, A. I. (1954a). *Rybnaya promshlennost* **6**, 38-41.

Smirnov, A. I. (1954b). *Trudy Soveshch. po. Vopr. Lososevogo Khoz. dal. Vostok* **4**, 94-110.

Smirnov, A. I. (1975). Biologiya, Razmnozhenie i Razvitie Tikhookeanskikh Lososei. Moscow State University, Moscow. 335 pp.

Soldatov, V. K. (1910). *Proc. Fish. Ind.* **12**, 493-505.

Soldatov, V. K. (1912). Untersuchungen über die Biologie der Salmoniden des Amur. *In* Die Fischereien des Fernen Ostens 7. St. Petersburg, Dept. Landwirtschaft. 223 pp.

Soldatov, V. K. (1915). *In* Material to understanding of Russian fish. *Ind. Publ. Agric. Dept.* **3**, 1-95. Petrograd.

Vasilev, I. M. (1954). *Trudy Soveshch. po Vopr. Lososevego Khoz. dal. Vostoka* **4**, 111-119. Moscow.

Vasilev, I. M. (1957). *Rybnoe Khozyaistvo* **33** (9), 56-62.

Vasilev, I. M. (1960). *Mater. Conf. Fish Culture. Fish Ind.* 61-62, Moscow.

Vasilev, I. M. and Yurovitskii, Yu, G. (1954). *Zool. Zh.* **33**, 1344-1348.

Vorobyev, A. V. (1926). *Bull. Fish Ind. Publ. Bureau Inst. Fish Ind.* **2**, 28-29. Moscow.

Vronsky, B. B. (1972). *Vopr. Ikhtiol.* **12**, 293-308.

Chapter 6

Salmon Propagation in Japan

T. KOBAYASHI

Hokkaido Salmon Hatchery, Sapporo, Hokkaido, Japan

INTRODUCTION

Three of the six species of salmon widely distributed in the northern Pacific inhabit Japanese waters: chum salmon or sake *(Oncorhynchus keta)*, pink salmon or karafuto masu *(O. gorbuscha)*, and masu salmon or sakura masu *(O. masou)*. The distribution of the three species forms the southernmost boundary of the genus *Oncorhynchus*, increasing in density from south to north, and the principal salmon production area in Japan is Hokkaido. The relationship between man and salmon has a long history: it is known from archaeological finds that salmon were eaten in prehistoric times, although only by the nobility because of the scarcity and high quality of salmon.

Salmon ranching in the ocean as now practised in Japan is the result of years of efforts to propagate salmon. The geographical and economic environment of Japan may have contributed largely to this technical development: because of religious commandments relating to diet, the Japanese people depended heavily on animal proteins from the sea, so the fishing industries had to make many technical innovations and contrivances to meet the demand for fish. The artificial propagation of salmon has been regarded as a promising way to enhance salmon stocks and revitalise the declining coastal fisheries in northern areas of Japan, so a high expectation is held for its further development. This chapter outlines the development, past and present, of Japan's salmon resources enhancement (i.e. salmon propagation) programme.

FISHING AND MIGRATION

Commercial fishing for salmon began in the sixteenth century in Hokkaido. It was not until 1700, however, that this fishing venture took a firm root, when an ethnic group called the Ainu caught salmon for food. The target of fishing was adult salmon ascending their home rivers and streams for spawning. At that time either beach seine or gill net was employed for commercial fishing operations carried out in estuarine waters. After 1800, coastal set nets were introduced, which helped to expand salmon fishing grounds in the coastal areas. Exploration and exploitation of new fishing grounds were conducted intensively, in addition to the development of fishing gear, after 1868 the year of Meiji Restoration, when Japan embarked on the road towards becoming a modern state. These efforts have contributed much to the development of today's salmon fishing industry. Recently, the salmon stocks in Hokkaido have increased, probably due to the salmon resource enhancement efforts, and expectations for a rejuvenation of the declining coastal fisheries in Hokkaido are high.

Over 90% of Japan's salmon catch is chum; the remainder is made up of 6% pink and 1% masu salmon. Chum fetches the highest market price. Most of the catch is salt-preserved, but some is destined for canning, freezing or smoking. The annual chum salmon catch in Hokkaido shows fairly large fluctuations (Fig. 1).

During the years 1879 to 1893, the average catch was about 7 000 000 fish, with a peak of 11 000 000 in 1889. During these years, which correspond to early development stages of Hokkaido, the salmon stocks were thought to have been in a healthy state and were supported by favourable environmental conditions for natural spawning. This was followed by about 70 years of poor production, with average annual catches amounting to about 3 000 000 fish (one to five million) up until 1970. In 1971 and thereafter, the annual catch has shown a significant increase, totalling 15 770 000 in 1975 and 10 210 000 in 1977. The catch of chum salmon in Honshu island has also increased, from one to two million fish per annum, in recent years. As for pink salmon, the catch was much less (see Fig. 2), 300 000-400 000 per annum in the years before 1968. However, the annual catch began to increase after 1969, and the periodicity (poor harvest year followed by good harvest year and so on) has become less marked in recent years. This indicates a recovery of pink salmon resources.

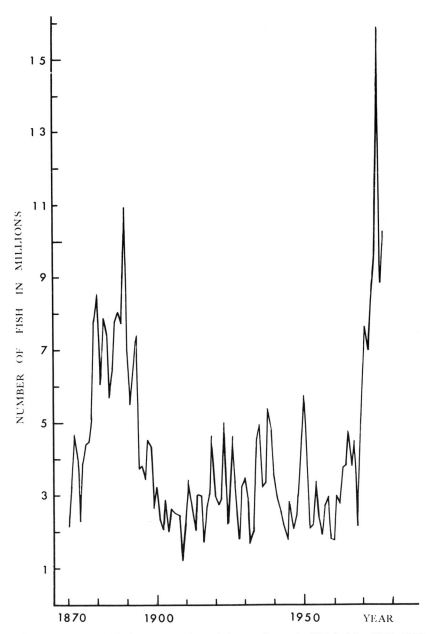

Fig. 1. Annual fluctuation of catches of chum salmon in Hokkaido, 1870-1977.

T. Kobayashi

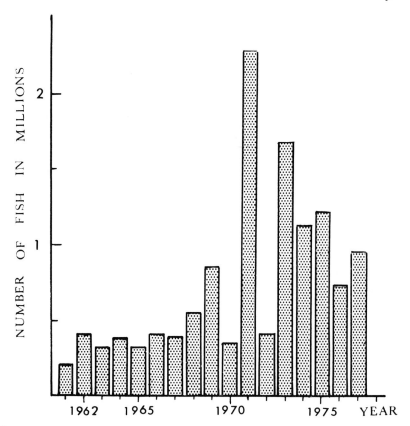

Fig. 2. Annual fluctuation in catches of pink salmon in Hokkaido, 1961-1977.

Commercial catches of masu salmon have been at an annual level of 200 000-300 000 fish. As well as the low level of stocks, game fishing of this species might have been partly responsible for the depletion of resources: masu salmon stay a full year in freshwater before they migrate to sea, so game fishing in freshwater systems is believed to affect the resources greatly.

The distribution of salmon extends far and wide in the northern Pacific except for the masu salmon, which is limited to the nearshore waters of Japan. Chum and pink migrate widely across the Pacific north of 40°N. However, the fate of chum and pink salmon after one to two months stay in coastal estuarine waters is not known. Their ocean life is not known in detail yet.

Figure 3 gives the estimated distribution and migration areas of Japanese chum salmon in the Pacific Ocean. In the years of homing migration, the chum salmon first appear in April and May in the south-western region of the Alaskan Gulf, then migrate through the Bering Sea in June and July, and finally move south along the Kamchatka Peninsula and the Kurile Island chain before reaching Hokkaido and Honshu in September and December (Kondo *et al.*, 1966). These are called autumn salmon since they spawn then. The catches of autumn salmon along the coasts constitute the principal salmon harvest in the coastal set nets. According to recent statistics, over 90% are caught along the estuarine coasts and the rest in rivers and streams for use in artificial fertilisation.

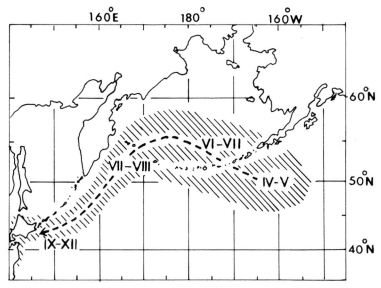

Fig. 3. Estimated area of distribution and migration route of chum salmon originating from Japan (Kondo *et al.*, 1965). Month is given in Roman numerals.

SALMON PROPAGATION IN JAPAN

There are two methods for increasing salmon stocks: by improving their natural spawning conditions and by artificial fertilisation followed by subsequent incubation, fry-hatching and their release into the streams. The latter method has been practised in Japan predominantly for resource enhancement of chum and pink salmon. Part of the masu salmon stock enhancement is dependent on natural spawning of the fish.

Human involvement in the propagation of salmon has a long history in Japan. Conservation measures to protect salmon resources by improving their natural spawning environment had already been employed in Honshu region in the 1750s. The usual method was *Tanegawa No Seido* (seed protection in rivers) in which the spawning of salmon was protected in certain streams and rivers designated by the feudal lord. In the late nineteenth century, a more positive means of salmon propagation, artificial fertilisation and incubation, was introduced.

The artificial propagation method attracted attention because of its effectiveness in increasing salmon stocks. It also enabled an examiner to enumerate the eggs used for propagation, and the assessment of a stock enhancement programme became easier and more precise than before. Although several difficulties hindered the development of this resource enhancement programme, various fishery associations began to practise the method with a view to increasing the salmon resources. The difficulties encountered included the failure of the administration to cope with environmental disruption, as well as failure in experimentation due to inexperience, poor technology and lack of knowledge of the biology of fish. In the initial years of the programme the status of salmon resources did not improve as much as had been expected. One reason was the deterioration of river conditions, due to dredging for gravel which led to the destruction of natural spawning beds and to the effluents of paper mills and starch plants which polluted the water. It was realised that this programme would not succeed unless the natural environment was well preserved.

Subsequent improvement of river conditions and public concern about the need for natural resources conservation helped to restore the salmon stocks and led to the development of the salmon resource enhancement programme of today.

Salmon Propagation Rivers

There are about 200 rivers with salmon populations in Hokkaido and 150 in Honshu. Of these, 123 in Hokkaido and 129 in Honshu are currently used for salmon propagation. Most are relatively short, less than 50 km in length; only six rivers in Hokkaido and 11 in Honshu are longer than 100 km. The environmental conditions in almost all these rivers have been unsuitable for the natural spawning of salmon because of deteriorated habitat for the fish. Human activities, often inadvertent, have in some way or other altered the otherwise pristine rivers from source to estuary. Dams for electric power generation, decrease in the volume of water flow due to increased use of water for various purposes, irregularity in the volume of water flow as a result of deforest-ation, water contamination caused by industrial effluents, and waste water and sewage from urban areas all stood in the way, directly or indirectly, of the spawning migration of mature salmon or fry descending rivers. Although some alteration of natural conditions in rivers is unavoidable, efforts must be made to prevent the deleterious effects these activities have on the water system. Maintaining a healthy environment should contribute to the development of the salmon propagation programme.

Artificial Salmon Propagation Programme

History of Hatchery Development
Artificial salmon hatching was introduced to Japan in 1876 but did not reach a large scale until 1888 when the State-run Chitose Central Salmon Hatchery was established on a tributary of the Ishikari River in Hokkaido. It was modelled after the Backsport Salmon Hatchery of Maine, U.S.A. The technical expertise gained at this hatchery helped to lay the foundation for Japan's salmon hatcheries.

Particularly in Hokkaido, many hatcheries were constructed in rapid succession. In the twenty years following the construction of Chitose Central Salmon Hatchery, as many as fifty salmon hatchery stations were built in Hokkaido; almost all were privately run except for two government-run hatcheries. At this stage problems arose in the management of privately owned hatcheries: since they were built and operated either by local fishery co-operatives or by fishery associations, the need to recover the cost of investment in addition to maintaining their hatchery operations took precedence, and they sought profit from the sale of parent fish carcasses after egg stripping. The income from this sale gradually became a large part of the profits of fishery co-operatives and associations but not all was re-invested in further development of the hatcheries. In other words, the very existence of the fishery co-operatives and associations came to depend on the number of parent fish caught and sold, thus defeating the original purpose of resource enhancement by depleting salmon resources. A vicious circle ensued, and the poor return of parent fish was followed by poor achievements of hatchery operations due to poor harvest. By 1930 a number of hatcheries had resorted to measures that ran counter to salmon propagation in order to tide over their financial difficulties. So, because of poor management, most of the private hatcheries were taken over by the Hokkaido government in 1934, primarily in the public interest.

In 1952 salmon propagation in Hokkaido was incorporated into a national development, and the administrative jurisdiction was transferred to the Fishery Agency in compliance with new legislation on the conservation of fishery resources which took effect in 1951. In recent years, however, an increasing number of privately run hatcheries have been built by fishery co-operatives and have helped to secure an adequate supply of fry for release into the rivers, in addition to those produced from national hatcheries.

At present, there are 37 national, 3 prefectural and 62 private hatcheries in Hokkaido. Most of the private hatcheries are small in scale and their total fry production accounts for only 30% of all production in Hokkaido. The development of salmon propagation in mainland Honshu followed a different pattern to that in Hokkaido. Initially, the protection of natural spawning streams commonly known as *Tanegawa No Seido* had been widely observed in the nineteenth century. This propagation method gradually gave way to artificial salmon hatching introduced from Hokkaido.

Almost all the hatcheries in Honshu were built and managed by the private sector, such as fishery co-operatives and associations. For various reasons, historical as well as regional, hatcheries in Honshu are not operated by the national government. In recent years, however, some governmental and prefectural subsidies have been granted to these hatcheries in order to alleviate their financial burdens.

Present Status of Salmon Propagation
In all the rivers in Japan, any kind of commercial and non-commercial fishing for salmon is prohibited except for collection of broodstock for artificial reproduction. To obtain eggs for the hatchery systems, adult

(mainly chum) salmon are caught in streams. In 1976, 129 streams were used for this purpose each in Hokkaido and Honshu. The number of streams from which mature broodstock of salmon are collected differs slightly according to the year.

Spawning escapement (Table I) fluctuates largely according to the year. Recently, however, securing 800 000-1 000 000 of escapement has been envisaged in Hokkaido to increase the chum resource, thereby ensuring a stable catch. The escapement in Honshu has been roughly one-third of that in Hokkaido. The average number of fry released has been 400-500 million in Hokkaido and 100-200 million in Honshu.

The return of 20 million salmon out of the release of 1000 million fry is set as a target figure to be achieved by the enlarged national salmon resources enhancement programme.

Table I. Annual total catch, escapement and number of fry released from 1967 to 1977 for chum salmon.

Year	Hokkaido			Honshu		
	Total catch[a] ($\times 10^6$)	Spawning escapement ($\times 10^3$)	Number of fry released ($\times 10^6$)	Total catch[a] ($\times 10^6$)	Spawning escapement ($\times 10^3$)	Number of fry released ($\times 10^6$)
1967	4·50	592	434	0·512	142	161
1968	2·14	230	207	0·375	115	121
1969	4·17	578	362	0·448	134	140
1970	5·29	627	442	0·573	148	145
1971	7·65	845	576	0·897	246	212
1972	6·96	614	476	0·927	229	225
1973	8·32	594	446	0·854	238	271
1974	9·63	600	485	1·145	244	272
1975	15·77	1174	802	1·912	362	344
1976	8·80	464	523	1·614	271	287
1977	10·21	872	693	2·351	374	408

[a]Includes coastal catch plus escapement.

Artificial salmon propagation starts with collecting parent fish (broodstock), followed by egg-stripping, artificial fertilisation, indoor incubation of the eggs, hatching, and finally the release of fry into streams. At each of these stages, rationalisation and labour-saving improvements have been put into practice. To attain satisfactory results from the artificial salmon resources enhancement programme, it is necessary (i) to secure a predetermined number of mature broodstock for reproduction, (ii) to obtain high-quality eggs from healthy stocks, (iii) to produce vigorous fry and (iv) to release them at the most appropriate time.

(a) *Broodstock and egg collection.* To obtain eggs for the hatchery systems, adult chum salmon are trapped in streams by means of river racks and traps, seines, fish wheels and gill nets. The most common method is a river rack with a V-throated box set across a stream, commonly called the Urai type fish trap (Fig. 4).

Fig. 4. River rack with V-throated traps for catching adult salmon.

Eggs are stripped immediately after the adults are caught and non-ripe fish are kept in an enclosure until they reach maturity. Egg stripping and subsequent artificial insemination are conducted by the so-called dry method. Eggs are first pressed out from the female into an appropriate pan, and the sperm is added and gently mixed with a feather. Fertilisation takes place almost instantly when water is poured into the pan.

(b) *Hatching and release of fry.* The fertilised eggs are incubated on trays until they hatch. Utmost care is taken in controlling water temperature, water flow rate, control of disease, etc. In early stages of development the eggs are particularly vulnerable to physical stimuli, so malachite green is commonly applied to them by mixing it with the water supply to prevent their infection by Saprolegnia and other fungal diseases, instead of removing the dead eggs.

The rates of egg development and hatching are primarily controlled by water temperature and they differ from one species to another. Table II shows the number of days needed for salmon to hatch under constant water temperature; this differs slightly from species to species. Chum salmon spawn (and their eggs hatch out) in springwater with constant water temperature in the wild environment; pink and masu salmon spawn on redds in the surface water where the bottom consistency provides good permeation of water (Kobayashi, 1968). The day of hatching is estimated from cumulative water temperature. Although the number of days until hatching differs from one species to another, the cumulative water temperature from the time of hatching to the absorption of yolk does not differ much among chum, pink and masu salmon. Initially the fry were released at this stage into nearby streams. However, to minimise the mortality rate in the early stage, the fry are now reared with artificial feed for about one month after yolk sac absorption before being released.

(c) *Release after feeding.* Experimental feeding before release was first conducted in 1962. Full scale feed-and-release practice began in the spring of 1967 (the fry of the 1966 brood year) employing dried artificial fish feed. The feed is manufactured from a combination of fish meal (main component) and mineral with vitamin additives. By feeding salmon fry it was expected that they would become more vigorous and viable, achieving as a result high rates of return.

Table II. Number of days until hatching.

Species	Water temperature (°C)	Number of days until hatching	Product of water temperature (°C) and days
Chum salmon	8	60	480
Pink salmon	8	70	560-580
Masu salmon	8	55	440

It is not known yet, however, when is the best time for the release of fry. Since wild salmon fry usually descend a stream in April and May, the release of the fry is timed to coincide with the natural outmigration period. The length of time feeding before release is one month and by this time fry have reached 0.6-1.0 g in weight. The standard quantity of feed per day is 2-4% of the fry's body weight.

A unique feature of the salmon fishery in Japan is that about 70-80% of the fry presently descending rivers to the sea every year have been reared artificially.

(d) *Feeding and releasing in sea water.* An experiment of feeding salmon juveniles with artificial feed in seawater and releasing them at the time of their seaward migration off the coast was conducted in 1967. Since the mortality of young (fry, parr, smolt and juvenile) is thought to be very high during their freshwater life stages, much is expected of this new venture. However, many technical problems still remain unsolved, for example, type of suitable facilities, kind and quality of feed, method of rearing and care, appropriate time of release, etc. So far, encouraging results have been reported in some instances.

Experiments on this feeding in seawater are presently being conducted in Iwate and Miyagi prefectures. Net enclosures are set out in coves where the waters are calm. The juveniles are reared for about two months and then released in mid to late May when wild salmon start their seaward offshore migration. By that time the juveniles reach 5-10 g in weight and their viability and chances of survival are expected to be much higher.

Effectiveness of Artificial Propagation

Return of Adults
There are two methods by which the effectiveness of artificial salmon propagation is measured: one employs the rate of return of marked fry and the other employs statistical data such as number of fry released and number of adults returning, by which the degree of contribution by hatchery fish to the whole population is measured. Marking is a reliable method of following the homing migration and is widely used to study behavioural ecology of the fish, including migration and growth. Fin-clipping is one of the most popular methods and is the main way of assessing contributions of artificial propagation. It is also used to determine the appropriate time, place and method of fry

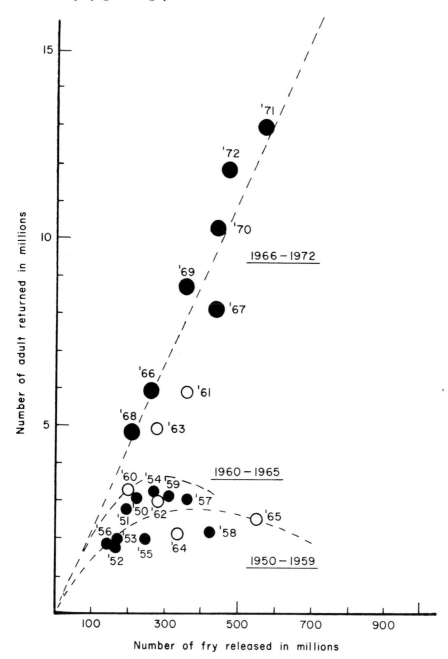

Fig. 5. Reproduction curves for chum salmon of Hokkaido origin in the brood years 1950-1972.

releasing, and to study the effectiveness of full feeding immediately prior to release. Application of the findings of marking experiments has contributed much to the recent increase in salmon stocks. In the following example, the relative effectiveness of artificial chum salmon rearing in Hokkaido is examined using the statistical method (Fig. 5).

For the brood years 1950-1959 about three million adults returned from the release of 300 million fry; eight million adults returned from the release of 400 million fry of the brood years 1966-1972. Thus, there have been significant changes in the results of the recent artificial salmon propagation (resource enhancement) programme. If Ricker's formula for the reproduction curve (Ricker, 1958) is applied to the brood years 1966-1972, it becomes $R = 2 \cdot 332 \ Ee^{-0 \cdot 01E}$, where E is the number of fry released ($\times 10^8$) and R is the number of adults returning ($\times 10^6$). From this equation the number of returns is likely to increase linearly until the number of fry released reaches 1000 million. Details of the rates of return are given in Table III.

Table III. Effectiveness of artificial salmon propagation as expressed by the rate of adult return in Hokkaido.

Brood Year	Rate of return		Number of adults returning per spawner	
	Range	Mean	Range	Mean
1952-1955	0·81-1·23	1·08	6·2- 9·5	8·3
1956-1960	0·51-1·67	1·09	4·1-12·9	8·4
1961-1965	0·49-1·84	1·13	3·7-14·2	8·3
1966-1970	1·89-2·41	2·22	14·9-18·6	17·1
1971-1972	2·24-2·49	2·37	17·3-19·2	18·3

The number of adult returns per spawner in brood groups before 1965 was 3·7-14·2, with annual means between 8·3 and 8·4. In the brood year groups after 1966, it increased markedly to more than twice the level of previous brood year groups, i.e., 14·9-19·2, with annual means between 17·1 and 18·3. In particular the recent increase in adult returns has been conspicuous in northern and eastern Hokkaido. The rate of return, for example, in major rivers flowing into the Okhotsk Sea has achieved 3·40-5·55%, with the mean of 4·33% in recent years.

This spectacular development after 1966 is thought to have been made possible mainly by the initiation of fry feeding and release at an appropriate time. Technological progress and improvements of hatchery facilities might have contributed to the development, helped by good management.

The rate of return of adults increases as the proportion fed before release increases (Fig. 6). It is understood that the high rate of survival of the fry has contributed to the resultant increase in the rate of returns. In other words, healthy and vigorous fry produced in the hatcheries brought about this satisfactory result. It is not clear whether such high rates of return will continue. If the productivity of the ocean can accommodate further increase of the salmon biomass, it will be possible to increase the size of salmon populations.

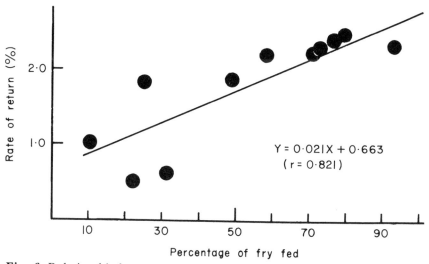

$$Y = 0 \cdot 021X + 0 \cdot 663$$
$$(r = 0 \cdot 821)$$

Percentage of fry fed

Fig. 6. Relationship between rate of adult return and percentage of fry which were fed before release in the population of chum salmon in Hokkaido.

Economic Effects

Almost all the major hatcheries in Hokkaido are owned and operated by the national government. Various beneficiary private organisations represented by fishery co-operatives shoulder a part of the budget to be used for the capture of parent fish and egg collection. The total annual budget in recent years including the governmental and private hatcheries has shown a sharp increase. This may attest to the

awareness of the people concerned of the need to enhance domestic
fisheries in view of the changing international fishery situation and it
has been encouraged by the satisfactory achievement of high rates of
return as a result of the salmon propagation programme. For example,
it was 476 million yen in 1966 and 1004 million yen in 1972 (see
Table IV).

Table IV. Production costs per fry and per fish returned in Hokkaido.

Brood Year	Total annual budget for salmon propagation (Yen × 10^6)	Production cost per fry (Yen)	Production cost per fish returned (Yen)
1962-1965	374-540	0·99-1·60	86·7-241·9
Mean	463	1·35	165·1
1966	476	1·74	79·5
1967	582	1·33	70·5
1968	603	2·90	126·0
1969	670	1·85	76·7
1970	767	1·74	75·9
1971	992	1·72	76·8
1972	1094	2·30	92·2
Mean of 1966-1972	741	1·94	85·4

Production costs per fry and per fish returned for each brood year
from 1966 to 1972 are shown in Table IV. The production cost of fry
can be reduced if the catch of parent fish is high. Similarly, the production cost per returning salmon from artificially released stocks will
be low.

If the average weight of an adult salmon returning during the period
1966-1977 was 3·5 kg, the mean cost of production per kg is estimated
to be 24·4 yen (85·4 yen/3·5 kg), which is only one-half of the cost of
such a fish before 1966. The landed price (first sale price) per kg for
returned adult salmon during the seven year period 1966-1972 varied
between 340 and 1000 yen, with a mean of 670 yen. The mean cost of
production per kg is only 3·6% of this price and since all chum are
hatchery produced, this fact shows that the present stock of chum

salmon has been maintained by about 4% of all the value in the coastal catch of this species. This low production cost per kg of salmon returned is an index of the relative effectiveness of recent salmon hatching and releasing activities (salmon ranching) in Japan.

REFERENCES

Japan Fisheries Resource Conservation Association (1966). "Propagation of chum salmon in Japan". JFRCA, Tokyo, 1-55.

Kobayashi, T. (1968). *Sci. Rep. Hokkaido Salmon Hatch.* **22,** 7-13.

Kobayashi, T. (1976). FAO Technical Conference on Aquaculture, Experience Rep. No. 75, 1-12.

Kondo, H., Hirano, Y., Nakayama, N. and Miyake, M. (1965). *Int. N. Pac. Fish. Comm., Bull.* INPFC **17,** 1-213.

Ricker, W. E. (1958). Handbook of computations for biological statistics of fish populations. *Bull. Fish. Res. Bd Can.* **119,** 300.

Sano, S. (1959). *Sci. Rep. Hokkaido Salmon Hatch.* **14,** 21-90.

Chapter 7

Salmon Ranching in the Atlantic Maritime Provinces of Canada

J. A. RITTER[1] and T. G. CAREY[2]

[1]Government of Canada, Department of Fisheries and Oceans,
P. O. Box 550, Halifax, Nova Scotia, Canada
[2]Government of Canada, Department of Fisheries and Oceans,
240 Sparks Street, Ottawa, Ontario, Canada

INTRODUCTION

The freshwaters of the Maritime Provinces of New Brunswick, Nova Scotia and Prince Edward Island on the east coast of Canada (latitudes 43-48°N; longitudes 60-69°W) (Fig. 1) generally consist of shallow, swift-flowing rivers, numerous small lakes, and ponds. The water is of low productivity (oligotrophic) except in some farming areas, and environmental conditions are extreme (e.g. water temperatures averaging 0° to 4°C for four months during winter, and reaching 25°C in summer).

This region is a major stronghold for the Atlantic salmon *(Salmo salar)*, a species well adapted to surviving the relatively harsh environment. They are present in most New Brunswick and Nova Scotia rivers and in a few small rivers on Prince Edward Island. After spawning in October-November and hatching in April-May, the young salmon remain 2-4 years in freshwater before migrating to sea as smolts at 12-20 cm. Most adults returning to their home rivers to spawn enter freshwater between May and October. They return as 1-sea-winter (grilse), 2-sea-winter and, to a lesser extent, 3-sea-winter salmon. The grilse generally range in size from 50-60 cm, the 2-sea-winter salmon

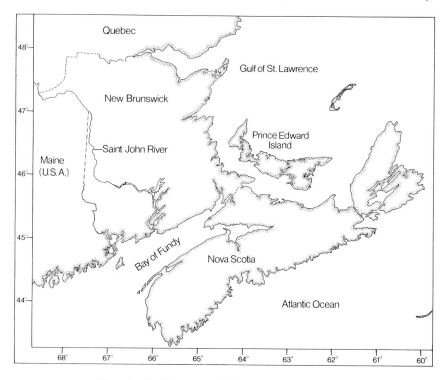

Fig. 1. Outline map of the Maritimes Region.

from 60-85 cm, and the 3-sea-winter salmon from 85-100 cm. Within virtually all spawning populations a few adults (<10%) are present that have spawned previously.

The production potential of salmon rivers in the Maritimes Region is roughly 500 000 adult salmon (Ritter *et al.*, 1979), one-third of the total for eastern Canada. Production from most rivers supporting salmon populations is below the potential of their freshwater habitat. Additional production potential from waters not presently supporting salmon is about 100 000 adults. Legislative and management responsibility for these stocks rests with the Canadian federal government.

Although over-exploitation is the prime reason for the present depressed state of existing stocks, degradation and loss of freshwater habitat as a result of man's industrial and development activities continue to be the main threats to the Region's salmon resource. These negative factors, recognised in the early nineteenth century, justified the construction of the first fish hatcheries in the Maritimes later that century. Their purpose was to augment salmon and, to a lesser extent, trout production in areas where stocks were either naturally low or had been reduced as a result of man's activities. Incubating eggs and releasing large numbers of fry was to result in heightened adult recruitments and consequent increased numbers of salmon and trout in the Maritime Provinces. This was the beginning of a long history of the application of various artificial culture techniques to support the maintenance and enhancement of the Region's salmonid resources.

In the early twentieth century it was decided that hatcheries should stock larger and older fish than fry, to ensure higher survival rates and increased contributions to fisheries. This led to development of extensive rearing programmes, and by 1940 more than 80% of the 26 000 000 salmon and trout distributed from the 14 hatcheries and 6 rearing ponds were fingerling size or larger. In the 1960s hatchery distributions decreased from roughly 30 000 000 to less than 5 000 000 fish annually, chiefly through increased production of salmon smolts and 15-cm yearling trout, and decreased distribution of underyearling fish. By 1970, 54% of the salmon and 17% of the trout, by numbers stocked, were smolts and 15-cm fish, respectively. Total production throughout this period was relatively constant at slightly less than 100 000 kg a year.

The development and expansion of hatchery rearing programmes has been costly, as expenditures for modification and construction of facilities at the older fish culture stations have accumulated. In the late 1960s amalgamation, consolidation and modernisation of facilities were required to justify the cost of the continued operation of several older stations. In view of the relatively large capital cost of renovation, a thorough evaluation of all hatchery programmes was needed before money was spent. This evaluation, beginning in 1968, marked the first step in the development of a direct biological support programme to fish culture operations and subsequently involved pathologists, physiologists and nutritionists. Genetic research has also come to the foreground with the opening of the North American Salmon Research Centre at St Andrews, New Brunswick, in 1974.

The biological support programme for federal government hatcheries in the Maritimes contributes technical advice and information to improve the effectiveness of fish culture operations and monitors the success of culture and stocking programmes and the general health and condition of the stocks produced. Annual assessment of quality (Frantsi *et al.*, 1972b) has led to a striking improvement in the smolts released, to improved survival of hatchery-reared fish, and to an overall increase in the contribution of hatcheries to fisheries and spawning escapements. The hatcheries distribute approximately 500 000 smolts annually and roughly the same number of fall fingerlings, i.e. 0 + parr released in the fall. These salmon originate from nine federal hatcheries and are distributed only in rivers where the need for intervention and the use of cultured stocks has been identified, and generally where adult returns to the river and the fisheries are monitored. Current federal policy sees hatchery-reared salmon being used primarily for transplanting stocks to new areas, for increasing the rate of reproduction of fish populations, and for overcoming deficient natural reproduction in specific areas (Carey, 1973). Such salmon are used in a variety of management and enhancement projects throughout the region (Lister, 1975), as at Mactaquac Hatchery, New Brunswick, the most modern Atlantic salmon hatchery in eastern Canada. This hatchery's entire production is released in the Saint John River, New Brunswick in support of the river's salmon management programme. This is the largest and most comprehensive salmon ranching project in the Maritime Provinces.

HATCHERY PROGRAMME FOR THE SAINT JOHN RIVER

The Saint John River is the largest river system in eastern North America south of the Saint Lawrence and east of Connecticut. Approximately 680 km long, it drains the northern section of the State of Maine, part of the Province of Quebec, and almost one-half of the 73 000 km² which comprises the Province of New Brunswick. Atlantic salmon inhabit the system as far upstream as Grand Falls (Fig. 2). Below the falls the river runs through the fertile Saint John River Valley, which has attracted human settlement for over 350 years. During this interval, man's industrial and development activities have caused environmental degradation and water pollution (Dominy, 1973), both of which have had adverse effects on the river's salmon resources (Elson *et al.*, 1973; Ruggles and Watt, 1975).

The river's size made it suitable for hydroelectric development, with dams being constructed for water storage and power generation at

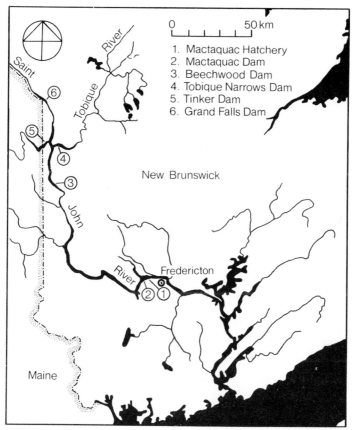

0   50 km

1. Mactaquac Hatchery
2. Mactaquac Dam
3. Beechwood Dam
4. Tobique Narrows Dam
5. Tinker Dam
6. Grand Falls Dam

New Brunswick

Fredericton

Maine

Fig 2. Map showing major features of the Saint John River in New Brunswick.

Beechwood (1957), Tobique Narrows (1952), Grand Falls (1928) and Tinker (1906). The Beechwood and Tobique Narrows dams had fish passage facilities for adult upstream migrants but no facilities to safeguard downstream migrant smolts. Major concern was therefore expressed for the salmon resource in the mid-1960s, when the New Brunswick Electric Power Commission proposed a fifth major dam at Mactaquac, near Fredericton. The salmon-rearing habitat above Mactaquac represented over 60% of the total in the system and, if eliminated, would have meant the loss of at least 70 tonnes of salmon from the commercial catch and 3500 fish from the recreational fishery (Penney, personal communication). Delays in smolt migration at the dams and multiple exposure to turbines were expected to cause mortality and injury that could eventually annihilate the Atlantic salmon above Mactaquac.

The federal government and the New Brunswick Electric Power Commission agreed that a hatchery should be built to rear sufficient salmon smolts to replace the loss in natural production above Mactaquac and also a trapping facility in the dam from which salmon and other migrating fish could be either transported to the hatchery or released upstream. The management scheme after 1967 called for the culture and annual release of 500 000 smolts. Adult broodstock in excess of hatchery requirements were to be released upstream for angling exploitation and some measure of spawning, although little contribution to exploitable stocks was expected from natural production above Mactaquac Dam.

Mactaquac Hatchery and Adult Collection Facilities

Technical Aspects
Mactaquac Hatchery and associated trapping facilities at the dam were built in 1967 by the New Brunswick Electric Power Commission for a cost of $3·5 million and are operated by the federal government. The hatchery is located on a six-hectare site and contains offices, hatching rooms, small and large rearing ponds, adult holding pools, migration/ effluent channel, and other associated facilities (Fig. 3).

The adult trapping facilities are operated throughout the salmon migration, from April to November each year. Non-salmonid species, including alewife *(Alosa pseudoharengus)*, blueback herring *(A. aestivalis)*, shad *(A. sapidissima)* and eel *(Anguilla rostrata)* are separated from the salmonids and immediately released above the dam. All salmonids (primarily Atlantic salmon) are transported for sorting at the hatchery, examined individually for tags or finclips, and either retained for broodstock or released upstream of Mactaquac Dam. Generally, 25%- 35% of the adults returning from hatchery-reared smolt releases are captured in the hatchery migration channel. Virtually all adult returns from smolts produced upriver of Mactaquac Dam by-pass the hatchery migration channel and are captured in the trap at the dam.

In October and November each year, broodstock are transferred from holding pools to special tanks where they are anaesthetised and spawned. Green eggs are disinfected and transferred to fibreglass

1 Mactaquac Dam
2 Saint John River
3 Aeration Tower
4 Rearing Pond Area
5 Migration Channel
6 Adult Sorting Facility
7 Spawning Shed and Broodstock
   Holding Pond Complex

Fig. 3. Aerial view of Mactaquac Hatchery.

incubation troughs in the main hatchery building. Eggs are incubated on surface water, developing to the eyed stage by January or February and hatching in April. Feeding fingerlings are transferred to 1·8 × 2·7-m concrete ponds in June/July and then to 11 × 11-m concrete ponds the following year. Smolts (primarily two-year) are released into the river via the effluent channel in April/May. All the rearing ponds are of the self-cleaning, Swedish design (see Chapter 9) that has proven to be very successful for culturing Atlantic salmon.

The water supply to the hatchery is piped 4 km from the headpond of Mactaquac Dam (from three levels) and pumped from one deep and three shallow wells on the hatchery property. Headpond water temperatures range from 1°C in winter to 20°C in summer; wellwater temperatures are relatively constant between 5°C and 9°C. All water supplies are aerated through a tower originally constructed to increase oxygen levels of hypolimnetic water from the headpond supply in summer, and from the wells. The tower was modified in later years to reduce nitrogen supersaturation of both surface and ground water supplies.

Biological Aspects

The original hatchery breeding programme was designed to ensure that run timing coincided with that of the wild salmon produced upriver of Mactaquac Dam, by using proportionate segments of each part of the wild run as broodstock. The genetic control of temporal pattern of return to a river has since been confirmed, progeny of early and late run parents returning early and late, respectively (Ritter, 1972). All broodstock used are collected as native stocks at Mactaquac, as tagging investigations have shown that survival of hatchery smolts varies inversely with the distance that stocks are transplanted from their native stream (Ritter, 1975), suggesting that migration of salmon is at least partially under hereditary control.

The breeding programme has excluded grilse from matings, to favour the older maturing salmon (Ritter and Newbould, 1977). Also, with the first returns from hatchery plantings 90% of matings were between hatchery-return fish, to maintain a broad genetic base while developing a stock adapted to both artificial culture and high survival at sea. This programme was aimed at meeting the original objective of producing fish for commercial and recreational fisheries in the river. Recently it has been altered as a result of much higher recruitments than expected from wild stocks released upriver of Mactaquac Dam. Objectives of the new hatchery programme are to contribute to the river fisheries, and to natural spawning and production in areas above the dam. Hatchery-reared broodstock are now mated with wild fish to ensure that the traits for spawning and surviving in the natural environment are maintained.

All hatchery stocks are fed commercially prepared dry diets by hand at the fry stage and with automatic feeders thereafter. Numerous feed trials have been conducted to assess the nutritional value of diets and their effects on general health and survival of the fish (Foda and Ritter, 1977). Nutrition is considered an important component of the hatchery operation, since the progeny must survive 1-3 years after release into the natural environment.

Recent improvements in water quality and management practices have reduced fish mortalities from disease. *Aeromonas hydrophila* is the most serious pathogen at this station and is presently controlled with antibiotics (oxytetracycline). Covert symptoms of Corynebacterial kidney disease (BKD) have recently been detected in both fingerling and yearling salmon, but no mortalities have been attributed to BKD. Enteric redmouth disease (ERM) was detected in one adult migrant in the Saint John River, but not in any of the hatchery stocks. Significant mortalities from gas bubble disease (nitrogen supersaturation), have been eliminated since the aeration tower was modified to degas the water supplies. Other diseases encountered at Mactaquac but which do not cause major mortalities include infectious pancreatic necrosis (IPN), bacterial gill disease, saddleback disease, fungus infections (*Saprolegnia* sp.) and finrot.

Maintaining fish health and assessing "quality" of smolts are high priorities. Quality rather than quantity was emphasised early: for example, the annual production objective was reduced from 500 000 to 250 000 smolts because of their small size and the high incidence of finrot. Subsequent increased survival rates proved that this drastic reduction in production was justified (Penney, 1976).

Contribution of Hatchery Stocks

Hatchery-reared salmon released in the Saint John River contribute to commercial fisheries off West Greenland, along the east and south coasts of Newfoundland, on the Atlantic coast of Nova Scotia, and in the Bay of Fundy. Recoveries off West Greenland and Newfoundland have each amounted to less than 10% of the total tag returns from all fisheries, plus those recovered at Mactaquac. Saint John River salmon contribute proportionally less to the distantly located fisheries than hatchery or wild stocks from Gulf of St Lawrence rivers (Ritter, 1972). Since 1972, when commercial salmon fisheries in and near the Saint John River, and in other areas of New Brunswick and the Province of Quebec, were banned temporarily, more than 70% of the adult recaptures of tagged, Mactaquac Hatchery smolts came from river fisheries (mainly recreational and Indian food fisheries) and the Mactaquac trap.

The hatchery now contributes over 40% of the total adult returns to the Mactaquac facilities (Table I). The majority originates from smolts released below Mactaquac Dam rather than from underyearling and post-yearling parr released upriver of the dam. In 1976 and 1977, hatchery returns exceeded 8000 grilse and large salmon (maiden multi-sea-winter salmon and previous spawners), but in 1978 dropped to 4600 fish, a record low for the past five years. This reduction was due to poor sea survival of the 1977 smolt year class, also evident in unexpectedly low returns of wild grilse to the Saint John River and other systems throughout Atlantic Canada.

Table I. Grilse and large salmon counts at Mactaquac (1967-78) and percentages originating from hatchery stocking.

Year	Grilse		Large salmon[a]	
	Number	% Hatchery	Number	% Hatchery
1967	1 181	—	1 271	—
1968	1 203	—	770	—
1969	2 572	—	1 749	—
1970	2 952	3	2 465	—
1971	1 910	18	2 303	2
1972	1 030	24	5 414	11
1973	3 614	49	2 842	17
1974	7 089	52	6 682	28
1975	11 060	48	8 058	23
1976	14 491	53	7 134	23
1977	9 684	64	9 315	22
1978	4 140	62	4 985	39

[a]Large salmon includes all maiden multi-sea-winter salmon and previous spawners.

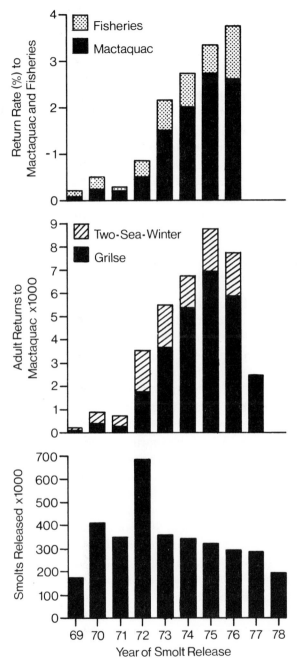

Fig. 4. Summary of smolt stocking programme in the Saint John River, New Brunswick, 1969-78: (Bottom) number of smolts released; (Middle) thousands of adult returns to Mactaquac; (Top) smolt-to-adult return rates (%) to Mactaquac and fisheries.

Returns to Mactaquac from annual smolt releases increased from less than 1000 grilse and two-sea-winter salmon from smolts liberated in 1971 to more than 8000 from smolts released in 1975 (Fig. 4). Adult returns from smolts released during this five-year interval increased despite the decrease in the numbers of smolts liberated since 1972. Smolt survival has increased tenfold over that recorded for the first three years of stocking (i.e. 1969-71), probably due to increased size (but see Chapter 3), improved fin condition, and general health at release. These gradual improvements in smolt quality have occurred throughout the Region's hatchery system, as rearing densities were reduced and as improvements were made in other culture practices.

Biology of Hatchery-reared Stocks

Most adult returns have been from two-year smolts, although some are derived from varying but smaller numbers of one-year smolts released in the Saint John River since 1970. Recently returns from two-year smolts marked with modified Carlin tags (Saunders, 1968) have been more than five times those from one-year smolts (3·9% v. 0·7%). This difference is at least partially attributed to size (Peterson, 1973; Ritter, 1977), as two-year smolts are usually greater than 19 cm fork length while most one-year smolts are less than 17 cm. The one-year smolts represent the largest 10% of the yearlings; the other 90% are retained for an additional year and released as two-year smolts.

The lower return produced by one-year smolts from Mactaquac is not attributed to age, as 2·0% returns are being recorded for one-year smolts reared at a southern hatchery and released in a Nova Scotia river. In this case they represent 90% of the entire population at fork lengths from 13 to more than 20 cm (Goff and Forsythe, 1979). Investigations in Sweden and Iceland have shown equal or better return rates for one-year smolts than for similarly sized two-year smolts (Peterson, 1973; Isaksson, 1976).

Adult returns to the Mactaquac trap show that the hatchery-reared stocks have, throughout the programme since 1969, consistently produced proportionately more grilse than the wild stocks. Recently, grilse:2-sea-winter salmon ratios produced by individual year-classes of hatchery-reared smolts have exceeded 3:1 compared to roughly 1:1 ratios produced by wild smolts. This is assumed to be partially due to differences in the sex ratios of hatchery-reared and wild smolts. The sex ratio of two-year hatchery smolts has been 1:1, whereas it is assumed that the ratio for wild smolts has favoured female migrants (Osterdahl, 1969; Pratt *et al.*, 1974; Jessop, 1975). As Saint John River grilse are roughly 90% male and 2-sea-winter salmon are more than 70% female, a difference in sex ratios of hatchery and wild smolts would favour earlier maturity of hatchery fish.

Furthermore early maturity of hatchery fish may relate to the large size of the two-year smolts being liberated. It has been suggested that coho *(Oncorhynchus kisutch)* smolts reared to a large size before liberation tend to mature sooner than smaller smolts (Hager and Noble, 1974; see also Chapters 16 and 17). Recently more than 90% of Mactaquac smolts have exceeded 19 cm in fork length; wild smolts seldom exceed 17 cm (Jessop, 1975). Other possible factors contributing to early maturation of hatchery stocks have yet to be identified.

Marshall (1975), as well as more recent investigations, showed that fewer hatchery-return adults move upstream following their release above Mactaquac Dam and that some drop back to be captured a second time in the Mactaquac trap. The annual re-entrapment rate of fish at Mactaquac has been 0-22% for hatchery-reared adults released 75 km upriver of Mactaquac Dam, compared with 0-6% for fish of hatchery origin released 170 km upriver. The latter had to pass over or through three hydroelectric dams; the former had their downstream movement obstructed by the Mactaquac Dam only.

The dropback behaviour noted among hatchery-return adults reduced their availability to anglers fishing upper segments of the river (Penney, personal communication). Hatchery-return adults are virtually absent from angling catches upstream of the upper release site. It is likely that this dropback behaviour also reduces the contribution of hatchery-return salmon to spawning and natural production from the upper river.

Opportunities for Improving the Effectiveness of the Hatchery Programme

Production of one-year rather than two-year smolts at Mactaquac hatchery is appealing: adults from one-year smolts would probably consists of proportionately fewer grilse than those from two-year smolts (Ritter and Newbould, 1977), twice the number of one-year migrants could be produced in existing rearing facilities, and one-year smolts usually have lower incidence of finrot and are healthier. Preliminary investigations into rearing one-year smolts, using heated water during the fry stage (Foda and Henderson, 1977), indicate that energy costs for converting the rearing schedule at Mactaquac Hatchery would be relatively low. Survival differences for one-year and two-year smolts should be reducable, and the weight of adult salmon produced should be increased with change to a one-year smolt rearing programme.

Besides producing smolts, numerous fry and other subsmolt stages could be reared for distribution in suitable habitats lacking viable stocks. Although many such areas have fish passage problems, opportunities exist in the Saint John River where subsmolt stages could be utilised. Greater usage of the Hatchery's capacity to produce large numbers of fry and fingerlings for the Saint John River would increase production of adults, and improve the cost-effectiveness of the Hatchery Programme.

FUTURE OF SALMON RANCHING IN THE MARITIMES

The application of Atlantic salmon culture for enhancing stocks in the Maritimes Region has been fragmented and relatively ineffective, despite the major efforts and expenditure on this activity over the past century. This has been due to slow development of technology, to the failure of culturists and fishery managers to recognise the full potential of the many culture and enhancement strategies available to them, and to conservative views on the value of using cultured fish in enhancement projects. The future of the Maritimes Atlantic salmon resource depends on the development of a long-term management plan that is holistic in scope, imaginative in its endeavours, and sensitive to the heightened demands for a resource which depends on a diminishing freshwater habitat base. In this plan, a broader application of existing and new stock-enhancement strategies is required, with their success being dependent on the selection and use of the most appropriate technology given the project objectives and local conditions.

Initially, the majority of projects will be publicly funded, with benefits being widely distributed to commercial fishermen, recreational fishermen, and native people. Interest and involvement in the culture of Atlantic salmon by the private sector are growing and are expected to accelerate as technology improves. The main thrust in the private sector has been towards sea-pen rearing, although interest in the possibilities of commercial sea ranching is growing.

While salmon culture in the private sector will need to be financially rewarding to its investors, economic justification of publicly funded programmes will also be a prerequisite for their development.

Enhancement Strategies

The main strategies for enhancing production of Atlantic salmon in the Maritimes are discussed below. Their application, if properly integrated in a management plan, would result in a greater abundance of the species for harvest by various users and increased social and economic benefits to residents in rural areas.

Colonisation

Atlantic salmon production could be increased by roughly 100 000 adult fish through colonisation of areas upstream of natural or manmade obstructions to fish passage and recolonisation of areas accessible to migrating salmon which, because of pollution and/or overexploitation, lack viable stocks (Ritter *et al.*, 1979). The seed stock for colonisation programmes would range from adults originating from nearby rivers to cultured juveniles. The cultured stocks could range from unfed fry to smolts, and could originate from a variety of culture facilities, including modern hatcheries, deep substrate incubators and semi-natural rearing ponds.

Supplemental Stocking

Cultured salmon will be used to rebuild diminishing native stocks and to alter the characteristics of others. Stock levels in many of the Region's smaller rivers have declined significantly, with adult returns less than 50% of that required for full seeding and maximum production. The selectivity of fisheries has altered run timing of some stocks and favoured production of younger maturing adults in others. Strategies employed to rebuild stocks or alter their characteristics will include the infusion of selected cultured stocks.

Sea Ranching

Sea ranching is defined here as the strategy of utilising cultured stocks to supplement or totally support fisheries beyond the natural salmon-producing potential of the available freshwater habitats. The extent of sea ranching will depend upon the availability of cultured stocks and the opportunities for project implementation. Projects would be located only in areas where they are not expected to interfere with production or harvest of naturally produced salmon stocks. It is expected that the majority of sea ranching programmes will depend on hatchery-reared smolts, although the occasional programme may be supported through the introduction of subsmolt stages into lakes and/or natural stream habitats of river systems in which the development of self-sustaining populations of Atlantic salmon is either not possible or not wanted.

Although the initial efforts in sea ranching will be publicly funded and will support public fisheries, the private sector is expected to show increased interest in this strategy as technology improves and leads to more economical operations. It is expected that, as the demand for hatchery stocks to support colonisation and stock maintenance programmes decrease, smolt production will be used increasingly for sea ranching. Experiments demonstrating the feasability of sea ranching where there was no salmon run previously have been underway in southern New Brunswick at the federal government's biological station since 1972 and at the North American Salmon Research Centre since 1976. Their technical success is encouraging although economic feasibility has yet to be demonstrated (Saunders, personal communication).

The use of exotic salmonid species, such as *Oncorhynchus spp.*, to satisfy public fishery demands or the interests of private investors will be explored under this strategy. The chief interest in introducing Pacific salmon to the Maritimes Region will be to increase salmon landings in the public commercial fisheries; the major concern will be the negative impact that introduction of exotics could have on native Atlantic salmon.

Culture Strategies

A wide range of culture and stocking strategies will be used to support initiatives in salmon enhancement envisaged for the future. Strategies will be specific to a project and be selected on the basis of their appropriateness in terms of biological effectiveness, broodfish availability, costs, and time frame.

Hatcheries

Hatcheries will be the chief source of cultured stocks for salmon enhancement and restoration projects. This would require replacing older stations with new hatcheries and upgrading others. The modernised system would initially have a production capacity of almost three times the present system and a potential for doubling that, should stocks be required. Adult salmon production from hatchery distributions alone could exceed 200 000 fish annually, should the modernisation scheme be fully implemented.

Hatchery production and distribution are expected to include all stages, from fry to smolt. Fry and fingerling stages are likely to be used in colonisation programmes when there are sufficient broodstock available. Although these subsmolt stages are less costly to produce than smolts, their survival rates are lower (MacCrimmon, 1954; Elson, 1957a; Ritter, 1972). Since smolts can be effectively used in almost all types of salmon enhancement projects, it is expected that they will dominate hatchery production and distributions in the future in spite of their relatively high unit cost and the large capital investment in production facilities. A shift in production to more one-year smolts and fewer two-year fish is expected for both economic and biological reasons.

Deep Substrate Incubation

Deep substrate incubators could be used to produce unfed fry and thus are an alternative to hatcheries as a source of seed stock for colonisation programmes (Porter and Meerburg, 1977). Capital costs for incubation boxes would be low relative to costs to construct hatchery rearing facilities. Egg-to-adult survival of fish derived from substrate incubation and unfed fry stocking appears to be lower than that for fish produced by hatchery programmes involving the production and stocking of either fall fingerlings or smolts (Elson 1957a, b; Ritter, 1972; Porter, personal communication). The low efficiency of the substrate incubation strategy is likely to restrict its use in the Maritimes Region, as most colonisation programmes are limited by the small numbers of suitable broodstock available.

Semi-natural Rearing

Although modern hatcheries have been selected as the basic method of support for salmon enhancement and restoration projects, less expensive rearing facilities, such as natural and man-made lakes and ponds, are also likely to be employed in the production of smolts. A pilot feasibility investigation carried out in a small Nova Scotia lake demonstrated that quality two-year smolts could be produced when yearling salmon were stocked and supplemental feeding was provided (Frantsi *et al.*, 1972a). The major problems encountered in this test programme were heavy predation by mink *(Mustela vison)* and otter *(Lutra canadensis)* and poor emigration of smolts from the lake because of low discharges. Both these problems would have been overcome had the investigation not been terminated because of fiscal constraints.

Considering the low capital and operating costs of this rearing technique and the high quality of smolts it produces, a revaluation of its feasibility and application to salmon enhancement projects is likely in the near future. This revaluation should include pilot investigations in lake rearing of salmon, with and without supplemental feeding and studies to determine the complementary benefits that could be derived from lake fertilisation. Should semi-natural rearing prove technically feasible and as cost-efficient as projected, it could become an important component in the region's salmon culture programme. Ponds and lakes used for semi-natural rearing would serve as satellite operations to local hatcheries, probably on river systems where there were major enhancement projects. The adoption of this strategy to support sea ranching should contribute to lowering freshwater rearing costs and thus improve economic feasibility.

Post Rearing and Delayed Releases of Smolts
The post rearing of hatchery-propagated Atlantic salmon smolts in sea-pens is expected to contribute to increased marine survival rates subsequent to their delayed release into the sea (Saunders, 1977). This delayed release strategy when applied to Pacific salmon stock enhancement projects has resulted in increased returns to fisheries local to the area of release (Kossov *et al.*, 1960; Baker, 1977; Kobayashi, 1976 and Chapter 6; and Novotny, Chapter 17). As the application of this strategy to public or private sea ranching programmes could result in increased adult returns and consequently greater benefits, further review and subsequent testing of it in Atlantic Canada appears imminent.

Kelt Reconditioning
Atlantic salmon kelts reconditioned in captivity could be an alternative

source of eggs for public and private culture operations supporting salmon enhancement projects and commercial aquaculture enterprises. Acceptable survival and maturation rates have been achieved with spent fish retained in land based tanks supplied with water ranging in salinities from 0 to 28 parts per thousand (Ducharme, 1972; Gray *et al.*, 1976; Hill, 1978). Good growth, followed by maturation of both males, and females and acceptable fecundities have been recorded for kelts retained in fresh, brackish and full salt waters. Suitable egg fertility and hatchability rates, although acceptable for eggs obtained from kelts retained in saline waters, have yet to be demonstrated for eggs produced by fish reconditioned in freshwater.

CONCLUSION

Salmon ranching, or the use of artificial propagation techniques in the management and enhancement of wild Atlantic salmon populations, has been undertaken by the federal government of Canada in the Maritime Provinces for more than 100 years. Strategies have progressed from the relatively unsophisticated method of hatching and releasing large numbers of fry to the combining of a variety of complex culture techniques for rearing juveniles for the many alternative enhancement options now available. Numerous changes and innovations have increased the effectiveness of the federal government's hatchery programme. The most recent improvements stem from the implementation of an intensive programme to assess the contributions of hatchery-reared stocks to fisheries and spawning escapement, and from the provision of biological expertise in the fields of fish diseases, nutrition, physiology and genetics.

Salmon ranching in its various forms is now a widely accepted tool in fisheries management and is expected to become increasingly important in management and enhancement of our salmon resources. Intelligent application of the many salmon-ranching strategies available in long-term management programmes for the region's Atlantic salmon will result in a greater abundance of salmon for exploitation and increased social and economic benefits to Atlantic Canada.

There has been virtually no involvement of the private sector in salmon ranching so far, but interest is growing in the potential for commercial seed (eggs or smolts) production, sea ranching, and ocean-pen farming of Atlantic salmon. Although an abundance of technology exists that could be employed in the commercial application of various aquaculture strategies, its adoption by the private sector is restricted by lack of seed stock and information pertaining to economic feasibility. There is a need to strengthen the framework of federal and provincial agencies that respond to, encourage or direct the interest of private entrepreneurs in aquaculture. Of major importance is the need for federal and provincial governments to prepare policies that define their future roles in stimulating, developing and supporting the industry. At the same time, short- and long-term development plans should be prepared for commercial aquaculture in the region. Without these basic building blocks, commercial aquaculture will continue in the haphazard manner that has characterised its development so far.

ACKNOWLEDGEMENTS

This chapter is dedicated to the many individuals that have been involved in the culture of salmonids in the Maritimes Region during the past century. Through their devoted efforts they have pioneered the development of the efficient and highly technical system of salmon culture that is practised today.

Thanks are extended to N. E. MacEachern, G. H. Penney, J. D. Pratt, K. E. Smith and Dr G. I. Pritchard for reviewing the chapter in manuscript.

REFERENCES

Baker, R. O. (1977). "Halibut Cove Pink Salmon Rearing Experiment". Report by Department of Fish and Game, Division FRED, Anchorage, Alaska.

Carey, T. G. (1973). Transactions of Canadian Society of Environmental Biologists, Atlantic Chapter Annual Meeting, 81-85.

Dominy, C. L. (1973). *Biol. Conserv.* **5** (2), 105-113.

Ducharme, L. J. A. (1972). Artificial reconditioning of Atlantic salmon *(Salmo Salar L.)* kelts. Internal Report of Resource Development Branch, Fisheries and Marine Service, Department of Fisheries and Environment, Halifax, Nova Scotia.

Elson, P. F. (1975a). *Canadian Fish Culturist* **21**, 7-18.
Elson, P. F. (1975b). *Canadian Fish Culturist* **21**, 25-32.
Elson, P. F., Meister, A. L., Saunders, J. W., Saunders, R. L., Sprague, J. B. and Zitko, V. (1973). International Atlantic Salmon Foundation. Special Publication Series **4** (1), 83-110.
Foda, A. and Henderson, T. K. (1977). International Council for the Exploration of the Sea. Anadromous and Catadromous Fish Committee, C.M. 1977/M:31.
Foda, A. and Ritter, J. A. (1977). International Council for the Exploration of the Sea. Anadromous and Catadromous Fish Committee, C.M. 1977/M:28.
Frantsi, C., Foda, A. and Ritter, J. A. (1972a). International Council for the Exploration of the Sea. Anadromous and Catadromous Fish Committee, C.M. 1972/M:15.
Frantsi, C., Ritter, J. A. and Foda, A. (1972b). Canada Department of the Environment, Fisheries Service, Resource Development Branch, Maritimes Region. *Prog. Rep.* **7**.
Goff, T. R. and Forsyth, L. S. (1979). Canada Department of Fisheries and Environment, Fisheries and Marine Service, Resource Branch, Maritimes Region. Tech. Rep. 841.
Gray, R., Cameron, J. D. and McAskill, J. D. (1976). Study on recycling Atlantic salmon *(Salmo salar L.)* kelts from three different rivers in Nova Scotia to improve the efficiency of broodstock utilization. Paper presented by R. Gray to the Northeast Fish and Wildlife Conference, Hershey, Pennsylvania, April 1976.
Hager, R. C. and Noble, R. E. (1974). *Progressive Fish Culturist* **38** (3), 144-147.
Hill, G. M. (1978). Reconditioning of Atlantic salmon *(Salmo salar)* kelts in freshwater. Paper presented by G. M. HIll to the Northeast Fish and Wildlife Conference, White Sulphur Springs, West Virginia, February, 1978.
Isaksson, A. (1976). *J. Agr. Res. Icel.* **8** (1-2), 19-26.
Jessop, B. M. (1975). Canada Department of Fisheries and Environment, Fisheries and Marine Services. Resource Development Branch, Maritimes Region. Tech. Rep. MAR/T-75-1.
Kobayashi, T. (1976). FAO. Tech. Conf. Aquaculture, Kyoto, Japan. FIR: AQ-Conf.-76-E.75.
Kossov, E. G., Lazerev, M. S. and Polikashin, L. V. (1960). *Rybnoe Khozyaistvo* **36**, 20-25.
Lister, D. B. (1975). Canada Department of Fisheries and Environment, Fisheries and Marine Service, Resource Development Branch, Maritimes Region. Internal Rep. MAR/I-75-2.
Marshall, T. L. (1975). Canada Department of Fisheries and Environment, Fisheries and Marine Service, Resource Development Branch Maritimes Region. Tech. Rep. MAR/T-75-4.
MacCrimmon, H. R. (1954). *J. Fish. Res. Board Can.* **11**, 362-403.

130   *J. A. Ritter and T. G. Carey*

Österdahl, L. (1969). *In* "Symposium on Salmon and Trout in Streams" (Ed. T. G. Northcote). pp. 205-215. H. R. MacMillan Lectures in Fisheries, University of British Columbia, Vancouver, Canada.

Penney, G. H. (1976). International Council for the Exploration of the Sea. Anadromous and Catadromous Fish Committee, C.M. 1976/M:19.

Peterson, H. H. (1973). International Atlantic Salmon Foundation. Special Publication Series 4 (1), 219-235.

Porter, T. R. and Meerburg, D. J. (1977). International Council for the Exploration of the Sea. Anadromous and Catadromous Fish Committee, C.M. 1977/M:22.

Pratt, J. D., Hare, G. M. and Murphy, H. P. (1974). Canada Department of Fisheries and Environment, Fisheries and Marine Service, Resource Development Branch, Newfoundland Region. Tech. Rep. NEW/T-74-1.

Ritter, J. A. (1972). Canada Department of Fisheries and Environment, Fisheries Service, Resource Development Branch, Maritimes Region. Prog. Rep. 5.

Ritter, J. A. (1975). International Council for the Exploration of the Sea. Anadromous and Catadromous Fish Committee, C.M. 1975/M:26.

Ritter, J. A. (1977). International Council for the Exploration of the Sea. Anadromous and Catadromous Fish Committee, C.M. 1977/M:27.

Ritter, J. A. and Newbould, K. (1977). International Council for the Exploration of the Sea. Anadromous and Catadromous Fish Committee, C.M. 1977/M:32.

Ritter, J. A., Côté, Y., Porter, T. R. and Tétreault, B. (1979). Issues and promises for Atlantic salmon management in Canada. *In* "Atlantic Salmon in the World of Tomorrow" (Ed. A. E. J. Went). Fishing News Books Ltd. Farnham.

Ruggles, C. P. and Watt, W. D. (1975). *J. Fish. Res. Board Can.* **32**, 161-170.

Saunders, R. L. (1968). *Progressive Fish Culturist* **30**, 104-109.

Saunders, R. L. (1977). International Atlantic Salmon Foundation. Special Publication Series **7**, 17-24.

Chapter 8

Salmon Ranching in Iceland

Á. ÍSAKSSON

Institute of Freshwater Fisheries, Reykjavik, Iceland

INTRODUCTION

Ocean ranching is defined as aquaculture in which fish range freely for feeding in the sea and are harvested at a specific location on their spawning migration. The Atlantic salmon is well suited for ocean ranching due to its precise homing to the place of release where it can be harvested in traps, nets or by a rod fishery. The average growth of Icelandic salmon is from 30 g to 2·5 kg in one year and to 6 kg in two. If return rates of released smolts are high, salmon can be ranched profitably.

In 1962 a government-owned salmon farm was opened at Kollafjordur to serve as a research facility and derive income from the sale of trapped adults resulting from the release of salmon smolts at the station. The first smolts were released in 1963. Although less than 0·5 m³/sec of water flowed from the station, the returns of marked two year smolts had exceeded 8% by 1966 (Gudjonson, 1973), and the foundation for ocean ranching in Iceland had been laid.

RATIONALE FOR SALMON RANCHING IN ICELAND

Salmon ranching in Iceland is of two types: enhancement of salmon stocks to improve sport fishing and releases of salmon smolts into non-productive streams, where returning adults are trapped and sold on the market. The hatchery may also be located on the same watershed as at Kollafjördur. Most of the information on the survival of hatchery-produced salmon in Iceland has been obtained here.

It has become increasingly clear that Icelandic salmon stocks probably enjoy a higher rate of return than in other Atlantic countries. This has only been confirmed in south-western Iceland, but the abundance of salmon in other parts suggests similar conditions. Oceanic survival of 20% of wild smolts to grilse size has been ascertained in an Icelandic salmon stream, whereas hatchery smolt survival obtained at Kollafjördur has been at best 10-15%.

Three factors are primarily responsible for the high survival rates: prohibition on fishing for salmon at sea, high proportion of grilse (1-sea-winter fish), and a great abundance of suitable food organisms for salmon around Iceland.

Ban on Commercial Sea Fishing

In 1932 the Icelandic parliament passed a law forbidding salmon fishing in the sea with any gear. Excepted were a few farms that had a traditional income from salmon fishing, mostly by land-connected gill nets. Today these farms account for approximately 1% of the total Icelandic catch. The farsightedness of this decision is noteworthy, as it can be considered the major reason for the suitability of Iceland for salmon ranching as opposed to many other salmon-producing countries.

Predominance of Grilse

An estimated 50-60% of the salmon caught in Iceland each year are grilse, averaging 2·5 kg. They do not migrate as far as the 2- and 3-sea winter salmon and are consequently not caught in foreign waters. The grilse proportion differs between different geographical areas. In the north and east of Iceland, which produce approximately 25% of all the salmon (Fig. 1) older fish predominate (>60%). In the south and west there is a 60% predominance of grilse, which probably is partly responsible for the greater numbers of salmon caught in these areas.

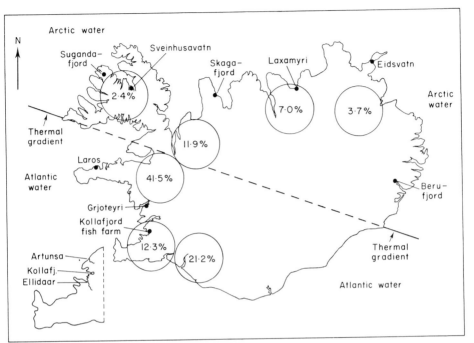

Fig. 1. Average contribution of the various areas in Iceland in the salmon catch (1971-76). The diagonal line shows the boundary between Southern and Northern stocks. Southern stocks constitute over 75% of the annual landings. Notice the vast areas with no salmon production. Also shown are various places of interest mentioned in the text.

Availability of Food

Capelin *(Mallotus villosus)* and small crustacea, known foods of salmon, are abundant off northern Iceland. Lancetfish *(Paralepsis* sp.) and squid are abundant in the more temperate waters off southern Iceland.

SUITABILITY OF DIFFERENT AREAS FOR OCEAN RANCHING

Some parts of Iceland may be better suited for ocean ranching than others, depending on the survival rate of salmon, which again is a function of the following:

(1) length of time spent at sea;
(2) proximity of feeding grounds and their vulnerability to fishing by other nations;
(3) the quantity and quality of food organisms and their availability in that area;
(4) possible adverse effects of hydrographic factors (temperature, salinity, etc.) on downstream migrants or adults.

Duration of Stay in the Ocean

Although grilse are more abundant in southern than in northern Iceland, there is no concrete evidence concerning the genetic or environmental control of maturation age in Icelandic salmon. Nævdal *et al.* (1976) found indications that maturation age in Norwegian salmon was genetically controlled. This may also be partly true in Iceland, although environmental influences must be taken into account. There are environmental differences between the two areas that might affect ocean age. The most important ones are the following:

Smolt Age
Smolts in northern Iceland stay in freshwater a year longer on average than in the south. They are slower growing in freshwater and could also be at sea.

Smolt Size
Wild smolts in southern Iceland average 12-13 cm (Gudjonsson 1978, Isaksson *et al.*, 1978). The smolts in northern Iceland may be smaller. Since hatchery work in Iceland has shown a strong positive relationship between smolt size and size on maturation as grilse (Isaksson and Bergman, 1978), it is possible that small smolts would not reach the size necessary for maturation in one year which would favour a higher ocean age. (See also Chapter 3.).

Time of Downstream Migration
Smolts migrate in southern Iceland in late May and early June (Gudjonsson, 1978). Their migration in northern Iceland is unknown but is probably late June-early July in view of cold spring temperatures. Thus northern smolts would lose a month's ocean feeding compared

with southern ones. Kollafjördur experiments indicate that such a reduction in feeding period is reflected in grilse size the following year (Isaksson and Bergman, 1978) and could also affect the number maturing as grilse.

Time of smolt arrival into the estuaries may vary between streams with the rate of warm-up and the distance travelled by the smolts. Streams originating at high altitudes warm up slower and later than those originating in the lowlands. This may explain why some streams that originate far inland but flow to the opposite coasts of Iceland in some cases have similar grilse/salmon ratios.

Ocean Temperatures

Smolts entering the sea off northern Iceland are exposed to colder water than those entering in the south. If sea-growth is a function of temperature, initial growth of these northern fish will be slower, thus favouring late maturation. Experience in Norwegian salmon culture shows that marine growth of salmon, although relatively unaffected by low sea temperatures (Gjedrem and Gunnes, 1978), is somewhat more affected during the first sea winter than later. Thus smaller smolt size, delayed migration and reduced oceanic growth could together lengthen the period until maturation in northern salmon stocks.

River Discharge

In some Icelandic rivers grilse females are rare, probably because life-history characteristics have evolved in response to specific physical characteristics of those rivers, such as water velocity.

Geographical Isolation

Pronounced geographical barriers exist between these populations (Fig. 1). On the north-west peninsula and the east coast the cold streams do not foster salmon. Sharp oceanic temperature gradients off the northwest and southeast coasts, where Atlantic water meets Arctic, may isolate the populations with respect to feeding areas. Thus many factors favour isolation and separate genetic evolution of southern and northern stocks and may have impact on homing and impede successful transplanting between the two areas. The relative importance of the factors in determining maturation age is unknown; they may work in combination.

The Feeding Grounds of Icelandic Salmon

Most information on feeding migrations of the Icelandic salmon has been obtained from Carlin tagged smolts released from Kollafjördur, and only represents southern stocks. Figure 2 shows the straying of salmon released at the fish farm as well as distant recaptures.

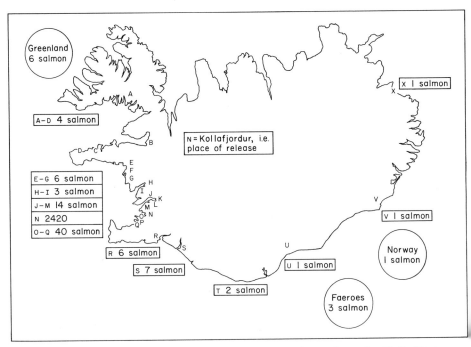

Fig. 2. Geographical distribution of recaptured salmon from the Kollafjördur Fish Farm (1966-1974).

Since the grilse are not harvested on their feeding grounds, the tagging experiments do not reveal their whereabouts. There have been returns of six salmon from Greenland and four from the Faroe-Norway area during eight years of tagging. These data indicate that some salmon from south-western Iceland which stay two or more years at sea mix with salmon stocks from Canada and various European countries off west Greenland and some go into the Norwegian Sea. This is insufficient to establish the feeding grounds of Icelandic salmon but can be used in conjunction with accepted theories on the high seas migration of salmon to find likely areas of feeding. For the northern stocks one must make a great deal of assumptions based on the same principles used for the southern ones.

It is not known whether the salmon orient to oceanic currents or navigate by other means. The applicability of the major theories on high seas migration of salmon can be evaluated from Icelandic tagging data.

High Seas Migration Theories

Theories on the high seas migration of salmon are of two types: passive or current-guided movements and hypotheses assuming celestial navigation (Hasler, 1966).

The former theory seems to be more widely accepted by analogy with the current-dependence of Pacific salmon in the North Pacific Ocean.

Taguchi (1957) noted that adult salmon bound for the Siberian coast and Japan were travelling with the oceanic currents. Later tagging studies confirmed this, but data on smolt migration at sea is lacking. Taguchi's observations gave rise to theories that Pacific salmon populations are tied to a local oceanic eddy during the feeding migration. Thus the Kamchatka-Sakhalin salmon are following the Kuroshio current and the Alaskan salmon a larger gyre in the Gulf of Alaska.

Similarly Mathisen and Gudjonsson (1978) suggested that Icelandic salmon are tied to eddies close to Iceland, utilising the productive mixing areas of cold arctic and temperate Atlantic water. These theories assume that the salmon follow the currents throughout their marine phase. Thus the grilse are assumed to occupy smaller eddies than salmon destined to stay two or three years in the sea.

Icelandic Evidence

The major eddies present around Iceland were first demonstrated in drift bottle experiments by Hermann and Thomsen (1946) and later confirmed by Einarsson and Stefansson (1953). The main ones off the south-west coast are the Irminger Sea eddy and a circular current around the southern tip of Greenland into the Davis strait (Fig. 3). Both these gyres would bring salmon on their return journey to the south coast of Iceland. According to Hermann and Thomsen (1946) it takes 225 days for a drift bottle to complete the circuit in the Irminger

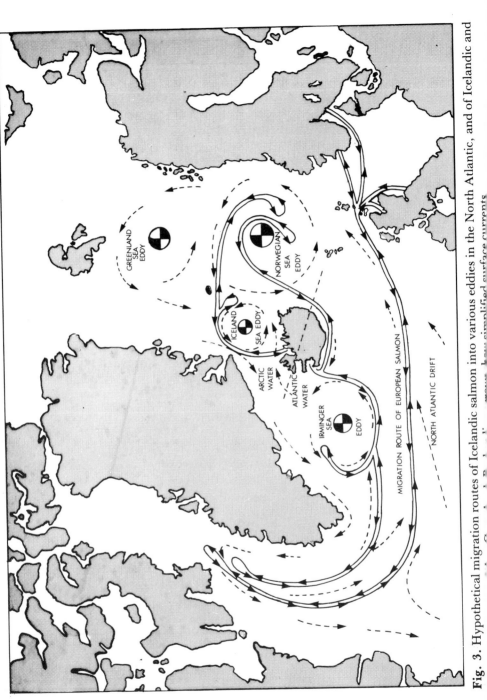

Fig. 3. Hypothetical migration routes of Icelandic salmon into various eddies in the North Atlantic, and of Icelandic and

Sea. If we accept the theory of denatant migration throughout the marine phase, this circuit is very well suited for salmon smolts from the southwest of Iceland, destined to stay one year in the sea (Mathisen and Gudjonsson 1978).

The straying pattern of returning salmon (Fig. 2) suggests that the fish from southern Iceland are approaching from a south to south-westerly direction, namely from the Irminger Sea. It is unlikely that any of these fish are feeding off the north or east coast or they would have strayed into some northern and eastern rivers. This straying pattern extends just about to the location where the cold and warm ocean masses meet.

Also Gudjonsson (1977) found that 2% of adult salmon tagged in the Ölfusá estuary on the south coast of Iceland were recaptured the same summer in the Borgarfjördur district in western Iceland. This suggests that some salmon destined for western Iceland approach the south coast and even enter southern streams before going on to their final destination (Fig. 4). Similarly Gudjonsson (1978) states that salmon enter streams later in the season as one moves northward in Iceland, possibly indicative of delay in arrival.

Finally, in summer 1976, 140 adult salmon were transported from Kollafjördur to a tributary of the Thjorsá river in Southern Iceland to be sportfished. The river was blocked but a few escaped in floods. A month later two returned to Kollafjördur (Fig. 4). The return journey involved a 50 km downstream migration and a 150 km saltwater migration around the Reykjanes peninsula. There is a definite westerly current along the south coast which it is likely that the salmon were following or navigating by more sophisticated methods. Smell could only have been important during the final stages. Such evidence suggests that the salmon are feeding in the Irminger Sea eddy and going with the current on their spawning migration.

Other observations suggest that salmon would not always have time to complete the circuit in the gyre. Atlantic, unlike Pacific salmon, do not die after spawning and kelts (spawned out fish) stay only two to three months at sea before re-entering freshwater. Furthermore, at Kollafjördur some very large male smolts (>20 cm), migrating out in May have returned in August for spawning. None could have completed the circuit in the Irminger Sea.

Some information obtained at Kollafjördur suggests that smolts may be positively rheotactic until mature, when they retrace their route with

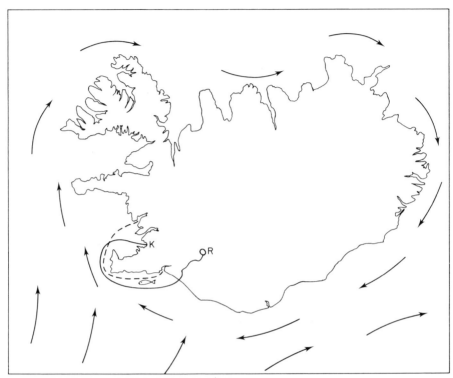

Fig. 4. Migration route of Atlantic Salmon adults from the Kollafjördur Fish Farm (K), transported by truck to location R where they were used for a put-and-take fishery. One month later two salmon had made the 200 kilometer trip back to the Fish Farm. The dotted line indicates the migration route of five salmon tagged in the Ölfusá estuary (Gudjonsson, 1977). The arrows show oceanic currents which the salmon may have been following around Reykjanes peninsula.

the current. Figure 5 shows likely distances travelled by grilse, kelts and oversize smolts as borne out by their release and return times. In 1975 smolts released early returned late the following year and were larger upon return than smolts released later in the spring (Isaksson *et al.*, 1978). A longer migration for the fish released earlier and consequently a longer return route result in a delayed return. Kelts released in late winter usually return very early in the next fishing season indicating a short migration. Such a contranatant pattern of outward migration would account for movement of European salmon

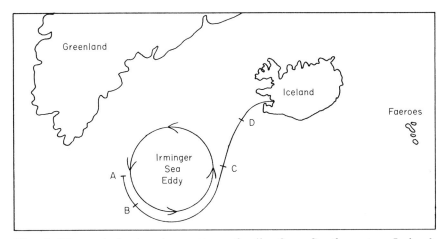

Fig. 5. Theoretical migration pattern of grilse from South-western Iceland into the Irminger Sea Eddy assuming a contranatant migration of smolts followed by a denatant one upon maturation. Arrow pointers indicate direction of current in the Eddy.
A: Smolts released in May—returning as adults in August of the following year.
B: Smolts released in June—returning as adults in July of the following year.
C: Kelt released in January—returning in July of the same year.
D: Oversize smolt released in May—returning as precocious males in August of the same year.

to west Greenland, since the prevailing currents are from west to east (Fig. 3).

The question of smolt orientation to oceanic currents is academic if the salmon are tied to oceanic eddies throughout their feeding period. That granted, the likely feeding areas for Icelandic salmon lie in the eddies close by (Fig. 3). The Irminger and the Iceland Sea eddies probably serve as major feeding grounds for grilse in southern and northern Iceland, respectively. From tagging experiments, older salmon in southern Iceland go to west Greenland and a few into the Norwegian Sea. The Norwegian, and to a lesser degree the Greenland Sea eddies, are likely feeding grounds for older northern salmon but no tagging data exist to support this.

If these ideas are true, the grilse populations from southern and northern Iceland are unlikely to mix on their feeding grounds while older salmon probably do. It is particularly important to establish the feeding grounds of Icelandic grilse, as they form the backbone of ocean-ranching programmes in Iceland today. Their return rates are much higher than those of older salmon and it is likely that Iceland can prohibit their exploitation in the sea if they are feeding within the 200-mile fishing limit.

As the quantity of available food in a certain area may limit the salmon ranching potential, it is also necessary for a successful venture to know the marine diet of salmon.

Food of the Icelandic Salmon

Information on the food of salmon at sea is fragmentary. The main food items in 32 salmon caught in the Irminger Sea were lancetfish *(Paralepsis)* and squid *(Brachytheuthis)* (Jensen, 1974). These findings have been confirmed by Jensen and Lear (1978). The waters of the Irminger Sea are too warm for arctic fish such as capelin, which seems to be a major food item in arctic waters.

There is no information on the food of salmon in the sea north of Iceland, but it is probably similar to that of salmon feeding in other polar areas. Lear (1971) found that over 75% by weight of food in salmon stomachs off West Greenland examined consisted of capelin *(Mallotus villosus)*. Sandeel *(Ammodytes)* made up some 12% with Euphausids and Amphipods, each comprising less than 2%.

No data exist on the feeding of smolts at sea. Large quantities of different fish larvae are present along the coast and presumably available to the young salmon as well as various species of Amphipods. It is not uncommon to find 10-100 000 4-cm capelin fry per nautical mile trawled on the continental shelf of Iceland (Vilhjálmsson and Fridgeirsson, 1975) in mid-summer, shortly after the salmon smolts have left freshwater. These capelin vary greatly in distribution between years, which may be responsible for yearly fluctuations in salmon abundance.

That salmon will feed on capelin is very encouraging for the salmon-ranching programme in Iceland. The total biomass of capelin around Iceland is several million tons (Vilhjálmsson, personal communication) with only a minor fraction harvested as yet. This resource is probably only utilised by some 100 000 salmon today, a figure which could be expanded into millions in spite of direct competition with a growing capelin fishery.

EXPERIMENTS WITH SALMON RANCHING

General Background

Kollafjördur Experimental Fish Farm had the following objectives (Gudjonsson, 1960):

(a) To perform hatching and rearing experiments with salmonoid fish.
(b) To develop and teach new rearing techniques.
(c) To perform selective breeding of salmon and trout.
(d) To perform ocean ranching experiments with salmon, marketing the returning adults.

These have been followed within the limits of available resources. To be financially independent, emphasis has been placed on mass production and sale of smolts and on the sale of returning adults. Work on the oceanic survival of hatchery smolts has enabled fish farmers to set certain criteria of smolt quality necessary for successful salmon ranching.

Besides Kollafjördur, ranching is carried out at Lárós on Snæfellsnes using a large lake to rear salmon fry and generate salmon runs. Adult traps are also located at Súgandafjördur and Sveinhúsavatn (Fig. 1), where salmon ranching has used hatchery smolts from distant areas.

Kollafjördur Experimental Fish Farm

Total Releases and Returns
Figure 6 shows the general layout of the station. In the standard "above-lagoon" release method the smolts migrate from the release ponds down a small brook into a large freshwater lagoon and from there through the adult trap out to sea. In the "below-lagoon" release method smolts have been transported from one of the rearing houses to below the adult trap.

The total run of salmon since 1964 has exceeded 20000, and total releases are in excess of 430000 smolts (Table I). The recapture rate of just under 5% is considered good, considering the variation in the quality of smolts released over the years. The yearly releases (1964-66) were quite satisfactory and better than the four years following (1967-70). In these early years two-year-old smolts were raised in outdoor ponds during their last freshwater winter. By 1967 the emphasis was on indoor rearing of one-year-old smolts, under artificial

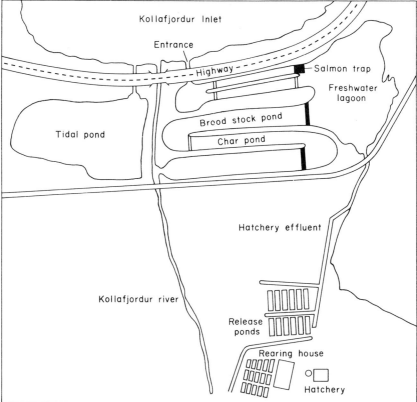

Fig. 6. (upper) The Kollafjördur Experimental Fish Farm. (lower) Diagram showing major rearing facilities, release sites and adult trap. Most smolt releases have been performed from the release ponds but some below the adult trap.

Table I. Yearly releases of smolts from Kollafjördur Experimental Fish Farm from 1963 through 1975 and subsequent returns to the adult trap.

Year of release	Number of smolts released	Number of adult returns	Number returning as grilse	Return as grilse (%)	Highest returns of tagged smolts (%)	Age of smolts in best group (years)
1963[a]	300	4	4	1·3	—	—
1964[a]	1 000	57	57	5·7	—	—
1965[a]	12 250	704	640	5·2	8·2	2
1966[a]	11 500	610	550	4·8	2·5	2
1967[a]	11 300	203	190	1·7	0·6	2
1968[a]	16 000	263	230	1·4	1·7	2
1969[a]	125 700	4 187	4 100	3·3	10·5	2
1970	95 000	516	350	0·4	0·01	1
1971[b]	17 500	681	600	3·4	4·7	2
1972[b]	14 000	1 956	1 600	11·0	9·8	2
1973[b]	23 300	3 065	2 850	13·0	14·8	1
1974	82 600	6 920	6 400	8·0	13·0	2
1975	26 400	2 094	1 500	5·7	14·4	1
Total	436 850	21 260 (4·9%)	19 071	4·4	—	—

[a]Gudjónsson, 1973.
[b]Ísaksson, 1976.

light throughout their rearing period. This had negative effects on oceanic survival as well as on smolt migratory behaviour. By 1972 one-year smolt production had improved by exposing the salmon smolts to natural photoperiod changes and total returns were greatly improved.

Although the techniques for rearing of one- and two-year smolts are established, the salmon returns are still relatively unpredictable. Judging from the high return rate of certain tagged smolts (Table I) it is safe to assume that the oceanic survival of hatchery smolts is more related to husbandry during the last few weeks in freshwater than to oceanic feeding conditions.

Returns of Tagged Smolts
Between 1966 and 1975 experiments have used differing rearing techniques, tagging and release methods (Table II). Fuller details of these are given in Gudjonsson (1973), Isaksson (1976a, b, c), and Isaksson and Bergman (1978).

"Above the lagoon" (Fig. 6) was the standard release, except in 1973. After 1973 "below lagoon" releases have been very unpredictable but occasional successes (1976, unpublished) have given rise to a new "below lagoon" release technique, using a release pond. Standard release time has been in late May and early June, when the primary migration of wild smolts in south-western Iceland takes place.

The types of smolts used were (Table II):

(a)   One or two year indoor; reared intensively under artificial light up to migrant size, irrespective of time of day or season.

(b)   One or two year photoperiod; exposed to natural photoperiod indoors for 10-35 weeks before release.

(c)   One or two year outdoor; kept in outdoor ponds for 10-35 weeks before release:

From 1966 to 1971 only indoor and outdoor smolts were released at the station. Indoor smolts gave practically no returns, irrespective of age. The best overall returns were from two-year smolts kept in outdoor ponds for 35 weeks. In 1971 one-year-old smolts were reared in outdoor ponds for the 10 weeks immediately prior to release. There was a significant increase in returns, comparable to a two-year-old control group (Table II). In 1972 natural photoperiod was imitated indoors using artificial lights, with considerable improvement in returns. In 1973, one-year smolts were reared under a transparent roof for 35 weeks before release resulting in a great increase in one-year-old smolt survival at sea, exceeding 14%. In 1974 this technique worked very well for two-year smolts also.

The 1974 and 1975 tagging experiments have confirmed that the one-year smolts are comparable to two-year smolts with respect to oceanic survival and will be the foundation upon which the salmon-ranching programmes in Iceland should rest. The proportion of grilse in the returns is equally high for one-year and two-year smolts released at Kollafjördur, usually over 90% of the returns.

Carlin tagging has been the main method used at Kollafjördur. The Carlin tag is an external dangler, attached with a steel wire in the dorsal musculature of salmon smolts. This tag gave dubious results if the smolts tagged were under 13-14 cm in fork length. The information obtained was therefore restricted to relatively large smolts. Nevertheless, the Carlin tag has given useful information about distant migration of Icelandic salmon and straying into various rivers within the country. It has also been useful in studying the relative survivals of different hatchery groups, and has given, in a few instances, returns exceeding 10%, which must be considered very satisfactory.

In 1973 the Carlin tag with a polyethylene attachment extensively used in other countries was tried. The recaptures were fairly good and no worse than the standard Carlin tag returns in that year (Isaksson 1976b) (Table II). Subsequent uses of these tags were not as successful and gave little improvement over the steel wire tags. The polyethylene tags may, however, yield returns on smaller smolts than the steel wire tags.

A major breakthrough in the tagging techniques at Kollafjördur came in 1974 when experiments were started using the microtag. Kollafjördur was considered ideal for the use of microtags since each returning adult is caught in a trap and inspected for marks. These tags should give more accurate indication of salmon survival, since tag related effects on the fish are minimal.

The microtagging technique was developed in the 1960s for Pacific salmon. Application and recovery are described by Bergman *et al.* (1968). They are very small encoded tags, injected into the snout of smolts, magnetised after injection, and found later, using a detector. As there are no external signs of the tag, adipose fin-clipping is used to aid recovery. In contrast to Carlin tags, the microtags are a group marking technique and do not allow individual identification. Considerable effort must be exercised to recover these tags from sports or high seas fisheries.

Table II. Returns of tagged salmon to the Kollafjördur Experimental Fish Farm, over a 10-year period from 1967 to 1976. Different smolt types are compared.

Year of release	Year of return	Type of tag	Type of smolt	Number tagged	Number returning	Return (%)	Release time and location
1966[a]	1967(68)	Carlin	1-year indoor	391	0	0	Late May above lagoon
			2-year outdoor 35 weeks	2114	54	2·5	Late May above lagoon
1967[a]	1968(69)	Carlin	1-year indoor	660	0	0	Late May above lagoon
			2-year outdoor 35 weeks	1566	9	0·6	Late May above lagoon
			2-year indoor	399	0	0	Late May above lagoon
1968[a]	1969(70)	Carlin	1-year indoor	1941	2	0·1	Late May above lagoon
			2-year outdoor 35 weeks	2636	45	1·7	Late May above lagoon
			2-year indoor	990	0	0	Late May above lagoon
1969[a]	1970(71)	Carlin	1-year indoor	2413	3	0·1	Late May above lagoon
			2-year outdoor 35 weeks	2305	243	10·5	Late May above lagoon
1970[b]	1971(72)	Carlin	1-year indoor	9200	1	0·01	Late May above lagoon
1971[b]	1972(73)	Carlin	1-year outdoor 12 weeks	5250	17	0.3	Late May above lagoon
			2-year outdoor 10 weeks	583	3	0·5	Late May above lagoon
			2-year outdoor 35 weeks	3775	176	4·6	Late May above lagoon
1972[b]	1973(74)	Carlin	1-year photoperiod 30 weeks	970	19	1·9	Late May above lagoon
			2-year photoperiod 30 weeks	1500	50	3·3	Late May above lagoon
			2-year outdoor 35 weeks	6600	397	6·0	Late May above lagoon
1973[b]	1974(75)	Plastic[d]	1-year photoperiod 35 weeks	2800	239	8·5	Early June below lagoon

Table II. *cont.*

Year of release	Year of return	Type of tag	Type of smolt	Number tagged	Number returning	Return (%)	Release time and location
		Adipose clip	1-year photoperiod 35 weeks	2300	340	14·8	Early June below lagoon
		Plastic[d]	2-year outdoor 35 weeks	1000	95	9·5	Late May above lagoon
1974[c]	1975(76)	Microtag	1-year photoperiod 35 weeks	3000	197	6·6	Late May above lagoon
			2-year photoperiod 35 weeks	3080	345	11·2	Late May above lagoon
			2-year outdoor 35 weeks	4000	355	8·9	Late May above lagoon
		Carlin	2-year outdoor 35 weeks	2500	149	6·0	Late May above lagoon
1975[c]	1976(77)	Microtag	1-year photoperiod 35 weeks	2000	218	10·9	May and June above lagoon
			2-year photoperiod 35 weeks	1000	47	4·7	May and June above lagoon
			2-year outdoor 35 weeks	2180	165	7·6	May and June above lagoon
		Carlin	2-year outdoor 35 weeks	1560	9	0·6	May and June above lagoon

[a]From Gudjónsson (1973)
[b]From Isaksson (1976)
[c]From Isaksson and Bergman (1978)
[d]Modified Carlin tag, polyethylene monofilament attachment.

Carlin tags and microtags were compared with respect to survival in several size classes of smolts (see Isaksson and Bergman, 1978). Double tagging with microtags was used to check on the loss of both standard and polyethylene-attached Carlin tags. Microtag loss was determined by the number of adipose clipped salmon returning without microtags. The major findings were as follows.

Of microtagged salmon 1·6 returned for each Carlin tagged released in the same numbers. The performance of microtagged smolts in the smallest size classes (10-13 cm) was outstanding, sometimes exceeding 10%. The performance of small hatchery smolts has been considerably underestimated in previous years due to a bias from Carlin tags. The loss of Carlin tags attached with steel wire was about 10%, those attached with polyethylene thread 24%, and microtags less than 2%. The negative effect of Carlin tags, as opposed to microtags, on oceanic growth was shown by the weight of returning adults. Similar effects were noted for ventral fin-clips.

Thus microtags provide a truer picture of salmon return rates, being more representative of untagged fish, especially those smolts under 13 cm, which correspond closely with wild smolt-sizes. One drawback is that the salmon has to be killed to read the microtag and a 10-mm diameter hole is left in the snout of the fish. This has not been a problem in selling the fish, which are considered such prime merchandise that the demand exceeds supply.

Transplants of Hatchery Smolts

Salmon smolts, both tagged and untagged have been planted into Icelandic streams for over 15 years. Judging from the recaptures many of these releases were of questionable value due to poor smolt quality, bulky tags and inferior release techniques. A controlled transplanting experiment was made in 1975 using the microtag at Ellidaár, a productive salmon stream flowing through the city of Reykjavík, and at Ártúnsá, an unproductive stream flowing from Mt Esja 25 km to the north (Fig. 1). Direct release methods were tested against the use of a release pond for adaptation before seaward migration. Wild smolts were microtagged for comparison with the hatchery fish (see Isaksson *et al.*, 1978, for full details).

The Productive Stream: Ellidaár (Fig. 7)
Unhandled hatchery smolts from the release pond had a return rate exceeding 8% spread over two years, more than double that from direct releases. The wild smolts had a survival rate of over 20%. Straying of the hatchery smolts to the hatchery, 10 km away, was only 3%. This experiment demonstrated that hatchery smolts can yield satisfactory returns when released into a salmon stream close to the parent stream or hatchery.

Non-productive Streams
It is important to salmon ranching in Iceland to create runs to relatively unproductive streams which have no natural run. This can

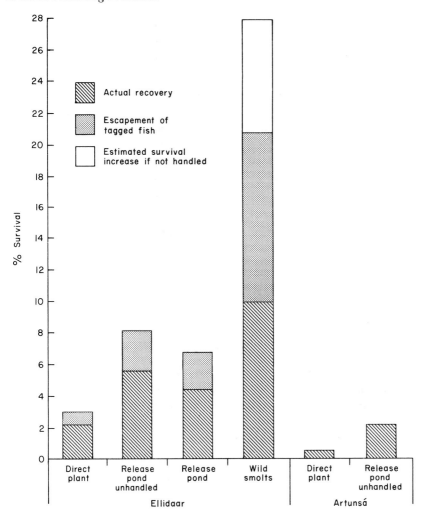

Fig. 7. Survival of hatchery and wild smolts at Ellidaár and Ártúnsá in the 1975 tagging experiment. (From Isaksson, Rasch and Poe, 1978.)

be done where the homing river receives hatchery effluent, but is the chemical composition (including the smell of salmon) important? If so, conditions must be created artificially in these streams.

Ártúnsá (Fig. 7). The smolts used at Ártúnsá were smaller and of lower quality than those used at Ellidaár due to shortage of smolts at Kollafjördur. Total returns were 2·4%, but of these over 25% strayed to Kollafjördur. The smell of salmon may not be strong enough at

Ártúnsá or the water chemistry at Kollafjördur and Ártúnsá may be too similar, since both get water from Mt Esja. If the latter were true, salmon destined for the Fish Farm would stray more into Ártúnsá than Ellidaár. Since the opposite is true, one tends to favour the first explanation.

Súgandafjördur (Fig. 1). The salmon release site in Súgandafjördur on the north-west peninsula is the only facility in Iceland entirely dependent on smolts from distant hatcheries for salmon ranching. Since its establishment in 1972 (on a hobby basis) 1000-3000 smolts have been released each year with 1-2% returns. With improved smolt quality and release technique survival should be improved, but the lack of local stocks is a problem. There are few salmon rivers in that area and no hatcheries within 200 kilometres. Canadian information suggests that smolt survival drops off with distance transported from their native stream (Ritter, 1975). The river at Súgandafjördur is very cold and unproductive and similar to Ártúnsá. The lack of salmon smell (pheromones) may also be a major problem. A similar but little-used release and recapture site is located at Grjóteyri in Borgarfjördur.

Current experiments. In 1977 financial support was obtained from the Nordic Council to do salmon-ranching experiments in Iceland. The grant is primarily aimed at establishing salmon ranching as a secondary occupation for farmers in isolated areas. In addition to the Kollafjördur Farm, whose established salmon runs will serve as a control, three sites will be used for the experiments: Berufjördur (eastern Iceland), Skagafjördur (northern Iceland) and Súgandafjördur. At the first two recovery will be done by seining because of the prohibitive cost of building adult traps.

During 1977 and 1978 release ponds were built in all locations and 6000 microtagged smolts released into each in 1978. Since the release locations are scattered all around Iceland, two different salmon stocks have been used: one native to Kollafjördur, representing southern stocks, and one native to Laxá-river from the Laxamýri hatchery, representing northern stocks. Both one-year and two-year smolts were included in the experimental groups.

The present experiments are the largest salmon ranching ventures attempted in Iceland outside Kollafjördur. The first returns are expected in the summer of 1979. It is likely that further fine-tuning will be desirable with respect to the salmon stocks used. Increased numbers of fish farms in Iceland should help to solve this problem in the future.

Natural Rearing Areas

In the early 1960s salmon fry were planted in salt and brackish water enclosures on the west coast of U.S.A. in the hope that they would utilise natural food resources and migrate to sea when they reached the proper size. The first use of this principle in Iceland was at Lárós (Fig. 1). In 1965 a dyke 300 m long was built across a tidal flat, creating a 165-hectare lake. A spillway and adult trap were built at one end of the dyke. In the early years this very productive area only had a small population of char *(Salvelinus alpinus)*, and it was then planted with salmon smolts and parr. The following discussion is based on release and return figures published by the owners (Sveinsson, 1967; 1968, 1973) whereas correlation of returns to specific releases was made by the Institute of Freshwater Fisheries (Table III).

The returns of salmon gradually increased after 1966, peaked at 2600 in 1971 and then stabilised around 500-1000 per year. There appeared to be two reasons for the decline in salmon runs to the rearing area (Isaksson and Kristjánsson, 1975). First, during the early years only 1-summer-parr and smolts were planted which had relatively good chances of survival compared to the sac-fry released after 1972. The sac-fry can only survive if planted on gravel beds and those are limited

Table III. Number of salmon returning to the Lárós rearing area as a function of previous releases.

Year of recovery	Number of salmon recovered	Sac-fry 4 years earlier	1-summer parr 3 years earlier	Smolts 2 years earlier
1966	2	—	—	—
1967	230	—	30 000	—
1968	320	—	10 000	64 300
1969	311	—	80 000	45 000
1970	620	—	25 000	9 000
1971	2 564	—	167 000	9 670
1972	1 308	75 000	5 000	—
1973	1 000[a]	30 000	—	—
1974	700[a]	550 000	—	—
1975	500[a]	400 000	—	3 000
1976	1 000[a]	800 000	200 000	—

[a]Sveinsson (personal communication).

to the shoreline of the lake which means that the total area of the lake is very poorly utilised. Secondly, the char population within the lake increased, the char being better adapted to live in a lake than the salmon which do best in a swift current. The char are therefore filling more of the habitat in the lake. Atlantic eels *(Anguilla anguilla)* also colonised some of the gravel beds.

Because of the great size of the lake, control of forage species is not practical. Adult char have been netted heavily during the summer but the fishing intensity has not been great enough, since large numbers are feeding in the sea at that time, entering the area in the fall when the main fishing pressure is over. There is, therefore, always a big spawning stock to maintain the char population.

With low running costs the owners claim that they are making some profit at the present return level (Sveinsson, personal communication). There are other recently constructed sites using the same principle at Sveinhúsavatn and Eidsvatn (Fig. 1).

ECONOMICS OF SALMON RANCHING

Salmon ranching can be profitably performed in Iceland. The potential in south-west Iceland is fairly well known, and success is dependent on the use of high-quality smolts and good release techniques. Ocean survival as a function of marine feeding conditions seems to be of lesser importance. There are a number of problems associated with the expansion of salmon ranching to outlying areas in Iceland. These are: the use of stocks suited for a specific location; homing to unproductive streams with dilute chemical characteristics; difficulty and prohibitive cost of transporting salmon smolts from distant rearing stations; and marketing of returning adults. The home market is limited so exports will have to be developed. The cost of producing smolts can be reduced considerably by building larger stations and increasing the efficiency of the rearing process.

Development of the salmon-ranching programme requires consider-able capital; this has not been available and has slowed down progress. It is conceivable that the development of large scale ocean ranching programmes comparable to those started by the Weyerhaeuser Corporation with Pacific salmon is too costly for the Icelandic people and international cooperation may be needed. Iceland has an enormous potential for salmon ranching (Joyner, 1976; Mathisen and Gudjonsson, 1978) and one must hope that full utilisation of this potential will become a reality in the very near future.

REFERENCES

Bergman, P. K., Jefferts, K. B., Fiscus, H. F. and Hager, R. C. (1968). A preliminary evaluation of an implanted coded wire fish tag. *Wash Dept. Fish. Res. Pap.* **3** (1), 63-84.

Einarsson, H. and Stefánsson, U. (1953). Drift-bottle experiments in the waters between Iceland, Greenland and Jan Mayen during the years 1947 and 1949. *Rit Fiskideildar* **1**.

Gjedrem, T. and Gunnes, K. (1978). Comparison of growth rate in Atlantic salmon, Pink salmon, Arctic char, Sea trout and Rainbow trout under Norwegian farming conditions. *Aquaculture* **13**, 135-141.

Gudjonsson, T. (1960). Tillögur Veidmálastjóra til landbúnaðarráðuneytisins um, að ríkið reisi fullkomna tilraunaeldisstöð (unpublished).

Gudjonsson, T. (1973). Smolt rearing techniques, stocking and tagged adult salmon recapture in Iceland. Int. Atlantic Salmon Found., Spec. Pub. Ser. **4** (1), 227-235.

Gudjonsson, T. (1977). Recaptures of Atlantic Salmon Tagged at the Estuary of the River Ölfusá-Hvíta, Iceland. ICES C.M./M:40, 6 pp.

Gudjonsson, T. (1978). The Atlantic Salmon in Iceland. *J. Agr. Res. Iceland* **10** (2), 11-39.

Hasler, A. D. (1966). Underwater "Guideposts". University of Wisconsin Press, 155 pp.

Hermann, F. and Thomsen, H. (1946). Drift-bottle experiments in the northern North-Atlantic. *Medd. for Komm. for Havundersögelser, Hydografi* **3**, 4.

Isaksson, A. (1976a). The Results of Tagging Experiments at the Kollafjördur Experimental Fish Farm from 1970 through 1972. *J. Agr. Res. Iceland* **8** (1-2), 3-13.

Isaksson, A. (1976b). Preliminary results from the 1973 tagging experiments at the Kollafjördur Experimental Fish Farm. *J. Agr. Res. Iceland* **8** (1-2), 14-18.

Isaksson, A. (1976c). The improvement of returns of one-year-smolts at the Kollafjördur Fish Farm 1971-1973. *J. Agr. Res. Iceland* **8** (1-2), 19-26.

Isaksson, A. and Kristjánsson, J. (1975). Rannsóknir í Lárósi, Fyrri hluti: Laxrannsóknir, M.S.

Isaksson, A. and Bergman, P. K. (1978). An evaluation of two tagging methods and survival rates of different age and treatment groups of hatchery-reared Atlantic salmon smolts. *J. Agr. Res. Iceland* **10** (2), 74-99.

Isaksson, A., Rasch, T. and Poe, P. (1978). An evaluation of smolt releases into a salmon and a non-salmon producing stream using two release methods. *J. Agr. Res. Iceland* **10** (2), 110-113.

Jensen, J. M. (1974). Salmon survey in the southern part of the Irminger Sea, 1974. ICES C.M./M:29, 2 pp.

Jensen, J. M. and Lear, W. H. (in press).

Joyner, T. (1976). Farming ocean ranges for salmon. *J. Fish. Res. Bd Can.* **33**, 902-904.

Lear, W. H. (1971). Food and feeding of Atlantic salmon at sea. ICNAF Res. Doc. 71/2 Serial no. 2487.

Mathisen, O. A. and Gudjonsson, T. (1978). Salmon management and ocean ranching in Iceland. *J. Agr. Res. Iceland* **10** (2).

Nævdal, G. M. H., Ingebrigtsen, O. and Møller, D. (1978). Variation in age at first spawning in Atlantic Salmon *(Salmo salar). J. Fish. Res. Bd Can.* **35**, 145-147.

Ritter, J. A. (1975). Lower ocean survival rates for hatchery reared Atlantic salmon *(Salmo salar)* stocks released in rivers other than their native streams. ICES. C.M./M:26, 10 pp.

Sveinsson, J. (1967). Fiskeldis- og fiskhaldsstöðin í Látravík á Snæfellsnesi, uppbygging hennar og fyrsti árangur. Árbók Félags áhugamanna um fiskrækt 1967.

Sveinsson, J. (1968). Láróslaxinn 1967 og 1968. Árbók Félags áhugamanna um fiskrækt 1968.

Sveinsson, J. (1973). Láróslaxinn. Árbók Félags áhugamanna um fiskrækt 1969-1973.

Taguchi, K. (1957). The seasonal variation of the Good Fishing Area of Salmon and Movements of the Water masses in the Waters of the Western North Pacific—II. The distribution and migration of salmon populations in offshore waters. *Bull. Jap. Soc. Scient. Fish.* **22** (9), 515-521.

Vilhjálmsson, H. and Fridgeirsson, E. (1975). A review of O-group surveys in the Iceland-East-Greenland area in the years 1970-1974. ICES C.M./H:34, 17 pp.

Chapter 9

Smolt Rearing and the Baltic Salmon Fishery

P.-O. LARSSON

Salmon Research Institute, Älvkarleby, Sweden

THE BALTIC SEA AREA

The Baltic drainage area consists of the Baltic Sea and adjacent gulfs, mainly east of longitude 13°E, and affluents from Denmark, Federal Republic of Germany, German Democratic Republic, Poland, U.S.S.R., Finland and Sweden (Fig. 1). The sea itself covers 373 000 km² and consists of a series of basins separated by ridges. The water is generally shallow, of average depth 55 m; depths of more than 100 m and 200 m make up 15% and 0·5% of the total area respectively. The climate of the sea is mainly moderate humid oceanic, but in the northern and eastern parts is strongly influenced by the surrounding continental territories.

Tidal movements are insignificant. The current system is closely connected with the interchange of oceanic bottomwater and brackish water. The outflowing upper water layers move as a southwesterly current of the Gulf of Bothnia along the east coast of Sweden and contribute to wind-conditioned anticlockwise surface circulation of the whole sea including its gulfs. The water is brackish, the salinity varying from about 3 parts per thousand in the north to 15 parts per thousand in the extreme west (Fig. 2). Further data on hydrography and climate are given by Magaard and Rheinheimer (1974) and Fonselius (1974).

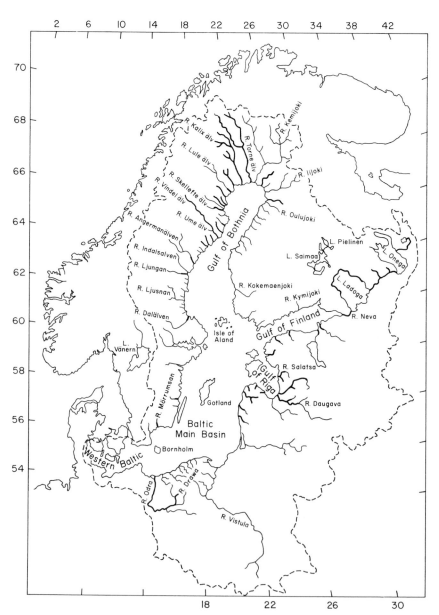

Fig. 1. Baltic drainage area. Rivers and reaches of rivers supporting salmon run in former time (thin line) and at present (thick line). From Christensen and Larsson (1979).

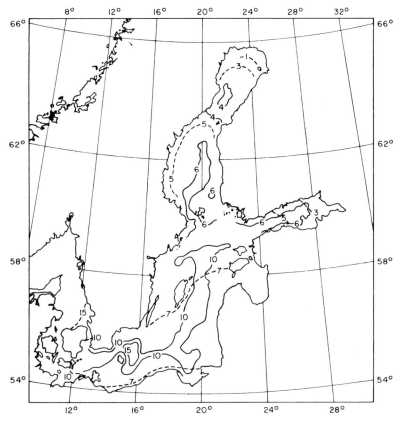

Fig. 2. Isohalines (in parts per thousand) of the Baltic Sea at the surface (broken lines) and at the bottom (continuous lines). After Deutsche Seewarte. From Ekman (1953).

BALTIC SALMON CHARACTERISTICS

Baltic salmon are a geographically isolated population of Atlantic salmon (*Salmo salar*, L.) but are not taxonomically discriminated by Berg (1948). Geographical variations in external morphology between individuals of Baltic and Atlantic stocks, if any, are not thought to be significant. Chromosome number is normally 60, but nuclei with 59 and 58 chromosomes also occur. With respect to chromosome morphology Baltic salmon differs from Atlantic salmon as well as from landlocked salmon from Lake Vänern (Prokofieva, 1934a, b; Svärdson, 1945).

Mean smolt age increases with latitude (Table I), reaching up to five years in northern rivers (Alm, 1934).

The Baltic Main Basin is the principal feeding area of the majority of salmon from the rivers of Gulf of Bothnia. The remainder, varying as to year class and river origin, remain in the Gulf of Bothnia, where salmon from southern Baltic rivers are reported also. (Chrzan, 1964; Backiel and Bartel, 1967; Bartel, 1976). Salmon in the Gulf of Finland are supposed to be generally of local origin, derived from U.S.S.R. affluents (Järvi, 1935, 1943; Halme, 1961, 1964; Thurow, 1968; Toivonen, 1973). Likewise, the Gulf of Riga on the whole does not harbour salmon of outside origin, but seems to be a transition area for postsmolts and spawning migrants (Alm, 1931; Mitans, 1970; Mitans and Rimsh, 1978). According to Swedish tagging experiments about 0·04% of recaptured salmon had migrated outside the Danish islands.

Table I. Age distribution of smolts in Baltic rivers based on analyses of smolt scales (from Christensen and Larsson, 1979).

River	Latitude (approximate)	Age (%)				Mean age		
		1	2	3	4			
Rickleån	64°N	—	25·2	73·8	1·0	2·75	1961-65	Österdahl (1969)
Salatsa	58°N	24·1	72·9	2·9	0·1	1·79	1964-70	Mitans (1973)
Mörrumsån	56° 30′N	80	20	+	—	1·20	1963-66	Lindroth (1977)

During the first year at sea growth of Baltic salmon is comparatively poor but improves in the following years. Grilse weigh only about 1·5 kg, while the 2- and 3-sea-winter spawners weigh 4-5 kg and 8-10 kg respectively (Fig. 3). Sex ratio in grilse is very high in favour of males, especially in the northern rivers, e.g. 99·5% in River Indal (Peterson, 1967). The intensive offshore fishery for feeding fish that has developed since 1950 (see below) has heavily affected the age-distribution of spawning migrants (see Table II).

The run of Baltic salmon is dependent on the latitude, being later and of shorter duration the more northerly the river. During the last decades the run has started later and later in the year (Table III).

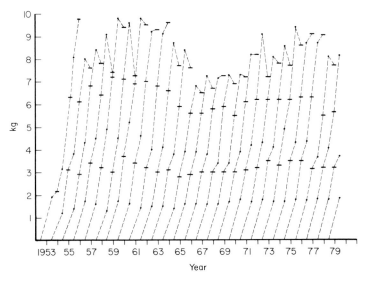

Fig. 3. Size fluctuation of recaptures from Swedish tagging experiments, offshore (—) and coastal (•).

Table II. Sea age distribution of spawning migrants in some Baltic rivers 1925-33, based on scale-analysis (Alm, 1934) and on results of smolt-tagging experiments, 1966. From Christensen and Larsson (1979).

	Sea age distribution in %, number of sea-winters								
	1925-33					From 1966			
River	1^a	2	3	4	5 or more	1	2	3	4	5 or more
Lule	34·2	19·9	35·4	10·6		32·1	46·7	17·4	3·0	0·8
Ume	3·4	31·5	55·7	9·4		31·1	63·5	4·1	1·4	
Ångermanälven	2·5	36·9	50·5	9·6	0·5	66·7	28·8	3·3	4·2	
Indalsälven	1·1	41·4	52·6	4·6	0·3	56·6	32·0	9·0	0·8	0·8
Ljusnan	2·1	21·6	67·3	8·8	0·3	35·2	50·0	11·1	3·7	
Dalälven	0·5	18·3	68·1	13·1		63·3	23·9	11·7	0·5	0·3

^{a}The proportion of 1-sea-winter salmon is probably underestimated on account of gear selection (R. Lule excepted).

Table III. Distribution by month (in percentage) of salmon catches in some Swedish rivers. From Christensen and Larsson (1979).

River		Mar.	Apr.	May	Jun.	Jul.	Aug.	Sep.	Oct.
Torneälv ⎤					24·7	74·0	1·3		
Umeälv ⎟	1920-30				40·9	55·0	3·9	0·2	
Dalälven ⎨	Alm (1934)			23·0	63·5	12·0	1·2		
Mörrumsån ⎦		0·7	5·7	35·2	34·6	16·1	4·7	1·4	1·6
Umeälv	1970				0·3	28·1	60·5	11·1	
	Johansson (1973)								
Mörrumsån	1974				3·1	12·4	10·1	7·0	8·5	58·9
	Persson (1975)								

SALMON FISHERY

Salmon fishing was originally confined to the capture of ascending spawners in the rivers. This way of exploiting salmon stocks was dominant until the end of the nineteenth century. At present less than 5% of the total yield of Baltic salmon accrues to the river fishery, mainly in Finland, Sweden and the U.S.S.R. In former times the most important methods of capturing salmon in the northern Baltic rivers were various weir constructions. The larger types are no longer in use. In the few rivers left in Finland the short bank weir *(forspata)* is still in use. Only floating gill nets are operated, as set gill nets are not permitted. Seine and brail fishing is also carried out (Toivonen, personal communication). In Sweden seines of various types are now most important. Some kinds of salmon traps are still working and brail fishing of spawners for stripping is maintained in the River Mörrumsån. In the U.S.S.R. fishing with gill nets, beach seines and special salmon traps is carried out in the lower reaches of the rivers (Lishev, personal communication). At present in Poland salmon are fished mainly for rearing purposes and by means of electrofishing. Formerly trammel nets were in use (Sych, personal communication).

Salmon fishing in the Baltic sea was reported as early as the middle of the seventeenth century (Jensen, 1964) but is certainly older. The sea fishery may be divided into coastal and offshore fishing, today represented by the operation of fixed gear for maturing salmon on spawning migration and drifting gear for feeding salmon, respectively. Coastal fishery was dominant until about mid-century; today only

15-20% of the total catches are coastal. As a consequence of the pre-war development of pelagic gear, offshore fishery surpassed the other fisheries and is now responsible for about 80% of the total catches.

In the Gulf of Bothnia salmon fishing is carried out mainly along the shores, especially near salmon rivers. In the northern part, fyke nets are the most common gear set for salmon as well as sea trout (*S. trutta*) and white fish (*Coregonus* spp.), but are now increasingly being replaced by bag nets. In the southern part of the Gulf fyke nets are now practically replaced by bag nets. Fixed hooks and gill nets set in a special crooked fashion are used in certain localities on the Swedish coast. In this part of the Gulf salmon drift nets and long lines are also operated in autumn and ice-free winters. The Gulf of Finland stock of salmon is exploited by Finland with long lines and drift nets offshore in autumn and late spring, and by U.S.S.R. with fixed gear on the coast. In the Gulf of Riga salmon fishing is carried out by pound nets and fyke nets in the estuaries and on the coast near the river mouths (Evtyukhova, 1971). In the Main Basin salmon are exploited offshore by drift net and long line vessels from Denmark, Federal Republic of Germany, Finland, Poland and Sweden. In 1974 the U.S.S.R. also started offshore fishing in this area.

Salmon drift nets were in use in the near offshore single-day fishery off southern Sweden and Bornholm at least from the middle of the nineteenth century (Smidt, 1861; Skrydstrup, 1875). Replacement of the hemp originally used as net material by synthetic fibres during the first half of the 1960s made drift nets the most important salmon gear in the Baltic. Drifting long lines were introduced in the Baltic salmon fishery by Danish fishermen in 1947 and dominated salmon fishing in the 1950s. Standing lines were in widespread use in coastal areas of the Main Basin up to middle of the present century. The lines were set up to 15 nautical miles offshore, from southern Sweden, the Islands of Gotland and Bornholm and along the coast from the Island of Rügen to the Baltic east coast.

In the Main Basin, drift netting is carried out most of the year, only interrupted by the closed season, 15 June to 9 September, mainly in the northern and central part during autumn, and further to the south during the spring. Long lines are usually operated from November to February throughout the Main Basin. Apart from November and December, drift nets dominate the fishery and are responsible for about 80% of the total offshore catches.

The general trend in the catch statistics is shown in Table IV. The decline in number of ascending spawners since 1976 is so severe that there is a shortage of females for stripping in several rivers dependent on artificial reproduction (Larsson, 1979).

Table IV. Nominal catch of Baltic salmon (metric tons). Five-year annual means. After Christensen and Larsson (1979).

Period	Offshore fishery for feeding fish	Coastal and river fishery for spawning migrants	Total
1900-04	225 + [a]	216 +	441 +
1905-09	210 +	163 +	373 +
1910-14	205 +	127 +	332 +
1915-19	380 +	368 +	748 +
1920-24	539	508 +	1047 +
1925-29	624	188 +	812 +
1930-34	721	622	1343
1935-39	448	525	973
1940-44	560	437 +	997 +
1945-49	2046	1466	3512
1950-54	2510	525	3135
1955-59	1913	457	2379
1960-64	2403	463	2866
1965-69	2661	349	3010
1970-74	2139	326	2465

[a] + indicates catch known to be bigger but data are missing from one or more nations.

ENVIRONMENTAL CHANGES AFFECTING BALTIC SALMON

Around the turn of the century spawning occurred in some 80 rivers. Since the era of hydroelectric development a large number of rivers and upper reaches have been cut off from salmon runs (see Fig. 1). Today spawning occurs regularly in 13 large Swedish rivers, of which one is the border river with Finland, River Torne, the only large Finnish river left. Two important salmon rivers in the U.S.S.R. are the Salatsa and the Daugava. River Drawa, a tributary to the River Odra, is the only Polish water where spawning occurs regularly, though scantily (Christensen and Larsson, 1979).

Other human activities, such as pollution, stream regulation, drainage, logging, and silting have also restricted spawning and rearing sites. The adverse effect on salmon reproduction of decreasing pH as a consequence of acid precipitation (airborne pollution) has not yet been observed, unlike the case in some Atlantic salmon rivers in Norway and western Sweden. In Finland, however, the low pH of the river water resulting from extensive agricultural and forestry draining has reduced the salmon habitats. Karlström (1977) found that destroying the structure of the river beds for the floating transport of timber reduced the density of parr by up to 15% compared with natural areas. Restoration of river beds resulted in a return to the original parr density (Karlström, 1977).

As pollutants, PCBs and heavy metals have a special impact on salmon. Jensen *et al.* (1970) reported PCBs as affecting egg mortality. Brånin and Paulsson (1971) likewise pointed out the toxicity of heavy metals for eggs and newly hatched fry. The effect of heavy metal pollution, examined in the rivers Rickleån and Emån, was shown by a large decrease of parr density, partly as a secondary effect as a consequence of reduced invertebrate fauna (Södergren, 1974).

Strong turbidity caused by discharge from a paper mill has also been shown to reduce parr density. On the other hand, higher population density and better growth resulted from the admission of drainage-sewage water to northern Swedish rivers on account of the fertilising effect (Karlström, 1977). In the southern rivers eutrophication is a problem by affecting the habitat with increased production of plants and loose sediments and favouring other species, mainly cyprinids. In the Swedish rivers Emån and Mörrumsån spawning grounds and parr habitat were successfully improved by removal of loose sediments and plants and adjustments of the water flow to prevent silting.

SALMON MANAGEMENT

Review of Baltic Salmon Management Problems (Christensen and Johansson, 1975; Christensen and Larsson, 1979)

In 1903, the year after the inaugural meeting of the International Council for the Exploration of the Sea (ICES), a committee was formed to consider the salmon and sea trout problems of great concern to the nations bordering the Baltic. Estimates were made of the level of the salmon fishery, and information was provided on hatcheries, on liberation of salmon and sea trout in Baltic rivers, and on the national measures taken to protect the salmon stocks. Because of the decreasing yield of the salmon fishery, suggestions were made for international agreements on propagation and protection of the stocks. In 1912 the main problem, namely the reason for the decline of the stocks in the Baltic rivers and the possibilities of an improvement in the situation, was considered. Five rivers situated in Russia, Sweden, Denmark, Finland and Germany respectively were chosen as subjects for observations and investigations. Henking (1913) described the salmon fishery in the Baltic and the research rivers, but the First World War interrupted co-operative work. However, Henking (1916) reported on catch statistics, tagging of adult salmon, natural and hatchery-reared smolts, scale analyses and other special studies. In 1927 ICES agreed to recommend an international size limit for salmon and sea trout in the Baltic, and in 1933 made more recommendations on salmon protection and improvement.

After the Second World War interest in Baltic salmon increased for two reasons:

(1) the immense peak in the coast and river catches, which unexpectedly occurred in the mid-1940s;

(2) the menace to natural propagation of salmon by the hydropower projects developed in Finnish and Swedish rivers.

In Sweden this led to the constitution of a Migratory Fish Committee (later the Salmon Research Institute, see below).

In 1953, on suggestions from Alm, ICES proposed to the Governments of Denmark, Federal Republic of Germany (F.R.G.), Finland and Sweden, that closed seasons, a minimum size for salmon, and minimum mesh and hook sizes were necessary, to restrict capture of the Baltic stock. This led to the Baltic Salmon Fisheries Convention of 1962 ratified by Denmark, Federal Republic of Germany (F.R.G.) and Sweden which came into force in 1966. Its most important Articles state:

Article 5. Minimum mesh size of salmon drift nets of natural and synthetic fibres: 170 and 160 mm respectively. Minimum gap (shortest distance between point and shaft) of salmon hooks: 19 mm.

Article 6. Minimum length of salmon: 60 cm.

Article 10. The establishment of a Permanent Commission in which each Contracting Party is represented. The duty of this Commission is to establish contracts with scientists and research institutes in order to promote conservation and rational exploitation of the stock of Baltic salmon and to consider the expediency of changes in and additions to the Convention.

In 1969 this Permanent Commission recommended closed seasons and the prohibition of pelagic trawling for salmon. In 1971 Poland also joined the Convention. In 1964 Finland had enacted regulatory rules similar to the Articles of the Convention. Until 1975 the U.S.S.R. exploited Baltic salmon only in rivers, river mouths and surrounding coastal areas, and so enacted no special legislation for the offshore salmon fishery, but observed a minimum size of 60 cm for salmon.

At the Baltic Sea Conference 1972 in Stockholm, it was stressed that strict protective measures were urgently required if the natural resource represented by salmon was not to be lost. Each state should therefore restore, or by stocking compensate for their former smolt production, establish new spawning areas by construction of fish ways, investigate the effect of different fishing methods, follow the fishery statistically and not allow too intensive fishing. As the most urgent step however the Conference agreed that all states should ratify the Baltic Salmon Fisheries Convention, and in addition proposed closed seasons and provisions regarding details of gear mounting and maximum amount of gear per fishing vessel. The articles of the 1962 Convention and the 1969 proposals of its Permanent Commission were adopted in 1976 as a Fishery Rule of the Convention on Fishing and Conservation of the Living Resources in the Baltic Sea and the Belts.

The closed season for drift-netting and long-lining of salmon in the sea is 15 June to 9 September, with the aim of reducing the catches of small feeding salmon in their second summer in the sea. The fishery was not subjected to any international limitations on efficiency and number of fishing units until 15 April 1978. Regulatory measures were then enforced inside the Swedish fishing zone, limiting the number of foreign boats and the amount of gear operated per boat (150 drift nets per crew member, maximum 600 per boat, and 2000 long line hooks per boat). Catch quotas for foreign vessels were introduced in 1978. For Polish rivers local provisions on length, depth and number of drifting gill nets linked together have been established. In Sweden local regulations restrict the number of hooks and the number of rods operated per boat fishing in some rivers. Protection zones around river mouths, permanently or for part of the year to ensure the spawning run into the rivers, have been established by national or local provisions. The bag net fishery is banned outside the Finnish salmon and whitefish rivers within a distance of 3 km, and in some few rivers even 5 km from the river mouth. Fishing is usually prohibited at fishpasses, dams, and outlet canals of power plants. Ascending salmon spawners in the rivers are protected by means of closed seasons. Duration and start vary from country to country and from one river and even part of a river to another, depending on the run of the local stocks.

As salmon are particularly sensitive to pollution, demands for environmental legislation and control are generally more rigorous when salmon rivers are concerned. Maximum values for permissable contents of organic matter and a variety of chemicals have been established for salmon rivers, as well as limits for thermal pollution. Standards for contents of heavy metals and other toxicants have also been developed.

Artificial Stocking

In Finland, Poland, Sweden and the U.S.S.R. reared smolts are produced for stocking mainly in order to compensate for the declining natural production. 50% or more of the Baltic salmon population is now maintained by hatchery-rearing (see below).

Other Management Measures

Numerous fishways of various designs have been constructed in Baltic rivers supporting salmon runs especially in connection with establishment of power plants, but few have proved completely successful (Sakowicz and Zarnecki, 1954; Zarnecki and Kolder, 1955; Grundström, 1946; Carlin, 1963); some exceptions are a fishway in the River Umeälv which fully maintains the local stock (Johansson, 1973; Lindroth, 1974), and in the River Mörrumsån a significant part of the run is dependent on a similar construction (Persson, 1975). In Sweden fishways are constructed at natural obstructions to make suitable spawning areas accessible to salmon, the first being constructed in 1892 in the River Dalälven (Trybom, 1893; Mattson, 1957; Ottosson, personal communication). In some Swedish rivers obstructed by power plants, spawners are caught below and released above the dam, if necessary transported by truck far upstream. The method was more commonly used in earlier years, before a sufficient rearing capacity was attained (Törnquist, 1935; Carlin, 1948; Lindroth, 1974). In order to lead ascending fish to fishways and to exclude descending fish from inlets of turbines, mechanical barriers, such as steel gates and boulders, electric screens and light screens have been tested.

SMOLT PRODUCTION IN SWEDEN

Around 1900 some 7·3 million smolts were produced annually in the Baltic rivers (Table V). In 1970 the remaining natural production was at about 2 million smolts, and has been reduced further since then.

The first salmon hatcheries in Sweden were built in the 1860s, and a century ago some 4 million eggs were incubated (Lundberg, 1879), which is roughly the same number as today. In those days only fry were released, however, and without any positive effect on stock size. The

Table V. Estimated annual smolt recruitment to the Baltic. From Christensen and Larsson (1979).

Countries	Original natural production (1900)	Remaining natural production (1970)	Released reared[b] production (1977)
Denmark	—	—	120 000
Finland	2 540 000	350 000[a]	101 000
F.R.G.	—	—	17 000
Poland	10 000	1 000	?
Sweden	4 000 000	1 400 000[a]	2 014 000
U.S.S.R.	700 000	204 000	(845 000)[c]
Total	7 250 000	1 955 000	(3 097 000)

[a]A further decrease occurred in the 1970s.
[b]U.S.S.R., mainly yearlings and one-year-old fish; other countries smolts aged two years.

same negative result was obtained by releasing one summer old parr. After preliminary studies by the Salmon Research Institute under the late Dr Börje Carlin, rearing of smolts started, and from the early 1950s Swedish courts decided amounts of smolts to be released annually to compensate for destroyed salmon reproduction. Special provisions and controls ensure the quality and weight (not less than 25 g) of the smolts released. Swedish plantings of salmon in Baltic rivers are shown in Fig. 4, and the number of smolts released in individual rivers from 1975-1979 is given in Table VI.

In 1945 the Swedish power industry set up the Migratory Fish Committee, which became the Salmon Research Institute in 1961. The aim was to explore new methods of salmon conservation. The funds are provided by the power industry, but the fishery authorities and the power industry are equally represented in the council and the board of management. Under these a director leads the work of the four laboratory divisions: fish biology, sea biology, pathology, and the salmon-rearing plant. In the hatchery (Fig. 5) rearing methods are developed and tested on a full industrial scale. The annual production capacity is more than 200 000 two-year-old smolts. The fish are reared under experimentally varied and controlled conditions, and survival, growth rate and health conditions are recorded in detail. Selective breeding is conducted to investigate the genetic variation in salmon.

The fish biology division supplements experiments by more detailed laboratory research on physiology. The main work concerns food, and the dry pelleted food for salmon rearing was developed there (Bergström, (1973). The work is now concentrated on testing different proteins, mainly single-cell proteins, and affecting smoltification by ingredients in the food.

The fish pathology division carries out basic research on fish diseases (Johansson, 1977), for the moment mainly on furunculosis (Johansson, 1972; Ljungberg and Johansson, 1977a; Johansson, in press), ulcerative dermal necrosis (UDN), which broke out in 1975 in some Swedish rivers (Ljungberg and Johansson, 1977b), and a new unnamed disease causing mortality in alevins (Johansson, personal communication). The pathology division is also the centre of a service organisation for disease control in all Swedish salmon-rearing plants.

The sea biology division studies the importance of release conditions on the results of stockings (see below) and the population of the Baltic salmon and sea trout stocks (Larsson, 1975). It also supervises all

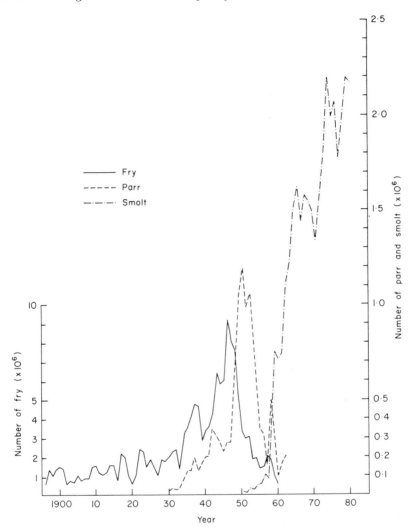

Fig. 4. Swedish plantings of salmon fry, parr and smolts 1900-1979. (Partly after Lindroth, 1965.)

tagging experiments with salmon and most of the experiments with sea trout in Sweden, including final tests of various rearing experiments, methods of transport and release, studies of the sea-life or monitoring the method of compensating damage on salmon stocks by releasing hatchery-reared smolts. The computerised handling of the recaptures (Carlin, 1971) is also done by this division.

Table VI. Hatchery-reared salmon smolts released in Swedish Baltic rivers.

River	No. of smolts				
	1975	1976	1977	1978	1979
Lule älv	616 513	687 499	609 794	582 358	663 612
Skellefteälv	155 565	156 006	161 699	154 436	138 375
Ume älv	99 561	78 887	193 208	102 722	241 410
Ångermanälven	328 840	310 640	326 200	713 184	329 525
Indalsälven	387 778	216 891	357 126	255 750	388 798
Ljungan	34 295	32 598	27 720	32 027	0
Ljusnan	305 076	175 078	254 906	244 710	271 913
Dalälven	51 400	57 000	39 200	53 700	71 400
Other rivers	83 508	50 500	43 724	58 500	72 800
Totals	2 072 536	1 765 099	2 013 577	2 197 387	2 177 833

SMOLT PRODUCTION METHODS

In Sweden, spawning migrants are caught in the rivers by special traps, seines, gill nets or electrofishing and retained for stripping (Lindroth, 1963; Carlin, 1966; Monten, 1969). In Poland reared salmon are also kept in freshwater ponds until sexual maturity. At the Swedish Salmon Research Institute fish were retained in freshwater ponds for the purpose of selective breeding but eggs from these fish suffered severe mortality from high concentrations of PCBs (Jensen et al., 1970). After stripping, the eggs are fertilised "dry", mostly in October and November in Sweden. Incubation time is 6-7 months. In some places with access to heated water incubation time is reduced by several weeks with the aim of producing one-year smolts (Peterson, 1973). The eggs in some hatcheries are regularly treated with malachite green to prevent growth of Saprolegnia. Incubation boxes are mostly made of wood or plastic, generally about 50 × 30 × 20 cm with a metallic grating bottom. Recent experiments with bottoms of artificial turf have given very promising results with increased size of alevins (Eriksson and Westlund, 1979).

At the Hölle laboratory, where the Swedish Salmon Research Institute was first located, a variety of tank types were tested. Tanks with marginal inlet and central outlet of water gave the best results and have since then been used in Swedish as well as Polish hatcheries. They

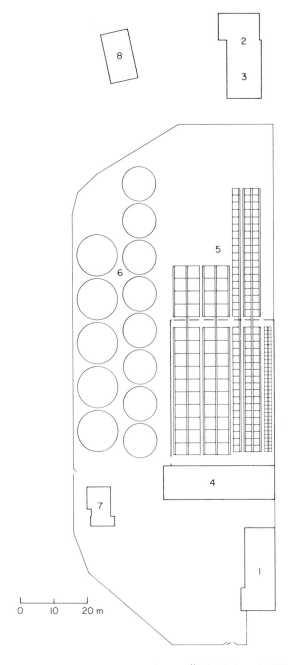

Fig. 5. Swedish Salmon Research Institute, Älvkarleby. 1. Division of fish biology; 2. Division of fish pathology; 3. Division of sea biology; 4. Rearing plant, office, hatchery, store, etc.; 5. Tanks and troughs, partly under roof for overwintering; 6. Ponds; 7. Water tower; 8. Store.

are all similarly organised and constructed like the production plant at the Swedish Salmon Research Institute in Älvkarleby (Fig. 5), built in 1961. Table VII lists the rearing units and the originally estimated production capacity of the Swedish salmon rearing plants. The production is now generally higher as an effect of increased density of fish in the ponds.

Tanks, troughs and ponds, mostly made of concrete or fibreglass, are constructed with horizontal bottoms and a central outlet consisting of a horizontal grating usually made of perforated stainless steel. The form may be circular or square with rounded corners and a diameter of 2-8 metres. Salmon during their first summer are usually kept in square troughs with a bottom area of 4-12 m², and during their second summer in circular ponds of 20-100 m². Water depth is 10-30 cm, and water flow is normally 10-15 litre $min^{-1}m^{-2}$ of bottom area. Stocking density is recommended to be 3 kg m^{-2} in the summer and 10 kg m^{-2} in winter (Carlin, 1966). The ponds in Swedish hatcheries are painted with an antifouling paint which considerably reduces the labour of cleaning them (Carlin, 1966).

Table VII. Data on Swedish salmon-rearing stations.

Plant	Built (year)	Rearing units					Production capacity number of smolts
		Type	Number	Size m²	Total area summer	winter	
Heden	1962	circular ponds	12	95	1 140	—	(600 000)
		concrete tanks	58	36	2 088	2 088	overwintering
					3 228	2 088	only
Kvistforsen	1961	circular ponds	20	95	1 900	1 900	200 000
		steel tanks	102	4	408	200	
		concrete tanks	16	4	64	64	
					2 372	2 164	
Norrfors	1960	circular ponds	16	94	1 504	1 504	180 000
		steel tanks	103	4	412	176	
					1 916	1 680	
Långsele	1959	circular ponds	8	94	752	—	190 000
	(1946)	concrete tanks	22	16	352	352	
		concrete tanks	6	56	336	336	
		concrete tanks	40	4	160	160	
					1 600	848	
Forsmo	1957	circular ponds	10	63	630	—	200 000
	(1946)	concrete tanks	74	12	888	888	
		fibreglass tanks	92	4	368	—	
					1 886	888	
Blatjärn	1957	fibreglass tanks	32	9	—	288	(50 000)
	(1947)						overwintering only

Table VII. *cont.*

Plant	Built (year)	Type	Number	Size m²	Total area summer	winter	Production capacity number of smolts
Hölle	1952	circular ponds	2	175	350	350	160 000
		concrete tanks	40	12	480	480	
		fibreglass tanks	13	4	52	—	
					882	830	
Bergeforsen	1955	circular ponds	4	100	400	400	500 000
		concrete tanks	14	115	1 610	—	
		concrete tanks	68	22	1 500	880	
		concrete tanks	202	5·6	1 130	280	
					4 640	1 560	
Galtström	1955	concrete tanks	16	16	256	256	30 000
	(1930)	concrete tanks	12	4	48	—	
		fibreglass tanks	60	4	240	—	
		earthen ponds	3		544	544	
					1 088	800	
		natural ponds	2		12 ha		
Bollnäs	1958	concrete tanks	11	63	693	693	175 000
		concrete tanks	4	15	60	60	
		concrete tanks	13	7	98	98	
		fibreglass tanks	46	4	184	184	
					1 035	1 035	
Ljusne	1953	circular ponds	2	254	508	—	120 000
		circular ponds	32	7	224	—	
		fibreglass tanks	15	4	60	—	
		wooden tanks	28	4	112	—	
					904	—	
Näs	1959	circular ponds	14	63	882	882	175 000
		fibreglass tanks	100	4	400	176	
					1 282	1 058	
Älvkarleby	1959	concrete tanks	13	23	299	207	130 000
	(1916)	concrete tanks	4	43	172	172	
		fibreglass tanks	60	4	240	128	
					711	507	
		natural pond	1		15 ha	15 ha	
Älvkarleö	1961	fibreglass tanks	68	0·9	61	61	175 000
(Salmon		circular ponds	5	94	470	470	
Research		circular ponds	8	62	496	496	
Institute)		concrete tanks	56	11·6	650	464	
		concrete tanks	108	3·4	367	184	
					2 044	1 675	
Långhult	1960	circular ponds	14	94	1 316	1 316	200 000
		steel tanks	100	4	400	176	
					1 716	1 492	
		earthen ponds	2	240	480		
Munka-Ljungby	1954	earthen ponds	20	400	8 000	8 000	
	(1925)	fibreglass tanks	20	4	80	—	
Laholm	1948	concrete tanks	16	16	256	256	20 000
	(1938)	concrete tanks	18	4	72	—	
					328	256	
Brattfors	1959	circular ponds	6	55	330	330	25 000
		fibreglass tanks	24	4	96	96	
					426	426	

Salmon kept in large earth ponds with a natural food production are of better quality than those intensively reared in densely populated troughs. For practical reasons the method is nowadays applied in few rearing plants in Sweden (Steffner, 1961; Arnemo, 1975a, b) but is more common in Finland (Ovaskainen, 1975; Toivonen, personal communication).

Swedish hatcheries now use pelleted dry food developed exclusively for salmon (Bergström, 1973). Feeding is facilitated by automatic feeders (Carlin, 1966; Svensson, 1970). In Poland, liver, fresh fish, yeast and vitamins are used as additional food (Bartel, personal communication).

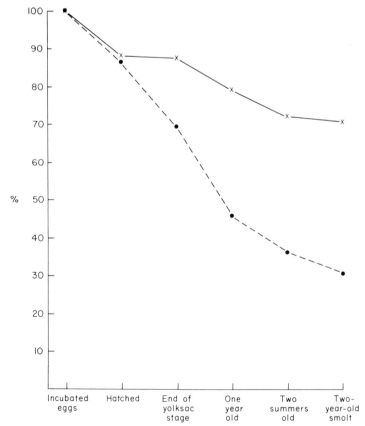

Fig. 6. Survival from incubated eggs to two-year-old smolts. Average for four hatcheries 1960-1966 (dashed line) and one hatchery 1970-1973 (full line).

A strict disease control is practised at all hatcheries, in Poland by the Veterinary Research Station, Fish Disease Laboratory and in Sweden by the Fish Pathology Division of the Salmon Research Institute.

The effectiveness of smolt rearing has gradually improved and now averages about 50% from incubated eggs to two-year-old smolts. The variation between hatcheries is considerable, mainly depending on differences in water quality and water temperature conditions during summer. The heaviest losses are normally from the start of feeding throughout the first summer, especially if the water temperature is high ($>20°C$). Figure 6 shows the average effectiveness of four hatcheries during the years 1960-1966 and of one hatchery with good water quality and temperature conditions during the years 1970-1973, with separate mortality during some stages.

CONTRIBUTIONS OF SMOLT PRODUCTION FROM OTHER BALTIC NATIONS

Denmark and FRG lack opportunities to rear salmon smolts themselves but in recent years have bought smolts from Swedish hatcheries with "surplus" (in 1977 120 000 and 17 000 respectively, Table V). This sea-ranching system is more pronounced from 1980, when Denmark and FRG have to pay for the release of the number of smolts that corresponds to their catch quota in the Swedish economic zone.

In Finland around 100 000 smolts have been released annually over a number of years. The first water court decisions similar to those in Sweden are now expected, meaning an additional annual output of more than one million smolts. The Finnish smolt production programme aims at releasing 1·5 million smolts by 1985.

In Poland salmon smolt production attempts have failed mainly due to very high summer temperatures. The famous Vistula seatrout—almost like a salmon in appearance, growth and behaviour—is easier to rear so all Polish hatcheries work with that species.

From the hatcheries in the U.S.S.R. most of the fish are released as yearlings or two-summer-old parr ($>90\%$). Increasing numbers of one-year-old smolts have been released in recent years and with fairly good effect (Mitans and Rimsh, 1978).

No smolt production is reported from the German Democratic Republic (G.D.R.).

PROSPECTS FOR THE FUTURE

According to the population models by Thurow (1966), Carlin (1959, 1962) and Larsson (1975, Table VIII) there are two main problems in the future management of Baltic salmon. The most important one is the over-exploitation of feeding fish. Of the population entering the second and third winter in the sea 55% and 67% respectively are caught during the season (Table VIII) according to Larsson's model,

Table VIII. Model of the population of reared salmon in the Baltic Sea. (From Larsson, 1975.)

	Years in the Baltic				
	1	2	3	4	5
NUMBER OF SMOLTS RELEASED (%)					
At start of year	100	14·55	4·16	0·70	0·08
Migrating for spawning	—	2·75	1·10	0·50	0·06
Left over in sea	—	11·80	3·06	0·21	0·02
Caught in sea	0·17	6·46	2·05	0·11	0·01
Eliminated by natural mortality	85·28	1·18	0·31	0·02	—
NUMBER OF SALMON AT START OF YEAR (%)					
Migrating for spawning	—	18·90	26·44	71·43	—
Caught in sea	—	54·75	66·99	52·38	—
Eliminated by natural mortality	85·28	10	10	10	—

leaving a correspondingly smaller fraction for spawning migration (Fig. 7). This is a terrible waste of salmon as a natural resource and even a threat to its existence. The population model was used by Larsson (1975) to estimate the effect of simulated changes in the offshore fishing intensity (Fig. 8). The simulations show that a complete ban on the fishing for feeding fish would be highly beneficial. The primary value of the total catch would be twice as high as now. Besides, the offshore fishery is much more energy consuming than the coast and river fishery.

After the establishment of economic zones in the Baltic (1978) the Swedish authorities have set catch quotas for 1980 that mean

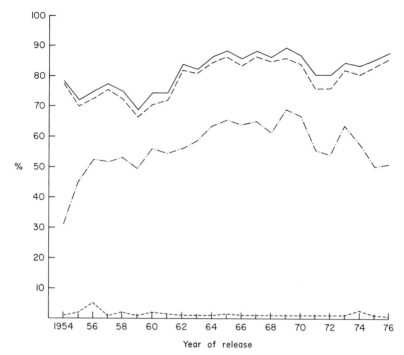

Fig. 7. Percentage distribution of recaptures on spawning migrators (above full line) and feeding fish separated on seasons.

reductions of offshore catches in the Swedish zone to about 30% of the average for 1960-1975. In the zones of the U.S.S.R., Poland and G.D.R. almost no offshore salmon fishing will be permitted and in the Bothnian Sea and Bay the Finnish and Swedish authorities have agreed on a limitation of the offshore catch.

From Table IX it is obvious that the offshore fishery is most important for Danish fishermen. As mentioned above the further Danish salmon fishery (from 1980) can be regarded as sea-ranching in which the extra number of released smolts, paid for by the Danes and produced in Swedish hatcheries, must correspond to the expected catch in the sea. The average return rate in tagging experiments, 500 kg adult salmon per 1000 smolts released, will be used as the base for calculations.

The second important problem to be emphasised in the near future is the high mortality due to predation immediately after release of the

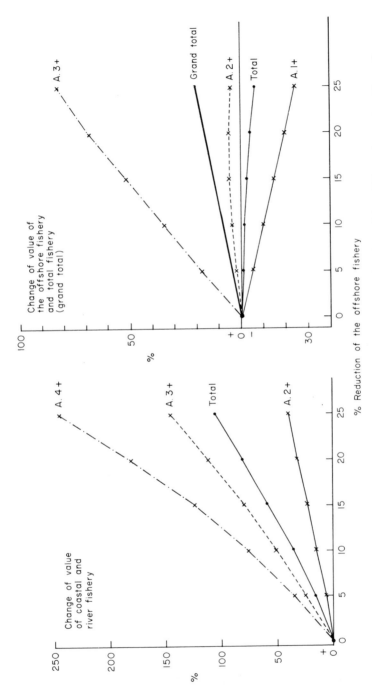

Fig. 8. Estimated change of value of Baltic salmon catches by simulated reduction of the offshore intensity. From Larsson (1975). A.1+, A.2+, etc. = sea age of fish at capture. A 25% reduction in intensity of the offshore fishery would result in: a 6% decrease in value of that fishery; a 100% increase in value of the coastal and river fishery; and a 17-18% increase in value of the total fishery.

Table IX. Annual catches in metric tons of Baltic salmon in the offshore fishery, 1969-1978. (After Christensen, 1979.)

Year	Baltic Main Basin						Gulf of Bothnia			Gulf of Finland	Total
	Denmark	Finland	F.R.G.	Poland	Sweden	U.S.S.R.	Denmark	Finland	Sweden	Finland	
1969	1469	169	134	30	366	—	0	69	33	140	2410
1970	1298	121	130	11	341	—	11	68	39	136	2155
1971	993	138	106	11	285	—	52	29	38	124	1776
1972	1034	122	117	13	277	—	11	50	47	138	1809
1973	1107	192	107	17	407	—	12	67	63	135	2107
1974	1224	282	52	20	403	21	0	109	68	111	2290
1975	1112	237	67	10	352	43	98	90	107	158	2274
1976	1372	181	58	7	332	40	38	150	88	81	2347
1977	951	134	77	6	317	31	60	175	101	75	1927
1978	810	143	16	4	252	26	—	95	80	82	1508

hatchery-reared smolts (Larsson and Larsson, 1975; Larsson, H.-O., 1977). Improved hatchery procedures seem no longer to increase survival significantly after release (Hosmer *et al.*, 1979) compared to the effects achieved by optimising release conditions (Larsson, P.-O., 1977; Larsson and Eriksson, 1979).

Attempts have been made to increase survival, mainly by reducing migration in the river where large populations of predators dwell, pike *(Esox lucius)*, burbot *(Lota lota)*, and birds being the most important. Releases in river mouths, at the coast or in the sea close to the river mouth do, however, affect the homing behaviour. The spawners stray around in the river mouth area for a long time and get caught there to an unacceptable extent. To avoid this, experiments have been started towing the smolts down the river in a net-pen and releasing them in the mouth or in the sea, thus attempting to imprint the river migration while the smolts are protected from predators. So far the survival has been 2·3 times higher for those fish than control fish released directly from the hatchery, but the effects on the homing behaviour are not yet clear (Larsson and Larsson, 1979).

REFERENCES

Alm, G. (1931). Resultaten av laxmärkningarna i Sverige åren 1924-1926. *Ny Svensk Fisk. Tidskr.* **40** (1), 1-6.
Alm, G. (1934). Salmon in the Baltic precincts. *Rapp. P.-v. Réun. Cons. int. Explor. Mer* **92**, 1-63.
Arnemo, R. (1975a). Limnological studies in Hyttödammen. The young salmon, its growth and food. *Laxforskningsinst. Medd.* 5.
Arnemo, R. (1975b). Limnological studies in Hyttödammen. Outlines of the ecosystem and its management. *Laxforskningsinst. Medd.* **8**.
Backiel, T. and Bartel, R. (1967). O efektach zarybiana smoltami troci na tle wyników ich znahowania. *Roczn. Nauk. Roln.* H-90, **3**, 365-388.
Bartel, R. (1976). The Drawa River salmon in the light of some recent tagging experiment. *ICES, Doc. C.M.* 1976/M:6 (mimeo).
Berg, L. S. (1948). "Fresh water Fishes of the Soviet Union and Adjacent Countries". Part 1. Moscow-Leningrad: 446 pp. Transl. from Russian by Israel Progm. Scient. Transl., Jerusalem 1962.
Bergström, Eva (1973). The role of nutrition in growth and survival of young salmon. In: the International Atlantic Salmon Symposium 1972. *Int. Atlant. Fnd., Special Publ. Ser.* **4**, 1, 265-282.
Brånin, B. and Paulsson, C. (1971). Långtidsförsök med tungmetaller på de första utvecklingsstadierna hos lax. *Laxforskningsinst. Medd.* **2**.

Carlin, B. (1948). Översikt över laxtransporter vid Ångermanälven 1945-1948. *Vandringsfiskutredn. Medd.* **2**.

Carlin, B. (1959). Results of salmon smolt tagging in the Baltic area. *Rapp. P.-v. Réun. Cons. int. Explor. Mer* **147**, 89-96.

Carlin, B. (1962). Synpunkter på frågan om Östersjöns laxbestånd i belysning av de svenska märkningsförsöken. *Laxforskningsinst. Medd.* **5**.

Carlin, B. (1963). The Salmon Research Institute and Salmon conservation in Sweden. *Svenska Vattenkraftfören. Publ.* **502**, 221-259.

Carlin, B. (1966). Salmon rearing in Sweden. *Laxforskningsinst. Medd* **5**.

Carlin, B. (1971). Data processing in Swedish Salmon Tagging Experiments. *Laxforskningsinst. Medd.* **3**.

Christensen, O. (1979). Catches of Baltic salmon in 1976-1978. *ICES, Doc. C.M.* 1979/M:27 (mimeo).

Christensen, O. and Johansson, N. (ed.) (1975). Reference report on Baltic salmon. *ICES Coop. Res. Rep.,* No. 45.

Christensen, O. and Larsson, P.-O. (ed.) (1979). Review of Baltic salmon research. *ICES Coop. Res. Rep.,* No. 89.

Chrzan, F. (1964). The movement and growth rate of tagged Drawa salmon. *ICES, Doc. C.M.* 1964/No. 77 (mimeo).

Ekman, S. (1953). "Zoogeography of the sea". London.

Eriksson, C. and Westlund, G. (1979). Ett pilotförsök med olika kläckningslådor. *Laxforskningsinst. Inf.* **4**.

Evtyukhova, B. K. (1971). "Baltic salmon Fishery—Biological Characteristics". Riga.

Fonselius, S. (1974). "Oceanografi". Stockholm.

Grundström, J. A. (1946). En originell laxtrappa i Byske älv. *Svensk Fisk. Tidskr.* **55** (11), 233-234.

Halme, E. (1961). Report on salmon tagged in Finland. *ICES, Doc. C.M.* 1961/No. 17 (mimeo).

Halme, E. (1964). Report on salmon tagged in Finland 1959-1964. *ICES, Doc. C.M.* 1964/No. 61 (mimeo).

Henking, H. (1913). Die Lachsfrage im Ostseegebiet I. *Rapp. P.-v. Reun. Cons. int. Explor. Mer* **16** (6).

Henking, H. (1916). Die Lachsfrage im Ostseegebiet II. *Rapp. P.-v. Reun. Cons. int. Explor. Mer* **23** (2).

Hosmer, M. J., Stanley, J. G. and Hatch, R. W. (1979). Effects of Hatchery Procedures on Later Return of Atlantic Salmon to Rivers in Maine. *Prog. Fish-Cult.* **41** (3), 115-119.

Järvi, T. H. (1935). Om laxens färdvägar i Östersjön. *Finl. Jakt- och Fiskeritidskr.* **30**, 53-63.

Järvi, T. H. (1943). Merkityt lohet. Suomen vesistä saatuja uusia tapauksia. *Suomen Kalastuslehti* **50**, 80-81.

Jensen, J. K. (1964). "Bornholmske Samlinger". Rønne.

Jensen, S., Johansson, N. and Olsson, M. (1970). PCB—Indications of effects on salmon. *Laxforskningsinst. Medd.* **7**.

Johansson, H. (1973). Fenklippning av laxsmolt i Ume älv 1970-1973. *Proc. from Salmon Rearing Conference, Visby 1973, Doc.* No. 8, 13 pp.

Johansson, N. (1972). Furunculosis in Swedish fish farms 1951-71. Symposium on the major communicable fish diseases, in Europe and their control. FAO/EIFAC, Amsterdam, April 1972.

Johansson, N. (1977). Studies on diseases in hatchery-reared Atlantic salmon (*Salmo salar* L.) and sea trout (*Salmo trutta* L.) in Sweden. *Acta Universitatis Upsaliensis,* **401**.

Karlström, Ö. (1977). Habitat selection and population densities of salmon (*Salmo salar* L.) and trout (*Salmo trutta* L.) parr in Swedish rivers with some reference to human activities. *Acta Universitatis Upsaliensis,* 404.

Larsson, H-O. (1977). The influence of predation after release on the result of salmon smolt planting. *ICES, Doc. C.M.* 1977/M: 44 (mimeo).

Larsson, H-O. and Larsson, P-O. (1975). Predation på nyutsatt odlad smolt i Luleälven 1974. *Laxforskningsinst. Medd.* **9**.

Larsson, P-O. (1975). En modell av Östersjöns population av odlad lax. *Laxforskningsinst. Medd.* **4**.

Larsson, P-O. (1977). The importance of time and place of release of salmon and sea trout on the results of stockings. *ICES, Doc. C.M.* 1977/M: 42.

Larsson, P-O. (1979). Avelslaxproblemet. *Proc. from Salmon Rearing Conf., Storlien 1979,* 55-57.

Larsson, P-O. and Eriksson, C. (1979). The impact of water temperature at release on the subsequent return rates of hatchery reared Atlantic salmon smolts, *Salmo salar* L. *Laxforskningsinst. Medd.* **3**.

Larsson, P-O. and Larsson, H-O. (1979). Preliminära resultat av utflytningsförsök med laxsmolt i Luleälven. *Laxforskningsinst. Inf.* **3**.

Lindroth, A. (1963). Salmon conservation in Sweden. *Trans. Am. Fish. Soc.* **92**, 286-291.

Lindroth, A. (1965). The Baltic Salmon Stock. *Mitt. int. Verein. theor. angew. Limnol.* **13**, 163-192.

Lindroth, A. (1974). Appraisal of the artificial salmon reproduction in Sweden. *Laxforskningsinst. Medd.* **6**.

Lindroth, A. (1977). The smolt migration in the river Mörrumsån (Sweden) 1963-1966. *ICES, Doc. C.M.* 1977/M:8 (mimeo).

Ljungberg, O. and Johansson, N. (1977a). Epizootological studies on atypical *Aeromonas salmonicida* infections of salmonids in Swedish fish farms, 1967-1977. *Bull. Off. int. Epiz.* **87** (5-6), 475-478.

Ljungberg, O. and Johansson, N. (1977b). Ulcerös dermal necros hos laxfiskar. *Svensk Veterinärtidning* **29** (4), 129-135.

Lundberg, R. (1879). Förteckning öfver Rikets Laxodlings-anstalter vintern 1879. *Fiskaren* **2** (4), 77-78.

Magaard, L. and Rheinheimer, G. (ed.) (1974). "Meereskunde der Ostsee". Berlin, Heidelberg, New York.

Mattson, E. (1957). Laxtrappa i Linafallet. *Svensk Fisk. Tidskr.* **66** (12), 190-195.

Mitans, A. P. (1970). The application of tagging in the investigations of salmon after their descent into the Gulf of Riga. *Sbornik Balt NIIRH* Riga, No. 7.

Mitans, A. P. (1973). Baltic salmon parr population estimation from change of composition caused by smolt descent. *ICES, Doc. C.M.* 1973/M: 14 (mimeo).

Mitans, A. P. and Rimsh, C. (1978). Distribution in the sea and rate of recaptures of Baltic salmon smolts from the Gulf of Riga rivers.*ICES, Doc. C.M.* 1978/M: 7 (mimeo).

Montén, E. (1969). Vattenfalls fiskodlingsverksamhet 1950-1968. *Laxforskningsinst. Medd.* **11**.

Österdahl, L. (1969). The smolt run of a small Swedish river. *Laxforskningsinst. Medd.* **8**.

Ovaskainen, R. (1975). Uppfödning av fisk i naturdammar i Finland. En aktuell översikt. *Proc. from Salmon Rearing Conf., Umeå 1975, Doc.* No. 15.

Persson, W. (1975). Redogörelse för kontroll av uppvandrande och nedvandrande vuxen lax och öring år 1973-1974 vid Mariebergs laxtrappa, Mörrum. *Laxforskningsinst. Inf.* **5**.

Peterson, H. (1967). Könsfördelningen hos grilse i Indalsälven. *Laxforskningsinst. Medd.* **15**.

Peterson, H. (1973). Adult returns to date from hatchery-reared one-year-old smolts. Int. Atlantic Salmon Symp., 1973. *Int. Atlant. Salm. Fnd. Spec. Publ.* **4**, 1, 219-226.

Prokofieva, A. (1934a). On the chromosome morphology of certain Pisces. *Cytologica* **5**, 395-525.

Prokofieva, A. (1934b). Investigations on the chromosome morphology of some Pisces and Amphibia. *Compte Rend. Acad. Sci. USSR,* 79-84.

Sakowicz, S. and Zarnecki, S. (1954). Przepławki komorowe. Biologiczno-rybackie zasady projektowania. (Pool passes. Biological principles of planning.) *Roczn. Nauk. Roln.* **69-D**, 1-164.

Skrydstrup, V. (1875). Laxefiskeriet ved Bornholm. *Nordisk Fiskeritidskrift* **2**, 15-30.

Smidt, A. J. (1861). "Beretning om Fiskeriernes Tilstand ved Bornholm og Christiansø". Copenhagen.

Södergren, S. (1974). Ecological effects of heavy metal discharge in a salmon river. *Rep. Inst. Freshw. Res. Drottningholm* **55**, 91-131.

Steffner, N. G. (1961). Hyttödammen åren 1938-1960. *Laxforskningsinst. Medd.* **4**.

Svärdson, G. (1945). Chromosome studies on Salmonidae. *Rep. Inst. Freshw. Res. Drottningholm* **23** (1), 1-151.

Svensson, K. M. (1970). Foderapparat för torrfoder, typ Svensson. *Fiskodlingshandbok, 1.43. Laxforskningsinst.*

Thurow, F. (1966). Beiträge zur Biologie und Bestandkunde die Atlantischen Lachses (*Salmo salar* L.) in der Ostsee. *Ber. dt. wiss. Komm. Meeresforsch.* **XVIII** (3/4), 223-379.

Thurow, F. (1968). On food, behaviour and population mechanism of Baltic salmon. *Laxforskningsinst. Medd.* **4**.

Toivonen, J. (1973). The stock of salmon in the Gulf of Finland. *ICES, Doc. C.M.* 1973/M: 17 (mimeo).

Törnquist, N. (1935). Fisktransporter vid Klarälven. *Svensk Fisk. Tidskr.* **44** (3), 61-66.

Trybom, F. (1893). Laxtrappan vid Domnarfvet i Dalelfven. *Svensk Fisk. Tidskr.* **2** (1), 1-6.

Zarnecki, S. and Kołder, W. (1955). Observacje nad przechodzeniem ryb przes przeplawki w Rosnowie i Czchowie. (Observations on the migration of fish through passes in Roznów and Czchów.) *Roczn. Nauk. Roln.* **69**-B-4, 501-525.

Chapter 10

Salmon Ranching in Ireland

D. J. PIGGINS

Salmon Research Trust of Ireland Inc.,
Farran Laboratory, Newport, Co. Mayo, Eire

LEGISLATIVE RESTRICTIONS

Sea ranching of Atlantic Salmon *(Salmo salar)*, in the sense of a commercially orientated operation with total culling of returning stock, is not practised in Ireland and indeed, would not be possible, under existing legislation, in the Republic of Ireland. A number of river traps operate commercially on the Rivers Shannon, Moy, Corrib, Boyne, Nore, Currane, Drowse, Lennon and Blackwater, but with the exception of Thomond Weir on the Shannon, part of the river is left untrapped (the "free gap") and traps are lifted for 48 hours at weekend close times. At Thomond Weir, the Electricity Supply Board is allowed to take 28% of the total run until 19 July each year.

A similar situation exists on the R. Bush in Northern Ireland. All ascending fish are trapped and a fixed proportion is released upstream as a spawning escapement, the surplus being sold commercially or maintained as hatchery broodstock. This would constitute the·closest approach to a true sea-ranching operation in Ireland.

Total trapping facilities exist also at the Salmon Research Trust's installations on the Burrishoole River system but these traps are used solely for monitoring annual runs of salmon and sea trout *(Salmo trutta)* and no commercial culling of stocks is permitted.

It would be difficult to formulate the necessary amending legislation for the Republic of Ireland which would enable commercial operators to cull the entire run of adult fish returning from a smolt-rearing operation. Of necessity, the rearing and release operations for smolts would require a site close to the outflow of a river system with an ample freshwater supply and in Ireland such a river system would hold wild stocks of salmon and/or sea-trout. The separation of wild and "reared" stocks at a trap, with the release of wild and culling of reared stocks would almost certainly have to be done under official supervision to safeguard the rights of upstream riparian owners.

Apart from the legislative aspect, other factors affecting the commercial viability of a sea ranching operation include the survival rates of reared smolts to adults as influenced by exploitation by coastal nets and intrinsic low viability, as well as the escalating costs of smolt production. These will be discussed in this chapter.

RESULTS FROM REARING INSTALLATIONS IN IRELAND

There are six salmon smolt rearing stations in Ireland, situated at:
Bushmills, Co. Antrim, River Bush, N. Ireland Dept. of Agric. & Fisheries;
Carrigadrohid, Co. Cork, River Lee, Electricity Supply Board;
Parteen, River Shannon, Electricity Supply Board;
Salmon Research Trust, Furnace, Newport, Co. Mayo. Burrishoole River system;
Virginia, Co. Cavan, River Boyne;
Cong, Co. Mayo, Upper Lough Corrib system.

Bushmills

The rearing station at Bushmills was partly operational by 1973 and the first yearling smolts were released in that year. (See R. Bush Salmon Project, Ann. Reps. 1973-77.) Considerable trouble has been experienced with water quality at this station and survival rates from ova to smolts have been poor, due largely to gill disease in the early stages and to furunculosis among the parr, both associated with stress from unsatisfactory water quality. For example, only 12·2% of the ova stock survived to end-of-year parr in 1974, 4·8% in 1976 and 8·4% in

Table I. Bushmills, Co. Antrim, N. Ireland. Survival rates from smolt to adult (including 2- and 3-sea-winter fish) at the Bush trap.

Hatch year	1 + smolts released (No.)	Adults recaptured (No.)	Adults recaptured (%)	2 + smolts released (No.)	Adults recaptured (No.)	Adults recaptured (%)
1972						
Tagged	181	4	2·2	946	22	2·3
Cold branded	94	11	11·7	1027	45	4·4
1973						
Tagged	1000	8	0·8	1250	8	0·6
Cold branded	1250	29	2·3	1250	20	1·6
1974						
Tagged	3568	0	0·0	5600	17	0·3
Cold branded	907	4	0·4	31770	445	1·4

1977; there was a total loss of the 1975 stock. Recent improvements to filter beds and water-quality monitoring to give advance warning of increased pollution load seem to have had beneficial effects on the 1978 stock.

Survival rates from smolt to adult (including 2- and 3-sea-winter fish) up to the 1974 releases are given in Table I. Returns from 10 557 1 + smolts released in 1976 are not yet known. The figures in Table II refer to River Bush stock, but some smolts from River Boyne stock were released (1800 × 1 +, 1974, 2700 × 2 +, 1975) with returns totalling 0·2%.

Table II. Bushmills, Co. Antrim, N. Ireland. Adult recoveries showing evidence of lost tags, or having unidentifiable brands.

Mark	Recovery year				Totals
	1974	1975	1976	1977	
Lost tag	0	27	10	17	54
Unidentifiable brand	0	55	39	167	261

It should be noted that on average the returns from branded smolts were three times better than those from tagged smolts, although the former suffered the disadvantage of not being noticed in the high seas or coastal netting recaptures. However, a number of salmon returning to the Bush trap were noted as having shed their tags or having unidentifiable brands (Table II). These figures increase the recapture rate of tagged fish by almost 100% and branded fish by almost 50%.

Carrigadrohid (see Ann. Fish. Reps. Electricity Supp. Bd. 1963-76)

Smolt rearing was undertaken by the Electricity Supply Board at Carrigadrohid, on the River Lee, in 1971, following a catastrophic decline in the numbers of fish returning to this river after it was harnessed for hydroelectric development. It appeared that the two dams created shallow reservoirs ideally suited to pike *(Esox lucius)* reproduction when descending salmon smolts were subjected to intense predation pressure. After the pike numbers were successfully reduced, brown trout took over the predatory role, and the count of ascending salmon at Iniscarra dam fell from a peak of 914 in 1965 to only 57 in 1972.

Carrigadrohid has a smolt-rearing capacity of 150 000 per annum and has been virtually disease-free since its inception, accounting for the high survival rate from ova to 1 + smolt which is seldom less than 70%. It has produced 1 + smolts of exceptional quality (averaging 40-50 g) in the following quantities:

1972	119 000
1973	131 418
1974	118 800
1975	126 000
1976	150 000

The returns of adult fish to Iniscarra dam showed an immediate improvement to:

1973	171
1974	494
1975	205
1976	419
1977	165

From 1973 onwards a very considerable number of the fish returning to Iniscarra were of hatchery origin, and by 1977 the River Lee was virtually dependent on hatchery-reared smolts for its existence as a salmon river. At the same time, there was increasing concern over the exploitation of these fish by coastal and riverine nets, accounting for the average return to the trap of 0·2% over the years 1973-77.

Parteen (see Ann. Fish. Reps. Elec. Supp. Bd. 1963-76)

Parteen rearing station on the River Shannon became operational in 1960 and was designed by the Electricity Supply Board to restore the declining runs of salmon in that river, following the building of an hydroelectric generating station at Ardnacrusha. The original installations were expanded until by 1966, it was capable of producing 200 000 smolts per annum. There are now 125 × 2 m, 14 × 6 m and 4 × 10 m ponds at Parteen and annual production was maintained at close on 200 000 yearling smolts, as well as large numbers of fry and parr, until 1972. From 1973 to 1976 the numbers of smolts released declined somewhat to an average of about 120 000, due in part to increased commitments for smolts for saltwater rearing operations and to increased mortality from disease, particularly a resistant form of furunculosis.

No figures can be quoted for survival from ova to 1 + smolt because the smaller underyearlings are graded out of the population several times a year and used for restocking of selected tributaries.

It is difficult also to ascribe precise rates of return of these smolts but it is believed (N. Roycroft, personal communication) that overall some 3-4% survive to the adult stage, returning to the River Shannon. This estimate would include fish taken in the estuarine nets and those counted at Thomond Weir, with further checks at counting devices maintained by the Electricity Supply Board at Ardnacrusha' and Parteen dams.

The counts of fish at Thomond Weir cease each year at the end of the fishing season for the weir (19 July). These counts provide a good indication of the extent of the upstream run but are not completely accurate in that some fish can bypass the weir through the ''Abbey River'' and from 400-1500 fish have been known to ascend the river after 19 July.

During the years 1970-76 an average of about 12% of fish killed for market at Thomond Weir were fin-clipped and therefore of hatchery origin. In 1977, this proportion rose to 18·5% and in 1978 to 20%, indicating that wild stocks were declining by comparison with relatively uniform numbers of reared smolts released each year. In 1974, 618 fin-clipped salmon were counted at Parteen, and in 1975, of 1845 fish examined in the Parteen trap, 1025 (55·6%) were of hatchery origin. As for the Lee smolt-rearing operation, considerable concern has been expressed by the Electricity Supply Board over the degree of exploitation of Shannon stocks by the coastal net fisheries and by illegal nets in the Shannon estuary.

Similar situations exist in two other river systems administered by the Board, where hydroelectric power stations have been installed. These are the Erne and the Clady/Crolly systems in Co. Donegal and counts of ascending fish have declined dramatically in both, largely as a result of uncontrolled netting. The Board has stated that restoration programmes of restocking cannot be undertaken in these rivers until exploitation is reduced and controlled by co-operation with local interests.

Salmon Research Trust (see Ann. Reps. Salmon Res. Trust Ire. 1962-77)

The Salmon Research Trust of Ireland began its smolt-rearing operations in 1956 and the first batch of yearling smolts was released in 1957. The original site on a small river has been abandoned and all smolt rearing is now conducted at the Furnace installations, between Loughs Feeagh and Furnace, on the Burrishoole river system. Rearing capacity has not been expanded since 1965 and although a new rearing complex was added in 1974, the added production has been utilised for an independent salt water farming project. However, a warmed-water facility was incorporated in the hatchery during 1971 and has effectively increased the annual smolt production by increasing the proportion of 1 + smolts in the yearling population. In general terms, 1 + smolts constitute 60-70% of the population when warmed-water treatment is given from the eyed ova stage for 10-12 weeks, compared with 20-30% 1 + smolts from early rearing at ambient temperature.

Annual smolt production ranged from 5000-9000 until 1967 but since then has ranged from 10 000-18 000 except for the years 1972 and 1973 when 2 + smolt production was severely curtailed by furunculosis in the early summer and "fungus disease" (allied with furunculosis) in the winter months. In a normal year, survival from ova to end-of-year parr exceeds 60%, and survival from yearling parr to 2 + smolt exceeds 80% although furunculosis is now endemic and increasingly difficult to control by normal antibiotic treatment.

The first significant returns from reared smolts were obtained in 1963, and in 1969 "reared" grilse constituted almost 40% of the total population. In 1972, after full adult trapping facilities had been installed in 1970, there was an overall return of 6·6% from reared smolts but this has proved to be the best return to date, with recaptures falling to less than 1% in 1977. It seems likely that the decline in survival rates is due firstly to reduced viability of reared smolts from residual furunculosis infection at the time of release. Although outwardly healthy, the stress of an hyperosmotic environment can cause a flare-up of latent disease with heavy losses during the first month at sea. This has been confirmed by transfers of smolts to sea-cages, both by the Salmon Research Trust and by Bradan Mhara Teoranta, in Connemara. A second and undoubtedly serious cause of the decline has been the increased exploitation of salmon stocks by coastal nets in recent years and this will be dealt with more fully in the succeeding section.

Table III gives the results of smolt-rearing operations by the Salmon Research Trust since 1966, when the recapture rates up to and including 1969 are the minimum figures, full trapping facilities having been available only since 1970.

Table III. Smolt release and adult recapture at Furnace, Co. Mayo

Year of recapture	Smolts released	Adults recaptured	Return of 2 + Smolts (%)	Return of 1 + Smolts (%)
1966	9764	62	0·62	0·83
1967	10 256	194	1·87	1·09
1968	14 260	490	4·41	2·91
1969	17 317	654	5·20	4·02
1970	16 637	312	3·64	1·25
1971	10 219	136	1·27	1·65
1972	10 237	682	7·00	4·08
1973	7 906	117	1·55	0·85
1974	5 479	60	1·10	1·08
1975	10 206	354	4·18	0·80
1976	15 674	253	1·62	1·60
1977	15 258	96	0·48	0·79
1978	17 922	N/A	N/A	N/A

Virginia

Virginia smolt-rearing station on the River Boyne is the newest installation of this type in the Republic of Ireland and has a projected capacity of 100 000 smolts. It was opened officially in 1978 and produced its first yearling smolts (20 000) in that year (N. O'Keefe, personal communication). It is hoped that the operation of this station will counteract the serious decline in the salmon stocks of the R. Boyne following *(inter alia)* an arterial drainage scheme. The annual catch of salmon on this river (nets, traps and rods) has fallen from a yearly average of around 20 000 to only 2000 in 1977.

Cong

The rearing station at Cong was built in the mid-1960s to supply fry and parr for re-stocking the Corrib system, following arterial drainage. The first yearling smolts (1000) were released in 1978, but some earlier 1 + smolt production was used in experimental sea-cage operations (N. O'Keefe, personal communication).

EXPLOITATION OF REARED SALMON STOCKS

It is therefore apparent that returns of reared salmon to traps situated at the rearing station have been poor. In the case of the Bush, the average return of tagged and branded smolts from the ova-hatch years 1972, 1973 and 1974 was 1·3% (618 fish from 48 843). The results from the Lee indicate that 1454 salmon returned to the Iniscarra trap from 1973 to 1977, from a total release of 645 218 smolts, or 0·22%. Returns to the Shannon are more difficult to estimate, but the figure of 3-4% cited in the text refers to possible total returns to the river and not to the smolt-rearing station plus Thomond Weir trap. It is possible to calculate, for example, that if 12% of the Thomond Weir catch in 1975 were added to the known total of 1025 fin-clipped fish at the Parteen dam trap, the grand total still represents less than 2% recaptures from the smolts released. Reared fish returns to the Salmon Research Trust have varied from less than 1% in 1977 to a maximum of 6·6% in 1972 but over the period 1966-77, 3410 salmon returned from a total release of 143 213 smolts, or 2·4%.

The factor of reduced viability in reared smolts compared with wild smolts is well known and is attributed to chronic disease in the smolts at release, as well as to physiological and behavioural deficiencies resulting from intensive rearing techniques. As a measure of this factor, 5230 wild smolts were tagged and released in the R. Bush during the three years 1974-76, with subsequent recaptures of 204 salmon and grilse, or 3·9%. Similar taggings of reared smolts gave 57 returns from 12 545 tagged, or 0·45%. The Salmon Research Trust operates downstream traps which allow an accurate count to be made each year of all wild smolts migrating out to sea. Counts of returning adults (grilse and salmon) in the upstream traps in the two succeeding years have given wild smolt survival rates ranging from 4·2% to 12·7% with an average of 8·3% for the years 1971-77. The comparable survival rate of reared smolts for the same period was 2·3%.

Apart, however, from this reduced viability of reared smolts, a further factor which affects the return of adults to a smolt rearing station is the degree of exploitation by high-seas and coastal nets. There is no evidence to suggest that, in the Irish context, ''reared'' salmon are more susceptible to this exploitation than the wild stocks, but sea-ranching, as a commercial enterprise would depend upon harvesting the maximum yield, with as small a contribution as possible to the public fishery, unless the operation were entirely State-sponsored.

The salmon drift-net fishery off the north, west and south coasts of Ireland has undergone a rapid expansion during recent years, with the employment of larger boats, longer nets and other technological advances. The catch increased from about 112 000 kg in the late 1950s to 1 498 500 kg in 1975 (E. Twomey, personal communication), but although official statistics are not yet available for 1976 and 1977 it is known that the estimated total has fallen to just over 1 080 000 kg, while the figure for 1978 is likely to be lower still. The number of drift-net licences issued reached 1046 in 1975 and is not thought to have increased significantly since then, being subject to some restrictions since 1974. This has had the unfortunate effect of increasing the number of illegal drift-nets, where the catch is sold privately or through contacts with the licensed market. The proportion of illegally caught fish marketed in 1978 has been estimated at from 20% to over 50%. The drift net fishery now accounts for over 75% of the total catch of Irish salmon.

From a number of samples of salmon and grilse caught by commercial nets in the summer of 1977, the Dept. of Fisheries estimated that fin-clipped salmon constituted 3% of the catch. If the commercial catch is taken as some 300 000 fish in that year, this gives a total of 9000 reared fish taken by coastal nets. Returns to all four rearing stations in Ireland totalled less than 2000 fish from total smolt release of about 312 000 in 1977.

More recently, a sample of 7657 salmon was examined in Galway by the Dept. of Fisheries between 19 June and 20 July, 1978; 592 fin-clipped fish were noted, constituting 7·73% of the overall catch. Most of the fish caught in this area are moving in a southerly direction so that the fin-clipped fish may be presumed to have originated from smolts released at the Parteen and Carrigadrohid rearing stations. The salmon returning to the Carrigadrohid station on the River Lee appear to be particularly heavily exploited by local nets, and in 1975 one bag net recorded almost 29% of its catch of 326 as fin-clipped fish (E. Twomey, personal communication).

ECONOMICS OF SALMON SEA-RANCHING IN IRELAND

A commercial sea-ranching operation requires large-scale annual outputs of smolts and the production costs of these fish would constitute the major debit item on the balance sheet. Costings produced in 1974 (Piggins and Lawrie, 1974) for a rearing installation producing 50 000 smolts per annum, examined various alternative schemes, such as release of 1 + smolts and sale or planting-out of the yearling parr as well as the production of mixed 2 + and 1 + smolts (70:30). The latter alternative appeared to be the most economical and the cost per smolt worked out at a minimum of 34p each. When these costings were updated in 1978, the cost per smolt had risen to 50p minimum.

Using a unit of 1000 smolts for cost-benefit analysis, the initial outgoings are £500, to which must be added a sum for the erection and maintenance of a trapping device in the river of release.

The market price of salmon and grilse to fishermen averaged £1.50 per lb in Ireland during 1978, so that to reach a minimum break-even point of £500 one would require: 6·6% return of 5 lb grilse; 5·6% return of 6 lb grilse; or, say, 3·7% return of 9 lb salmon. Bearing in mind that these return rates do not allow for the cost of trap maintenance, rates and taxes or profit margin, then salmon sea-ranching as a private commercial enterprise seems unlikely to be popular in Ireland. As a

State-sponsored enterprise, however, various other options and factors become operative, such as maintenance of coastal salmon fisheries as a social obligation, disposal of surplus yearling parr as a national re-stocking policy and the use of an entire river system for smolt production, with culling of all surplus adults, as is being attempted on the River Bush, in N. Ireland.

It is interesting to compare the costings of a private commercial sea-ranching operation with those of a sea-farming operation. Where these latter have been derived by extrapolation from actual costings of a pilot-scale sea-farming project conducted by the Salmon Research Trust from 1974-77, taking the same unit of 1000 smolts, the minimum expected yield after one year (or less) in sea cages, would be 700 fish, averaging 1·35 kg in weight. By marketing before and after the main grilse run, these fish should realise a minimum of £2500 at 1978 prices. A rough breakdown of production costs for the 1000 smolt unit would be:

	£
smolts	500
food	850
labour	300
cage and moorings	140
supervision	100
	1890

This leaves a probable profit margin of some £600. If this were added to the sea-ranching production costs of £500 (minimum) it would be necessary to achieve a return rate of 12·2% of grilse averaging 2·7 kg in weight, from these smolts in order to achieve a comparable income.

CONCLUSIONS

Sea-ranching of Atlantic salmon, as a private commercial enterprise in Ireland, would seem, at present, to be a non-viable proposition, in that:

(a) amended legislation would be required for the operation of river-mouth traps, to cull the entire returning stock;

(b) survival rates of reared smolts to the adult stage are poor, due to a combination of low viability of such smolts and increasingly heavy exploitation by coastal nets.

As a State-sponsored enterprise, however, with benefits accruing to all sections of the salmon-fishing community, some large-scale enterprises could be justified and may well prove necessary, as a conservation measure. There are indications that artificially reared smolts have made a significant contribution to total commercial catch in 1978. The only problem remaining is that of increasing the viability of reared smolts, and this is where considerable research work remains to be done on physiological and behavioural deficiencies, allied with disease prophylaxis by means of vaccines, rather than the current techniques of antibiotic therapy and chemotherapy.

ACKNOWLEDGMENTS

I am indebted to Miss Eileen Twomey, Dept. of Fisheries, Dublin, and Mr. Noel Roycroft, Electricity Supply Board, Parteen Rearing Station, for helpful discussions and production of data incorporated in this chapter.

REFERENCES

Annual Reports, Salmon Research Trust of Ireland, 1962-77. St. James's Gate, Dublin, 8.

Annual Fisheries Reports, Electricity Supply Board of Ireland, 1963-76. Lr. Fitzwilliam St., Dublin 2.

Piggins, D. J. and Lawrie, J. P. (1974). Costs of Production of Artificially Reared Salmon Smolts. App. I, Ann. Rep. Salm. Res. Trust Ire. No. XIX, 40-47.

Report of the Inland Fisheries Commission, 1975. Govt. Stationery Office, Dublin.

River Bush Salmon Project, Annual Reports, 1973-77. Dept. of Agric., Fisheries Divsn., Belfast BT4 3TA.

Twomey, E. (1976). The Restoration of Salmon Stocks of the River Lee. Anad. & Catad. Fish Comm. Paper M 14. ICES, Copenhagen.

Chapter 11

Salmon Ranching in Britain

Department of Agriculture and Fisheries for Scotland,
Freshwater Fisheries Laboratory, Pitlochry, Scotland

Salmon ranching, as defined in Chapter 1, is potential rather than actual in Britain. Until recently, the nearest approaches to this exploitation system have been some limited augmentation programmes practised by river management authorities. To gain a clear picture of the situation in Britain it is pertinent to trace the historical development of salmon propagation in the country.

Atlantic salmon (*Salmo salar* L.) were once widespread in European rivers along the Atlantic, Baltic and Arctic Ocean seaboards. As a consequence of increased human use of river systems from the late eighteenth century onwards many of these stocks have been exterminated or severely depleted (Netboy, 1968). In Britain most rivers would once have carried a salmon stock, but now the species is restricted to a few rivers in England and Wales and most of those in Scotland. Where the species has been exterminated its absence is obvious: restriction of stocks to levels below those of the former carrying capacity of rivers is not certain, since at no time has there been a method in operation on any British river allowing a complete census of total stocks in that river. Decline of stocks can only be inferred, and then from fishery data which have varied in their method of collection and dependability. Nevertheless it has been assumed that fishery data indicate declines of stock, and artificial propagation of salmon has been seen as a means of compensating for the detrimental practices which have induced these declines.

Artificial propagation became possible after Jacobi (1763, 1765) discovered the method of stripping adult salmonids and fertilising their eggs. Details of salmon life history were obscure at this time: a century earlier Willughby (1686, in Day, 1885) had stated that they spawned in the upper tributaries in November, and the eggs gave rise to "samlets", and the old fish then descended to the sea. In the early nineteenth century it was recognised that the young salmon descended to sea in the spring, but the time span of the life-history was uncertain, giving rise to some heated disputes. Several experiments were undertaken to resolve these. The first (Shaw, 1836) showed that the progeny of salmon in southern Scotland spent at least one year after hatching before silvering and migrating seaward. Others, by Buist, in the Stormontfield ponds on the River Tay (Brown, 1862), showed that a proportion of the young fish required two years in freshwater before emigrating seaward.

In Buist's experiments several hundred smolts were marked, either by fin-clips, holes punched in the opercula, or the attachment of silver rings. Recoveries of these fish were few but they led the experimenters to believe that marine growth of salmon was dramatically rapid and that "grilse" returned to spawn 3-4 months after emigration as smolts. There is some mystery about the data from these experiments, as several successive years' information is quoted in support of this conclusion. Added to that, the Duke of Atholl marked kelts (spent adults) in the upper reaches of the River Tay at about the same time (March 1859) and claimed from the recoveries of these that they were capable of growth from 5 to 8·5 kg by mid-summer. Either feeding conditions and salmon responses have changed drastically in the last 150 years, or else there are some mistakes in the records (as Calderwood (1924) considered): nowadays smolts emigrating in the spring do not return as mature fish for at least 14-15 months, and kelts recovering so rapidly and increasing in size at this rate would be highly exceptional.

Throughout these experiments it was assumed that survival of progeny from artificially spawned fish was substantially higher than that from wild fish. The evidence for this assumption is not clear, and the marking experiments were quite inadequate to test it. However, the belief persisted, and although subsequently called in question in a series of government reports on salmon fisheries (see Hutton *et al.*, 1933) the practice of stripping salmon in the autumn for distributing eyed eggs or early fry over "suitable" habitats was widespread by the beginning of the twentieth century. Under a system of District Salmon Fishery Boards in Scotland, and Regional Water Authorities in England and Wales, this rather arbitrary system of supposed conservation value persists in one form or another, and in most cases without adequate means of assessing its value in terms of increased return of adults to the fisheries and the rivers (Harris, 1978). The 1932 government committee (Hutton *et al.*, 1933) recommended a publicly funded experiment to evaluate the artificial propagation of salmon, and this recommendation included experiments in which the fish were to be reared to the adult stage. Three Scottish rivers, the Conon, Halladale and Spey, were considered suitable sites,. but the experiments were never undertaken.

A stimulus to more systematic salmon propagation for augmentation purposes came with the development of hydroelectric power in Scotland after World War II. The North of Scotland Hydro-Electric Board reared salmon to the smolt stage at their Invergarry hatchery for liberation into rivers where it was assumed that construction of dams and power-stations, or diversion of water, had been to the detriment of the salmon stocks there. Also a consequence of power development, the Freshwater Fisheries Laboratory was set up at Pitlochry, initially to investigate the biology of trout (*Salmo trutta* L.), but very soon its attention was turned to salmon also. Since the 1960s a substantial part of this laboratory's programme has been concerned with the growth and survival of juvenile salmon in streams (e.g. Egglishaw and Shackley, 1977) and under hatchery conditions (e.g. Marr, 1963, 1966; Thorpe, 1977) and with methods of rearing juveniles in hatcheries and releasing them into the wild.

The principal findings of these studies relevant to salmon ranching have been that:

(a) Salmon alevins show the most efficient usage of their yolk supply in growth when reared in an environment that minimises stimuli to locomotion (Marr, 1963, 1965, 1966);

(b) Salmon fry take up station on stream riffles, in contact with the substrate, thus occupying territories that are two-dimensional living spaces (unlike trout, which also use the water column and thus possess three-dimensional territories) (Egglishaw, 1970);

(c) Territory consists of the possession of an exclusive space from which food can be acquired easily and which is actively defended (Wankowski and Thorpe, 1979a);

(d) At all sizes and developmental stages in freshwater salmon select food particles preferentially, with a maximum width of 2·2-2·6% of their own body length (Wankowski, 1977; Wankowski and Thorpe, 1979b);

(e) At all stages of development until the smolt transformation in the spring, juvenile salmon show an increased level of activity at night, and with increasing temperature, within the range 0-20°C (Morgan and Thorpe, in preparation);

(f) Juvenile salmon up to the smolt stage prefer a dark non-reflecting surface to a bright reflecting one and respond rapidly and positively to overhead cover (Thorpe, in press);

(g) They occupy stations at relatively high water velocities (2·5-8·3 body lengths per second) (Wankowski and Thorpe (1979), and show evidence of developing most rapidly to the smolt stage at flows of approximately 5 body lengths per second (Thorpe and Morgan in preparation);

(h) Smolting rate (proportion of a sibling stock becoming smolts at age 1) is influenced by both environmental and hereditary factors; currently evidence points to a dominant influence of the male parent in this regard (Simpson and Thorpe, 1976; Thorpe, 1977; Thorpe and Morgan, 1978b);

(i) The incidence of maturation of male parr has genetic controls (Thorpe, 1975);

(j) The progeny of male parr tend to grow at least as well, and develop faster than, the progeny of sea-run males (Thorpe and Morgan, in preparation (b));

(k) The downstream movement of smolts is primarily passive, aided by a progressive reduction of intensity of behavioural characteristics which have served to maintain station in the current—namely territoriality, rheotaxis, contact with the stream bed, and swimming against high current velocities (Thorpe and Morgan, 1978a; Tytler et al., 1978; Morgan and Thorpe, in preparation).

This information has been used in hatchery practice in various ways. Marr's (1963, 1965) ideas about the survival value of burial of eggs in gravel redds, and the demonstration that absence of light, low level of mechanical disturbance and physical support by a rough surface resulted in the production of a larger fry at first feeding (cf. Bams' work with *Oncorhynchus* spp. (1972)), have been translated into simple corrugated plastic mouldings fitted to the floor of hatchery trays (Fig. 1), held in troughs with a low water flow under red light of wavelength >690 nm, outside the salmon's visible range (Ali, 1975). At first feeding, the elements of territory have been provided in a tank environment by introducing food particles with the water-flow vertically on to the centre of the tank floor (Fig. 2), so that both water and food travel radially across that floor to a circular peripheral drain

Fig. 1. Corrugated plastic mouldings on the floor of a hatchery tray, providing the physical support for alevins, and inhibiting swimming.

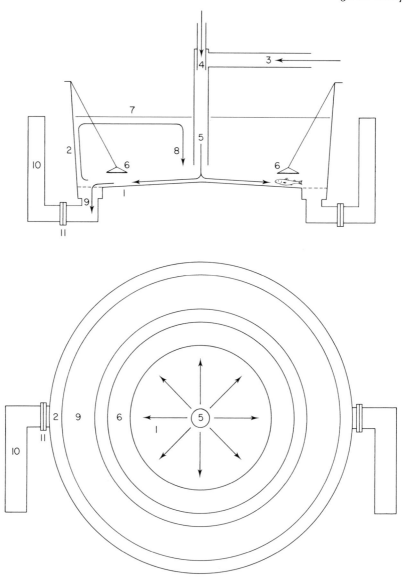

Fig. 2. Radial flow tank: *(upper)* side view; *(lower)* top view. (1) Tank base; (2) Tank side; (3) Main water input; (4) Food input; (5) Central water inlet; (6) Cover ring suspended from tank rim; (7) Water Surface; (8) Current cell; (9) Peripheral drain, with perforated cover; (10) Adjustable standpipe; (11) Swivel joint. (From Thorpe, J. E. (in press). Rearing salmonids in freshwater. *In* A. D. Hawkins (ed.) Fish keeping. Academic Press, London and New York.)

channel (Minaur, 1973; Thorpe and Wankowski, 1979). The floor was coloured matt black to meet the fishes light preferences, and the sides white, for the same reason (Thorpe, in press). An annular aluminium cover was suspended in the tank, at a height above the floor equivalent to one fish body depth, to exploit the propensity of salmon for hiding under overhead cover. Exposure to specific flow rates has been controlled by opening inflow valves, or by narrowing the inner radius of the cover, as the fish take up station with head under the inner circumference of the cover. Water velocity over the floor has been calibrated against a volume flow-meter on the inflow. Food was dispensed in measured rations on a preset schedule, governed by time-switches, into a subsidiary water supply which re-entered the main flow before entering the tank. Under such rearing conditions high pro-portions of 1-year smolts are achievable (50-90%, partly dependent on choice of parents) without use of heated water, and high survivals are characteristic (85-95% from first feeding to 1 year). The advantages of such high performance at the freshwater stage could be annulled if transfer to the wild were made under inappropriate conditions. Since the motivation and mechanics of downstream migration of smolts are inadequately understood, it is not possible yet to specify the optimal time or environmental conditions for release of smolts into the wild, and therefore indirect methods are being tested. The simplest of these uses the occurrence of wild smolts in the river supplying the hatchery as the time cue, at which hatchery smolts are transferred from their tanks to a 3 × 3 m steel mesh holding-cage staked into the river bed (Fig. 3). The 15-cm wide aperture at the apex of a triangular downstream extension of this cage is closed by fine wire mesh for 2-7 days after transfer of the fish, and then opened, permitting the smolts to leave this protected area of the river bed at will. Recoveries of marked adults have been higher from such releases than from direct liberation of smolts into the river simultaneous with transfer of smolts to the release cage. Return rate is also influenced by parental type. As reported by Sahlin (personal communication) for Baltic salmon and by Ritter (1975) for Canadian salmon, sea age and freshwater age appear to be inversely related, so that within one sibling population fish smolting early tend to return from the sea as large 2-sea-winter fish, and those smolting late as smaller 1-sea-winter fish (Table I). As the proportion smolting at 1 year old is genetically influenced (Simpson and Thorpe, 1976; Thorpe, 1977; Thorpe and Morgan, 1978), so that proportion

Fig. 3. Simple release cage at Almondbank.

Table I. Smolt age and return age among marked Atlantic salmon (*Salmo salar* L.) from the Almondbank smolt-rearing station, Scotland (*Triennial Review of Research*, 1976).

Smolt age	Sea "age" (winters)	
	Salmon (2 +) (%)	Grilse (1) (%)
1	60·0	40·0
2	28·7	71·3

returning as grilse (1-sea-winter fish) is influenced by parental type (Table II). (See also Piggins, 1974.) But as noted by Ricker (1972) for salmon species generally, most characteristics of development are influenced by both genetic and environmental factors: this is the case for smolting rate (Thorpe, 1977; Thorpe and Morgan, 1978b, in press) and likely to be the case for maturation rate at sea (Simpson and Thorpe, 1976; Simpson, personal communication; Mitchell, personal communication).

Table II. Percentage return of tagged Atlantic salmon (*Salmo salar* L.) reared at the Almondbank smolt rearing station, Scotland and released as 2-year-old smolts into the Tay estuary in April 1976. All recoveries were made at the grilse stage (1977) by commercial seine netting in the Tay estuary.

Parental type		Percentage return to
Male	Female	the commercial nets
Grilse (2·1)	× Grilse (2·1)	5·7
	× Salmon (2·2)	3·8
Salmon (2·2)	× Grilse (2·1)	1·2
	× Salmon (2·2)	0·5

In addition to hatcheries, small lakes have been used as nursery areas for rearing salmon, to augment natural production (Jones and Evans, 1962; Munro, 1965; Sinha and Evans, 1969; Harris, 1973). While it has been possible to rear salmon under such conditions, initial success in producing smolts has not always been maintained over successive stockings, as was found in the Loch Kinardochy experiments in Scotland (*Triennial Review of Research,* 1976). The reasons for this have not been elucidated, but it might be inferred from knowledge of social and feeding behaviour of the fry (Kalleberg, 1958; Wankowski, 1977; Wankowski and Thorpe, 1979a) that relatively deep bodies of almost static water would not permit efficient use of the salmon fry's repertoire of innate responses, and unless trophic conditions were exceptionally favourable, survival and smolt production would not be particularly high. Although wild Atlantic salmon are not known to make extensive use of such water bodies as nursery grounds, it has been recommended recently (Harris, 1978) that reservoirs and lakes free of predatory fish be used for smolt production. Critical evaluation of this proposal is lacking.

To date, recovery of adult salmon released through the research programs has relied on commercial and recreational fisheries. The commercial fisheries consist of fixed nets along the coasts, sweep-nets within the estuaries, and limited drift-netting off the north-east coast of England; the recreational fisheries are by rod and line in the rivers and lakes. As conservation legislation enforces limits to the fishing seasons and forbids the use of total traps on rivers, recovery of adults is necessarily incomplete. This shortcoming has to be remedied before the full potential for ranching can be assessed. A pilot ranching scheme on a small Scottish west coast river has recently been launched, which should help to provide a reliable basis of information on which to build future commercial ranching undertakings.

Current commercial interest in ranching is extensive, some 18 organisations considering entering the field, but it is active only in isolated instances. The absence of an adequate framework of law to support such an industry holds back its development, and existing law relating to salmon fisheries is not appropriate to this form of exploitation. Present legislation is designed to safeguard the wild resource and control the level of exploitation to ensure its sustained productivity; however, ranching has inbuilt safeguards for that productivity—close seasons are unnecessary, since the spawning ''escapement'' is under the control of the rancher. No biological benefit is gained by banning the harvest of a ranched stock during a close season. Moreover, potential ranchers are reluctant to invest heavily in rearing units if the bulk of fish returning to them is intercepted along the coast by traditional fisheries and their harvest at the release site is only a modest one. The reality of the assumption on which this misgiving is based has yet to be demonstrated. As noted elsewhere in this book (Chapters 4 and 19) the situation is common to most ranching fisheries, and can usually be accommodated economically, with some promising manipulations to help (for example, Chapter 17). Nevertheless, a move towards overall management of the U.K. salmon resources, both wild and manipulated (ranched), is desirable, and it has been argued elsewhere (Saunders, 1977; Thorpe, 1979 and Chapter 20) that this should be on a river stock-unit basis, implying exploitation in rivers and ranching units only, and not along open coasts or on the high seas.

REFERENCES

Ali, M. A. (1975). Retinomotor responses. *In* "Vision in Fishes" (Ed. M. A. Ali) pp. 313-355. Plenum Press, New York and London.

Bams, R. A. (1972). A quantitative evaluation of survival to the adult stage and other characteristics of pink salmon *(Oncorhynchus gorbuscha)* produced by a revised hatchery method which simulates optimal natural conditions. *J. Fish. Res. Bd Canada* **28**, 1151-1167.

Brown, W. (1862). "The Natural History of the Salmon". Thos. Murray, Glasgow, 136 pp.

Calderwood, W. L. (1924). The artificial and the natural breeding of the salmon. *Fish. Bd for Scotland, Salm. Fish.* 1924 II, 20 pp.

Day, F. (1885). On the breeding of salmon from parents which have never descended to the sea. *Trans. Linn. Soc. Lond. 2nd. Ser.* **2**, 447-468.

Egglishaw, H. J. (1970). Production of salmon and trout in a stream in Scotland. *J. Fish. Biol.* **2**, 117-136.

Egglishaw, H. J. and Shackley, P. E. (1977). Growth, survival and production of juvenile salmon and trout in a Scottish stream, 1966-75. *J. Fish. Biol.* **11**, 647-672.

Harris, G. S. (1973). Rearing smolts in mountain lakes to supplement stocks. *Int. Atl. Salm. Found. Spec. Publ. Ser.,* **4** 1, 237-252.

Harris, G. S. (ed). (1978). *Salmon propagation in England and Wales.* National Water Council, London. 62 pp.

Hutton, J. A., Johnston, W. D., Menzies, W. J. M. and Pryce-Tannatt, T. E. (1933). The artificial propagation of salmon. *Fish Board Scot. Salm. Fish.* 1932 **7**, 13 pp.

Jacobi, S. L. (1763). Method of breeding fish to advantage. *Hannöver Mag.* 1763, No. 23.

Jacobi, S. L. (1765). On the breeding of trout by impregnation of the ova. *Hannöver Mag.* 1765, No. 62.

Jones, J. W. and Evans, H. (1962). Salmon rearing in mountain tarns—a preliminary report. *Proc. zool. Soc. Lond.* **138**, 499-515.

Kalleberg, H. (1958). Observations in a stream tank of territoriality and competition in juvenile salmon and trout *(Salmo salar* L. and *S. trutta* L.). *Rep. Inst. Freshwat. Res. Drottningholm* **32**, 55-98.

Marr, D. H. A. (1963). The influence of surface contour on the behaviour of trout alevins, *S. trutta* L. *Anim. Behav.* **11**, 412.

Marr, D. H. A. (1965). The influence of light and surface contour on the efficiency of development of the salmon embryo. *Rep. Callenger Soc.* **3**, No. 17.

Marr, D. H. A. (1966). Influence of temperature on the efficiency of growth of salmonid embryos. *Nature* **212**, 957-959.

Minaur, J. (1973). Smolt rearing at Almondbank, Perthshire. *J. Inst. Fish. Mgmt.* **4**, 65-68.

Morgan, R. I. G. and Thorpe, J. E. (in prep). Changes in behaviour of Atlantic salmon smolts, *Salmo salar* L., prior to emigration to sea.

Munro, W. R. (1965). The use of hill lochs in Scotland as rearing grounds for young salmon. *ICES. CM. 1965/58.* 6 pp.

Netboy, A. (1968). "The Atlantic Salmon. A vanishing species?". London, Faber and Faber. 457 pp.

Piggins, D. J. (1974). The results of selective breeding from known grilse and salmon parents. Salm. Res. Trust of Ireland Inc., Ann. Rep. **18**, 35-39.

Ritter, J. A. (1975). Relationships of smolt size and age with age at first maturity in Atlantic salmon. *Fish. and Mar. Serv. Tech. Rep.* Mar./T.75-5. 7 pp.

Saunders, R. L. (1977). Sea ranching—a promising way to enhance populations of Atlantic salmon for angling and commercial fisheries. *I.A.S.F. Spec. Publ. Ser.* **7**, 17-24.

Shaw, J. (1836). An account of some experiments and observations on the parr and on the ova of the salmon, proving the parr to be the young of the salmon. *Edinburgh. New Philos. J.* **21**, 99-110.

Simpson, T. H. and Thorpe, J. E. (1976). Growth bimodality in the Atlantic salmon. *ICES CM 1976:* M.22, 7 pp.

Sinha, V. R. P. and Evans, H. (1969). Salmon rearing in mountain tarns. The scales and growth of the fish of Llynau Dyrnogydd, Teryn and Cilan. *J. Fish. Biol.* **1**, 285-294.

Thorpe, J. E. (1975). Early maturity in male Atlantic salmon. *Scot. Fish. Bull.* **42**, 15-17.

Thorpe, J. E. (1977). Bimodal distribution of length of juvenile Atlantic salmon (*Salmo salar* L.) under artificial rearing conditions. *J. Fish. Biol.* **11**, 175-184.

Thorpe, J. E. (1979). Ocean ranching: general considerations. pp. 152-164. *In* "Atlantic Salmon: its future" (Ed. A. E. J. Went). Fishing News Books, Farnham.

Thorpe, J. E. (in press). Rearing salmonids in freshwater. *In* "Fish Keeping" (Ed. A. D. Hawkins). Academic Press, London and New York.

Thorpe, J. E. and Morgan, R. I. G. (1978a). Periodicity in Atlantic salmon, *Salmo salar* L., smolt migration. *J. Fish. Biol.* **12**, 541-548.

Thorpe, J. E. and Morgan, R. I. G. (1978b). Parental influence on growth rate, smolting rate and survival in hatchery reared juvenile Atlantic salmon, *Salmo salar. J. Fish. Biol.* **13**, 549-556.

Thorpe, J. E. and Morgan, R. I. G. (in press). Time of divergence of growth groups between potential 1 + and 2 + smolts among sibling Atlantic salmon. *J. Fish. Biol.*

Thorpe, J. E. and Morgan, R. I. G. (in prep. a). Influence of water flow on smolting rate in juvenile Atlantic salmon, *Salmo salar,* L.

Thorpe, J. E. and Morgan, R. I. G. (in prep. b). Growth and development of progeny of 'precociously' mature male Atlantic salmon, *Salmo salar* L.

Thorpe, J. E. and Wankowski, J. W. J. (1979). Feed presentation and food particle size for juvenile Atlantic salmon, *Salmo salar* L. pp. 501-513. *In* Tiews, K. (Ed.) *Proc. World Symp. on Finfish Nutrition and Fishfeed Technology.* Berlin.

Triennial Review of Research (1973-1975) (1976). Freshwater Fish Laboratory, Pitlochry. 45 pp.

Tytler, P., Thorpe, J. E. and Shearer, W. M. (1978). Ultrasonic tracking of the movements of Atlantic salmon smolts (*Salmo salar* L.) in the estuaries of two Scottish rivers. *J. Fish. Biol.* **12**, 575-586.

Wankowski, J. W. J. (1977). The role of prey size in the feeding behaviour and growth of juvenile Atlantic salmon (*Salmo salar* L.). Ph.D. Thesis, Univ. of Stirling, Scotland.

Wankowski, J. W. J. and Thorpe, J. E. (1979a). Spatial distribution and feeding in Atlantic salmon, *Salmo salar* L., juveniles. *J. Fish. Biol.* **14**, 239-248.

Wankowski, J. W. J. and Thorpe, J. E. (1979b). The role of food particle size in the growth of juvenile Atlantic salmon (*Salmo salar* L.). *J. Fish. Biol.* **14**, 351-370.

Chapter 12

The Pink Salmon Transplant
Experiment in Newfoundland

W. H. LEAR

*Department of Fisheries and Oceans, Research and
Resource Services, P.O. Box 5667, St John's,
Newfoundland, A1C 5X1, Canada*

INTRODUCTION

The first serious effort to introduce the Pacific pink salmon *(Oncorhynchus gorbuscha)* into the north-western Atlantic was in Maine during the period 1913-1917 (Bigelow and Schroeder, 1953). Smaller efforts had been made in 1906, 1907, and 1908, when 559 000, 12 000 and 421 000 fry, respectively, were released into various streams in Maine. The eggs of the odd-year cycles of 1913, 1915, and 1917 were derived from a Skagit River stock (Puget Sound); the eggs of the even-year cycles of 1914 and 1916 were from an Afognak Island stock (Alaska) (Ricker, 1972). There were about 7 000 000 fry released from each of the four successive year-classes of 1913-16 while about 1 000 000 fry were released from the 1917 year-class. There were returns from fry of the Skagit River stock but none from the two releases of Afognak stock. Ricker (1972) stated that the homing migration of Afognak pinks is generally northward and that of the Skagit pinks is southeastward, neither of which was correct for getting pinks back to Maine.

During 1921, 1923, and 1925, about 445 000, 590 000, and 1 130 000 eggs were collected from wild fish and the resultant fry were planted in the Dennys and other rivers nearby. Natural reproduction did not

213

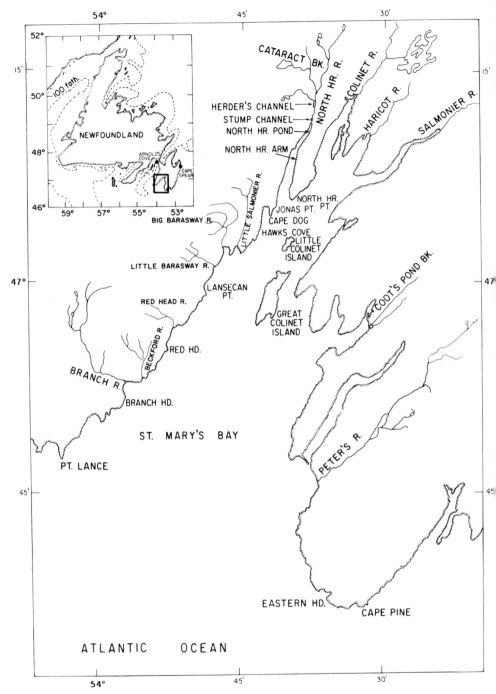

Fig. 1. St Mary's Bay, Newfoundland, showing place names mentioned in the text.

appear to be successful since very few were ever reported after 1927 (Bigelow and Schroeder, 1953).

There was also one small attempt made towards the introduction of pink salmon into James Bay at the southern end of Hudson Bay. During January 1956, about 513 000 eyed eggs and sac fry from the Lakelse run on the Skeena River, B.C. were introduced into Goose Creek near Port Severn. An additional 225 000 fingerlings were planted during the spring of 1956. Although fyke net operations resulted in the capture of about 500 fingerlings on their downstream migration, no adult pink salmon were reported from Goose Creek or other streams in Hudson Bay (Ricker and Loftus, 1968).

An introduction of pink salmon from British Columbia to Newfoundland was begun in 1958. Five transplants of eyed eggs were made in 1959, 1962, 1964, 1965, and 1966 to North Harbour River, St. Mary's Bay, Newfoundland (Fig. 1) (Lear, 1975; Lear and Day, 1977).

INITIAL PLANNING AND DEVELOPMENT OF THE NEWFOUNDLAND PROJECT

This project was requested by the Newfoundland Wildlife Branch and was sponsored by the Fisheries Research Board of Canada. Pink and chum *(Onchorhynchus keta)* salmon were recommended for initial transplantation to eastern Canada because:

(1) The primary objective was to establish a commercial fishery which required fish in large numbers, the production of which would not be limited to suitable freshwater lakes and streams as would be the case with sockeye salmon;

(2) In freshwater chum salmon required very little food and pink salmon no food, so they did not compete with native fish for food;

(3) They were the most cold-tolerant of all five species of Pacific salmon and hence best able to cope with the cool waters that prevail off the Atlantic coast during much of the year.

Newfoundland was considered the best place for the initial introduction for several reasons. The Canadian Atlantic fishing area would benefit by the addition of a new, valuable and easily sold major fish resource. This was especially true of Newfoundland, where the salt cod industry was in perennial difficulties because of the low market value of the product. The establishment of one or more species of Pacific salmon in commercial quantities would broaden the resource base, diversify the fishing industry, and thus help to boost the Atlantic fishing economy. Newfoundland was centrally located with respect to the part of the ocean most favourable for salmon and had not been subjected to DDT spraying, a factor which was strongly in favour of the survival of the salmon fry.

There was evidence that a salmon's ability to survive and return to its stream of origin in satisfactory numbers was partly hereditary, so the process of establishing a new run could be considered as a speeded-up process of adaptation by natural selection, with a consequent poor rate of return during the first few generations. Ricker (1954) suggested two desirable characteristics for any programme of transplantation:

(1) Relatively large plantings (>10 million) should be made to one or a few neighbouring sites. This would allow an adequate expendable surplus to allow for losses by natural selection of genotypes that were maladaptive to the new situation; 15-20 million eggs (i.e. 10 000-13 300 female pinks) would be needed to establish a moderate-sized run.

(2) Donor stocks should be selected carefully to match up the freshwater and marine conditions of existence of the old and the new sites as closely as possible. Because the sea is cool around the new site, other fish from more northerly portions of the Pacific would probably take hold most quickly. On the other hand, if the latitudes of the two sites must be matched because the fish may navigate in the ocean due to an innate response to incident light, then the most southerly stocks should be chosen as donors because the south shore of Newfoundland is at 47°N Another possibility was that most salmon of an east Pacific stock would tend to migrate east as they approach maturity, hence a donor stock from e.g. southern Kamchatka would be a more suitable donor than any American stock.

It has been suggested that fluctuations in the stock from less than the spawning population to more than 20 times the number of spawners could be caused by the environment (Wickett, 1958). Consistently high-producing streams have a low gradient and loose clean gravel that is not subject to scouring or drying (Wickett, 1958). Incubation temperatures below 4°C during the pre-eyed stage, i.e. up to 200 degree-days, cause high mortality (Combs and Burrows, 1957). The numbers of predators in the stream and estuary have a bearing on the minimum number of fry that produces a self-sustainable stock (Hunter, 1959).

To make the best use of transplanted eggs, provision must be made to provide optimum freshwater conditions in the initial stages of the project so as to guarantee high survival.

The general requirements of pink and chum salmon are shown in Table I.

Table I. General requirements of pink *(Oncorhynchus gorbuscha)* and chum *(O. keta)* salmon.

	O. gorbuscha		*O. keta*	
	Fry	Adults	Fry	Adults
Stream:				
temperature (°C)	2-8	8-12	2-8	6-10
gradient	0·001-0·01	0·001-0·01	0·001-0·01	0·001-0·01
flow (m s⁻¹)	even flow	0·2-0·6	even flow	0·2-0·6
depth (m)	0·2-0·5	0·2-0·5	0·2-0·5	0·2-0·5
substrate (cm) (loose clean gravel)	1·3-5·0	1·3-5·0	1·3-5·0	1·3-5·0
Ocean:				
temperature (°C)	4-12	4-15	4-12	4-15
salinity (coastal) (parts per thousand)	32	32	32	32

It was finally recommended that the donor streams would be one or more of the Tsolum, Oyster, Koeye or Lakelse rivers, and that pink salmon eggs were to be used for the first three years at least, since these would give answers on returns most quickly.

The project was to be in two phases:

(1) Experimental phase (1959-60) would consist in transplanting up to 1 000 000 eggs to check on freshwater survival more fully and to familiarise personnel with shipping, planting, and incubation problems.

(2) Pilot plant phase (1960-61) would be the first real test of sea survival. It was recommended that 10-25 million eggs would be transplanted to one stream for each of these two years. The results would be first seen in 1962 (W. P. Wickett, personal communication).

Transplant Site

During 1958, 14 streams in Newfoundland were rated for gravel, water-flow, presence of side channels for planting and incubation, public relations, presence of predators, and ease of transportation. Four in St. Mary's Bay on the Avalon Peninsula were well suited to the purpose. North Harbour River at the head of St. Mary's Bay was recommended for the first transplant, as it met the above-mentioned criteria and ocean and freshwater properties (Table I) appeared favourable. It was not too far removed from the St. John's Biological Station and the airport and presented a minimum of interference to native salmonids, because the stock of Atlantic salmon *(Salmo salar)* in this river was very low.

Two controlled-flow spawning channels were used for the egg plantings. Stump Channel, 0·8 km from the river mouth, was 111 metres long, of which 84 metres were gravelled, and 3 metres wide. Herder's Channel, which was also the spawning site for most of the naturally spawning fish that returned to the river, was 4 km from the river mouth, 540 metres long overall with 480 metres of gravelled area, and 5 metres wide (Fig. 1).

METHODS

Pink salmon eggs were collected on the spawning grounds in three British Columbia streams (see Table IV), and transported when eyed in insulated cases to North Harbour River. They were planted at densities of 1900-4300 m^{-2}, at 20 cm depths in 30 cm of gravel. Emerging fry were counted using traps, and in later years survival was estimated using batches of 25 eggs in perforated aluminium or plastic containers within the gravel. In the main river after 1969 the Bailey (1951) mark-recapture method was used to estimate migrating fry.

Visual estimates were made of fry moving through North Harbour Pond and Arm, and St. Mary's Bay, from May to July and irregularly thereafter. Juveniles were sampled by beach seine.

In the 1960s fish were gill netted in North Harbour Arm during May and June to investigate potential predation on pink salmon fry. Downstream migrant Atlantic salmon, brook trout *(Salvenlinus fontinalis)*, brown trout *(Salmo trutta)*, eels *(Anguilla rostrata)*, and smelt *(Osmerus*

Table II. Dates of entire runs, 75% modes of runs, and peak week of runs of pink salmon fry in North Harbour River during 1960, 1963, and 1965-76.

Year	Entire run	75% of run	Peak week
1960	Apr. 11-May 31	May 12-18	May 15-21
1963	May 7-June 16	May 21-25	May 19-25
1965	Apr. 29-June 19	May 26-June 5	May 30-June 5
1966	Apr. 30-May 31	May 16-23	May 15-21
1967	Apr. 31-May 31	May 16-23	May 14-20
1968	Apr. 2-May 23	May 5-11	May 5-11
1969	Apr. 16-May 16	Apr. 20-May 3	Apr. 27-May 3
1970	Apr. 9-May 10	Apr. 24-27	Apr. 26-May 2
1971	Apr. 14-May 5	Apr. 22-27	Apr. 25-May 1
1972	Apr. 13-May 18	May 2-6	Apr. 30-May 6
1973	Apr. 19-May 18	May 6-10	May 6-12
1974	Apr. 24-May 20	May 10-15	May 12-18
1975	Apr. 18-May 19	May 13-17	May 11-17
1976	Apr. 19-May 19	May 8-13	May 9-15

Table III. Means and standard deviations of surface water temperatures (°C) during entire fry run, 75% mode, and peak week of fry run in North Harbour River and during entire fry run and 1 month after fry run in North Harbour Arm.

	North Harbour River						North Harbour Arm			
	Entire run		75% mode		Peak week		Entire run		Month after run	
Year	Mean	SD	Mean	SD	Mean	SD	Mean	SD	Mean	SD
1960	8·66	4·82	12·55	2·18	11·64	1·89	6·30	1·62	10·04	1·67
1963	9·29	3·98	11·35	3·14	11·14	3·13	5·50	0·71	10·11	1·00
1965	10·85	3·18	10·33	2·22	10·70	1·69	5·34	2·21	10·38	2·55
1966	8·58	3·49	9·38	2·55	8·64	2·24	6·58	1·78	8·00	1·98
1967	7·55	2·89	8·94	2·42	8·41	2·67	4·07	1·56	7·35	3·04
1968	6·51	3·13	7·43	1·11	7·43	1·11	3·70	1·15	7·19	1·64
1969	7·54	1·85	6·71	1·31	7·55	0·66	3·13	1·32	6·56	1·75
1970	6·57	3·34	8·09	3·33	8·32	2·67	5·19	1·26	7·03	0·88
1971	7·80	2·06	7·77	1·03	6·26	1·71	5·02	0·75	8·54	1·88
1972	6·23	2·20	6·15	1·78	6·21	1·72	2·78	1·05	7·85	3·40
1973	7·55	2·19	6·86	1·26	7·73	2·05	2·51	1·13	5·92	2·00
1974	6·21	2·60	8·06	0·96	8·43	1·50	3·97	0·67	4·46	1·66
1975	5·88	2·63	9·76	0·95	9·40	1·22	No data		No data	
1976	7·54	1·94	8·30	1·32	8·74	1·30	No data		No data	

mordax) were sampled for the same purpose from the counting trap in the river.

Adult returning pink salmon were counted at a fence (see Blair, 1957) 366 m up the North Harbour River, and nearby rivers were checked visually. Other reported sightings were checked, and commercial fishermen and anglers recorded their catches. Samples of adults were obtained from the fishery and from rivers.

Water temperatures were recorded in North Harbour River and Arm (Tables II and III) and at Cape Spear (Fig. 1).

RESULTS

Egg-to-fry Survivals (Table IV and Fig.2)

In 1959-60 the low rate of survival (38%) was thought to be due to excessive silting in the Stump Channel. In subsequent plantings survivals were about 85% on average. Fry have been observed at the mouth of North Harbour River during mid-May to early June, in the pond and in North Harbour Arm between mid-May and early June, and in St. Mary's Bay from late May to the end of July. Survival from egg to fry from natural spawnings after 1966 has averaged about 75%.

Fry Predation (Tables V and VI)

In North Harbour River, stomach contents of samples of migrant fish have revealed that brook trout fed more heavily than other species on pink salmon fry. On the basis of their size and behaviour these fry should be an ideal prey for eels. Since eels feed mainly at night, and the samples were collected by day, predation by these fish may be grossly underestimated. In North Harbour Arm brook trout were again the principal predators. Of 89 cod *(Gadus morhua)* and 19 Atlantic salmon caught commercially, and 1010 capelin *(Mallotus villosus)* seined during spawning in June, none contained any fry.

Distribution of Fry and Juveniles

Pink salmon fry were observed to leave North Harbour Arm and move along the western side of St. Mary's Bay (Fig. 3), close to shore,

Table IV. Transplants of eyed eggs of pink salmon from British Columbia to North Harbour River, Nfld., during 1959, 1962, and 1964-66, eggs deposited by natural spawning fish during 1966-75, and subsequent fry migrants.

Transplant no.	Eggs Year	Eggs No. millions	Fry migrants Year	Fry migrants No. millions	Fry migrants % of eggs	British Columbia Donor Stream	Lat.	Newfoundland Egg Channel North Harbour R.	Lat.
1	1959	0·25*	1960	0·10	38	Indian R.	49°N	Stump	47°N
2	1962	2·5*	1963	2·15	87	Glendale R.	51°N	Herder's	47°N
3	1964	3·4*	1965	2·86	83	Lakelse R.	54°N	Herder's	47°N
		(0·02)	1966	3·00	91				
4	1965	3·3*	1967	5·10	82	Lakelse R.	54°N	Herder's	47°N
5	1966	5·9*	1968	3·80	87	Lakelse R.	54°N	Herder's	47°N
		(0·5)	1969	0·86	76				
	1967	(4·4)	1970	0·67	72				
	1968	(1·1)	1971	0·87	70				
	1969	(0·9)	1972	0·27	72				
	1970	(1·2)	1973	0·04	79				
	1971	(0·4)	1974	0·035	71				
	1972	(0·05)	1975	0·010	67				
	1973	(0·05)	1976	0·026	70				
	1974	(0·014)							
	1975	(0·037)							

*Transplanted; ( ) = deposited naturally.

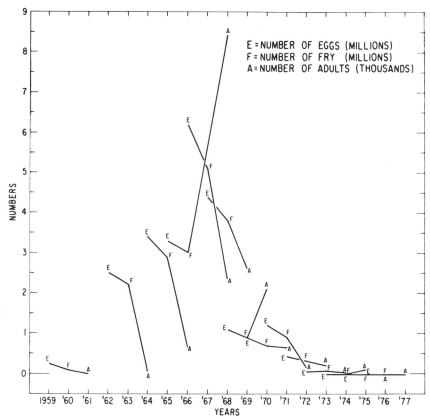

Fig. 2. Numbers of eggs, fry and subsequent total adult returns of pink salmon, 1959-77.

Table V. Predation on pink salmon fry in North Harbour River by brook trout brown trout, Atlantic salmon smolts, eels, and smelt during 1963, 1965-68, and 1970.

Species	No. of fish examined	No. of fish with fry	No. of fry	Average no. of fry/fish
Brook trout	1067	87	1091	1·02
Brown trout	332	25	95	0·29
Smolts	100	5	10	0·10
Eels	173	3	4	0·02
Smelt	310	1	1	<0·01

Table VI. Predation on pink salmon fry in North Harbour Arm: 9688 potential predators, caught in gillnets in 1963, 1965-68. The numbers of each species examined were calculated from the samples for 1963, 1966-67 and were adjusted up to the total number examined (factor of 1·90). For 1965 and 1968 the only data available were the numbers of each species with fry and the numbers of fry found.

Species (descending order of numbers caught)	No. of fish examined	Number with fry	Total fry found
Atlantic herring *(Clupea harengus)*	6971	1	6
Cunner *(Tautogolabrus adspersus)*	815	1	1
Winter flounder *(Pseudopleuronectes americanus)*	483	0	0
Short-horn sculpin *(Myoxocephalus scorpius)*	460	2	2
Atlantic cod *(Gadus morhua)*	409	1	1
Brook trout *(Salvelinus fontinalis)*	203	15	27
Rainbow smelt *(Osmerus mordax)*	139	0	0
Capelin *(Mallotus villosus)*	87	0	0
Thorny skate *(Raja radiata)*	32	0	0
Brown trout *(Salmo trutta)*	32	0	0
Atlantic tomcod *(Microgadus tomcod)*	21	0	0
Atlantic mackerel *(Scomber scombrus)*	17	0	0
Atlantic salmon *(Salmo salar)*	11	0	0
Haddock *(Melanogrammus aeglefinus)*	6	0	0
Northern wolffish *(Anarhichas denticulatus)*	2	0	0
Total	9688	20	37

frequenting tiny coves and inlets with heavy seaweed growths; possibly they used the seaweed cover as protection from predators. Juveniles were also seen on the western shore (Fig. 4), but also at Arnold's Cove, Placentia Bay, nearby, during August-October. Fork lengths of these fish are given in Table VII.

Adult Returns (Table VIII and Figs 5-9)

The percentage return of adults to Newfoundland waters increased sharply over the first 4 plantings of eggs, but declined again with the 1966 planting. Thereafter the total return fluctuated between 0·010%

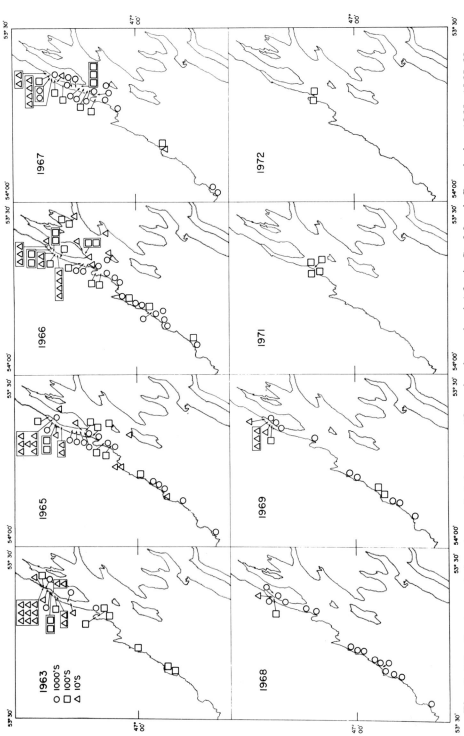

Fig. 3. Distribution and abundance of pink salmon (*Oncorchynchus gorbuscha*) fry in St. Mary's Bay during 1963, 1965-69,

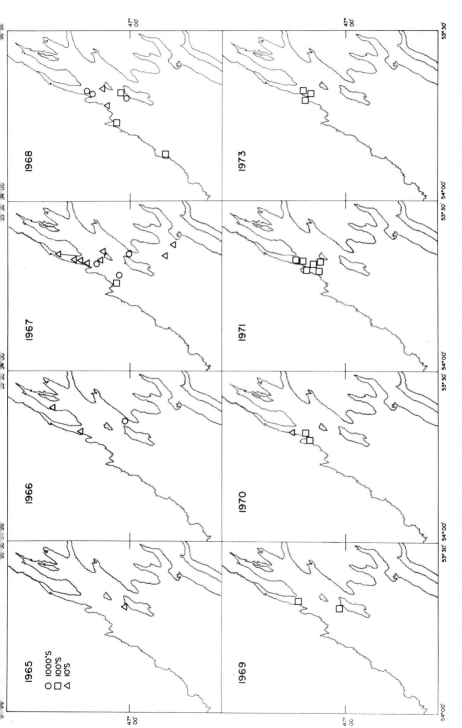

Fig. 4. Distribution and abundance of juvenile pink salmon in St. Mary's Bay during 1965-71 and 1973.

Table VII. Average fork-lengths of juvenile pink salmon sampled in 1966-67.

Date		No.	Mean lengths (mm)
1966:	16 June	25	45·1
	21 August	3	135·0
	5 October	5	188·2
	20 October	1	192·0
	25 October	9	213·0
1967:	29 June	6	38·2
	5 July	2	52·0
	17 July	25	60·0
	12 October	14	180·3

and 0·206% of the estimated egg deposition but without any clear trend. However, as only the parent stocks of 1968 and 1973 gave rise to adult generations more numerous than themselves, the absolute numbers of returning adults declined steadily. This decline was aggravated by straying and by exploitation in coastal nets such that only 60% of all recorded adults were found in North Harbour River; 18% were taken in St. Mary's Bay or its inflowing rivers exclusive of North Harbour River, and the remaining 22% ranged from Nova Scotia to Labrador, with the bulk caught along the eastern coasts of Newfoundland.

Length Distributions

Fork lengths were obtained from samples of adult pink salmon captured by commercial fishermen in St. Mary's Bay during 1964 and 1966-73. Analyses of variance revealed that annual differences in fork lengths were significant ($P < 0.001$) for both the even-year cycles ($F_{4283} = 10.74$) and the odd-year cycles ($F_{3359} = 8.56$). There was a trend towards decreasing fork length from 1969 to 1973 in both odd- and even-year cycles (Fig. 10). Overall average fork length of pink salmon of the odd-year cycle (54·98 cm) was significantly greater ($P < 0.001$) than that of the even-year cycle (49·22 cm). The average fork lengths were regressed against the sea surface temperatures in the southeastern Newfoundland area during the entire life span of each pink salmon run

Table VIII. Adult returns of pink salmon.

Year of release	Adults recorded			North Harbour River			St. Mary's Bay (exc. N.H. River) No.	Elsewhere No.
	Total No.	% of eggs	% of fry	No.	% of eggs	% of fry		
1959	1	<0·000	0·001	1	<0·000	0·001	0	0
1962	49	0·002	0·002	25	0·001	0·001	24	0
1964	638	0·019	0·022	419	0·012	0·015	219	0
1965	8500	0·258	0·283	5334	0·162	0·178	1221	1945
1966	2426	0·038	0·048	1353	0·021	0·027	762	311
1967	2603	0·059	0·069	1116	0·025	0·029	336	1151
1968	2091	0·190	0·243	1489	0·135	0·173	360	242
1969	624	0·069	0·093	468	0·052	0·070	128	28
1970	117	0·010	0·013	58	0·005	0·007	56	3
1971	174	0·044	0·064	60	0·015	0·022	72	42
1972	28	0·056	0·070	18	0·036	0·045	6	4
1973	103	0·206	0·294	46	0·092	0·131	13	44
1974	8	0·057	0·080	8	0·057	0·080	0	0
1975	6	0·016	0·023	4	0·011	0·015	2	0

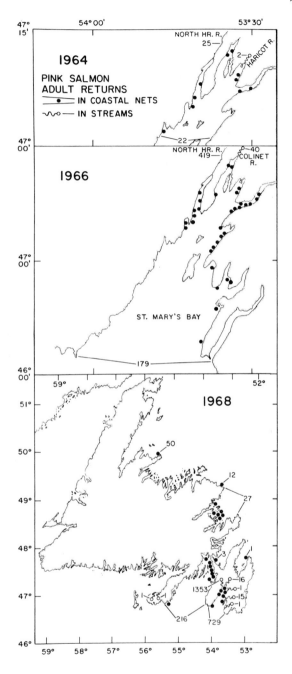

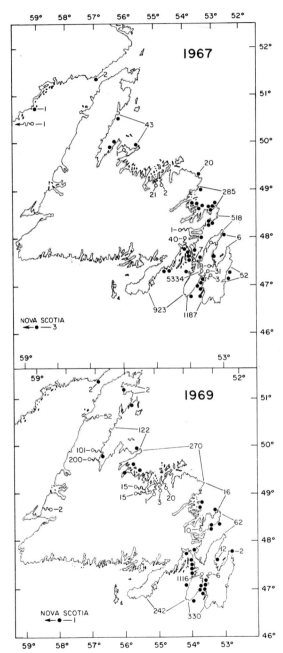

Fig. 5. Distribution of adult pink salmon during 1964, 1966-69 in North Harbour River, in coastal nets, and other streams.

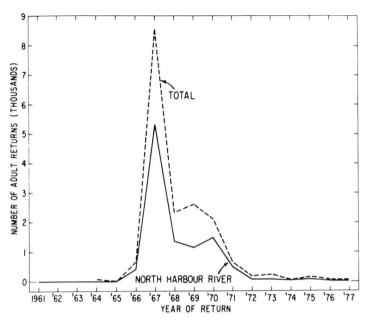

Fig. 6. Annual returns of pink salmon adults to North Harbour River (solid line) and total returns to all areas (broken line), 1961-77.

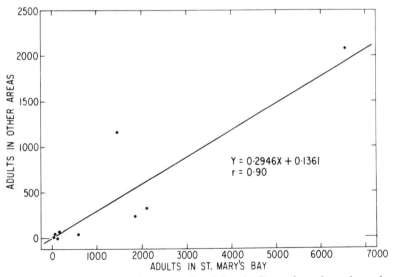

$$Y = 0.2946X + 0.1361$$
$$r = 0.90$$

Fig. 7. Returns of pink salmon to St. Mary's Bay plotted against those reported from other areas during 1967-75.

of the odd- and even-year cycles as well as the monthly and combined monthly averages during winter, spring, and summer of the return year. The only significant correlation ($r = 0.90$, $P < 0.05$) was that found between the average fork lengths of pink salmon of the even-year cycle and the average sea surface temperature at Station 27 during January-August of the return year; linear regression of fork length on temperature was $Y = 5.3709X + 35.8039$.

Other Species

Species of fish other than pink salmon migrating downstream were also enumerated at a down-stream counting trap which was kept in operation from the first week of May to late June or mid July during 1961-68 and 1971-74. The down-stream counting fence was not in operation during 1969-70 and has not been since 1974.

The numbers of migrating Atlantic salmon smolts fluctuated between 1495 and 2708 during 1961-64 and then decreased to 423 during 1965 and increased to 977 in 1966. During 1971-74, the numbers remained stable varying only from 648 to 671 (Fig. 11). The numbers of adult Atlantic salmon entering North Harbour River have been very low, varying from 13 to 52 during 1961-71 when total counts were obtained (Lear and Day, 1977). During 1972 and 73, the number of adults entering the river decreased to 6 and 4 respectively, but increased to 16 during 1974. The decrease in the number of adult Atlantic salmon returning is possibly related to exploitation of the smaller salmon (grilse) in the coastal fisheries. The pink salmon transplant does not appear to have affected the Atlantic salmon population in North Harbour River. If large numbers of pink salmon were successfully established in Newfoundland, however, there are at least two ways in which they might affect Atlantic salmon. Firstly, if pink salmon were allowed to spawn in large numbers in an Atlantic salmon river, their eggs, deposited in September, might release pheromones causing avoidance in Atlantic salmon which spawn in October. If this happened, the altered spawning behaviour of Atlantic salmon could lead to reductions in the Atlantic salmon population in the river. Secondly, there might be competition for food at sea. Stomachs of pink salmon (1.4-2.7 kg) taken in coastal nets set for Atlantic salmon contained capelin in about the same quantities as Atlantic salmon grilse of the same size. Thus, if large numbers of pink

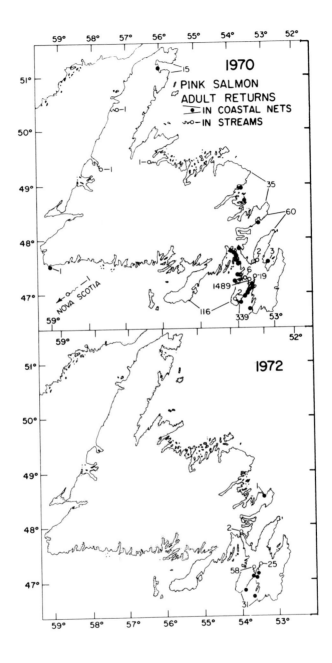

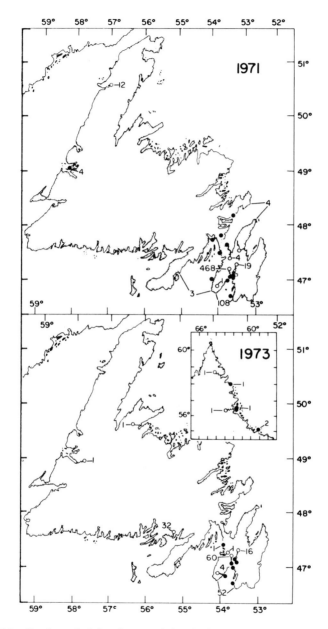

Fig. 8. Distribution of pink salmon adults during 1970-73 in North Harbour River, in coastal nets and other streams.

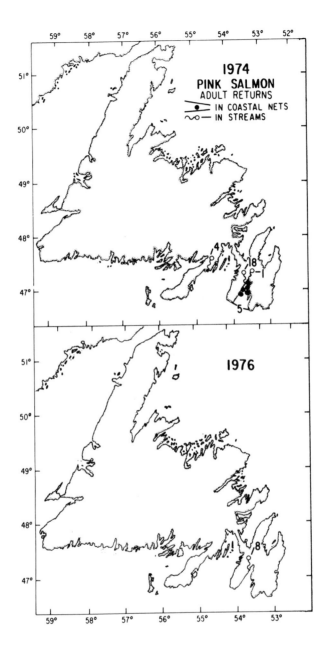

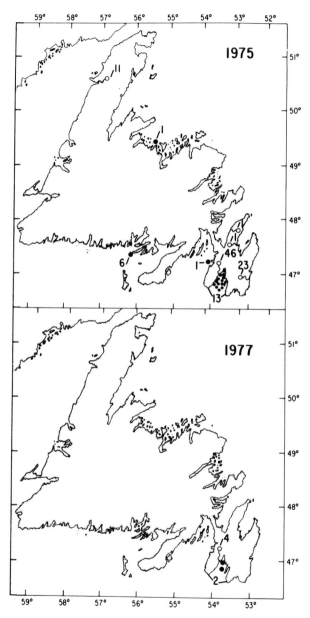

Fig. 9. Distribution of pink salmon adults during 1974-77 in North Harbour River, in coastal nets and other streams.

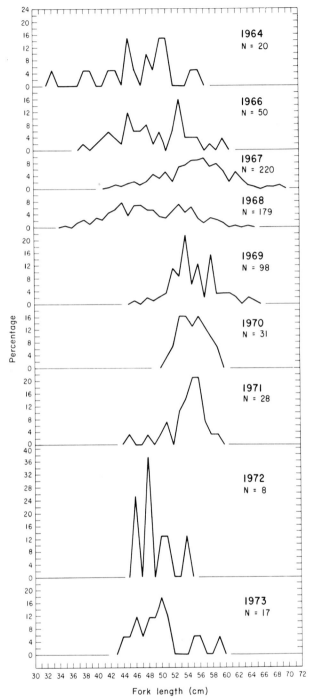

Fig. 10. Length distribution of adult pink salmon caught in commercial nets and taken in North Harbour River during 1964, 1966-73.

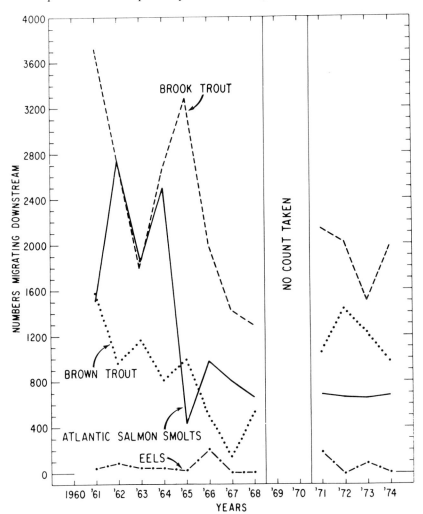

Fig. 11. Numbers of Atlantic salmon smolt, brook trout, brown trout, and American eel migrating downstream in North Harbour River during 1961-68 and 1971-74.

salmon were feeding in a bay or estuary during May-July, the competition might be detrimental to Atlantic salmon stocks feeding in the same area if the supply of capelin were a limiting factor.

The numbers of brook trout migrating have fluctuated greatly also but have increased from the 1968 low of 1298 to around 2000 during 1971, 1972, and 1974.

The runs of brown trout decreased from 1569 during 1961 to 138 during 1967 but have been increasing since then to around 1000-1400 during 1971-74. These brown trout are not native to the river but have increased as a result of straying from other systems into which they were introduced on the Avalon Peninsula, especially in the St John's area.

The numbers of American eel counted at the fence remained very low, varying from 1-193 during 1961-68, 1971-74.

In general, however, the transplant of pink salmon to North Harbour River, especially considering the small numbers returning, was not detrimental to the stocks of other species in the river at the time.

DISCUSSION

Possible Causes of Decline in Numbers

In the Pacific Ocean, the average marine mortality of pink salmon between the fry stage and returning mature adults, exclusive of fishing, is around 95% (Neave, 1953; Hunter, 1959). Severe departures from this figure have been observed; e.g. Hunter (1959) found that the marine mortality of pink salmon in the area before fishing took place varied from 89·2 to 99%.

Wickett (1958) presented data which gave estimated adult stock sizes of pink salmon produced by known numbers of fry at Hooknose Creek. The oceanic survival over a 9-year period varied from 0·6% to 5·2%. He suggested that the marine survival of pink salmon was related to temperature and salinity in the ocean in June (the month just after the fry enter the sea), with low temperature and reduced salinity being unfavourable. Vernon (1958) reported that the best single factor for predicting the rate of return of Fraser River pink salmon appeared to be the mean April to August seawater temperature in Georgia Strait. There was an inverse relationship between the mean temperature and the subsequent survival rate.

Survival rates of the odd- and even-year cycles, and the combined cycles of the 1964-75 year-classes were regressed on average surface temperatures in the North Harbour River during the entire fry run, the peak week of the run, and the 75% mode of the run. These same survival rates were also regressed on average temperatures at the surface and at 25 m depths, at Station 27 near Cape Spear (Fig. 1) during June and July. The only significant relationship ($P < 0.01$) was a positive one between survival of the odd year cycle (1965-71) and surface temperature in North Harbour River averaged over the entire fry run (Lear, 1975). These temperatures decreased significantly ($P < 0.01$) from 1965 to 1975, and could therefore be a contributory cause of fry mortality.

Henry (1961) obtained a good correlation between the first-year-ocean scale growth and percentage sea survival of sockeye salmon from the Fraser River, B.C. An 11% increase in first-year-ocean scale growth corresponded to a 220% increase in survival from 5% to 16%. The survival rates of pink salmon of the even, odd, and combined cycles of the 1962, 1964-69 year-classes were plotted against all, and part of, the first-year-ocean growth using the numbers of circuli in the entire first-sea-year, the number in the first half of the first-sea-year, and the number in the second half of the first-sea-year. There was no significant correlation between any of the indices of first-year growth and adult survivals of the even, odd, or combined cycles.

Hunter (1959) found that predation was important in reducing the numbers of fry. Gilhousen (1962) stated that, in south-eastern Alaska, herring were feeding on young pink salmon and postulated that the fluctuations of Fraser River pink salmon might be attributed to variable predation on pink salmon fry by the fish populations in Georgia Strait. It was hypothesised that the predation by herring and mackerel might account for variation in the return rates of pink salmon to North Harbour River, and it was assumed that the predation rate would be proportional to the stock sizes of herring and mackerel in the area. Thus the survival rates of pink salmon, of the even- and odd-year cycles and combined cycles of the 1964-75 year-classes, were compared with the herring stock sizes, calculated by virtual population analyses (Moores and Winters, 1977), in the St Mary's Bay-Placentia Bay area. No significant correlation was found. However, Lear (1975) found a significant inverse correlation ($P < 0.05$) between the survival rates of pink salmon of the even year cycle (1964-70 year-classes) and the herring stock sizes in the St Mary's Bay-Placentia Bay area.

This would suggest that there may be some relationship between herring stock sizes and consequent predation rates by herring and the marine survival rates of the pink salmon fry from North Harbour River. The survival rates of pink salmon fry of the even, odd, and combined cycles (1964-75 year-classes) were compared with the indices of mackerel abundance based on stock sizes of 1 + mackerel (Anderson, 1977). These analyses produced no significant correlations.

Aro and Shepard (1967) report that, in northern and central British Columbia, pink salmon are abundant in both even- and odd-year lines, but in some areas either the even- or odd-year stock vastly outnumbers that of the opposite line. Of the four largest egg transplants, three were of even-year stocks from southern British Columbia. The transplant that produced the largest returns (almost four times the next largest) was the odd-year stock of 1965. Thus the use of even-year stocks could also contribute to the lack of success of the transplant.

It appeared that the most serious predators on the pink salmon fry both in the river and in the estuary were the brook trout. It also is suspected that the predation rate in North Harbour Pond, between the river and the estuary, was higher than in the river or estuary, since the brook trout do not migrate directly to sea but inhabit the pond for periods varying from a few days to several weeks. In such an enclosed area the predation pressures on the fry may be considerable. In view of the pattern of distribution and migration of the pink salmon fry along the west side of St Mary's Bay during the summer, a high predation rate by anadromous brook trout near Big Barasway River, Little Barasway River, Red Head River, Beckford's River, and Branch River is highly possible. It is postulated that a significant portion of the fry mortality can be attributed to brook trout predation, although it is quite possible that eels may also be quite significant predators.

CONCLUSION

The experimental transplant of Pacific pink salmon from British Columbia to Newfoundland has obviously been a failure. However, this does not necessarily mean that further transplants of pink salmon to the Newfoundland area would not be successful in terms of maintaining a self-sustaining population.

Although the recommended level of egg planting was 10-25 million eggs annually for two consecutive years, this was not achieved as the plantings were of the order of 2·5-3·4 million, except for one year only, when 5·9 million eggs were planted. With such low numbers of eggs the population may not have been large enough to allow for the natural selection process to weed out the unfavourable individuals and at the same time to recover from years of low marine survival due to adverse environmental factors. Better results might have been obtained from larger plantings in which eggs were drawn from several stocks so as to increase the genetic variation and possibly increase the chances of survival of the offspring of the fish that subsequently would be spawning naturally.

The eggs for this transplant were taken from the eastern Pacific. Better results might have been obtained with eggs from the western Pacific since the migration patterns of western Pacific pink salmon might be more compatible with current systems in the North-west Atlantic. In view of the distribution of returning pink salmon prior to the spawning period, it is likely that a river on the north-east coast of Newfoundland may have proven more successful than a south coast river.

It may also enhance the probability of success of a future transplant if fry were held for a longer period before they were allowed to migrate to sea. This would enable them to attain a larger size, especially if they were fed with high-protein food, and would give them an advantage, since it has been shown for sockeye salmon fry that larger fry have an increased swimming performance and a greater ability to avoid predators than the smaller fry (Bams, 1967).

ACKNOWLEDGEMENTS

This project was possible only with the excellent co-operation and considerable effort devoted by the staff of the Nanaimo Biological Station and the Pacific Management Branch of the Department of Fisheries. I am particularly grateful to Mr W. P. Wickett for providing the information on the initial planning and development of techniques for the transplant. The following people played key roles in planning, developing techniques, selecting donor stocks, collecting eggs, incubating eggs, and transporting eggs: Drs W. E. Ricker, A. A. Blair, J. L. Kask, W. Templeman, A. W. H. Needler, Messrs W. P. Wickett, F. C. Withler, W. Caulfield, R. Humphries, and F. A. Day.

242   *W. H. Lear*

Dr A. A. Blair conducted and co-ordinated the transplant operation
at North Harbour River during 1958-69. Dr A. W. May was in charge
of the project during 1969-71. Mr F. A. Day was the senior technician
on the transplant site and supervised most of the technical operations
and the collection of environmental data.

REFERENCES

Anderson, E. D. (1977). Assessment of the Northwest Atlantic Mackerel
    Stock. ICES. Pelagic Fish (Northern) Committee, C. M. 1977/H:40. 26 pp.
Aro, K. V. and Shepard, M. P. (1967). Salmon of the North Pacific Ocean—
    Part IV. Spawning populations of North Pacific salmon. 5. Pacific Salmon
    in Canada. *INPFC Bull.* **23**, 225-327.
Bailey, N. T. J. (1951). On estimating the size of mobile populations from
    recapture data. *Biometrika* **38**, 293-306.
Bams, R. A. (1967). Differences in performance of naturally and artificially
    propagated sockeye salmon migrant fry, as measured with swimming and
    predation tests. *J. Fish. Res. Board Can.* **24**, 1117-1153.
Bigelow, H. B. and Schroeder, W. C. (1953). Fishes of the Gulf of Maine.
    U.S. Fish Wildl. Serv. Fish. Bull. **74**, 577.
Blair, A. A. (1957). Counting fence of netting. *Trans. Am. Fish. Soc.* **86**,
    199-207.
Combs, B. D. and Burrows, R. E. (1957). Threshold temperatures for the
    normal development of chinook salmon eggs. *Prog. Fish. Cult.* **19** (1), 3-6.
Gilhousen, P. (1962). Marine factors affecting the survival of Fraser River
    pink salmon. *In* "Symposium on Pink Salmon". H. R. MacMillan
    Lectures in Fisheries. pp. 105-111.
Henry, K. A. (1961). Racial identification of Fraser River sockeye salmon by
    means of scales and its applications to salmon management. *Int. Pac. Salmon
    Fish. Comm. Bull.* **12**, 97.
Hunter, J. G. (1959). Survival and production of pink and chum salmon in a
    coastal stream. *J. Fish. Res. Board Can.* **16**, 835-886.
Lear, W. H. (1975). Evaluation of the transplant of Pacific pink salmon
    (Oncorhynchus gorbuscha) from British Columbia to Newfoundland. *J. Fish.
    Res. Board Can.* **32**, 2343-2356.
Lear, W. H. and Day, F. A. (1977). An analysis of biological and environ-
    mental data collected at North Harbour River, Newfoundland, during
    1959-75. Fish. Mar. Serv. Res. Dev. Tech. Rep. 697, 61 pp.
Moores, J. A., and Winters, G. H. (1977). Production and yield of the
    Placentia-St. Mary's herring stock. CAFSAC Res. Doc. 77/30, 15 pp.
Neave, F. (1953). Principles affecting the size of pink and chum salmon
    populations in British Columbia. *J. Fish. Res. Board Can.* **9**, 450-491.
Ricker, W. E. (1954). Pacific Salmon for Atlantic Waters. *Can. Fish. Cult.* **16**,
    6-14.

Ricker, W. E. (1972). Hereditary and environmental factors affecting certain salmonid populations. *In* "The Stock Concept in Pacific Salmon". H. R. MacMillan Lectures in Fisheries, p. 27-160.

Ricker, W. E. and Loftus, K. H. (1968). Pacific salmon move east. Fish. Counc. Can., Annu. Rev. pp. 37-39, 43.

Vernon, E. H. (1958). An examination of factors affecting the abundance of pink salmon in the Fraser River. Int. Pac. Salmon Fish. Comm. Prog. Rep. 5: 49 pp.

Wickett, W. P. (1958). Review of certain environmental factors affecting the production of pink and chum salmon. *J. Fish. Res. Board Can.* **15**, 1103-1126.

Chapter 13

The Introduction of Pink Salmon into the Kola Peninsula

E. L. BAKSHTANSKY

*All-union Research Institute of Marine Fisheries and
Oceanography (VNIRO), Moscow, U.S.S.R.*

ACCLIMATISATION: METHODS AND RESULTS

Intensive practical work on pink salmon *(Oncorhynchus gorbuscha)*
(Fig. 1) acclimatisation has been carried out in the Barents and White
Sea basins since 1956 (Fig. 2). Eggs are collected chiefly in the Sakhalin
rivers, with a few from western Kamchatka and the Magadan district.
They are incubated in hatcheries until the eyes are pigmented and then
transported by plane in isothermal cases, keeping the temperature at
1-4°C. Each case can include about 250 eggs, the thickness of each of
two layers being 15 cm. They are transported over a period of 3-7 days,
during which their mortality rate is 0·5-6%. For their further
incubation the majority is introduced into hatcheries of the Kola
Peninsula, at Taybola 80 km from the estuary of the Kola River, at
Uraguba 4 km from the estuary of the Ura River, which enters the
Motovsky Gulf, and at Umba, on the Umba River 4 km from the sea.
A small number of eggs of pink and chum salmon *(O. keta)* were also laid
down at the Kandalakshsky and Knyazhegubsky hatcheries, lying on
the Kandalakshsky Gulf of the White Sea. In the last few years eggs
have been supplied chiefly to the Umbsky and Onezhsky hatcheries in
Arkhangel'sk District. Larvae are hatched from October to January and
are kept in Atkins-type concrete troughs at about 30 000 per m²,
initially. At the beginning of acclimatisation in 1957 and 1958, pink

Fig. 1. Adult male pink salmon *(Oncorhynchus gorbuscha).*

and chum salmon fry were released under the ice at Taybolsky and
Umbsky hatcheries in January and April. The first years of work on
acclimatisation were spent assimilating the methods of egg-transport-
ation, familiarising the fish-culturists of the Murmansk District with
new species, and enlarging the areas for egg incubation and rearing the
larvae. However, the pink and chum salmon did not return. All fish
returned to us by fishermen appeared to be Atlantic salmon *(Salmo
salar)* of unusual shape, char *(Salvelinus alpinus),* or even ide *(Leuciscus
idus).* From 1959 the fish-culturists of the Murmansk District began to
grow pink and chum salmon using the methods of the Sakhalin
specialists. During the short period of growth the density of the young
fish decreases to 15 000 to 10 000 per m². The young salmon were fed
eggs of cod *(Gadus morhua)* and lumpfish *(Cyclopterus lumpus),* ovaries
with their membranes of redfish *(Sebastes marinus),* capelin *(Mallotus
villosus),* cod liver and other items. The Kola Peninsula pink salmon
begin to swim 1-1·5 months later than those in the Sakhalin hatcheries,
at the end of May, when all but 15-20% of the yolk-sac is resorbed and
the temperature rises above 3°C. At 3-5°C pink salmon are kept in the
upper part of the hatchery, at 7-8°C in its lower section, and at about

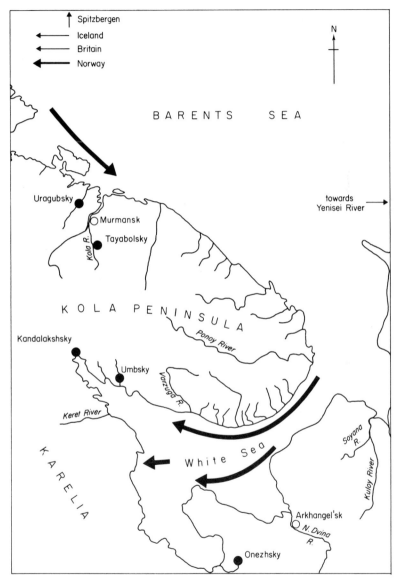

Fig. 2. Map of Kola Peninsula area.

12°C, and when the water is polluted by food, the young salmon may perish, so they are released. Their mass almost doubles due to growth, and the period of release is shifted to June. During twenty years of acclimatisation work the hatcheries have released about 200 000 000 pink salmon, of which almost 3 000 000 were from eggs collected on the Kola Peninsula (Fig. 3). During the first years (1957-1964) more than 50 000 000 chum were released as well, but only a few dozen returned.* Pink salmon started to return in 1960, varying between years from a few individuals to several hundred thousand per annum (Fig. 4). Actual numbers returning were about twice those reported in the

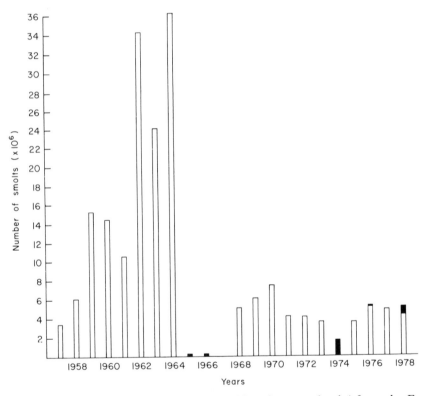

Fig. 3. Number of juvenile pink salmon *(Oncorhyncus gorbuscha)* from the Far East (white columns) and from locally produced stock (black columns) released from hatcheries in the Barents and White sea area.

*In 1933-1939 chum were acclimatised by release of fingerlings into the Kola and Onega Rivers, but only a few individuals returned.

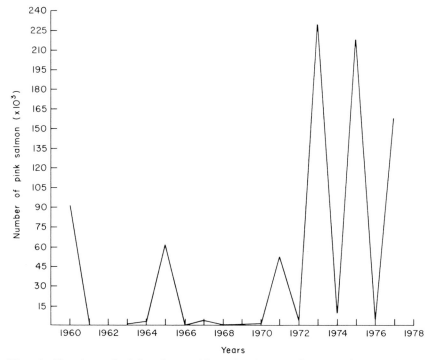

Fig. 4. Number of pink salmon *(O. gorbuscha)* caught or estimated in the White, Barents and Norwegian Sea areas by different years.

catch: pink salmon are caught by the same gear as the Atlantic salmon and thus the intensity of their catch is 50%.

In practice it is difficult to obtain stable high returns of pink salmon from hatcheries as survival of their small ''smolts'' is dependent on environmental conditions in their river or marine habitat. For instance, a high percentage return was obtained from the release of 15 000 000 smolts in 1959; subsequently (1960-1964) the return was very small, though the number released varied from 10 000 000 to 36 000 000.

PINK SALMON RETURN MIGRATION AND SPAWNING

In the first years of return, despite the fact that all pink salmon had originated at hatcheries, they entered rivers and streams of the White, Barents, and Norwegian Seas. The greatest number was caught in the area of fry release, especially on the southern coast of the Kola Peninsula in the White Sea, where most were taken by marine set nets and a much smaller number by set nets in rivers. A substantial number were also caught in Karelia and the Arkhangel'sk District, and they have been taken as far east as the rivers of the Yamal Peninsula and in the Yenisei River. The Norwegian catches of pink salmon are considerable, and a few individual salmon have been encountered in Great Britain, Iceland, and Spitsbergen. Usually the run begins off the north coast of Norway and the northern coast of the Kola Peninsula; the fish then migrate along the southern coast of the peninsula, appearing some time later off the Arkhangel'sk District and Karelia coasts. They are almost the same size as those observed in the Pacific, fluctuating somewhat between years, but fish size does not depend on their abundance. Their coloration is mainly pure silver, and their gonads are usually at maturity stages 3-4. Sometimes those migrating partially into rivers show signs of change associated with spawning. Some move more than 300 km upstream from the estuary in the Ponoy and Tanya Rivers, overcoming low rapids and falls, although not quite as well as the Atlantic salmon. Pink salmon stay in the river for 1-2 months before spawning, and the timing of migration and spawning differs by years: in 1960 the fish entered the rivers from June to October, spawning from late September to early October; in 1965 they ran from late June to early September, and spawned from late August to early September. The middle of the run most often occurs in August, and the middle of spawning in the first half of September. The timing of collection of local pink salmon eggs by the hatcheries corresponds to the period of mass spawning: in 1960 eggs were taken at the Umbsky hatchery from 11 September to 12 October, and in 1965 from 22 August to 5 December. Usually they spawn 2-4 weeks earlier than the Atlantic salmon: thus they improve the salmon rivers by clearing the bed of sand and mud. However, sometimes part of the pink salmon spawning coincides with that of the Atlantic salmon, and their spawning areas coincide with the exception of the headwater areas accessible only to the Atlantic salmon. Pink salmon redds are found to a depth of 0·2-0·9 m at sites where the river-flows range from 0·3-1 m per sec, and in a sand-gravel substrate or even among large stones. Ice may form to a thickness of 70 cm over the redds in winter, but the water is not frozen at all over the redds in some areas (Azbelev et al., 1962). Sometimes pink salmon spawn in estuaries, as in 1977 in the

Porya River where salinities became high during the flood tide. The adults dying after spawning are eaten mainly by acclimatised American mink *(Mustela vison)*, brown bears *(Ursus arctos)*, ravens *(Corvus corax)* and gulls *(Larus canus)*. Survival of eggs has been studied in some years by opening up the redds, but spawning success is best understood from data on the survival of local pink salmon eggs at the hatcheries and from the results of observations on the downstream migration of wild juveniles (Fig. 5). Often almost all the eggs die; this means that the spawning success of this species appears to be very variable, and a good run of adults very seldom coincides with a good survival of eggs and larvae. One can conclude that the downstream migration was successful enough in 1962, 1966, 1974, 1976, and 1978, when millions of migrants left from all the rivers of northern Europe. The mortality of local eggs, often observed in the spawning areas and in the hatcheries as well as the appearance of large numbers of

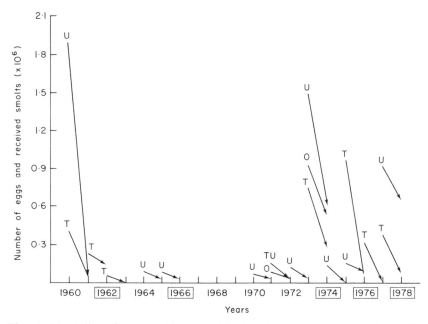

Fig. 5. Mortality of eggs and larvae of the local "Atlantic" pink salmon *(O. gorbuscha)* at the fish hatcheries (T = Taybolsky; U = Umbsky; O = Onezhsky) and the years of considerable downstream migration of wild juveniles (boxed).

deformed larvae, is a consequence of late deposition of eggs: the necessary 200 degree-days of heat cannot be obtained before the water temperature falls to its winter level of 0°C, and the embryos do not reach the safe eyed stage (Azbelev and Yakovenko, 1963). If spawning occurs early or if the autumn is warm and long, the eggs develop normally and larvae hatch in late autumn or early winter. Otherwise the eggs develop slowly and die throughout the winter. For example, live eggs were found in different rivers of the Peninsula throughout winter 1960-61 up to April; later, eggs and larvae died and no migrating smolts were found, despite very thorough searches, especially in the Umba River, where the greatest number of pink salmon were spawning. The north European rivers draw most of their water from surface run-off, so that there is a synchronous change in the temperature of many rivers over large areas, and it is quite natural that all the deposited eggs can perish under such conditions in a cold autumn or a late spring. Other causes also hamper spawning. There are numerous lakes and bogs on the rivers of the north, and the proportion of river-bed suitable for making redds, that is with stones, or pebbles and sand, is very small; for example, the total surface covered by pebbles in the comparatively large Keret River does not exceed 3000 m² (Gritsevskaya, 1963). Unreliability of pink salmon reproduction in northern Europe was well illustrated when the supply of eggs from the Pacific was temporarily interrupted between 1964-1966: in 1965, 65000 salmon were recorded, in 1967, about 3000, and in 1969, only 200.

Latterly the natural reproduction of pink salmon has become more remarkable: in 1971 more than 50000 returned, in 1973 about 240000, in 1975 about 230000, and in 1977 about 165000. The fact that they enter the rivers of the northern Europe throughout a large area in the odd years may allow a temporary pink salmon population to last longer than did those in Maine, U.S.A., and in Newfoundland, Canada (see Chapter 12).

BIOLOGY OF JUVENILES

In the first years of work with pink and chum salmon there were no returns, so it was necessary to study the juveniles released from the hatcheries and the conditions affecting their survival. Experiments in the laboratory showed that juveniles withstood considerable fluctuations in abiotic conditions, namely temperature, salinity, and oxygen content. The larvae and smolts survived well, even at instant transfer from freshwater to seawater at 5-10°C. When freshwater and seawater temperatures were lowered below 3°C the smolts became less mobile; at seawater below 1°C they did not move at all, sank to the bottom, and their mortality increased (Bakshtansky, 1964b, 1965).

It is very likely that the larvae released in January and April 1958 in the Umba River were carried into the sea by a strong current and died there, as the sea temperature was about —1°C at that time. In all subsequent years the smolts were released when the sea temperature near the coast was about 10°C. It is unlikely that slight fluctuations in seawater temperature could affect survival of the immature fish so greatly that the number of returning adults could fluctuate by a factor of a thousand.

Successful tolerance of unfavourable abiotic conditions is also shown in the survival of pink salmon in a small Arctic lake covered by ice for seven months within a year (Bakshtansky, 1962a), where they were kept alive to reach age 2 + .

Juvenile pink and chum salmon grown in hatcheries migrate downstream at the time of maximum zooplankton development in the coastal area of the Barents and White Seas. Fingerlings feed intensively at sea, their stomach fullness index ranging from 15-70 parts per thousand. There is some difference in diet between the two species, but the bulk of their food consists of harpacticoids, gammarids, and pupal tendipedids (Bakshtansky and Nilova, 1965). Predators affect the survival and even the behaviour of the immature fish greatly. Their effect should be considered at the same time as the characteristics of the downstream migration of the smolts. Early on in the acclimatisation work it was noted that immature pink and chum salmon migrate down the Kola River very slowly, and feed actively in the shallows and backwaters. As a result large ones may be caught about 50 km below the release area. (The mean length of pink salmon migrants can be 5 cm, and their mean weight over 1 g.) The larger the juvenile pink and chum are at their release into the Kola River, the faster their downstream migration. In 1959 the mean weight of pinks was 0·22 g, and their migration lasted 8 ten-day periods; in 1960 it was 0·36 g, and 5 ten-day periods; and in 1961 0·55 g and 2 ten-day periods. The immature chum behaved similarly. Some juveniles of both species are found in the river up to August (Bakshtansky, 1962b, 1963). Those released by the Uragubsky hatchery usually reached the sea on the day of release, a distance of about 4 km. When only a small group (200 000-300 000 fingerlings) were released, the fish did not reach the river but remained in the 2 km length of the hatchery brook. Their further migration was interrupted by frequent predatory attacks by young sea trout *(Salmo trutta)* and Atlantic salmon (Table I). When the number released was greater, the schools were larger, the same predators presented less of an obstacle to downstream migration, and the fingerlings reached the river and the Uragubinsky Gulf. The constant high light intensity of the polar day and the fact that the juveniles are always persecuted by freshwater and marine fish, whose splashes are seen at a great distance, allow long observations on the same small school of fingerlings. Among birds, the terns *(Sterna paradisea)* pursue pink and chum fingerlings intensively and successfully, a fact which also helps the observer. When the small fish reach the head of the gulf, the effect of the predators on their abundance increases considerably. Young cod, haddock *(Melanogrammus aeglefinus)*, and especially saithe *(Pollachius virens)* hunt for salmon so successfully, both close to the coast and at some distance from it, that a small school became few in number while we watched. The young salmon entering small gulfs and bays are blocked and detained there by the young cod and become stranded at the ebb, being forced to the edge of the water. The chum are more susceptible here, due to their more littoral mode of life (Bakshtansky, 1963, 1964a). The Umbsky hatchery releases the young salmon into the Umba River some 4 km from the estuary, where, due to a strong current, the majority moves down into the White Sea during the first

Table I. Number of pink and chum smolts found in predators' stomachs.

Fish species	Number of stomachs examined	Total number of smolts found	Greatest number of smolts in one stomach
Pike	41	182	180
Sea trout	26	315	165
Atlantic salmon	9	20	3
Cod	190	76	4
Saithe	20	62	6
Stickleback	220	5	1
Herring	102	304	23

day. An insignificant number are eaten by sea trout, young Atlantic salmon, pike *(Esox lucius)* and terns in the river, but herring *(Clupea harengus)* are a great danger to the smolts at sea. In 1962, the author observed a massacre of young pink and chum by herring. At night, when the greatest number of young salmon moved downstream herring entered the river mouth and even the fresh water. Up to 23 smolts of pink and chum salmon were recorded in the stomachs of 15-cm herring (Bakshtansky, 1964c). From 1959-1965 pink salmon catches were only large when herring had not been caught close to the Umba River at the time of the smolt migration. However, direct observations reveal the effect of predators on young salmon than much better the data of Table I. The pink and chum could be observed longer and further from the hatchery when the number of predators in the release area was lower. A month after moving downstream pink salmon caught at sea weighed about 1 g, and chum about 1·5 g.

Wild pink salmon move down the Kola Peninsula rivers in June-July over a period of about a month (Fig. 6), beginning as the temperature rises to 5°C and becoming more intense at 7-8°C. Though a great number of spawning areas are not far from estuaries, most of the fry move down without a yolk-sac, by schools as in the estuaries of large Pacific rivers. Kamyshnaya (1967) reprorted that "the shoals moved

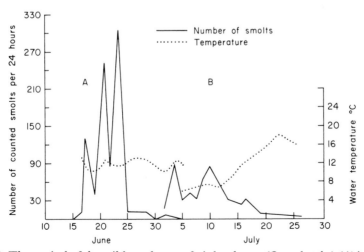

Fig. 6. The period of the wild smolt run of pink salmon *(O. gorbuscha) (A)* in the southern Kola Peninsula (Porya River) and *(B)* in the northern Kola Peninsula (Sydorovka River), 1974.

slowly in a river. They were feeding actively in the inlets and backwaters.'' The number of migrants is very difficult to determine, as under the polar day conditions the schools can avoid trap-nets with a small opening, as used in the Pacific ocean basin. Large pink salmon fry are seldom caught by these nets, but trap-nets overlapping a river will take the larger young. Therefore all counts of wild smolts are very rough (Fig. 5). It is unlikely that the number of wild pink migrants could be greater than tens of millions in the European north, and the highest count of these was recorded in 1978 when about 260 000 migrated downstream from the small Porya River alone (Data of Salmor and Neklyudov). The size of the wild smolts always increases with time during the migration in different rivers. Very large smolts were observed in the Soyana River throughout the migration period in 1974, the largest reaching 3 g and 7 cm.

The young pink salmon feed mainly on benthos in the drift of rivers. In 1963 their stomach content index was high, at over 40 parts per thousand, when caught close to the spawning areas of the Ponoy River affluents. Pupal chironomids and larval midges mainly were eaten; larval chironomids, mayfly nymphs, springtails and water mites were eaten to a lesser extent (Grinyuk and Shustov, 1977). In the Soyana River their intensity of feeding was considerably lower (1-90 parts per thousand). In this river their increase in size and reduction of fat content may be explained as follows: young pink salmon must migrate tens of kilometres past a great number of grayling *(Thymallus thymallus)* and young Atlantic salmon, under polar day conditions and very transparent water. Besides that, their number was very small. These circumstances hinder their migration and their feeding, and they apparently often have to hide among stones, as evidenced by the presence of gobies *(Cottus gobio)* up to 1·2 cm in length in their stomachs. Large pink salmon smolts, like those of Atlantic salmon, feed mainly on caddis-fly pupae, mayfly larvae, and adult insects (Bakshtansky and Chucksina, 1977).

DISCUSSION

Pink salmon always attract the attention of acclimatisers due to their high abundance and early downstream migration of young, but their return is seldom a success in a new area. In the 1920s they achieved successful runs in the State of Maine, U.S.A.; several generations reproduced in rivers of this area, but later they disappeared. At the end of the 1960s pink salmon returned successfully in Newfoundland, Canada, over a number of years, but then this temporary population disappeared as well (Lear, Chapter 12). When the causes of disappearance of temporary pink salmon populations from these areas are sought, the climatic peculiarities of the acclimatisation area are usually studied very thoroughly, as well as the area of origin of the eggs, the number of eggs transported and young released, and other factors. Attention is rarely paid to the peculiarities of the fish itself; its population structure and the necessity for a very wide specific spawning area create the greatest difficulties in attempting to acclimatise this species (Bakshtansky, 1968; Gritsenko and Bakshtansky, 1975). Almost all pink salmon become mature at age 1 + . If the whole population of eggs or young in a river dies, as has been observed in the Pacific, the area of pink salmon habitation would be reduced and the species could disappear. In such a situation other salmons are protected by a complex age structure and repeated spawning. As opposed to char, trout and several other salmons which may be characterised as having "protection in time", pink salmon has "protection in space", through an enormous abundance of small downstream migrants, large spawning and feeding areas, and an imprecise homing instinct, allowing it to reoccupy lost spawning areas.

The spawning area of pink salmon is not only larger than that of a number of other salmon but, more importantly, the conditions for development of the eggs and survival of the young are very variable. In their native range their rivers have a mixed source of water: a surface supply from snow or rain, and a subsurface one from groundwater. Dependent on the ratio of these two sources, the temperature regimes of the rivers vary considerably. Such conditions guarantee the pink salmon a successful reproduction over at least a part of the area, and explains why it is difficult to create stable pink salmon populations in a new area at their acclimatisation.

The greatest amount of work on pink salmon acclimatisation has been carried out in the Barents and White Sea basins over the past 20 years. During this period the hatcheries released about 200 000 000 smolts both in the north and the south of the Kola Peninsula, and in Arkhangel'sk District. The large scale of this programme has permitted some success. During the recent odd years migration became regular in the White, Barents and Norwegian Seas, and Soviet and Norwegian fishermen have studied this subject carefully because it helps them to increase their salmon catches.

Good condition and high fat content (about 10%) show that pink salmon find adequate food in the Atlantic ocean, so it is possible to increase the salmon catches in the northern Atlantic considerably, with the help of a complex of measures connected with their reproduction and acclimatisation.

Besides the topics covered in this chapter, details of pink salmon development north of the Arctic circle have been studied, as well as the possibility of regulating their maturation processes, and the effects of parasite infestations. Much time and effort were spent on observations of the spawning runs of pink salmon, the condition of eggs in the redds, and their downstream migration. Many problems remain to be solved in the future.

ACKNOWLEDGEMENTS

Much help has been given me during field and experimental studies by many colleagues of the Polar Research Institute of Marine Fisheries and Oceanography (PINRO), to whose Deputy Director, M. Y. Yakovenko, I am extremely grateful for the use of the Institute's data during the preparation of this chapter. My great thanks are also due to the chief of the Fish Culture Department of Glavrybvod, L. V. Polikashin, who helped me greatly in obtaining data on the pink salmon runs, counts, and survival at the hatcheries of the local "Atlantic" pink salmon eggs; and to J. E. Thorpe, who helped in the preparation of this Chapter.

REFERENCES

Azbelev, V. V., Bakshtansky, E. L., Surkov, S. S., Hushin, R. S. and Yakovenko, M. Y. (1962). The results of Soviet investigations into the acclimatization of pink salmon (Oncorhynchus gorbuscha) in the waters of the Barents Sea and White Sea. Conceil Permanent International Pour l'Exploration de la Mer. Annales Biologiques, Salmon and Trout, vol. XVII, pp. 240-242.
Azbelev, V. V. and Yakovenko, A. A. (1963). Materials on acclimatization of pink salmon in the basins of the Barents and White Seas. Trudy PINRO, issue 15, pp. 7-26, Moscow.

Bakshtansky, E. L. (1962a). Pink salmon inhabiting a lake. Scientific-technical Bulletin. PINRO, No. 4 (22), pp. 46-47, Murmansk.

Bakshtansky, E. L. (1962b). The descent of pink and chum salmon down the Kola Peninsula Rivers. ICES, Salmon and trout comm. No. 105, p. 3.

Bakshtansky, E. L. (1963). Observations for the downstream running of the pink salmon and chum in the European North. Trudy PINRO, issue 15, pp. 35-43, Moscow.

Bakshtansky, E. L. (1964a). Estimation of the detriment caused to salmon young by cod. Collection of articles of scientific-technical information. Issue I, pp. 40-41, Moscow, VNIRO.

Bakshtansky, E. L. (1964b). Experiments on the survival of the pink salmon young at different temperature of marine water. Collection of articles of scientific-technical information, issue 4, pp. 21-27, Moscow, VNIRO.

Bakshtansky, E. L. (1964c). Effect on predators on pink salmon young *Oncorhynchus gorbuscha* (Walb.) and *Oncorhychus keta* (Walb.) in the White and Barents Seas. Voprosy Ichtyologii, 4, issue 1 (30), pp. 136-141, Moscow.

Bakshtansky, E. L. (1965). The impact of the environmental factors on survival of the Far Eastern young salmon during the acclimatization of the latter in the North-west part of the USSR. ICNAF, Spec. publ. No. 6, pp. 447-479.

Bakshtansky, E. L. (1968). Peculiarities of pink salmon population due to their acclimatization in the Northern Atlantic. Collection of articles. The problems of acclimatization of fish and invertebrates in the basins of the USSR.'' pp. 46-50. Science Publishing House, Moscow.

Bakshtansky, E. L. and Nilova, O. I. (1965). Feeding of pink salmon and

Bakshtansky, E. L. (1970). Downstream running of pink salmon and chum and the reasons explaining their later approach into the Kola Peninsula Rivers. Collection of articles of VNIRO, v.XXIV, pp. 129-143, Moscow.

Bakshtansky, E. L. and Niolova, O. I. (1965). Feeding of pink salmon and chum in the White and Barents Seas. Collection of articles MMBI, issue 9 (13). pp. 106-111. Science Publishing House, Moscow and Leningrad.

Bakshtansky, E. L. and Chucksina, N. A. (1977). Some data on feeding and food relationships of young downstream-migrant pink salmon and Atlantic salmon. ICES, Anadromous and catadromous fish comm., M:5, pp. 1-12.

Grinyuk, I. N. and Shustov, Y. Q. (1977). Biology of chum yearlings and the young of other fish species of the Ponoya River basin. Collection of articles of PINRO, issue 32, pp. 79-80.

Gritsenko, O. F. and Bakshtansky, E. L. (1975). Perspectives of acclimatiz-ation of the Pacific salmon *Oncorhynchus* genus. Collection of articles of VNIRO, v.CVI, pp. 114-122, Moscow.

Gritsevskay, G. L. (1963). Hydrological conditions in the rivers of Karelia pouring into the White Sea. Materials of the fishery research investigations of the Northern Basin. Collection of articles N 1, pp. 36-39, Murmansk.

Kamyshnania, M. S. (1967). Downstream running and behaviour of acclimatized young of pink salmon. Rybnoye Chozyaistvo, No. 1, pp. 9-12.

Chapter 14

Salmon Ranching in South America

T. JOYNER

1515 4th Avenue North, Seattle, Washington 98109, U.S.A.

INTRODUCTION

Western Civilisation reached the southern end of South America with
Ferdinand Magellan in the year 1520, but it was not until the latter
part of the nineteenth century that it became sufficiently well established there to bring about significant changes in the regional ecology.
Between 1826 and 1836, extensive surveys of the southern South
American coast were conducted by the British Admiralty with the ships
Adventure and *Beagle*. Spurred by concern that British activity in the area
might threaten its sovereignty in the Strait of Magellan, Chile
established the first permanent settlements on the Strait at Fuerte
Bulnes in 1843 and at Punta Arenas in 1849. The latter quickly became
the commercial and administrative centre of the region. An Argentine
presence in the area began to develop in the last quarter of the
nineteenth century in response to Argentina's need to support its
territorial claims in southern Patagonia and in Tierra del Fuego, which
were being contested by Chile. The Chilean and Argentine settlements
in the far south soon produced ecological effects common to the
advance of Western Civilisation in other parts of the world. Native
organisms that were valuable or were nuisances to the new colonists
were rapidly depleted, and exotic organisms were introduced, either
inadvertently or deliberately. Sheep, cattle and salmonid fishes are
notable examples of the latter.

Early in the twentieth century, sport fishermen in Chile and

Argentina instigated the importation into their countries of European and North American stocks of trout and salmon. This was followed by the development of hatcheries for the propagation of the introduced stocks. These efforts are being continued in both countries, where they are regulated by governmental resource management agencies. As a result, several species of trout and a landlocked variety of Atlantic salmon were successfully established and became popular targets for

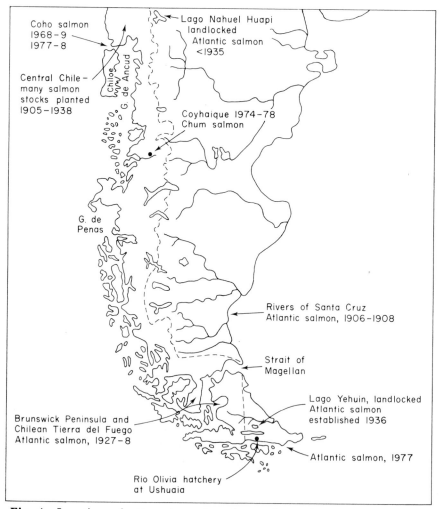

Fig. 1. Location of attempts to introduce salmon into southern South America.

sport fishermen. On the other hand, attempts to introduce sea-going salmon species have consistently failed.

The similarities of climate and hydrology with those parts of the Northern Hemisphere in which salmon are abundant that inspired sport fishing enthusiasts to try repeatedly to introduce salmon into southern South America, have recently attracted the attention of prospective commercial salmon ranchers. To evaluate the prospects for

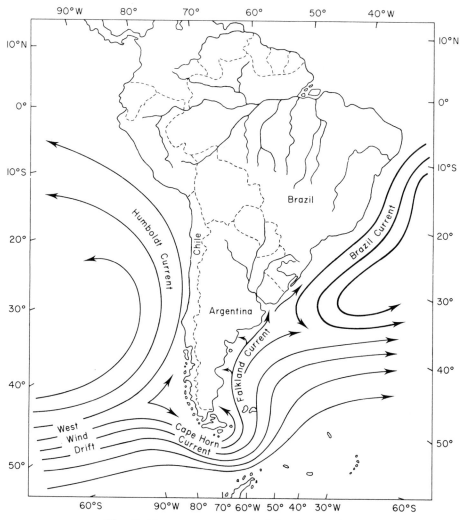

Fig. 2. Ocean currents around South America.

salmon ranching in that part of the world properly, all the environments that salmon would be likely to encounter, as well as their
probable migration routes, should be considered. There may also be
some valuable lessons in the records of previous attempts to introduce
salmon into South America that can be uncovered. The following
paragraphs and Fig. 1 present what I have been able to learn of that
history in Chile, Argentina and Brazil. My sources were the very
sparse records that are available and personal communications with
those involved. I have also reviewed briefly the major surface current
patterns prevailing around the coasts of southern South America (Fig.
2) which should help to provide interested readers with a preliminary
basis for making reasoned guesses as to where salmon, released along
these coasts, might possibly go during their ocean migrations.

CHILE

Chileans have long dreamed of introducing salmon into their country.
The dream has been doubly reinforced: first, by the successful introduction into Chile from Europe of several species of trout; and
secondly, by the successes in New Zealand with the introduction of
quinnat salmon, a sea-going species better known as chinook, from
California.

Introductions of trout and salmon began in Chile in the year 1905
(Club Deportivo de Pesca y Caza de Punta Arenas, 1954). The first
shipments, from Hamburg, Germany contained fertilised eggs of
brown *(Salmo trutta)*, rainbow *(Salmo gairdneri)* and brook trout *(Salvelinus
fontinalis)* and of Atlantic salmon *(Salmo salar)*. Subsequent shipments of
coho *(Oncorhynchus kisutch)*, chinook *(O. tschawytscha)*, and sockeye
salmon *(O. nerka)* eggs came from the United States. These
introductions depended entirely on fertilised eggs shipped from abroad
until 1914, when a hatchery newly built on the banks of the Rio Cautín
near the town of Lautaro, began to produce eggs and fry for stocking in
the streams and lakes of Chile. Other hatcheries were subsequently
built, and large numbers of salmonids were planted in the rivers and
lakes between 33° and 42° S. latitude. The stocking of the rivers and
streams in the vicinity of the Strait of Magellan began in 1927. Two
successive shipments were received in Punta Arenas from the hatchery
at Lautaro in 1927 and 1928. Each contained 400 000 eggs, mostly of

brown trout, but also some of Atlantic salmon. These were planted in relatively small lots in a number of streams on the Brunswick Peninsula, Última Esperanza and in Chilean Tierra del Fuego. In 1936, 4000 eggs of rainbow trout were planted in a small creek flowing into Seno Skyring. In 1941 and 1942, additional plantings of brown and rainbow trout eggs, totalling 600 000, were made in the rivers of the Brunswick Peninsula, especially those flowing into Seno Otway.

The introductions of trout were a stunning success. They exploded into ecological niches left vacant by the devastation to freshwater life wrought by Pleistocene glacial advances. Aided by the diligent, often arduous efforts of dedicated sport fishermen, who packed eggs into remote areas far beyond the reach of roads, trout have spread to nearly every stream between central Chile and Cape Horn, a distance of over 2500 kilometres. In the far south, some of these trout take up sea-run life. Browns and rainbows especially sometimes leave their native rivers to feed on the abundant plankton in the fjords, channels and sounds of the Chilean Archipelago. When they return to their natal streams to spawn, many of these large, red-fleshed sea trout weigh over 5 kg. These specimens, called ''salmon'' by local inhabitants, are highly prized by sport fishermen. At Puerto Bories on the Golfo Almirante Montt, they are sometimes caught in the set nets of commercial fishermen as they move through a narrow strait on their way to spawning beds in the Río Serrano.

All attempts at introducing salmon into Chile have so far failed. Between 1905 and 1938, stocks of Atlantic, coho, chinook and sockeye salmon were repeatedly planted in Chilean lakes and streams. The record is woefully incomplete with respect to the numbers planted and the lakes and rivers to which they were distributed. The records of the hatchery at Lautaro do show the dates and numbers of the eggs of several species of salmon that were incubated there. It would appear that except for those planted in the vicinity of the Strait of Magellan in 1927, 1928, 1936, 1941 and 1942, most of the plantings were made in the area between Valparaiso and Puerto Montt. I was unable to find any reliable evidence relating to the results of these plantings. From time to time, sportsmen fishing for trout in the rivers of central Chile have reported catching unusually large specimens that they are prone to call ''salmon''. The few seen by competent taxonomists have usually turned out to be sea-run brown trout. The old records from the Lautaro hatchery show what appears to be the continuous production of Atlantic salmon from 1916 to 1938. A substantial egg take peaked in 1932 at 1 120 000. This would suggest that the operators of the hatchery had available to them a population of about 500 adult female Atlantic salmon and enough males to fertilise the eggs. Whether these fish were from a stock landlocked in freshwater or from a successfully established migratory stock is not clear. There is no evidence of such a stock anywhere in Chile today.

Interest in the prospects for introducing salmon into Chile began to build again in the 1960s. In 1965 and 1966, the Instituto de Fomento Pesquero undertook extensive surveys of potential salmon habitats from Puerto Montt to Tierra del Fuego. In a report summarising the results of these surveys, De Witt and Soto Bussard (1969) concluded that the entire region surveyed appeared favourable for the introduction of salmon. They based their conclusion on an analysis of stream gradients, potential obstacles to fish passage, textures and porosities of stream beds, water quality, availability of suitable food organisms and the apparent lack of predators in potential nursery waters. De Witt and Soto Bussard suggested coho for salmon stocking experiments in Chile. They felt that, for this species, the high levels of costs and effort required for the long period of rearing would be more than offset by higher post-release survival and earlier returns than could be expected with earlier-smolting species.

According to Basulto (1969), a total of 180 000 fertilised eggs of coho salmon were obtained from Oregon and Washington in 1968 and 1969. They were taken to the hatchery of Río Blanco, North-east of Santiago, high on the slopes of the Andes mountains. After incubation was completed, the fry were reared for one full year in water from a mountain spring. The smolted fry were transported in a semi-anaesthetised state to a planting site near Puerto Montt, a distance of about 1300 kilometres. The coho were reared at Río Blanco rather than at the hatcheries at Lautaro or Polcura which are closer to Puerto Montt, because during the Chilean summer the water temperatures at the latter two are too high for the satisfactory incubation of eggs begun at the onset of the northern winter in Oregon and Washington. The stream in which the coho were planted flows into Reloncaví Sound, a semi-enclosed body of saltwater that opens into the Gulf of Ancud. The latter separates the mainland from the island of Chiloé. The smolts were reported to have survived the long trip from Río Blanco in good condition. Since they were planted close to an arm of the sea where they might be expected to find suitable feed and sufficient space to avoid heavy predation by trout, there were high expectations for success. However, there is no evidence that these coho ever returned to the planting site, or that any were ever captured in the fisheries of Reloncaví Sound or the Gulf of Ancud.

In 1969, Chilean interest in the introduction of Pacific salmon received a further stimulus from Japan. Experts from the Japan Fisheries Association, working with biologists from the Chilean Agriculture Ministry's Division of Fisheries Protection, undertook a two-year survey of the potential of Chilean waters resources to support the acclimatisation and culture of Pacific salmon. After a wide search, the interest of the Japanese experts narrowed to the Río Simpson watershed in the south central zone of Aisen. In 1971 the work continued with the assistance of the Japan International Cooperation Agency. A site was selected on the Río Claro near its junction with the Simpson, at the town of Coyhaique. The hatchery site is about 70 kilometres upstream from the head of navigation on Aisen Fjord.

In November 1972 (Nagasawa and Aguilera, 1974), 150 000 eyed eggs of cherry salmon *(Oncorhynchus masou)* from the September run in the Mena River in Hokkaido were shipped by air to temporary rearing facilities in the Río Claro. In January 1973, the 85 000 surviving fry were released into the Claro and their subsequent growth was monitored in the river for a period of 56 days. The rate of growth proved to be higher than in their native river in Hokkaido. This is not surprising, as the growth occurred during the Chilean summer rather than in the winter in Japan. In 1974, the seeding experiments were continued with chum salmon *(O. keta)* from the Tokachi River in Hokkaido (Nagasawa and Aguilera, 1976). By 1975, a permanent hatchery with a capacity for incubating 5 000 000 eggs was completed near Coyhaique. Built with Chilean funds, it was named in honour of Dr Yoshikazu Shiraishi, a Japanese ecologist who died in Coyhaique while working on the project. From 1974-76, 2 000 000 eggs were shipped each year from Japan to Coyhaique. The shipments were increased to 4 000 000 in 1977. The fry are being released in January and May, just after yolk-sac absorption. It is planned to continue the releases through 1978.

Although there were no returns from the 1973 release of cherry salmon, none was expected: it was merely a small-scale experiment for observing the growth of the fry in the river. There were hopes for returns in 1977 of up to 2700 adults from the 1974 release of chum salmon but none appeared. Only time will tell whether the subsequent introductions of chum salmon into Aisen will prove successful.

In 1975 and 1976, an international team of Chilean, American and British experts surveyed the potential for salmon ranching in the southernmost Chilean zone of Magallanes (Nash *et al.*, 1976). Funding was provided by the Rockefeller and Tinker Foundations and logistic support by the Chilean Navy, the Institute for Fishery Development, and the Division of Fisheries Protection. The team concluded that: (1) freshwater suitable for hatcheries was available in the zone; (2) the fjords, channels and sounds of the region were suitable for becoming nurseries for juvenile salmon; and (3) offshore currents should carry seaward migrants to ocean feeding areas from which it should be possible for them to return.

In 1976, the Union Carbide Corporation in Chile, aided by experts from the Union Carbide subsidiary, Domsea Farms, Inc. of Bremerton, Washington, began an experimental salmon-ranching venture near the town of Ancud on the island of Chiloé. During the summer of 1977-78, 100 000 coho smolts were released from the small lake in which they had been reared into an outlet stream that flows into the Gulf of Ancud. These cohos were from a stock native to the Baker River in Washington. It remains to be seen whether these latest releases of coho into the Gulf of Ancud will be any more successful than those of 1968-69 (see Chapter 20).

ARGENTINA

The factual information relating to Argentina was kindly provided by Dr Pedro H. Bruno Videla, who has been involved personally with the production and management of salmonids in Argentina for many years. Its interpretation, as presented here, is entirely the responsibility of the author.

In common with several other countries in the temperate parts of the Southern Hemisphere, salmonid stocks from North America and Europe were imported into Argentina early in the twentieth century. The first Argentine attempts to acclimatise salmon began in 1905 and continued through 1910. Quinnat *(Oncorhynchus tschawyscha)*, coho, sockeye and Atlantic salmon, along with several species of trout were all planted during this period, but without success. However, by the 1930s, permanent stocks of landlocked Atlantic salmon (Sebago Lake variety), brown trout, rainbow trout, and brook trout had become established at San Carlos de Bariloche on Lake Nahuel Huapi, in the mountains of the Territory of Río Negro. Eggs of Sebago salmon, shipped from Bariloche to Lago Yehuin in Tierra del Fuego by Dr Bruno Videla during the years 1935-37, resulted in the successful acclimatisation of a salmon species in the far south. These salmon, along with the brown, rainbow and brook trout, also successfully introduced in Tierra del Fuego, are now highly prized by sport fishermen and are rigorously protected by the government.

Among the unsuccessful attempts to acclimatise sea-going salmon in Argentina during 1905-1910, were those of 1906 and 1908, in which eggs of Atlantic salmon were planted in the penultimate southern territory of Santa Cruz. Largely due to the high esteem that Argentines hold for Atlantic salmon, particularly the Sebago Lake variety which they do have, another attempt is currently being made to introduce sea-going Atlantics, this time in Tierra del Fuego. A hatchery has been built on the banks of the Río Olivia at Ushuaia on the Beagle Channel. It has a heated incubation room with a capacity for hatching and holding 700 000 eggs through the period of yolk-sac absorption. Outside are 18 cement raceways for the rearing of fry. In addition, a stretch of the river in front of the hatchery that is bounded upstream by impassable waterfalls and downstream by the sea, can be used as a kilometre-long raceway.

In 1975 and 1977, fertilised eggs of Atlantic salmon were shipped from Moncton, New Brunswick (via Montreal) to the Río Olivia hatchery at Ushuaia. The 1975 shipment consisted of 100 000 eggs; that of 1977 contained 83 500. Owing to the extreme coldness of the hatchery water (in the bitter winter of 1976 it dropped to 0°C for three months), the growth of the 1975 hatch was very slow. Nevertheless, by the summer of 1977, 40 000 surviving fingerlings were distributed to a number of rivers throughout Argentine Tierra del Fuego. Since Ushuaia lies in the rain shadow of nearby mountains, it receives a substantial amount of winter sunshine. Dr Bruno Videla is planning to take advantage of this by installing solar heating units to boost the temperature of the water supplied to the incubators and indoor rearing tanks.

BRAZIL

The following information concerning the attempt to transplant
chinook salmon from California to Brazil was obtained from Mr
William Ellis Ripley, Fisheries Adviser to the United Nations Development Programme in New York.

In 1958, while working with the U.S. Agency for International
Development, Mr Ripley arranged for the shipment of 400 000

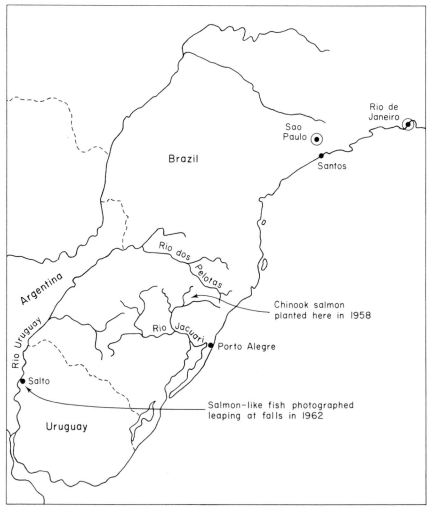

Fig. 3. Experimental planting of chinook salmon in Brazil and possible
recovery in Uruguay.

fertilised eggs of chinook salmon to the State of Río Grande do Sul, Brazil. The eggs came from the Nimbus hatchery on the American River in California and were carefully planted in artificial nests in the upper reaches of the Río Caí, the Tainhos and the Río dos Antos, tributaries of the Río Jaquarí (Fig. 3). The nests were built where the conditions in the stream beds closely resembled those of the spawning beds of the parent stock in the American River. Control samples, planted in Vibert boxes, produced a hatch of 70%.

Although there were no subsequent reports of adult salmon returning to the Río Jaquarí, four years after the planting of the eggs a number of large fish of a species unknown to the local residents, were seen leaping at the impassable falls at Salto on the Río Uruguay. This behaviour continued for a period of two to three weeks. A photograph of the leaping fish was shown to Dr Emilio Varoli, former director of the Fish and Game Division of the State of Sao Paulo, who reported that they appeared to him to be salmon.

ANALYSIS

When several species of trout and a landlocked variety of Atlantic salmon were brought from Europe and North America to southern South America, they adapted readily to the new environment. Sea-run variants of brown and rainbow trout exhibiting salmon-like appearance and behaviour soon developed. Along with the obvious similarities of climate and topography with Northern Hemisphere countries where salmon are native, these successful acclimatisations stimulated repeated attempts to transplant sea-going salmon to the southern half of the continent. To date, these efforts have failed to produce a single sustaining population of such fish anywhere in South America. Although the evidence is far from conclusive, it does seem possible that some of these fish may have returned successfully from the sea, but at locations inappropriate for their proper identification by competent observers, and in numbers insufficient for the establishment of self-sustaining stocks.

The possible reasons for these failures are many, but those that seem most likely can be grouped conveniently into the following categories: excessive freshwater mortality, too great disperson in planting, and selection of planting sites without sufficient consideration of the offshore conditions to be encountered by salmon migrating out to sea.

Excessive Freshwater Mortalities

These could have been induced by inappropriate handling of eggs and fry or by poor water and stream-bed conditions (freezing, floods, dry-outs, siltation). However, conceding that, for the most part, great care was probably taken with incubation, planting and the selection of good water and gravel, a likely major cause of freshwater mortality may well have been predation on salmon fry by previously established stocks of trout.

Planting too Thinly

Many of the sport fishermen and sport fishery managers who conducted the early attempts to transplant salmon into the southern part of South America were mainly interested in seeding as many streams as possible within their areas of interest. They had observed that small plantings could be spread over a wide area to produce dominant populations of trout and landlocked salmon in virgin lakes and streams. The technique did not work with sea-going salmon stocks. They apparently failed to consider the fact that the number initially needed to produce a breeding population must be far greater for sea-going salmon than for freshwater trout. Compared to the relatively limited space of the lakes and rivers inhabited by the trout, the vast spaces of the open ocean into which salmon venture can easily swallow up the small populations produced by limited plantings.

Point of Entry into the Sea

Ocean currents are features of the environment of great significance to salmon, but are only rarely encountered by trout and were therefore seldom considered by the trout-fishing enthusiasts who instigated the early attempts to introduce salmon into South America. An exception was Basulto (1969), who noted that immature salmon generally swim with the current. Young salmon entering the sea for the first time do so in search of more and better food. If offered a choice, they will pursue targets of a size appropriate to the size of their bite. According to Antezana (personal communication), the size of the zooplankton samples caught during a cruise in the channels of the Chilean Archipelago increased as the sampling progressed seaward. One would therefore suspect that salmon released along the Chilean coast would move seaward as they grew. This would soon subject them to the influence of the ocean currents that impinge upon that coast. Assuming that their pursuit of prey would be more random than directional, they would move generally along with the current unless unusual changes in the concentration of food, or of temperature and salinity, impelled them to move across or counter to the direction of the current. Studies by Royce *et al.* (1968), French and McAlister (1970), and Bakkala (1970) suggest that ocean currents and seasonal changes in the environment do indeed exert powerful influences on the distribution in the North Pacific Ocean of immature sockeye salmon from Alaska's Bristol Bay.

In the Southern Ocean, the principal feature of surface flow is the circumpolar West Wind Drift. The flow diverges where part of it strikes the coast of South America at about latitude 50°S. The northern component becomes the Humboldt Current, which sweeps northward along the Chilean coast and then veers offshore off the coast of Peru. Flowing to the north-west, it mingles ultimately with the westward-flowing South Equatorial Current. The inshore part of the southern component of the divergence, the Cape Horn Current, swings around the southern end of the continent to become the Falkland Current. This cold current flows northward over the Patagonian Shelf. It is bounded offshore by the warm, southward-flowing Brazil Current, producing a situation not unlike that prevailing off the coasts of Labrador and north-eastern Japan, where cold, equatorward-moving currents are bounded offshore by warm, poleward-moving currents.

CONCLUSIONS

Chile

The numerous attempts to introduce salmon during the first half of the twentieth century were special cases of the largely successful effort to establish trout as a game fish in that country. The repeated failures with salmon probably resulted from: (1) excessive mortalities in salmon fry resulting from predation by trout already established in the streams in which the salmon were planted; (2) planting too thinly and in numbers insufficient to overcome the high initial ocean mortalities to be expected with transplanted salmon stocks; and (3) planting at locations where offshore currents carried sea-going salmon into waters from which they could not return. Although the second factor has probably not been significant in the recent attempts to introduce chum salmon into Chile, the first and third could be causing problems. The third factor may well have prevented the return of the 1968-69 releases of coho into the Gulf of Ancud and could cause difficulties with the current attempts to introduce the same species at the same general location.

It would seem that the best opportunities for the successful establishment of salmon ranching in Chile could be gained by releasing large numbers of smolts, vigorous and ready to go to sea, of carefully chosen stocks below latitude 50°S. The inner channels and sounds of Última Esperanza and Magallanes, with their low-salinity water and abundant zooplankton, should prove to be excellent nurseries for juvenile salmon. Smolts migrating seaward through the outer channels would encounter the Cape Horn Current, which should lead them to satisfactory ocean pastures in the Atlantic off the coast of Argentina.

Argentina

Attempts early in this century to introduce salmon into the Territories of Santa Cruz and Tierra del Fuego probably failed from a combination of heavy predation by trout and by planting too thinly. Unlike the situation in Chile, however, the planting sites were favourably located with respect to offshore currents. Without sufficient numbers heading seaward from any given planting site, the probabilities of return of the initial year classes were apparently insurmountably small. It is significant that, in Argentina, landlocked Atlantic salmon did become established, whereas sea-going stocks of the same species did not. The attempt currently being made to introduce sea-going Canadian stocks into Tierra del Fuego may encounter the same difficulties as those experienced in earlier attempts, as the fry, so carefully reared in the new hatchery at Ushuaia, are being scattered rather thinly over a large number of streams.

Brazil

The 1958 experiment, in which 400 000 fertilised eggs of California chinooks were planted in several tributaries of the Río Jaquarí in Brazil's state of Río Grande do Sul (Fig. 3), presents some intriguing possibilities. In the first place, the apparent survival through hatching of 70% of the transplanted eggs, even with a subsequent river mortality of 90%, would have produced 28 000 smolts ready to go to sea. The seaward migration would have been during the southern winter, when the influence of the Falkland Current with entrained freshwater from the Río de la Plata would have been at its northernmost maximum off the coast of southern Brazil. The seaward migrants would not have had much opportunity for straying because of the nearness, to the north and east, of boundaries of warm water from the Brazil Current. The young salmon would have been confined close inshore, with their only option for travelling being a southward route toward favourable ocean pastures over the Patagonian Shelf.

The sighting of salmon-like fish trying to leap the falls of the Río Uruguay four years after the planting of the chinooks in nearby Brazil, suggests that salmon, having survived 3 + years in the ocean off the coast of Argentina, may have headed back to the north upon reaching maturity. When they encountered the freshwater plume of the Río de la Plata (the northward extension of which they might have encountered when they first ventured out to sea from Brazil), they could have turned into the enormous La Plata estuary. With several forks to choose from once within the estuary, it may be significant that the Río Uruguay (the one in which the salmon-like fish were photographed) rises in the same swamp that serves as headwaters for the Jaquarí, the river system in which the eggs were originally planted.

Whether salmon did return from the South Atlantic to ascend the Río Uruguay in 1962 cannot be established definitely. However, analysis of the environmental circumstances that would have been encountered by these fish, shows that conditions along the east coast of southern South America could be quite favourable for the properly planned and executed experimental introduction of salmon.

REFERENCES

Bakkala, R. G. (1970). Distribution and migration of immature sockeye salmon taken by U.S. research· vessels with gillnets in offhsore waters. Bull. 27, Int. North Pac. Fish. Comm. (1971), 70 pp. (original source: NMFS INPFC Doc. 1293, 1970).
Basulto, S. (1969). Actualidad nacional. Hay no salmones en los rios chilenos. *Orbita* **2** (3), 77-84.

Club Deportivo de Pesca y Caza de Punta Arenas, Chile (1954). Origen de las especies salmonidas en los rios Magellanicos. Report. Sept. 1954. 15 pp.

De Witt, J. W. and Soto-Bussard, S. (1966). Survey of potential salmon habitats and the feasibility of introducing salmon into Chile. Report. Instituto de Fomento Pesquero, Santiago.

French, R. R. and McAlister, W. B. (1970). Winter distribution of salmon in relation to currents and water masses in the northeastern Pacific Ocean and migrations of sockeye salmon. *Trans. Am. Fish. Soc.* **99** (4), 649-663.

Nagasawa, A. and Aguilera, P. (1974). Introduction into Aisen, Chile of Pacific Salmon. No. 1. Report. Japan International Cooperation Agency, Tokyo. 21 pp.

Nagasawa, A. and Aguilera, P. (1974). Introduction into Aisen, Chile of Pacific Salmon. No. 2. Report. Japan International Cooperation Agency, Tokyo. 26 pp, plates.

Nash, C. E., Joyner, T. and Mayo, R. (1976). Seeding the Southern Ocean with Salmon. Report. International Center for Living Aquatic resources Management. Honolulu.

Royce, W. F., Smith, L. S. and Hartt, A. C. (1968). Models of oceanic migrations of Pacific salmon and comments on guidance mechanisms. *U.S. Fish and Wildl. Serv., Fish. Bull.* **66**, 441-462.

Chapter 15

Salmon in New Zealand

G. D. WAUGH

*Ministry of Agriculture and Fisheries, Fisheries
Research Division, P.O. Box 19062, Wellington, New Zealand*

SALMON INTRODUCTIONS

Atlantic Salmon *(Salmo salar)*

The early attempts to introduce Atlantic salmon to New Zealand are
well documented by Nicholls (1882). He describes how the first living
ova were received at Otago by the Local Acclimatisation Society in
1868. Such societies originally consisted of groups of interested settlers,
who introduced all manner of animals and plants from their native
countries into New Zealand, and had been created by Government and
given statutory powers to manage game fish and animals in their
respective districts (Fig. 1). The majority of the salmon fry from the
first consignment of ova died, but 500 survived and were subsequently
released into the Molyneux River (now the Clutha River) in November
1869 (Fig. 2). In 1873 about 600 fry survived from a consignment of
approximately 50 000 ova and in 1876 about 10 000 young fish were
hatched.

Brown trout *(S. trutta)* were also imported, released and grew to a
very large size; some even became sea-run but there is no evidence that
any Atlantic salmon released to sea ever returned. Despite the lack of
returns the various Societies persisted in bringing out ova, hatching
them and releasing either the fry or smolts. Thomson (1922) was very
critical of the lack of co-ordination and of the competition between the
Societies. However, this competition may help to explain why more

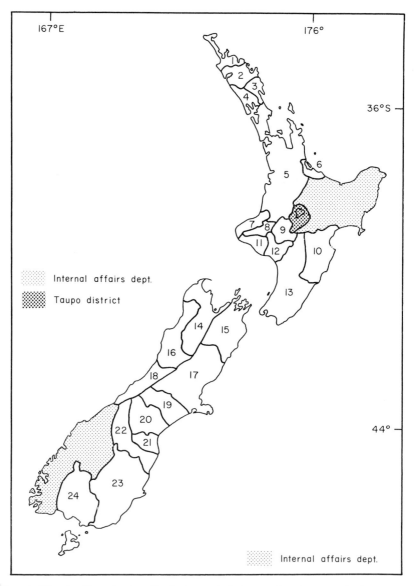

Fig. 1. The Acclimatisation Societies and their districts in New Zealand. The shaded regions are those administered by the Department of Internal Affairs, which acts as a Society in the Rotorua/Taupo and Southern Lakes districts.

(1) Mangonui-Whangaroa	(9) Waimarino	(17) North Canterbury
(2) Bay of Islands	(10) Hawke's Bay	(18) Westland
(3) Whangarei	(11) Hawera	(19) Ashburton
(4) Hobson	(12) Wanganui	(20) South Canterbury
(5) Auckland	(13) Wellington	(21) Waimate
(6) Tauranga	(14) Nelson	(22) Waitaki
(7) Taranaki	(15) Marlborough	(23) Otago
(8) Stratford	(16) West Coast	(24) Southland

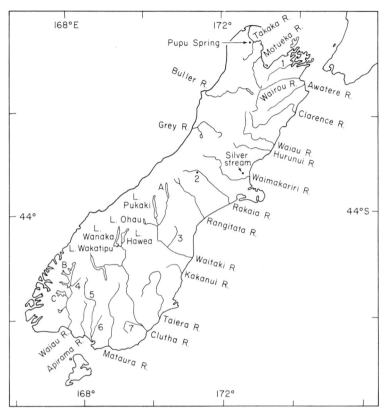

Fig. 2. Principal rivers and lakes of the South Island to which reference is made in the text.

(1) Pelorous R.   (5) Oreti R.   (A) L. Tekapo
(2) Glenariffe Stream   (6) Makarewa R.   (B) L. Te Anau
(3) Hakataramea R.   (7) Waipahi R.   (C) L. Manapouri
(4) Upukerora R.

than 5 million salmon eggs were imported to New Zealand and hatched and released during the period 1868 to 1911 despite the lack of evidence that a single specimen had ever returned from sea. The only success was the establishment of a freshwater stock in the L. Te Anau-Waiau River system (Calderwood, 1927; Hefford, 1927). Though there was no impediment to them doing so, the salmon did not migrate to sea but spawned in the tributaries and ranged widely in the lake. Whether these fish were derived from sea-going stock in the first place has been queried by Stokell (1955), who speculated that the fish may have originated from a 1905 consignment of American landlocked salmon. However, he also pointed out that some of the salmon hatched from earlier imports were retained at hatcheries until mature and that these fish were spawned and their fry subsequently released. Thus there is some possibility that fish were produced which lacked seaward migrating behaviour.

The effort to establish Atlantic salmon did not cease after 1911. The Southland Society, perhaps emboldened by the acclimatisation of quinnat salmon, *Oncorhynchus tschawytscha*, and believing that success might be achieved with salmon which did not migrate long distances, imported ova from Scotland in 1956 (Scott, 1960) and from Baltic stocks during the period 1960 to 1964. Proposals for the work to be done and reports on progress are contained in the Society's Annual Reports for the period from 1960 to 1965, but once again there was no success and the population seems to have declined. Graynoth (1971) showed that in the southern lakes the percentage of Atlantic salmon in the anglers' catch declined from 24% to 1% between 1947 and 1967.

Quinnat Salmon *(Oncorhynchus tschawytscha)* (Fig. 3)

The first consignment of Chinook or quinnat salmon was obtained by the Hawkes Bay Society in 1875 (Stokell, 1955) but, as many of the eggs were dead and others were hatching, they were immediately planted out in North Island rivers, principally the Waikato. In 1876 over 150 000 eggs were imported, of which 84 000 were sent to Southland for hatching. The Napier Society received 60 000 and other smaller lots were distributed through various North Island rivers. In 1877 about 275 000 ova were imported and again widely distributed, mostly in the North Island. However, some were sent to the South Island where 10 000 fry were liberated in the Waimakariri River, 10 000 in the Rangitata River and 3000 each in the Kakanui and Waipahi rivers. The Southland Society placed 35 000 eggs or fry in the Oreti River, 18 000 in the Makarewa and 10 000 in the Waipahi. A further importation was made by the Auckland Society in 1878, and some fry or smolts were liberated in an unspecified river in 1880. No further imports were made until 1901 when the government policy of intensive stocking for this species was implemented (see Ayson, 1910). In that year a shipment of 50 000 ova from California was divided between the Hakataramea (Fig. 4) and Lake Ohau hatcheries, and in

Fig. 3. A well-grown 4-year-old quinnat salmon.

Fig. 4. The old Hakataramea hatchery on a tributary of the Waitaki River. The hatchery was established in 1901 and continued to function until 1942 (C. L. Ayson).

1902 23 000 yearlings were liberated in tributaries of the Waitaki River. In 1903 32 000 two-year-old fish were liberated in the Hakataramea River. At the same time about 5400 fish between 3 and 4 years old were released together with 12 000 yearlings. Further shipments in 1906 and 1907, of half a million eggs each time, were divided between Ohau and Hakataramea but the greatest effort was devoted to the latter. By this time adult sea-run fish were returning, being stripped at the hatchery, and their progeny released. From then on the number of eggs stripped increased, with most of the fry and older fish released into the Hakataramea, so that by 1910 it was possible to export 25 000 ova to Tasmania and to release fish elsewhere in the South Island on both east and west coasts. No further importations were made but stripping of acclimatised fish continued until 1940. As a result of this policy a worthwhile run was developed in the Waitaki and was extended either by widespread liberation or straying to other rivers. By 1915 quinnat salmon were being taken by anglers at the mouths of the Waitaki, Rangitata and Rakaia rivers (Fig. 5) and by 1921 they had extended north to the Waiau and south to the Clutha.

Fig. 5. Anglers at the mouth of the Rakaia River at the beginning of the salmon season.

There are no records to show just when the fish began to return. Stokell (1955) quotes some inferential evidence to suggest that odd individuals may have been returning as early as 1898. However, the main point was that by 1907 a few sea-run fish were being caught. After protracted and prodigious effort plus considerable expenditure of funds, a salmon with an ocean-going phase in its life cycle was finally established in New Zealand waters.

Sockeye Salmon (Fig. 6)

Comparatively little attention seems to have been paid to the efforts to introduce the sockeye salmon *Oncorynchus nerka*. Only one successful consignment of 500 000 ova was received from Canada in 1901-1902, and from this about 150 000 fry were hatched at the Hakataramea hatchery. Of these, 5000 were liberated into tributaries of the Waitaki River, 90 000 into streams flowing into Lake Ohau, and 20 000 were retained at the hatchery. In 1903 10 000 eleven-month-old fish were released into the adjoining river and in 1903-1904 a further 6000 two-and-a-half year olds were liberated. By the end of 1904 about 2000 three-year-olds were left in the hatchery ponds and these too were released. Some were reported as returning to the Hakataramea to spawn and some were also taken in Lake Ohau. However, the fish were said to be small and in poor condition even though they were then thought to be sea-run. It seems rather surprising that if this were true, no further efforts were made to introduce the fish, but presumably the subsequent success of quinnat salmon reduced interest in the sockeye, which is, however, firmly established in Lake Ohau and regularly migrates between it and its tributary streams (Graynoth, in preparation). Some still enter the Hakataramea River to spawn and though able to migrate to sea have apparently developed a freshwater limited population. They appear to have been largely forgotten until the 1960s though they were known to occur in the Larch Stream (Flain, 1972). Recent work suggests that the stock could be increased in the Ohau system and the Waitaki River where they still persist in substantial numbers: 16 000 fish were estimated as spawning in the Larch Stream in 1977 with others spawning elsewhere. Four-year-olds were dominant with small numbers of 3- and 5-year-olds (Cameron, 1978). Sizes vary with season and lake of residence, but fish 52 cm long

Fig. 6. A 45-cm male sockeye salmon caught in the Larch Stream, L. Ohau (E. Graynoth).

and weighing 1·8 kg are not uncommon. With more knowledge of the requirements of the fish it may be possible to extend their range to other systems (Waugh, 1974; McDowall, 1978).

ESTABLISHMENT AND SPREAD OF QUINNAT SALMON

Although the Atlantic salmon and the trouts were introduced purely for sporting purposes and the attempts by the Societies to introduce quinnat salmon were for the same purpose, the government's objective in its concentrated efforts to introduce quinnat salmon into the Waitaki River was to establish a commercial fishery similar to that of the west coast of North America.

From 1925 to 1952 the fishery was managed by the then Marine Department. Rod selling licences were issued which permitted the holder to sell rod-caught fish. Commercial netting was also permitted under licence, but the total number of rod and netting licences issued each year was small and the catch of little significance. After 1952 the licences were abolished, but the Acclimatisation Societies of the Canterbury area undertook to supply for sale not less than 750 quinnat salmon each year. Most of these were taken from the tail race below the Highbank Power Station on the Rakaia River (see Hardy, 1972), but as water abstraction increased, the numbers of fish decreased and since 1959 none have been taken and no fish are marketed commercially, though the requirement still remains in force (Cunningham, 1972).

Either as a result of deliberate stocking (the records are not clear) or meandering by returning adults, the fish are widespread in the rivers of the east coast of the South Island from the Waiau south to the Clutha. They also occur in small numbers in the West Coast rivers and have been reported as occasionally occurring in rivers to the north, even in a few in the North Island. However, it seems that the fish, because of lack of suitable spawning sites, temperature limitations, or oceanic circulation may now have occupied all of the rivers available to them.

AGE AND GROWTH OF QUINNAT SALMON

For a number of years it was believed that the fish introduced to New Zealand grew less well than their North American counterparts.

However, Parrott (1971) and Flain (1972) exhaustively studied the scales from fish in all the principal rivers of the South Island and established that the average age of returning adults was younger than in North America. The dominant group in New Zealand is the three-year age class, followed by the four-year class. The two-year class is third most abundant and five-year-old fish are uncommon (Table I). None older than five years have been recorded.

Table I. Age-frequency distribution, mean lengths and mean weights of sea-run, angler-caught spawning quinnat salmon (from Galloway, 1976).

| Age-frequency distribution | | Mean lengths (cm) | Mean weights (kg) |
Age	(%)		
2	9·0	28	2·3
3	70·0	76	5·0
4	21·0	89	6·8
5	0·1	102	10·0

The size of the fish at any given age in the Northern and Southern Hemisphere is comparable but because no six-, seven- or eight-year-old salmon are present in New Zealand waters the average size of returning adults is substantially less than in North America.

There is no simple explanation for the earlier maturity in New Zealand, but recent work on Atlantic salmon (Thorpe, 1977) suggests that some hatchery-reared fish may develop more quickly and return to the waters in which they have been released at a younger age than wild stocks. If correct, this may help to explain why there are no New Zealand fish older than five years.

There may be a further explanation. Flain (1970) has described the characteristics and occurrence of precocious one-year-old males in New Zealand, where they are proportionately more abundant than in North America. They are fully mature and, if they remain in fresh water, are capable of surviving for a second or even third year (Flain, 1971). Gebhards (1960) has shown that in the U.S.A. such small fish participate in the spawning act. No similar observations have been made in New Zealand but if they do spawn and the small males are more abundant and survive to spawn again, there may be some continuing genetic selection for early maturation amongst the wild stocks. It further suggests that by selection of suitable males and females for stripping and subsequent rearing, the reverse may be possible and that a larger proportion of late-maturing fish could be developed. The availability of coded wire tags in New Zealand (Hopkins, 1977) now makes possible the evaluation of such manipulation of the stocks either at the Ministry of Agriculture and Fisheries hatchery at Silverstream or by commercial operators if their ocean ranching developments are successful.

FACTORS LIMITING THE SIZE OF STOCKS

The Recreational Nature of the Fishery

From 1959 to 1972, despite the fact that it was technically possible to take salmon for sale, none were marketed officially. The anglers and the Societies were strenuously opposed to any commercialisation of their recreational pursuits. They upheld the law which prohibited the sale of trout in New Zealand and contended that it should apply equally to salmon.

Except for a very few enclosed waters, all lakes and rivers are vested in the Crown and so are available for public use. Primarily to prevent the alienation by landowners or entrepeneurs of this unique right, a Bill to permit farming of salmon and trout was opposed by most of the Societies and by the Department of Internal Affairs, which manages the Rotorua/Taupo and Southern Lakes Conservancies in a manner similar to that of the Societies. The Bill became law in late 1972, but following a change of government it was substantially modified before the end of the year to permit only salmon farming and then only under a number of constraints.

In the meantime, despite representations by Society spokesmen and individual anglers, major modifications continued to be made to the freshwater environment to the detriment of the salmon (Waugh, 1975). Finally, most of the South Island Societies plus the Salmon Anglers Association, realising that their rivers were being progressively changed by impoundment and abstraction, and in some cases pollution, agreed that salmon runs must be augmented. Furthermore they recognised that this could best be done via commercial development—e.g. ocean ranching—of the salmon fisheries. With proper safeguards included in the commercial permits, the run of fish available to the anglers would be increased and at the same time a more readily identifiable value could be placed upon the rivers. Whether a more reasonable attitude by the anglers earlier would have secured better protection for the fisheries cannot now be answered, but the fact remains that in many rivers spawning tributaries have been inundated and barriers impassable to returning adults have been created on the rivers without compensating conditions for the fishes (Anderson, 1972).

The Seasonal Cycle

The principal spawning runs of salmon take place in summer and autumn. Fish begin to appear off the river mouths in November-December and the main upstream spawning takes place in March-April. It is during this period that river flows are reduced and upstream migration, even under natural flow conditions, tends to be restricted.

The Riverine Environment

None of the South Island east coast rivers is very long, and all except the Clutha are braided with unstable boulder strewn channels which cross the plains below the Southern Alps (Fig. 7). On the West Coast the rivers are even shorter and generally less stable. Many of the South Island rivers carry heavy loads of glacial flour which discolours them and causes silting away from the main channels. This heavy siltation plus the unstable nature of the river beds must limit the available food as well as the numbers of suitable spawning areas.

The upland tributaries suitable for spawning are generally fairly short and fast flowing, with few areas of quiet water. Even these tributaries are subject to flash floods which can destroy redds and so markedly affect the subsequent runs of returning adults. Galloway (1976) has shown that at Glenariffe on a tributary of the upper Rakaia river (Fig. 8) where the Ministry of Agriculture and Fisheries has established a salmon trap, the runs varied from a minimum of 424 to a maximum of 3045 in the period 1965 to 1978. Observations at the trap also show that at least 95% of the fry are swept out of the spawning streams into the main river within 48 hours of swim-up. This river, which is the least modified of those of the east coast, has little holding

Fig. 7. The lower Rakaia river, approximately 18 miles from the sea, showing the typical braided structure. At this point the river is 1·1 miles wide (National Publicity Studios).

water downstream and a very short estuary. Thus it is believed that few, if any, of the fry which leave their natal stream remain in the river and survive the rapid transition to the marine environment (Woolland, personal communication).

In all probability the lack of suitable holding water, either in the spawning streams or the main rivers, in which the fry can grow to the smolt stage, was the principal reason for the failure of fish to build up larger stocks. Local censuses and anglers diary schemes have been undertaken in the past (Graynoth, 1971, 1974; Graynoth and Skrsynski, 1974) but the results proved inconclusive in providing a realistic estimate for the actual size of the resources or a reliable indication of whether there has been any significant reduction in the size of the stocks following modifications to the various rivers. More detailed estimates for the total adult run in the Rakaia river in 1975-1976 and of the angler catch, have been made by West (in preparation) but even these estimates are subject to a substantial margin of error.

Fig. 8. The Ministry of Agriculture & Fisheries trap at Glenariffe on a tributary of the upper Rakaia river. Homing fish are deflected by the angled screen to the pound *(right centre)* where they are weighed and measured before passing further upstream. Outmigrant smolts that reach the trap are conveyed along to the small counting house to the left.

Impoundment and Abstraction

New Zealand depends to a substantial degree on hydroelectric power and the South Island rivers, which descend steeply from the Southern Alps before crossing the coastal plains, are convenient for impound-ment. Substantial dams (Fig. 9) have been created, i.e. Roxburgh on the Clutha river and Benmore and others in the Waitaki river, which

Fig. 9. The Benmore Dam on the upper Waitaki river. The dam retains a man-made lake 30½ square miles in area. The power station was commissioned in 1965 and is the second largest in New Zealand (National Publicity Studios).

completely deny access to spawning streams by returning adults. Many of the spawning streams themselves have been inundated by the storage lakes created behind the dams. In only two cases have any attempts been made to compensate for lack of spawning streams. The fish pass on the Waitaki river hydro dam was ill designed and never functioned satisfactorily, and the spawning race (Fig. 10 a, b) built lower down on the Waitaki below the Aviemore Dam was also not properly designed, has not been adequately managed, and has never been wholly successful.

Apart from impoundment for electricity generation there is a considerable demand for water for irrigation in the Canterbury and Otago areas, which are in the rain shadow of the Alps. Here again, until recently little or no provision was made to screen the river intakes, so that many out-migrating smolts are diverted to the irrigation systems and some are inevitably deposited on the land (Cunningham, 1972).

Fig. 10 (a). The Aviemore dam downstream from Benmore showing the spawning race in a hairpin to the left of the photograph. The fish ladder is close to the face of the dam (National Publicity Studios).

Fig. 10 (b). The Aviemore spawning race (C. J. Hardy).

A further factor resulting from the reduced flows is that sand bars, which are present at the mouths of several of the rivers, persist for far longer than previously and also impede upstream movement of the fish. Thus thirty years of endeavour which culminated in the establishment of a unique Southern Hemisphere stock of sea-run salmon has, until recently, been ignored in the interests of economic progress to the extent that the overall abundance of the fish is undoubtedly less now than it was in the 1920s.

Oceanic Circulation and At-sea Distribution

As yet little is known of the at-sea distribution of the quinnat salmon. They have been reported as being caught from time to time by commercial vessels, but in the last two or three years quantities appear to have increased considerably. However, as the possession of salmon is illegal unless they have been caught on rod and line and by the holder of an angling licence, it is little wonder that information is mainly hearsay.

It was suggested by Eggleston (1972) that the fish inhabit the cooler water of the Southland current on the east coast and are therefore confined close inshore during their marine phase (Fig. 11). This does not explain the fact that some fish, albeit in small numbers, do enter some of the west coast rivers to spawn. Heath (1973) suggested that a cool counter current with an onshore component moves south along the west coast. If this is the case and temperature is a limiting factor, a mechanism may also exist on that coast to confine the fish. Certainly the behaviour of the New Zealand whitebait (McDowall, 1968) suggests that a mechanism exists which either returns the larvae of the various galaxiid species back to the coast or retains them close to the spawning rivers during their 6 months at sea. They are poor swimmers, particularly in the early stages of development, and appear to be quite widely distributed (McDowall *et al.*, 1975), yet they still manage to re-enter the west coast rivers in large numbers. This observation suggests that the quinnat salmon might also be established on the west coast provided there were better natural spawning facilities. Alternatively hatchery-reared smolts could be released into selected rivers though the problem of collecting returning adults, in rivers subject to very rapid changes in level due to flooding, would remain. Whatever the reason, the basic assumption is that the fish only migrate

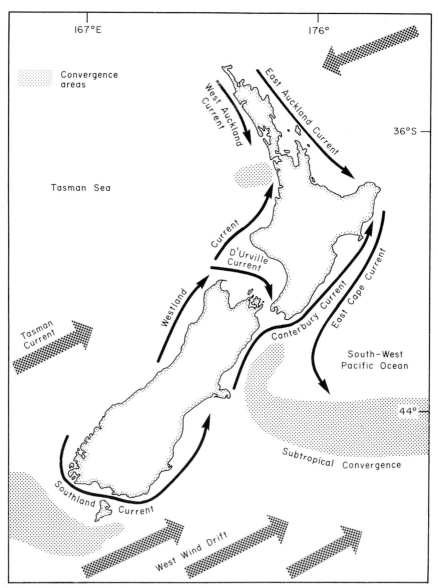

Fig. 11. Principal ocean currents around New Zealand (after Brodie, 1960, *NZ Jl. Geol. & Geophys.* **31**, 249).

over fairly short distances; this is why they have become successfully established. Whether there has been an adaptation to the New Zealand environment or whether the ova from the Sacramento river were from fish which already had a limited migration is uncertain. It was earlier suggested that the failure of *Salmo salar* to establish was because it migrated over long distances and lacked the orientation in the South Pacific to return it to its natal river. The ova of Baltic salmon imported from 1960-1965 were taken specifically because these fish migrated over shorter distances (Scott, 1961, 1962) but they too failed to return. This suggests that other factors, possibly sea temperatures, also influence the fish.

Offshore sea temperatures do not vary greatly between summer and winter around the New Zealand coast and also vary comparatively little between north and south (Eggleston, 1972). However, closer inshore they are probably marginal for the at-sea survival of salmon i.e. they exceed 15-16°C north of Kaikoura on the east coast. This may explain why the salmon are limited to the rivers south of the Waiau.

The important point is that wherever they occur, as far south as the Clutha river, there is no evidence that the sea or feeding conditions are in any way limiting. The adult returns are comparable with those in the North Pacific and the size at any particular age is similar or even better (Flain, 1972). Thus there are good reasons for believing that if the output of the smolts is augmented there should be a bigger return of adults.

EXPLOITATION OF QUINNAT SALMON

The quinnat salmon is currently regarded solely as a recreational fish. In the rivers in which it occurs and on which there are fisheries, management is by the Acclimatisation Societies. The South Island Council, on which the various societies are represented, has established its own Salmon Committee. This decides matters such as licence fees, bag limits, allocation of adults and ova for rearing purposes and the subsequent release of smolts in terms of location and quantity. Through the Council it has also provided extra funds for additional research (Hopkins, 1977). Local Societies also pass their own by-laws with respect to fishing areas and techniques. Anglers, usually Society nominees, are also represented on some local catchment boards. These boards are now charged with taking "due account of fisheries" when considering applications for water usage. However, the attention paid to fisheries interests varies considerably from region to region.

Basically, the present exploitation of the salmon is in the hands of the anglers alone, whilst the well-being of the fish and the fisheries is a bone of contention between the anglers and environmentalists on the one hand and the other users of the water on the other. Until now the angler, and therefore the fish, has lost out to the farmer and the developer.

FUTURE PROSPECTS

Is ocean ranching of quinnat salmon feasible? If it is, can it be undertaken on a large enough scale to become economic? If it does become economic, will the government and water users generally then accord it sufficient status to ensure the survival of the fisheries in perpetuity? On the answers to these three questions depends the fate of the New Zealand stocks of salmon.

The fact that the fish had been reared in hatcheries to which they subsequently returned suggests that ocean ranching is feasible. On this basis the possibility of developing an induced run back to a hatchery is now being investigated by the Ministry of Agriculture and Fisheries from its hatchery at Silverstream (Fig. 12) on a tributary of the Waimakariri river. The first releases were made in 1974 and the number of returning adults is still quite limited. In the three years 1977-1979 the numbers of adults returning have increased from 36 to 89 to 333. Although returns are still small, it is proposed to continue the project until 1981 so that a realistic evaluation can be made. As previously stated the Societies, upon whom the responsibility for management of the fisheries rests, have to agree via the Salmon Committee of the South Island Council to the removal of fish from the wild for stripping and rearing at Silverstream. They subsequently have to agree on the allocation of ova, fry or smolts for release. However, as is inevitable where a government agency is involved, there are those among the angling fraternity who seek to denigrate the work for lack of immediate results. Until home runs of mature fish are established these criticisms will continue.

In the meantime, with the goodwill or acquiescence of the anglers,

Fig. 12. The Ministry of Agriculture & Fisheries salmon hatchery on the Silverstream which discharges via the Kaiapoi river into the Waimakariri river (C. J. Hardy).

two commerical groups had begun attempts at evaluating the practicality of ocean ranching of salmon. In the first case smolts from Silverstream were released from sites in the Waitaki and Clutha rivers in 1977 and subsequent years. By 1979 one or two tagged fish had returned to the release points. Numbers have been particularly small, and the inability to recover fish may be due to the problem of establishing traps on the rivers. There are very wide fluctuations in flow, depending upon irrigation draw off or hydroelectric demands for storage or release, which in turn make the operation of a trap extremely difficult.

The second commercial operation is based in Pu Pu Springs (Fig. 13) which discharge into the Takaka river near its mouth. The volume of water produced by the springs is considerable (2×10^9 litres per day), but as the river discharges into the fairly shallow waters of Golden Bay at the north end of the South Island, where temperatures are relatively high, there is some doubt whether returning adults will penetrate the thermal barrier which is created. Because of the reluctance of the

Fig. 13. The salmon rearing facilities in early stages of construction at Pu Pu Springs on the Takaka river. The spring rises at the top left of the picture, the early raceways are in the left centre and the river originating from the springs discharges across the foreground (N. Boustead).

Salmon Committee to agree to the removal of wild fish for stripping by commercial operators as well as the limited capacity of the Silverstream hatchery, the source of young for the Pu Pu Springs development has been fry from Glenariffe (Fig. 14). With the agreement of the Societies concerned, escaping fry have been collected from below the trap and

Fig. 14. A floating fry trap below the Glenariffe salmon trap. This trap which was designed to sample out-migrating fry, has also been used as a collector for fry which have been transferred elsewhere for onward culture.

flown direct to the Springs in 1977 and 1978. The two consignments each of 250 000 fry, were grown on in newly built raceways. In 1979 eyed ova were despatched from the hatchery and reared in Washington trays. In Autumn 1979 a few fish were reported to have returned. Most of the smolts have been released into the river, though some have been reared to pan size for market evaluation. It was suggested that the Wairau river might make a more suitable release site but permission to transfer smolts from Pu Pu Springs for this purpose has so far been refused by the Marlborough Acclimatisation Society.

An advantage of such commercial developments, provided they are successful and not unduly obstructed, will be that the anglers will have a better opportunity to pursue their sport. Under the schemes proposed the fisherman has first opportunity to angle for the salmon as they return to the rivers. On this basis the recreational facilities could well be considerably enhanced. At the same time a definable value could be placed upon the stocks and the waters they inhabit, which can then be offset against other economic values of the water.

With respect to the scale of operations it has already been suggested that the near shore environment is not limiting at present, but if the fish are confined to a fairly narrow band of water close to the coast there will obviously be an upper limit to the stock this water will support. This, in turn, will mean that the fishery will never develop to the same scale as in the North Pacific but nevertheless there is undoubtedly room for considerable expansion.

In terms of utilisation and markets the Southern Hemisphere maturation and spawning offers some opportunity for exports of fresh fish during the Northern Hemisphere off-season. Furthermore the flesh quality and colour of samples of New Zealand fish sent to various importing countries for evaluation and comment is said to be particularly good. The local market, including the tourist and hotel trade, is as yet untapped and, because of prohibition on sales, there is no convenient way of assessing the likely demand that might be created for fresh or lightly processed fish. On the other hand recent imports of canned products have been between $3·5 and 4·0 million per annum, which suggests a potential local market for at least this equivalent. A further advantage that is enjoyed by the New Zealand salmonid stocks generally is freedom from disease. Of the known serious diseases which affect salmonids only whirling disease is present and, though now considered endemic, it is still confined to the waters of the Otago

District (Hewitt and Little, 1972; Cameron, 1978).* Prohibition of movements of fish within New Zealand without prior certification as to freedom from disease should continue to keep the disease localised. Few parasites or other diseases have been recorded in salmon (Hewitt and Hine, 1972) and none of the viruses and other pathogens which afflict salmonids in the Northern Hemisphere have been detected (P. M. Hine and N. Boustead, personal communication). The total prohibition on the importation of salmonids or their ova except in the fully processed state, should enable New Zealand to preserve a disease-free stock. This resource could in itself be of value at some later stage for developing new fisheries elsewhere in the world or restoring others which have been damaged by pollution, disease etc.

It is difficult for the uncommitted layman, who is not a fisherman, to appreciate the importance of fishing, and particularly a short season of salmon fishing, to the dedicated angler. Whenever there has been conflict of interest between the recreationalist, to whom quiet outdoor pleasure is of paramount importance, and the worldly economic interests of the majority of the population, the former has almost always suffered. Unless the overall economy is sound, the luxury of purely recreational fishing is unlikely to be retained in the face of steadily increasing demand for energy and the even more rapidly increasing costs of energy. Once again the fisheries will suffer at the hands of the developers unless there is a greater public awareness of the potential value of the fisheries. Realisation of the economic value of a salmon fishery which is a low consumer of energy—the fish return to be caught—but a producer of very high quality protein could result in a major change in attitude to the salmon and to their preservation. This will in turn benefit the angler.

In Canada, the United States of America, Japan and Russia considerable effort is being devoted to preserving and/or enhancing the traditional salmon fisheries (see Chapters 1 to 7). At the same time attempts are being made or will be made, to introduce various species to South America (Nagasawa and Aguilera, 1974, 1976 and Chapter 14) in the hope of building up new large stocks capable of harvesting the productivity of the Southern Ocean. Except in the latter case, the principal reason for trying to maintain or improve the stocks seems to be directed as much to improving commercial returns as it is to increasing food production. Even in South America the principal objective, which is said to be increased food production,

*Since this account was written whirling disease has been discovered among rainbow trout reared at Silverstream, and a trace-back programme has established its presence in four catchments in the South Island.

will still be dependent upon the development of a viable commercial fishery.

New Zealand, after a great deal of expenditure of time, money and effort over a great many years, finally and perhaps by a lucky accident of nature, now possesses self-perpetuating stocks of quinnat salmon which until recently were regarded solely as entertainment for an elite group of anglers. Regrettable as it may be, the future survival of the salmon stock in worthwhile numbers is unlikely to be safe in their hands. Such a comment is in no way intended to denigrate the efforts of a great many enthusiastic amateurs who have spent long hours in unpleasant conditions improving streams and clearing spawning areas and who have also spent considerable sums of their own money in seeking to preserve their sport. But, time and again, their efforts have been negated by wholesale modifications to the rivers and the catchments without any recognition of the needs of the fish.

It seems, therefore, that the preservation of the salmon itself and of the recreational pursuit of the angler will depend on the success of the present experiments in ocean ranching and a more enlightened attitude on the part of the Government.

REFERENCES

Anderson, C. R. (1972). *Fish. tech. Rep. N.Z. mar. Dep.* **83**, 10-15.
Ayson, L. F. (1910). *Bull. Bur. Fish. Wash.* **281**, 969-975.
Calderwood, W. L. (1927). *Salm. Trout Mag.* **48**, 241-252.
Cameron, M. L. (1978). *Chairmans Report, Freshwater Fisheries Advisory Council 1978.* Ministry of Agriculture & Fisheries Wellington, N.Z. pp. 1-51.
Cunningham, B. T. (1972). *Fish. tech. Rep. N.Z. mar. De.* **83**, 16-30.
Eggleston, D. (1972). *Fish. tech. Rep. N.Z. mar. Dep.* **83**, 68-76.
Flain, M. (1970). *N.Z. Jl. mar. Freshw. Res.* **4**, 217-222.
Flain, M. (1971). *N.Z. Jl. mar. Freshw. Res.* **5**, 519-521.
Flain, M. (1972). *Fish. tech. Rep. N.Z. mar. Dep.* **83**, 52-66.
Galloway, J. R. (1976). *Fish. Res. Div. inf. leaf.* **8**, 1-17.
Graynoth, E. (1971). *Fish. tech. Rep. N.Z. mar. De.* **64**, 1-20.
Graynoth, E. (1974). *Fish. tech. Rep. Minist. Agric. Fish.* **135**, 1-70.
Graynoth, E. and Skrzynski, W. (1974). *Fish tech. Rep. Minist. Agric. Fish.* **90**, 1-41.
Gebhards, S. V. (1960). *Prog. Fish. Cult.* **22**, 121-123.
Hardy, C. J. (1972). *Fish. tech. Rep. N.Z. mar. Dep.* **83**, 125-152.
Heath, R. A. (1973). *N.Z. Jl. mar. Freshw. Res.* **7**, 331-367.
Hefford, A. E. (1927). *Salm. Trout Mag.* **48**, 253-262.

Hewitt, G. R. and Little, R. W. (1972). *N.Z. Jl. mar. Freshw. Res.* **6**, 1-10.
Hewitt, G. R. and Hine, P. M. (1972). *N.Z. Jl. mar. Freshw. Res.* **6**, 69-114.
Hopkins, C. L. (1977). *Catch '77.* **9**, 4, 17.
McDowall, R. M. (1968). *Fish. Res. Bull. N.Z.* **2**, 1-84.
McDowall, R. M. (1978). *New Zealand Freshwater Fishes, a guide and natural history.* Heineman Educational Books (N.Z.) Auckland. pp. 1-230.
McDowall, R. M., Robertson, D. A. and Saito, R. (1975). *N.Z. Jl. mar. Freshw. Res.* **9**, 1-10.
Nagasawa, A. E. and Aguilera, P. M. (1974). *Japan International Co-operation Agency.* pp. 1-21.
Nagasawa, A. E. and Aguilera, P. M. (1976). *Japan International Co-operation Agency.* pp. 1-26.
Nichols, A. (1882). *The Acclimatisation of the Salmonids at the Antipodes: Its history and results.* Sampson, Low, Marston, Searle and Rivington, London. pp. 1-238.
Parrott, A. W. (1971). *Fish. tech. Rep. N.Z. mar. Dep.* **63**, 1-66.
Scott, D. (1960). *Southland Acc. Soc. Ann. Rep. 1960.* pp. 10-11.
Scott, D. (1974). *New Zealand's Nature Heritage.* Paul Hamlyn, Wellington. pp. 502-506.
Stokell, G. (1955). *Freshwater Fishes of New Zealand.* Simpson and Williams, Christchurch. pp. 1-145.
Thomson, G. M. (1922). "The Naturalisation of Animals and Plants in New Zealand." Cambridge University Press, Cambridge, pp. 1-607.
Thorpe, J. E. (1977). *J. Fish. Biol.* **11**, 175-184.
Waugh, G. D. (1973). In "The Natural History of New Zealand." (Ed. G. R. Williams) pp. 251-84. A. H. & A. W. Reed, Wellington.
Waugh, G. D. (1975). *Catch '75.* **2**, 10, 3-4.

Chapter 16

Experimental Releases of Coho Salmon in British Columbia

H. T. BILTON

*Department of Fisheries and the Environment, Fisheries and
Marine Service, Resource Services Branch, Pacific Biological Station,
Nanaimo, British Columbia, V9R 5K6, Canada*

INTRODUCTION

Salmon ranching as a profit-oriented enterprise is not permitted at
present in British Columbia, but a number of hatcheries exist which
produce juvenile salmon for enhancement. Recently, the Canadian
Federal Cabinet accepted, in principle, a salmonid enhancement
proposal aimed at doubling the harvest of adult Pacific salmon. To
increase production from hatcheries, rearing channels, and other
salmon-ranching facilities, it is necessary to know the best combination
of size and time at which to release smolts to the sea in order to
maximise yield (the biomass of fish to the fishery per smolt released).
There is evidence from United States hatcheries that survival of
juvenile coho *(Oncorhynchus kisutch)* and chinook salmon *(O. tshawytscha)*
can generally be improved by increasing the size of smolts at release
(Johnson, 1970; Wallis, 1968). A more recent study of coho salmon
(Hopley and Mathews, 1975) indicates that both time and size at release
of yearlings influence the survival and the size of adults (fish that
matured in their third year of life). It was shown that a later release of
smolts of any given size resulted in a higher rate of return of adults to
the hatchery. Also, on any release date, larger size at release resulted in
a higher rate of return to the hatchery.

Bilton (1978) determined the combined effects of time and size at release of juvenile coho salmon in British Columbia on their subsequent survival, growth, and age at maturity, measured by the contribution the various experimental groups made to the escapement. Information on the contribution to the fisheries is incomplete. The results of this experiment are summarised here (for full details see Bilton, 1978).

MATERIALS AND METHODS

Location, Experimental Stock, Incubation and Rearing of Fry

The experiment was carried out at the Rosewall Creek hatchery, which is operated by the Pacific Biological Station, Nanaimo, British Columbia, and located on the east coast of Vancouver Island 80 km north of Nanaimo.

About 200 000 coho eggs were collected in November and December, 1973, from the Big Qualicum River 24 km south of Rosewall Creek. The eggs were incubated in Heath-type hatchery trays until February, 1974. The "eyed" eggs were then transferred to the Rosewall Creek hatchery into 45 Heath trays at a loading density of about 4500 eggs per tray.

In March 1974 resultant fry were transferred in equal groups into six Burrows ponds. Throughout rearing, fish were offered Oregon moist pellets every 15 minutes during daylight hours using automatic feeders. Water temperatures were partially manipulated by using either creek or ground water or a mixture of both. (For more specific information on growth of fry, temperatures, etc., see Bilton and Jenkinson, 1976.)

Experimental Design

The object of the experiment was (1) to rear three populations of juvenile coho to three average sizes (11, 15, and 22 g) by using three temperature regimes; (2) to release one-third of each of these populations at three different times—April, May, and June; (3) to compare the returns from each release. The three populations were replicated once (two Burrows ponds per size group), making a total of six experimental populations. In order to compare the returns from different size components within each population, fish in the six groups were graded* into subsize categories, small, medium, and large, based on their length (Fig. 1). Fish of each release were tagged with a coded wire nose tag.

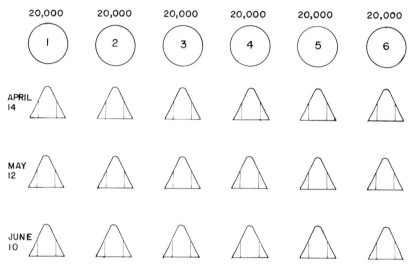

Fig. 1. Experimental design as explained on p. 304.

Nose Tagging, Marking, and Release

Once the size categories had been determined, all fish were marked by removal of their adipose fin, graded into respective size categories, and tagged with a binary-coded wire nose tag (Bergman *et al.*, 1968). A specific code was used for each size category for each of the six populations and for each release, making a total of 54 codes. Tagged fish were then transferred to a release pond where they were held from 14 to 19 days to acclimatise them to a more natural environment before release. Approximately 50 tagged fish from each of the 18 groups were held in netpens in the pond to provide an estimate of tag retention, size

*Size categories were determined for fish from each population on the basis of a sample of 300-500 fish that were removed without known bias, anaesthetised, measured for length, and returned to the population. A length-frequency curve was derived from these data and was used to determine the limits of the three size categories. Arbitrarily, it was decided on the basis of this curve that the first 25% of the fish on the left-hand side of the curve would be classified as small, the 50% in the middle of the curve as medium, and the 25% on the extreme right-hand side of the curve as large.

of fish, and sex composition in each of the groups released. Fish were released after dark on April 14, May 12, and June 10, 1975. At the same time, fish held in netpens were sampled.

About 7000 coho remained after the third release and these were released on July 8. In this case, only one population (the excess from the six populations released earlier) was released. They were also graded into three size categories and tagged with binary-coded wire nose tags (Fig. 1).

Recovery of Jacks and Adults

Jacks (males that mature at age 1·0*) were recovered from Rosewall Creek in the fall of 1975 and adults (males and females that mature at age 1·1) in the fall of 1976. All marked fish were killed, measured, weighed, sexed, and scaled. The heads were frozen for subsequent examination of the nose tag at the laboratory. The number of tagged fish recovered from each of the 57 groups of smolts was determined. From the percentage that returned as jacks and adults and the average length and weight from each group, various correlation coefficients (Pearson r) and regression formulae were calculated. Those comparing percentage return to size of smolt could be derived using either the six values for the six populations or the values for each of the three size categories within each of the six populations, making a total of 18 values. We decided to use the 18 values for each release because they provided a greater range of smolt sizes, improving the regression relationships. It can be argued, however, that the three size categories of smolts within each population may have been genetically different. If this were so, genetic and non-genetic factors could determine the relationship between size and their subsequent return as jacks and adults. In view of this, relationships based on the size categories within each population were examined statistically by analyses of variance (Li, 1964). This analysis indicated that although there were some differences in slopes and intercepts for regressions between size groups within releases, they did not differ significantly ($P > 0.05$) when all three releases were considered together. Hence, we concluded that it was valid to use the 18 values.

*The European system of age designation (Koo, 1962) is used here. The first digit indicates the number of annuli formed in fresh water and the second the number formed while fish were in the ocean.

RESULTS

Smolts

The numbers of tagged smolts from the six populations released in April ranged from 6751 to 7178; in May from 7393 to 7553; in June from 4217 to 7475; and in July it was 6937. The numbers by sex and size categories ranged between 148 and 2365 fish. The average sizes of smolts among the 57 groups varied markedly within and between releases. In April, they ranged from 5·1 to 18·8 g; in May, from 7·7 to 25·8 g; in June, from 12·1 to 32·1 g; and in July, from 14·9 to 33·1 g. Thus, the smolts continued to grow as the season progressed, despite attempts to retard growth by manipulating the water temperature. We decided against retarding growth by reducing food as this could have unknown stress effects.

Jacks (Age 1·0)

Return of Jacks
A total of 1417 tagged jacks was recovered at Rosewall Creek. As expected, all were males. The percentage return was lowest from smolts released in April (0·25%) and highest from those released in June (1·88%). The percentage return from smolts released in May was 1·64.

Smolt Size, Jack Return, and Jack Size
Among fish of each of the three releases (April, May, and June) there were highly significant positive correlations between the average size of smolts at release and the percentage that returned as jacks ($r = 0·76$, 0·95, and 0·91, respectively; $n = 18$ in each case; $P < 0·001$) (Fig. 2). The later release (except April), the lower the percentage that returned as jacks.

Jacks from the July release were smallest (average weight 263·4 g), followed by those from the June release (364·5 g) (Fig. 3). Those from the April and May releases were largest (515·8 g each).

Among fish of each of the three releases (April, May, and June) there were significant positive correlations between the average weight of smolts at release and of jacks that returned ($r = 0·92$, 0·74, and

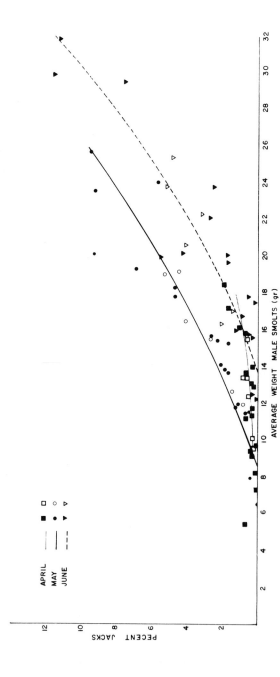

Fig. 2. Compares the percentage return of jack coho originating from male smolts of different sizes released in April, May, and June. Open symbols indicate values for each of the 6 populations. Closed symbols indicate values for each of the 18 sub-groups.

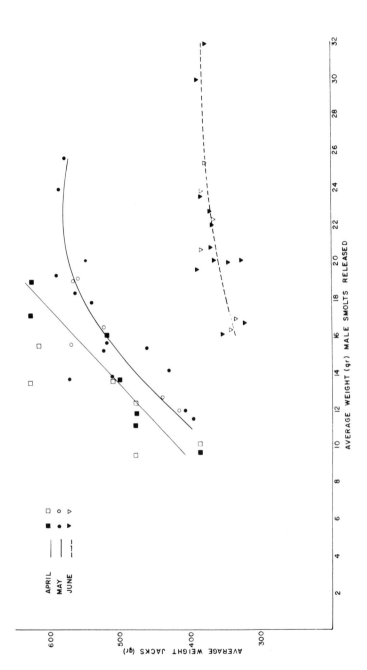

Fig. 3. Compares the average weight of jack coho originating from male smolts of different sizes released in April, May, and June. Open symbols indicate values for each of the 6 populations. Closed symbols indicate values for each of the 18 sub-groups.

0·60, respectively; n = 7, 14, 12; $P < 0·05$) (Fig. 3). For smolts of the same size, the later the release, the smaller the size of the returning jacks.

Adults (Age 1·1)

Return of Adults

A total of 2885 tagged and marked adults originating from April to July releases was recovered at Rosewall Creek. The percentage return of adults was lowest from smolts released in April (0·82%) and highest from those released in June (4·40%). The percentage returns from smolts released in May and July were 1·82 and 1·77, respectively.

There were significantly more females than males ($P < 0·05$) among adults of the April and May releases, while the June release showed equal proportions of both sexes ($P > 0·05$). Males of the July release significantly outnumbered females. However, this trend changed substantially when jacks were added to the male count. The ratio of total males to females in the return from the April release did not differ significantly, whereas there were significantly more males than females among each of the three later releases.

Smolt Size, Adult Return, and Adult Size

There were significant negative correlations between average weight of smolts at release and the percentage that returned as male adults for the April and May releases (r = —0·66, —0·56, respectively; n = 18 in each case; $P < 0·02$) (Fig. 4). A negative relationship was also indicated among fish from the June release, but the correlation was not significant (r = —0·37; n = 18; $P > 0·1$). However, when the probability values for each release were combined and a single test of significance of the aggregate was made (Fisher, 1950), the χ^2 value was significant at the 1% level (χ^2 = 20·302; df 6, $P < 0·01$). Thus, there is a trend towards a lower return of male adults with increased smolt size.

For smolts of the same size, the later the release (up to June) the higher the percentage return of male adults (Fig. 4). The July return of male adults fell between those of May and June (Fig. 4).

There were significant negative correlations between average weight of smolts at release and the percentage that returned as female adults for the April and June releases (r = —0·64, —0·53, respectively; n =

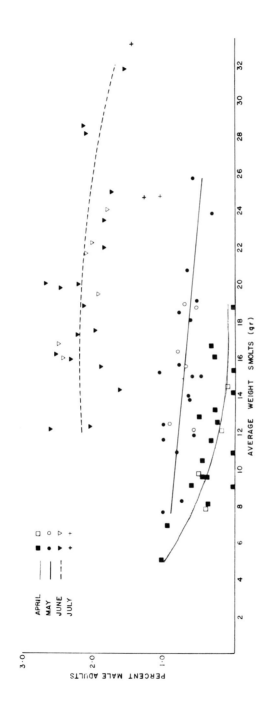

Fig. 4. Compares the percentage return of male adult coho originating from smolts of different sizes released in April, May, June, and July. Open symbols indicate values for each of the populations. Closed symbols indicate values for each of the 18 sub-groups.

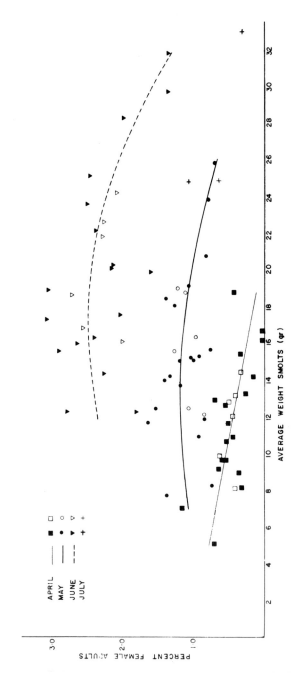

Fig. 5. Compares the percentage return of female adult coho originating from smolts of different sizes released in April, May, June, and July. Open symbols indicate values for each of the 6 populations. Closed symbols indicate values for each of the 18 sub-groups.

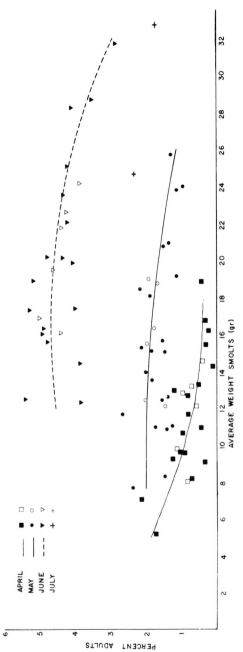

Fig. 6. Compares the percentage return of adult coho (males plus females) originating from smolts of different sizes released in April, May, June, and July. Open symbols indicate values for each of the 6 populations. Closed symbols indicate values for each of the 18 sub-groups.

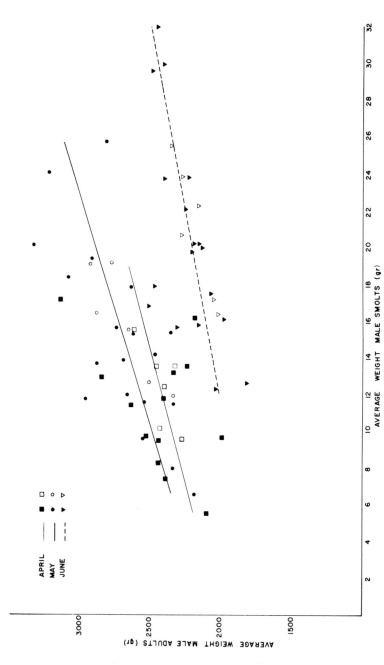

Fig. 7. Compares the average weight of male adult coho originating from smolts of different sizes released in April, May, and June. Open symbols indicate values for each of the 6 populations. Closed symbols indicate values for each of the 18 sub-groups.

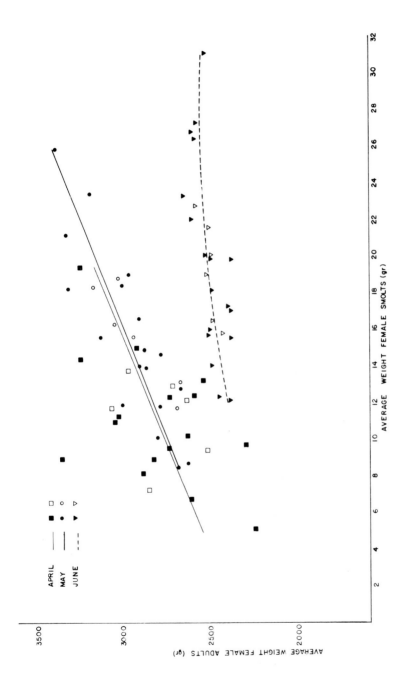

Fig. 8. Compares the average weight of female adult coho originating from smolts of different sizes released in April, May, and June. Open symbols indicate values for each of the 6 populations. Closed symbols indicate values for each of the 18 sub-groups.

18 in each case; $P < 0.05$) (Fig. 5). A negative but non-significant correlation ($r = -0.35$; $n = 18$; $P > 0.1$) was indicated for fish from the May release. However, when all three probability values were combined, the χ^2 value was significant at the 1% level ($\chi^2 = 19.806$; df 6; $P < 0.01$). Thus, the results indicated a trend towards a lower return of female adults with increased smolt size.

For smolts of the same size, the later the release (up to June), the higher the percentage return of female adults. The July return was most similar to that of the May release.

Combination of the data for male and female adults from each release (April, May, and June) resulted in significant negative correlations between average weights of smolts at release and the percentage return of adults ($r = -0.71$, -0.50, and -0.61, respectively; $n = 18$ in each case; $P < 0.05$) (Fig. 6). Hence, the data indicate that increased size of smolts at release result in a decrease in the percentage return of adults.

Returning females were larger than males in the escapement. Male and female adults from the May release were largest in size (Figs 7 and 8) and those from the June and July releases were smallest. The average weights of both sexes in the returns from the May and June releases were significantly and positively correlated with the average weight of the smolts from which they originated (for May, males and females, $r = 0.71$ and 0.86, respectively, $n = 18$ in each case, P $P < 0.001$; for June, males and females, $r = 0.75$ and 0.56, respectively, $n = 18$ in each case, $P < 0.02$). For males and females from the April release there were positive but non-significant correlations (for males, $r = 0.39$, $n = 13$, $P > 0.1$; for females, $r = 0.48$, $n = 16$, $P > 0.05$). When the probability values for each were combined the χ^2 values were significant at the 0.1% level (χ^2 for the males $= 32.236$, df 6, $P < 0.01$; for the females $= 27.762$, df 6, $P < 0.001$). Thus, for both males and females there was a significant trend towards larger smolts producing larger returning adults. For smolts of the same size, the later the release, the smaller the size of the returning adults.

Jack and Adult Returns

The size and the time at which smolts were released influenced the returns of both jacks and adults. Highly significant negative correlations between the percentage return of jacks and the percentage return of

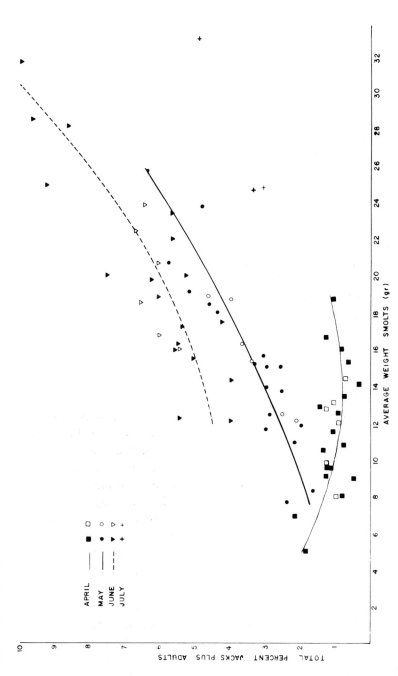

Fig. 9. Compares total percentage return of coho (jack plus adult) originating from smolts of different sizes released in April, May, June, and July. Open symbols indicate values for each of the 6 populations. Closed symbols indicate values for each of the 18 sub-groups.

adults (for April, May, and June, r = —0·54, —0·55, and —0·66, respectively, n = 18 in each case, P <0·02) indicate that as the percentage of jacks increased, the percentage return of adults decreased. Hence, an increase in numbers of jacks reduced the production of adults.

The total percentage returns of jacks plus adults in the escapement from the May and June releases were significantly and positively correlated with the size of the smolts from which they originated (for May, r = 0·92, and June, r = 0·88, n = 18 in each case, P <0·001) (Fig. 9). For those from the April release, there was a negative but non-significant correlation (r = —0·43, n = 18, P >0·05). Hence, for smolts released in May and June there was a higher total return from larger smolts, but for those released in April there was a suggestion of the reverse.

There was also an effect of time of release on the total returns to the escapement. For smolts of the same size, the total return from those released in June was highest, followed by those released in May, then July, and lastly April.

DISCUSSION

The data show clearly that both size and time of release of coho smolts have an effect on the proportion of fish that return in their first ocean year as jacks. Larger smolts produced more jacks; however, later releases produced fewer jacks. Larger jacks tended to come from larger smolts and earlier release times. Loss in size associated with later release is probably associated with the length of feeding time in the ocean. Similar results were reported by Hager and Noble (1976), who found that large, fast-growing males were most likely to mature earlier as jacks. They also observed that the average size of the returning jacks reflected the original size-differences present among the smolts at release.

The highest return of adults resulted from smolts released in June, and the lowest from smolts released in April. For both male and female adults, there was a decrease in percentage return to the escapement with increasing smolt size. Among smolts released in June, the highest return of adults was from smolts averaging 15-16 g (small to medium size). These findings are contrary to those of Hopley and Mathews (1975) and Hager and Noble (1976), who found an increase in the percentage of adults in the escapements with increasing smolt size. The reasons for the differences in results cannot be explained at present. It can be argued that our escapement data may have been biased by selection of the fishery, and, therefore, the conclusions are subject to error. For example, the observed differences in the returns of adults from the three releases to the escapement may have been caused by differences in exploitation rates rather than differences in survival. Further, the relationship between size of smolt and return of adults might not be as described when the fishery catch data are included. Even though most of the catch data are not yet available, a preliminary examination of some was made. Sport catch data listing the tag recoveries up to September, 1976, from each group of fish were analysed (Anon., 1976). The percentage return of adults in the escapement from the June release was 5·4 times greater than that of the April release and almost twice that from the May release. Almost identical differences between releases were shown for the sports fishery data (June 5·7 times greater than April and almost double that of May). Therefore, it can be concluded that the observed differences among fish from the releases in the escapement reflected differences in survival rather than in rates of exploitation by the fishery.

The average size of smolts was negatively correlated to the percentage escapement of adults. Tag recoveries in the sports fishery indicated a similar trend among April release fish ($r = -0·68$; $n = 18$; $P < 0·01$) but differed among fish from the May and June releases. Among those from the May release, a non-significant positive correlation was indicated ($r = 0·28$; $n = 18$; $P > 0·1$), suggesting a slight increase in adult recoveries from the smolts of larger size. Among those from the June release, there was a significant positive correlation ($r = 0·50$; $n = 16$; $P < 0·05$). As in the escapement data, however, the relationship was best expressed as a curve, with the percentage recoveries decreasing among the larger fish over 22 g in weight. The smaller fish were not as well represented in the catch as in the escapement, and therefore may have been subjected to a lower rate of exploitation by the fishery. Possibly many of the fish that originated from the smaller smolts escaped the fishery. Any firm conclusions on the representation of the various groups of experimental coho in the catches must await complete and detailed analyses of recoveries in the sport and commercial fisheries. The present example of catch data does, however, suggest that the escapement data reflects the relative differences in total returns of the different groups.

An important conclusion from this study is that there is no increase in the production of adults when larger smolts are released but there is a substantial increase in the production of jacks. There is an optimum combination of size and time to release smolts which will either maximise the production of jack or adult biomass. Usually, the objective of hatchery managers is to maximise the production of adult flesh to meet the needs of both commercial and marine recreational fisheries. However, in some instances it might be desirable to maximise jack production to create stream recreational fisheries for fish of a relatively small size.

What is the best combination of size and time of release that will maximise either the yield of jack or adult flesh? We attempted to answer this question by using a model based on combinations of release and sex for average smolt weight, and percentage return and weight of jacks, adult males, and adult females, respectively.

Estimates of the average resultant biomass of jacks and adults per smolt of different sizes released in April, May, and June are shown in Figs. 10 and 11. Some of these estimates of biomass involved extrapolation from the data. For April, estimates of biomass from smolts weighing 19-32 g, for May, from 5-8 g and 26-32 g, and for June, from 5-12 g are extrapolated values.

The model shows that for coho salmon maximum yield of jack flesh would be achieved by releasing smolts weighing at least 32 g in May, followed by smolts of the same size released in June and then in April. Maximum yield of adult flesh would be achieved by releasing smolts in June at a size of 19 g, followed by those released in May at a size of 15 g and then by those released in April at a size of 5 g.

In summary, if maximum production of adult flesh of coho salmon is the goal, then it would appear that smolts should be released at a moderate size (around 19 g) late in the season (early June). Hence, coho salmon production facilities should have a cool source of water, which would allow for later releases of fish at a smaller size. Release of fish at a smaller size would have the further advantage of increasing the rearing capability of the facility. Use of cooler water for rearing would also reduce the possibility of outbreak of disease, which is frequently associated with rising temperatures.

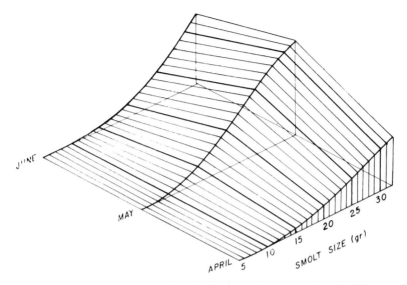

Fig. 10. Model shows yield of jack biomass from smolts of different sizes (g) released in April, May, and June.

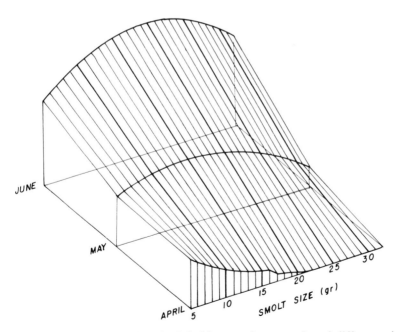

Fig. 11. Model shows yield of adult biomass from smolts of different sizes (g) released in April, May, and June.

REFERENCES

Anon. (1976). Georgia Strait Salmon Head Recovery Program. *Fish. Mar. Serv. Bull.* **29**, 16 p.

Bergman, P. K., Jefferts, K. B., Fiscus, H. F. and Hager, R. C. (1968). *Wash. Dep. Fish. Fish. Res. Pap.* **3**, 63-84.

Bilton, H. T. (1978). *Fish. Mar. Serv. Tech. Rep.*, 72 p.

Bilton, H. T. and Jenkinson, D. W. (1976). *Fish. Mar. Serv. Data Rec.* **7**, 16 p.

Fisher, R. A. (1950). *In* "Statistical Methods for Research Workers," p. 99. Hafner Publishing Company, New York.

Hager, R. C. and Noble, R. E. (1976). *Prog. Fish. Cult.* **38**, 144-147.

Hopley, C. W. and Mathews, S. B. (1975). Unpublished MS. Salmon Culture Division, Wash. Dep. Fish., 15 p.

Johnson, K. A. (1970). *Res. Rep. Oreg. Fish. Comm.* **2**, 12 p.

Koo, T. S. Y. (1962). *In* "Studies of Alaska red salmon," pp. 37-38, Univ. Wash. Press, Seattle, Washington.

Li, J. C. R. (1964). *In* "Statistical Inference." Vol. 1, 658 p., Edwards Bros. Inc., Ann Arbor, Michigan.

Wallis, J. (1968). *Oreg. Fish. Comm. Processed Rep.*, Clackamas, 61 p.

NOTE ADDED IN PROOF

Since this chapter was written the analysis of all the data (the fishery catch plus the escapement) has been completed. The results indicate the highest return of adults was realised from the June release (36·8%). This return was approximately five times that (7·3%) from the April release and more than double the returns from the May and July releases (15·9% and 15·3%, respectively). The data were also subjected to response surface analysis. Predicted maximum adult returns of 43·5% (catch plus escapement) were associated with computed release of 25·1 g coho juveniles on 22 June, 1975. There was a significant interaction between release time and size: maximum returns from early (14 April) releases would be expected from release of 16-17 g juveniles. Predicted returns of jacks would be maximised from early release of large juveniles.

REFERENCES

Bilton, H. T. (1980). *Can. Tech. Rep. Fish. Aquat. Sci.* **941**, 41 p.

Bilton, H. T., Alderdice, D. F. and Schnute, J. Unpublished MS.

Chapter 17

Delayed Release of Salmon

A. J. NOVOTNY

*Northwest and Alaska Fisheries Center, National Marine Fisheries
Service, National Oceanic and Atmospheric Administration,
2725 Montlake Boulevard East, Washington 98112, U.S.A.*

INTRODUCTION

The customary time of release for cultured fish from most salmon
hatcheries is about the time when wild stocks in the watershed
reach the peak of their seaward migration; the exact time of release
may vary due to floods, siltation, elevated temperatures, uncontrollable
diseases, and even economic problems. It was essentially a need to
respond to the declining sports angler harvest in the inner Puget
Sound, Washington that led to the development of delayed salmon
releases; that is, extending the artificial rearing periods beyond the
time of normal release or migration.

The saltwater catch of salmon by the sport fishery in Puget Sound,
Washington (Fig. 1) reached a peak in 1957, when anglers harvested
208 000 chinook salmon *(Oncorhynchus tshawytscha)* and 220 000 coho
salmon *(O. kisutch)*. Within 12 years, the catch of chinook declined to a
quarter of the 1957 peak and coho, to an eighth. This decline occurred
despite increased hatchery production, increased numbers of adult fish
returning to the hatcheries, and a relatively constant angling pressure.
Extensive marking studies in 1967-69 showed that Puget Sound
hatchery coho released at the normal time migrated northward and
westward into Canadian waters, where commercial trollers caught 10
times more fish west of Vancouver Island (Canada) than anglers did in

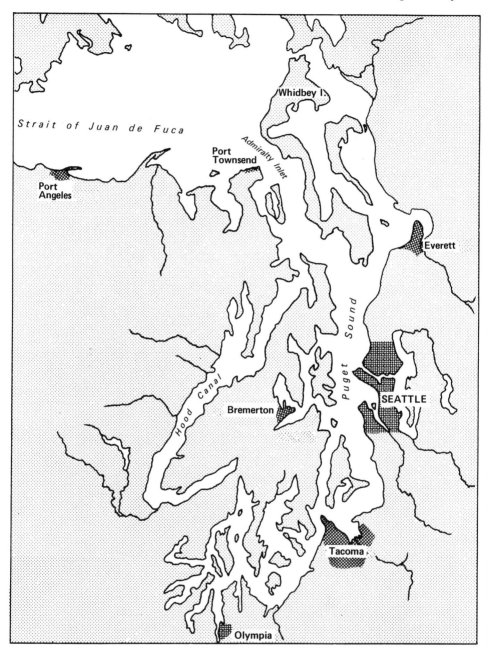

Fig. 1. Region of the most concentrated delayed release programmes in Washington State.

Puget Sound. Moreover, because hatchery coho were reluctant to feed in Puget Sound as adults, the harvests there were almost entirely by commerical net fisheries. In fact, many coho caught by anglers were taken as immature fish (an accepted management practice in Puget Sound) and were determined to be resident fish, primarily from local wild stocks.

Biologists with the Oregon Department of Fish and Wildlife conducted a controlled growth experiment and found that by simultaneously releasing coho averaging 17 g and 45 g, the latter would contribute at twice the rate of the smaller fish to the coastal fisheries (Johnson, 1970). Washington State Department of Fisheries (WDF) chose to rear coho salmon for an extended time to achieve a greater size at release, rather than control growth or grade out larger fish (Hager and Noble, 1976). In 1971, 57 g coho salmon released from Minter Creek Hatchery contributed 60 times as many fish to the Puget Sound salmon sport fishery as did 23 g coho salmon from a normal April release (Washington State Department of Fisheries, 1971).

Since that pioneering effort, delayed-release studies, sometimes referred to as extended rearing studies, have been applied to other species of Pacific salmon and trout. Their objectives include: altering oceanic migration routes, increasing marine survival, increasing contributions to certain types of fisheries, creating new fishing areas by altering migration routes, and imprinting to new "homing stations". In this chapter, techniques of delaying releases and imprinting salmon and trout are described and a number of studies discussed.

TECHNIQUES EMPLOYED IN DELAYING RELEASES

Freshwater Releases

Extended Fry Rearing
Most delayed release programmes in freshwater concern seaward migrating fish, but National Marine Fisheries Service (NMFS) biologists in Alaska conducted extended rearing experiments with sockeye salmon *(O. nerka)* fry to enhance survival to the migrant smolt stage in Auke Lake, Alaska. The sockeye salmon are normally released as unfed fry. In 1974, however, 11% of the cultured fry released into the lake at 0·38 g smolted at age 1 + and 2% more at age 2 + . This

quadrupled the total number of seaward migrants (at age 1 + and 2 +) that survived from hatchery plants (Northwest Fisheries Center *Monthly Report,* July 1976).

Wild chum salmon *(O. keta)* and pink salmon *(O. gorbuscha)* migrate to the sea in the spring as fry, shortly after emergence from the gravel. Hatchery programmes of WDF for pink salmon include freshwater rearing to 1 to 2 g prior to release. Some Japanese hatcheries practise a form of extended rearing of pink fry by ponding and feeding but allowing the fish to migrate freely at any time (Moberly and Lium, 1977). In WDF hatcheries, chum salmon fry are reared to 1·5 g before release, whereas in Japan they delay release until there is a combination of preferred stream and estuarine temperatures as well as a spring plankton bloom in the estuaries (Mathews and Senn, 1975). As prolonged freshwater rearing of chum and pink salmon may reduce oceanic survival, extended rearing must be manipulated carefully to maximise the returns to the fisheries and hatcheries.

Delayed Release of Fall Chinook Salmon

Recoveries. On the Pacific coast of North America, fall chinook salmon are normally released from hatcheries at 3-10 g in their first spring (age 0), which coincides with the early May to mid-June migration of most wild stocks. Size of fall chinook at release affects survival: 0·18% of Washington State's 1971 brood Puget Sound hatchery fall chinook released at 5 g returned to the release sites, whereas 1·5% of the University of Washington hatchery fall chinook released into Puget Sound at 11 g returned to the hatchery.* Differences in diets, environment, disease, genetic stock, and husbandry techniques can influence size at release but, in general, delayed-release fish are larger than average. The most extensive data available for the delayed release of fall chinook salmon from freshwater hatcheries are for the 1971 and 1972 brood years in Washington State, the first years of wide use of the coded-wire tag (Tables I and II; Figs 1 and 2).† The release sites range from northern to southern Puget Sound, and no general rule applies for all results. For example, yearlings released at

*Stephen B. Mathews, Associate Professor, College of Fisheries, University of Washington (Seattle). Data presented at June 23, 1977 meeting of the American Salmon Growers Association.
†Most hatchery reared fall chinook salmon in Washington State return as 3, 4, or 5-year old adults.

Table I. Survival and geographic distributions of 1971 brood normal and delayed release fall chinook salmon from Washington State Department of Fisheries hatcheries in Puget Sound, Washington. The data are summarised as percentages estimated from coded-wire tag recoveries in all fisheries sampled. Estimates of sport fishery recoveries in Puget Sound are indicated in ( ). (Data from Washington State Department of Fisheries.)

Stock no.	Release site	Stock origin	No. of rearing days	Average weight at release (g)	Date released	No. of tagged fish released	Total recovery[a] (%)	Distributions (%)						
								Alaska	British Columbia	Washington coast	Puget Sound	Oregon coast	Columbia River	Escapement
1-1	Skagit R.	Green R. X	124[b]	3.3	15/6/72	97 117	0.16	0.0	37.3	7.0	50.0(13.3)	0.0	0.0	5.7
1-2	Skagit R.	Skagit R.	149	4.5	11/7/72	66 486	0.10	0.0	29.8	0.0	55.2(3.0)	0.0	0.0	14.9
1-3	Skagit R.	Skagit R.	198	16.2	29/8/72	47 549	0.25	0.0	31.7	2.5	58.3(10.8)	0.0	0.0	7.5
1-4	Skagit R.	Skagit R.	298	34.9	7/12/72	39 622	0.99	0.5	14.7	5.6	72.3(48.2)	0.0	0.0	6.9
1-5	Skagit R.	Skagit R.	425	82.5	11/4/73	37 100	3.04	0.0	30.6	3.7	56.5(29.0)	7.1	0.7	1.3
1-6	Skagit R.	Skagit R.	441	75.7	1/5/73	28 624	5.62	0.0	19.6	3.5	65.5(58.7)	0.0	0.0	11.4
1-7	Minter Ck.	Minter Ck.	386	64.9	12/3/73	20 698	6.55	0.0	3.3	2.7	90.8(75.2)	0.0	0.6	2.7
1-8	Green R.	Green R.	100[b]	4.6	19/5/72	70 749	0.31	0.0	38.9	5.0	43.9(12.2)	0.0	0.0	12.2
1-9	Green R.	Green R.	125	8.4	22/6/72	64 137	0.46	0.0	36.3	3.4	38.4(9.9)	0.0	0.0	21.9
1-10	Green R.	Green R.	302	32.4	15/12/72	28 882	0.03	62.5	0.0	0.0	37.5(0.9)	0.0	0.0	0.0[d]
1-11	Nooksack R.	Nooksack R.	112[b]	4.2	18/5/72	69 806	1.26	0.2	61.5	9.9	24.6(14.6)	1.6	0.0	2.3
1-12	Nooksack R.	Nooksack R.	141	8.3	16/6/72	52 113	6.13	0.0	38.1	5.6	54.7(11.0)	5.6	0.0	1.6
1-13	Nooksack R.	Nooksack R.	182	15.1	27/7/72	31 361	5.44	0.0	34.7	8.0	55.1(8.8)	0.6	0.0	1.8
1-14	Nooksack R.	Nooksack R.	235	30.3	18/9/72	27 501	1.09	0.0	37.1	1.3	56.5(10.0)	1.3	0.0	3.7
1-15	Nooksack R.	Nooksack R.	440	90.8	11/4/73	18 092	6.77	0.0	26.2	1.5	71.6(31.8)	0.2	0.0	0.5
1-16	Capitol L.	Deschutes R.	125[b]	7.0	5/6/72	76 392	0.62	0.0	23.8	11.3	38.6(17.0)	0.0	0.0	26.3
1-17	Capitol L.	Satsop R. X	182	15.1	17/8/72	27 965	1.18	0.0	23.6	5.8	52.1(28.8)	0.0	0.0	18.5
1-18	Eld Inlet[c]	Deschutes R.	195	22.7	30/8/72	19 000	0.71	0.0	65.9	5.2	24.4(20.0)	0.0	0.0	4.4

[a] Estimated from coded-wire tag recoveries in all fisheries sampled in the Pacific Northwest (including Canada and Alaska) plus escapement.
[b] Normal rearing time and release for fall chinook salmon for that hatchery.
[c] Saltwater release site.
[d] There were only eight estimated recoveries from this release.

Table II. Survival and geographic distribution of 1971 brood normal and delayed release fall chinook salmon from Washington State Department of Fisheries (WDF) hatcheries in the Hood Canal-Juan de Fuca (Washington) region. The data are summarised as percentages estimated from coded-wire tag recoveries in all fisheries sampled. Estimates of sport fishery recoveries in Puget Sound are indicated in ( ). (Data from Washington State Department of Fisheries.)

Stock no.	Release site	Stock origin	No. of rearing days	Average weight at release (g)	Date released	No. of tagged fish released	Total recovery[a] (%)	Distributions (%)						
								Alaska	British Columbia	Washington coast	Puget Sound	Oregon coast	Columbia River	Escapement
2-1	Dungeness River	Elwha R.	442	64·9	19/4/73	37 513	0·16	1·7	26·0	4·0	62·8(61·4)	0·6	0·0	4·8
2-2	Hood Canal[c]	Hood Canal	97[b]	3·1	9/5/72	82 757	0·23	0·0	33·7	4·7	50·6(7·4)	0·0	0·0	11·0
2-3	Hood Canal	Hood Canal	91[b]	3·6	23/5/72	46 976	0·13	0·0	52·4	11·1	31·7(11·1)	0·0	0·0	4·8
2-4	Hood Canal	Hood Canal	99[b]	3·6	23/5/72	18 000	0·20	2·8	27·8	44·4	19·4(8·3)	0·0	0·0	5·6
2-5	Hood Canal	Hood Canal	191	20·6	31/8/72	28 684	0·02	0·0	83·3	0·0	0·0	0·0	0·0	16·7[d]
2-6	Hood Canal	Hood Canal	370	50·4	26/2/73	20 083	6·59	0·5	20·3	32·3	28·9(21·3)	3·1	0·2	14·6
2-7	Elwha R.	Elwha R.	369	64·9	31/1/73	10 974	0·49	3·7	50·0	5·6	31·6(16·7)	0·0	0·0	9·3
2-8	Hoko R.	Hood Canal	146	9·9	11/7/72	31 144	0·13	0·0	100·0	0·0	0·0	0·0	0·0	0·0
2-9	Pysht R.	Elwha R. X Hood Canal	146	9·9	11/7/72	30 881	0·35	1·9	53·7	0·0	44·4(13·9)	0·0	0·0	0·0

[a] Estimated from coded-wire tag recoveries in all fisheries sampled in the Pacific Northwest (including Canada and Alaska) plus escapement.
[b] Normal rearing time and release for fall chinook for that hatchery.
[c] WDF hatchery at Hoodsport (Hood Canal) releases its fish directly into the mouth of Finch Creek on this saltwater fjord. Fish can be conditioned in this hatchery with pumped seawater.
[d] There were only six estimated recoveries from this entire group.

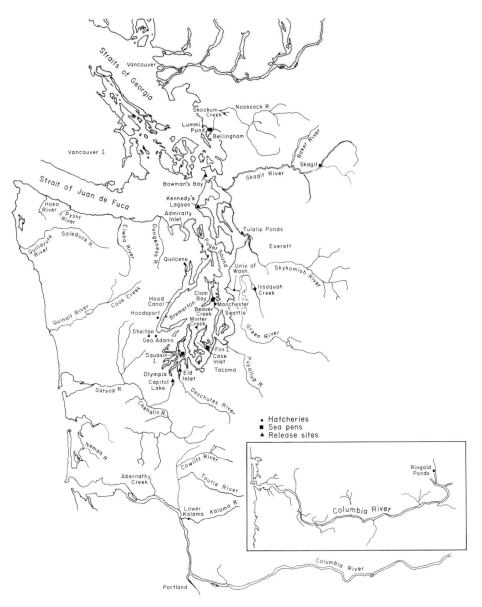

Fig. 2. Composite map showing the delayed-release areas discussed in the text.

the Skagit River Hatchery yielded 35 times the total recoveries of a normal release. Recoveries of fish from the same procedure at the Nooksack River Hatchery, however, yielded only 5 times those of normal releases (Table I). Similarly, extending the rearing from a normal 112 days to 141 days at the Nooksack River Hatchery produced a fivefold gain in recovery, but a similar procedure at the Skagit River Hatchery produced no benefits at all (Table I). In the Juan de Fuca and Hood Canal (Washington) regions (Figs 1 and 2), a spring release of yearling fall chinook from the Hoodsport Hatchery produced 33 times the normal total recovery, but a later summer delayed release of 0-age fish resulted in a tenfold decline (Table II). This could be due to seasonal abiotic factors in the release area, where surface temperatures can exceed 20°C, and dissolved oxygen concentrations become marginal.

Recovery patterns are reversed for serial delayed releases in the coastal Nemah River (Table III), where an early August release in the first year produced a fourfold recovery compared to a slightly delayed mid-May release. Genetic experiments with exotic strains complicated results from this region, as with stock 3-9 (Table III), yearling chinook salmon from a lower Columbia River stock hybridised with a southern coastal Oregon stock, which produced an unusual 9·19% recovery when released from a coastal Washington stream (Fig. 2). Differences in genetic stock and size of fall chinook are apparent in delayed-release experiments on the Columbia River (Table IV). There were benefits in rearing fall chinook from Kalama River Hatchery to a larger size in distant (Ringold, Wash.) spring-fed ponds before transporting them back to the hatchery for a delayed June release in the Kalama River (stocks 4-5 versus 4-6). Fourfold increases could be gained by releasing larger fish of the Ringold pond stock in late September from the Kalama River Hatchery (4-10) than of the native stock of the Kalama River Hatchery (4-7); midwinter delayed release (4-3) at the Toutle River Hatchery produced four times the recoveries of mid-fall releases (4-2), whereas midwinter releases from the Kalama River Hatchery (4-8) showed no benefits at all.

Migrations. Recoveries of coded-wire tagged salmon in commercial fishery samples from California to Alaska as well as the Washington State salmon sport fishery are revealing migratory patterns for both chinook and coho salmon. Fall chinook do not appear in the coastal sport fishery until age-2 nor in the commercial fisheries until almost

Table III. Survival and geographic distribution of 1971 brood normal and delayed release fall chinook salmon from Washington State Department of Fisheries hatcheries in the coastal (Washington) region. The data are summarised as percentages estimated from coded-wire tag recoveries in all fisheries sampled. Estimates of sport fishery recoveries in Puget Sound are indicated in ( ). (Data from Washington State Department of Fisheries.)

Stock no.	Release site	Stock origin	No. of rearing days	Average weight at release (g)	Date released	No. of tagged fish released	Total recovery[a] (%)	Distributions (%)						
								Alaska	British Columbia	Washington coast	Puget Sound	Oregon coast	Columbia River	Escapement
3-1	Nemah R.	Nemah R.	117[b]	5·3	17/5/72	33 718	0·86	15·0	41·8	21·9	0·3(0·3)	1·0	0·0	20·2
3-2	Nemah R.	Nemah R.	144	7·6	17/6/72	55 787	1·40	12·9	44·0	18·0	2·6(2·6)	0·4	0·0	21·9
3-3	Nemah R.	Nemah R.	192	14·2	3/8/72	32 248	3·73	11·5	33·1	26·4	0·6(0·6)	0·2	0·0	28·3
3-4	Nemah R.	Abernathy R.	137[b]	5·3	17/5/72	66 616	0·35	0·0	37·2	54·7	4·2(3·8)	0·0	0·0	3·8
3-5	Nemah R.	Abernathy R.	155	7·6	17/6/72	43 354	0·22	2·1	14·5	64·9	12·4(12·4)	0·0	0·0	6·2
3-6	Satsop R.	Nemah R. X Deschutes	376	75·7	13/3/73	41 972	1·83	1·2	44·9	33·1	6·3(6·3)	0·0	0·0	3·0
3-7	Soleduck R.	Nemah R. X Cook Ck.	98[b]	4·6	28/6/72	97 954	0·24	21·9	42·0	19·7	0·0	0·0	0·0	16·3
3-8	Soleduck R.	Cowlitz R. X	260	30·3	21/9/72	42 463	2·39	12·4	45·1	10·2	16·3(16·3)	0·8	0·0	15·5
3-9	Soleduck R.	Umpqua R.	496	141·9	8/5/73	26 819	9·19	5·9	57·3	14·6	4·5(4·5)	1·6	0·0	16·1
3-10	Soleduck R.	Quillayute R.	423	141·9	8/5/73	23 028	2·25	18·0	68·3	9·3	4·4(4·4)	0·0	0·0	0·2

[a] Estimated from coded-wire tag recoveries in all fisheries sampled in the Pacific Northwest (including Canada and Alaska) plus escapement.
[b] Normal rearing time and release for fall chinook salmon for that hatchery.

Table IV. Survival and geographic distribution of 1971 brood delayed release fall chinook salmon from Washington State Department of Fisheries hatcheries in the middle and lower Columbia River (Washington) region. The data are summarised as percentages estimated from coded-wire tag recoveries in all fisheries sampled. Estimates of sport fishery recoveries in Puget Sound are indicated in ( ). (Data from Washington State Department of Fisheries.)

Stock no.	Release site	Stock origin	No. of rearing days	Average weight at release (g)	Date released	No. of tagged fish released	Total recovery[a] (%)	Distribution (%)						
								Alaska	British Columbia	Washington coast	Puget Sound	Oregon coast	Columbia River	Escapement
MIDDLE COLUMBIA RIVER														
4-1	Columbia R.[b]	Lower Kalama R.	150	23·9	29/6/72	46 127	3·66	0·1	10·2	55·1	1·9(1·9)	5·7	26·8	0·1
LOWER COLUMBIA RIVER														
4-2	Toutle R.	Toutle R.	209	18·9	20/10/72	38 200	1·08	0·5	47·7	25·3	0·0	0·0	18·4	7·9
4-3	Toutle R.	Toutle R.	316	26·7	15/1/73	25 517	4·12	1·9	49·1	28·0	5·3(5·0)	0·3	8·9	6·7
4-4	Toutle R.	Toutle R.	394	56·8	10/4/73	21 376	12·06	0·3	38·2	39·9	2·4(2·4)	2·0	8·8	8·5
4-5	Lower Kalama R.	Lower Kalama R.	150[c]	23·9	29/6/72	38 198	1·96	0·1	16·2	61·3	2·0(2·0)	4·7	8·5	7·1
4-6	Lower Kalama R.	Lower Kalama R.	157	7·0	30/6/72	68 030	0·97	1·1	52·0	23·1	5·3(5·3)	0·9	14·7	3·0
4-7	Lower Kalama R.	Lower Kalama R.	233	18·9	21/9/72	39 762	1·58	0·0	49·9	33·0	4·3(4·3)	0·6	8·4	3·6
4-8	Lower Kalama R.	Lower Kalama R.	306	32·4	4/12/72	20 190	0·88	0·0	38·4	25·5	14·7(6·8)	0·0	18·6	2·9
4-9	Lower Kalama R.	Lower Kalama R.	424	78·3	1/4/73	20 088	8·77	0·3	35·6	46·5	2·6(2·6)	1·0	10·4	3·8
4-10	Lower Kalama R.	Ringold	250	64·8	21/9/72	17 566	6·85	0·2	21·9	57·5	2·9(2·9)	1·0	5·9	10·5

[a]Estimated from coded-wire tag recoveries in all fisheries sampled in the Pacific Northwest (including Canada and Alaska) plus escapement.
[b]Initial rearing at Lower Kalama hatchery; transported up the Columbia River to Ringold Pond for extended rearing and release.
[c]Reared at Ringold Pond and transported back to the Lower Kalama for release.

age-3, because of restrictions in net mesh size and strict regulations in the offshore troll fishery (Wahle and Vreeland, 1978). However, in Puget Sound (where there is no commercial troll fishery) sport anglers may keep chinook over 50-cm fork length—a size that is reached the winter after their second year. Puget Sound has a mild climate and is protected from oceanic storms. Consequently, small-boat anglers are able to catch many feeding chinook salmon during an intensive winter sports fishery. Any increase in fish residency increases the potential catch per angler day. If fishing remains persistently good, the rate of exploitation may be increased as more anglers are attracted into the fishery.

Migrational patterns of fall chinook salmon vary with geographical origin. Lander (1970) reported that contributions of fall chinook from Columbia River hatcheries to Alaska fisheries (from 1961-1964 brood year marking studies) were very low, as were those from the 1971 brood for some of the coastal stocks (Table III). The highest contributions to Alaskan fisheries of the latter stocks (3-7; 21·9%) came from a normal release, whereas the lowest had some extended rearing. In 75% of the delayed-release groups from coastal hatcheries, the recoveries from Washington coastal waters and Puget Sound were high. Contributions of 1971 brood fall chinook to the Oregon coastal fishery from any of the Washington State hatchery releases listed were negligible (Tables I-IV).

All Puget Sound recoveries from coastal releases (Table III) and most of the Puget Sound recoveries from Columbia River releases (Table IV) were from the sport fishery. Evidently large numbers of these fish turn into Puget Sound to feed as immature fish and leave before the late summer commercial net fishery begins.

Some delayed releases of coastal hatchery stocks (Table III, stocks 3-5 and 3-8) were of definite benefit to the Puget Sound sport fishery, even though they were of mixed origin. In comparison with normal releases, delayed releases of fall chinook salmon in the Hood Canal-Juan de Fuca region (Table II) were responsible for higher percentages of recovery in the Puget sound sport fishery (2-1, 2-6, and 2-7) as were delayed releases from Puget Sound hatcheries (Table I). Although some delayed release groups had a relatively poor showing in the Puget sound sport fishery (1-2, 1-3, 1-9, 1-10, 1-13, and 1-14), several of these releases had a very good showing.

Large numbers of chinook salmon that originate in Washington are caught in the Canadian commercial fishery off the British Columbia Coast. This includes a high percentage of recoveries of normal releases from Puget Sound hatcheries (Table I; 1-1, 1-8, 1-11; 3 out of 4) and some of the delayed releases (1-9, 1-12, 1-13, 1-14, and 1-18; 5 out of 14). Delaying the release of chinook salmon from hatcheries in other regions of Washington has an inconsistent effect on migration to Canadian waters. Although some shifts in the population movements occur, they are not *en masse*, and it would appear that the schools break up—some to residualise and others not. What determines this is not known.

Delayed Release of Coho Salmon

Recoveries. Coho salmon are normally released from Pacific Northwest hatcheries in the spring as yearlings (age 1 +). This coincides with normal migration time and age of most wild stocks, except for some colder Canadian and Alaskan waters, where coho may smolt at age 2 or even 3. They normally spend one winter at sea, and return as adults the following fall. Normal migrations lead these fish into the food rich coastal waters from northern California to Alaska.

However, some coho salmon spend their entire sea life inside Puget Sound. This resident group originally came from native wild stocks and contributed heavily to the important Puget Sound salmon sport fishery, at an average size at maturity smaller than ocean-run fish. Mathews and Buckley (1974) estimated that the natural mortality of these resident coho during their last winter in the sea was 48%. This high figure would justify a size limit lower than that for chinook and, indeed, there is no size limit on coho at this time inside Puget Sound. However, Buckley and Haw (1978) concluded that catches were declining from 1949 to 1967 due to decreases in the numbers of resident coho and that delaying the release of hatchery stocks (especially in the southern part of Puget Sound) might induce residency. In 1969, two groups of coho were marked and released at Minter Creek Hatchery (southern Puget Sound)—one at the normal time and another after extended rearing. The delayed-release group contributed 21 times more to the Puget sound recreational fishery, 3 times more to the ocean sport fishery, and 32 times more to the Washington commercial troll fleet than the group released at the normal time. The tests were expanded with the 1970 brood coho, releases of marked fish were made in May (control), June, July, and August. The June release had the greatest total contributions to Washington's fisheries (11·8%), but the recovery of the August release (9·3% total) was 3·8 times higher than the June release in the Puget Sound sport fishery. Using the May group as a control, the comparative benefits of the delayed releases to sports angling in all Washington waters were: June 7·5:1; July, 10·9:1; August, 16·0:1.

The coded wire tag was the major technical break-through that enabled subsequent expansion of experiments by the WDF biologists at the Minter Creek Hatchery and other WDF hatcheries (Tables V and VI) and confirmed that delayed releases could increase the total recovery but that the time of release and size at release were usually critical. Excessive extended rearing in fresh water may have contributed to the lower survival of stocks 5-4 and 5-10 (Table V), and 6-3 (Table VI), and was probably related to declining photoperiod (Hoar, 1976).

Tagged 1972 brood coho salmon were released from the Toutle River (Tributary to the Columbia River) Hatchery at intervals from early March until the end of June (Table VI). The earliest releases (No. 6-9) had the lowest recovery (of 5-11, Table V), and releasing larger fish gave greater benefits after the photoperiod started increasing (No. 6-12 and 6-15). The greatest recoveries came from normal sized smolts released at the beginning of June (6-16), and larger fish at the end of June (6-17). Thus, an 8·7% extension in rearing time over the normal release (6-13) produced 1·9 times more fish, and a 16·2% extension in rearing time produced 3·9 times more fish.

Migrations. Coho salmon in the Puget Sound, Admiralty Inlet, Hood Canal, and Juan de Fuca region can appear in the Washington sport fishery early because there is no size limit, unlike the coastal commercial troll and sport fisheries (which moreover are closed during the winter and early spring months). As the seasons progress, recruitment into the coastal fisheries accelerates, whereas increasing fish size and improving weather attract more Puget Sound anglers and recruitment here also increases. All fisheries peak in late summer and early fall as the rapidly maturing fish migrate toward their release areas. Late in the season the commercial drift gill-netters and purse-seiners enter the fisheries.

Migratory patterns differ between normal and delayed releases of coho salmon (Table V and VI). The percentage of the total recovery of the normal release from the Skykomish River Hatchery (No. 5-3) was

Table V. Survival and geographic distribution of 1971 brood normal and delayed release coho salmon from Washington State Department of Fisheries hatcheries in Puget Sound and Hood Canal (Admiralty Inlet), Washington. The data are summarised as percentages estimated from coded-wire tag recoveries in all fisheries samples. Estimates of sport fishery recoveries in Puget Sound are indicated in ( ). (Data from Washington State Department of Fisheries.)

Stock no.	Release site	Stock origin	No. of rearing days	Average weight at release (g)	Date released	No. of tagged fish released	Total recovery[a] (%)	Distribution (%)					
								California	British Columbia	Washington coast	Puget Sound	Oregon coast	Escapement
5-1	Skagit R.	Baker R.	359	18·9	1/5/73	39 886	3·11[b]	0·0	38·3	23·0	8·8(4·2)	1·9	28·1
5-2	Skagit R.	Skagit R.	488	45·4	30/7/73	19 998	2·77	0·0	26·0	20·0	23·8(11·5)	5·1	25·1
5-3	Skykomish R.	Skykomish R.	385	22·7	1/5/73	17 499	8·40[c]	0·0	40·0	22·8	17·0(1·0)	4·4	15·7
5-4	Skykomish R.	Skykomish R.	474	42·0	29/7/73	17 882	4·59	0·0	33·2	25·4	25·7(13·7)	3·3	12·5
5-5	Tulalip Ponds	Skykomish R.	—	28·4	15/6/73	18 700	6·28	0·0	44·7	16·9	33·1(3·5)	5·4	0·0
5-6	Green R.	Green R.	400	22·7	23/4/73	18 280	13·29[c]	0·0	35·4	17·2	12·9(3·4)	3·3	31·1
5-7	Puyallup R.	Green R.	470	37·8	5/7/73	20 000	7·53	0·0	21·0	9·3	35·8(13·9)	1·7	32·4
5-8	Minter Ck.	Minter Ck.	386	25·2	16/4/73	17 173	15·61[c]	0·7	27·2	17·2	29·2(4·6)	2·9	22·8
5-9	Minter Ck.	Minter Ck.	435–509	—	Jun–Aug	21 545	14·69[d]	0·0	27·6	15·6	32·2(4·2)	3·6	20·9
5-10	Minter Ck.	Minter Ck.	509	113·5	16/8/73	5 207	7·86	0·0	9·3	1·7	42·6(24·7)	0·0	46·4
5-11	Geo. Adams	Geo. Adams	366	18·2	1/3/73	30 183	1·97[e]	0·0	45·2	20·9	15·6(4·5)	9·0	9·3
5-12	Hoodsport	Hoodsport	515	56·8	31/7/73	26 325	4·76	0·0	11·5	9·3	18·1(12·8)	1·2	59·8

[a] Estimated from coded-wire tag recoveries in all fisheries sampled in the Pacific Northwest (including Canada and Alaska) plus escapement.

[b] Approximately normal release for that hatchery, but the stock is one that returns exceptionally early.

[c] Normal rearing time and release for coho salmon for that hatchery.

[d] Volitional releases from the hatchery pond.

[e] An example of a stock released earlier than normal and slightly smaller than those from a normal release.

Table VI. Survival and geographic distribution of 1972 brood normal and delayed release coho salmon from Washington State Department of Fisheries hatcheries in Puget Sound, coastal Washington, and the Columbia River regions. The data are summarised as percentages estimated from coded-wire tag recoveries in all fisheries sampled. Estimates of sport fishery recoveries in Puget Sound are indicated in ( ). (Data from Washington State department of Fisheries.)

Stock no.	Release site	Stock origin	No. of rearing days	Average weight at release (g)	Date released	No. of tagged fish released	Total recovery^a (%)	Distribution (%)						
								California	British Columbia	Washington coast	Puget Sound	Oregon coast	Columbia River	Escapement
6-1	Skagit R.	Baker R.	377	20·6	15/5/74	41 022	6·80^b	0·7	17·5	19·0	17·6(2·1)	1·7	0·0	43·5
6-2	Skagit R.	Skagit R.	385	25·2	15/5/74	31 923	6·28^c	0·0	23·3	16·4	36·0(2·4)	1·2	0·0	23·1
6-3	Skagit R.	Skagit R.	450	25·2	1/8/74	20 743	3·64	0·0	14·4	10·4	24·8(6·6)	4·8	0·0	45·5
6-4	Puyallup R.	Puyallup R.	386	22·7	30/4/74	30 205	9·40^c	0·0	24·7	19·5	50·0(4·3)	0·9	0·0	4·6
6-5	Puyallup R.	Puyallup R.	—	37·8	20/7/74	20 400	11·62	0·0	19·4	14·3	53·6(13·7)	3·0	0·0	9·9
6-6	Green R.	Green R.	487	32·4	31/7/74	20 221	7·41	0·0	18·6	15·0	49·8(26·7)	0·7	0·0	15·9
6-7	Nemah R.	Nemah R.	415	22·7	2/5/74	29 690	2·99^b	3·5	2·6	41·3	0·0	37·1	0·0	15·5
6-8	Nemah R.	Nemah R.	477	30·3	2/7/74	18 589	5·78	6·5	1·9	30·4	0·5(0·3)	42·9	0·0	17·9
6-9	Toutle R.	Toutle R.	296	22·7	1/3/74	52 220	3·47^d	10·3	0·3	22·7	0·0	41·1	1·3	24·4
6-10	Toutle R.	Toutle R.	327	15·1	1/4/74	49 050	3·72^e	13·2	0·5	19·0	0·0	37·5	2·4	27·3
6-11	Toutle R.	Toutle R.	327	22·7	1/4/74	42 000	4·25^f	15·7	0·0	20·1	0·0	39·5	0·0	24·7
6-12	Toutle R.	Toutle R.	327	32·4	1/4/74	31 668	4·94^d	12·1	0·7	14·6	0·0	46·9	0·8	24·9
6-13	Toutle R.	Toutle R.	357	21·6	1/5/74	42 756	4·17^c	14·3	0·1	28·3	0·0	32·3	1·1	23·9
6-14	Toutle R.	Toutle R.	357	15·1	1/5/74	41 820	4·11^g	8·8	0·2	18·0	0·2(0·2)	37·3	4·5	31·0
6-15	Toutle R.	Toutle R.	357	32·4	1/5/74	30 944	6·40^h	7·1	0·5	18·1	0·0	43·8	3·1	27·1
6-16	Toutle R.	Toutle R.	388	22·7	1/6/74	41 340	8·11^i	12·2	0·4	22·0	0·0	40·4	5·0	19·8
6-17	Toutle R.	Toutle R.	415	37·8	27/6/74	31 068	16·21	7·6	0·5	26·0	0·0	40·5	4·0	21·3

^a Estimated from coded-wire tag recoveries in all fisheries sampled in the Pacific Northwest (including Canada and Alaska) plus escapement.

^b Approximately normal release for that hatchery, but the stock is one that returns exceptionally early.

^c Normal rearing time and release for coho salmon for that hatchery.

^d An early release of large fish (normal smolt size).

^e An early release of small fish.

^f An early release of fish of normal (smolt) sized fish.

^g A release of small fish at the normal time.

^h A release of large fish at the normal time.

^i A delayed (late) release of normal (smolt) sized fish.

1·8 times that of the delayed release (No. 5-4). However, the proportion of recoveries of the delayed release in the Puget Sound sport fishery was 13·7 times that of the normal release and less in Canada and Oregon. A chronological examination of the Puget Sound sport fishery recoveries in 1974 reveals how these shifts occurred (Fig. 3). Some of the delayed-release group probably never left Puget Sound, but the controls contributed more heavily to the British Columbia troll fishery than fish in the delayed-release group that migrated out of Puget Sound; 19·1% of the delayed-release and 24·9% of the normal release recoveries came from fisheries off southwestern Vancouver Island (Canada), and 1·1% and 7·3% (respectively) came from fisheries off

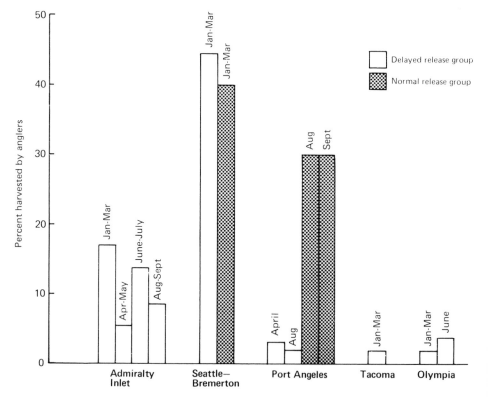

Fig. 3. Estimated 1974 recoveries in the Puget Sound sport fishery of normal and delayed release fish of the 1971 brood release (5-4) Skykomish River Hatchery coho. The time of the recoveries and the percentages of the estimated 1974 Puget Sound angler harvest *(above)* are shown in relation to the geographical reporting areas, and their distances from the estuary *(right)*.

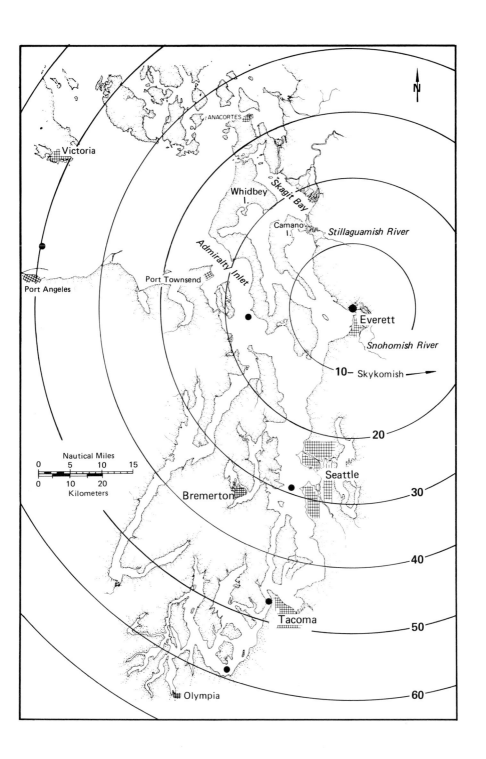

N

Victoria

ANACORTES

Whidbey
I.

Skagit Bay

Camano
I.

Stillaguamish River

Admiralty Inlet

Port Townsend

Port Angeles

Everett

Snohomish River

10— Skykomish ⟶

20

Nautical Miles
0   5   10   15

0   10   20
Kilometers

Seattle

30

Bremerton

40

Tacoma

50

60

Olympia

northwestern Vancouver Island (from unpublished WDF data not included in the tables).

Shifts in the distributions of other delayed-release stocks from the 1971 brood WDF hatchery coho also favoured the Puget Sound sport fisherman as "resident" coho and did not contribute as heavily to the northern Canadian fisheries (Table V; 5-2, 5-7, 5-10, and 5-12) as did the normal release groups (5-3, 5-6, and 5-8).

The delayed releases of the 1972 brood from the Skagit River Hatchery (Table VI, No. 6-3) contributed only 2·8 times more than the controls (6-2) to the Puget Sound sport fishery; the percentage distributions to the Canadian and U.S. commercial fisheries (except Oregon) was down, but the percentage of escapement was almost double the control. The average fork length of the delayed release escapement was 53 cm and of the control, 63 cm. This size disparity would favour heavy exploitation of the control fish by the intense, selective commercial gill-net fishery. Other 1972 brood delayed-release coho from WDF hatcheries in Puget Sound produced proportionately better populations, including resident fish (6-5 and 6-6).

As with most Columbia River hatcheries, very few of the 1972 brood Toutle River coho salmon (No. 6-9 through 6-17) were recovered in the Canadian fisheries or in Puget Sound. The major 1975 recoveries were from the Washington, Oregon, and California coastal fisheries; in the latter, major exploitation was from the commercial troll fleet. In coastal sport fisheries, 0-1% were recovered in California, 5·4 to 11·3% in Oregon, and 7·2 to 17·9% in Washington (from unpublished WDF data not included in the tables). As the range of total Washington coastal recoveries was only 14·6% (No. 6-12) to 28·3% (No. 6-13), these Toutle River Hatchery release groups contributed heavily to the coastal sport fishery. Although the contributions to the Washington coastal sport fishery of the control (No. 6-13; 16·5%) and those of the late June delayed release (No. 6-17; 17·9%) differed little, the latter contributed almost 4 times as many fish to the sport fishery as the controls—an impressive figure.

Saltwater Releases

Floating Net-pens

Floating net-pens for the culture of Pacific salmon were adapted from Japanese and Norwegian techniques for rearing rainbow trout *(Salmo gairdneri)* and Atlantic salmon *(S. salar)* in the sea. In 1969, the NMFS studied the feasibility of culturing coho and chinook salmon for market in net-pens in Clam Bay, Puget Sound, near the town of Manchester. During the course of a large pilot farm study, many excess coho and chinook salmon were made available for delayed saltwater release to study distributions and contributions to the sport fishery.

University of Washington and WDF biologists tagged 800 yearling chinook salmon weighing an average of 150 g with Carlin dangler tags and released them in Clam Bay and Case Inlet in southern Puget Sound. Within a year, the total contributions to the Puget Sound sport fishery were approximately 10%, with Case Inlet fish contributing heavily in southern Puget Sound and Clam Bay releases almost exclusively to middle Puget Sound (Haw and Bergman, 1972). After 17 months, 12·5% of the chinook were recovered from the Clam Bay release group and 14·3% from the Case Inlet group. Hundreds of coho salmon were tagged by WDF with the same external tag and released in the same areas with similar results. Coho salmon that escaped from the pilot farm net-pens in the winter of 1971-72 were in excellent condition and weighed from 200 to 400 g. Their caudal fins were rounded (presumably from the effects of high-density rearing). This distinguishing feature became well known to Puget Sound anglers, and their movements could be traced by the reports of heavy sport fishery catches of "round-tailed" coho. The total releases from this pilot farm, including excess potential brood fish, were approximately 10 metric tons and had a large impact on the local sport fishery.

These early successes in sport fishery enhancement through net-pen culture resulted in more organised studies, not all of which were encouraging. For example, over 70 000 yearling Minter Creek Hatchery coho salmon were released by NMFS and WDF biologists from floating net-pens in Clam Bay on 2 July, 1971, at an average weight of 45 g (Novotny, 1975), but recoveries in the Puget Sound sport fishery were approximately one-fifth those of a simultaneous delayed release of the same stock directly from the hatchery. Inventories in net-pen culture have always been a problem; the estimate of the number of fish released on 2 July, 1971, was probably too high—but not high enough to produce the difference in recoveries observed. Subsequent studies of releases of net-pen cultured chinook salmon at NMFS's Manchester facility on Clam Bay indicated that sport fishery recoveries could indeed be very poor. Moring (1973) estimated a contribution of only 0·1% from a 1973 release of 1971 brood fall chinook in Clam Bay. Releases of 1971 brood fall chinook in early 1973 from a net-pen rearing density study in Clam Bay contributed a meagre 0·3% to the resident sport fishery, and this failure was attributed to repeated epizootics of furunculosis and vibriosis during the saltwater culture stages (Novotny, 1978). In late August, 1974, NMFS released 95 externally tagged net-pen culture 1972 brood coho in Clam Bay. The average weight at releases was 554 g, and mortalities from tagging were expected to be low. Sport anglers returned 13·7% of the tags within three months after release, all from central Puget Sound (Fig. 4). The total recovery was 20% (including recaptures in a trap at the head of Clam Bay), but nothing further was seen of this tagged group after December, 1974.

The 1971 brood fall chinook salmon reared at the WDF Hoodsport Hatchery in Hood Canal (Fig. 5) were transported by truck and transfer barge to the floating net-pens near Squaxin Island (Fig. 6). Four groups bearing coded-wire tags were released in 1972 and 1973, including one that had been fed a dry, pelleted ration (instead of Oregon moist pellets) for part of the rearing period (Table VII). The percentage of recovery was not high for any group, but spring releases of yearling fish increased overall survival by as much as 29:1 over fish released the previous summer and improved the contributions to the Puget Sound sport fishery by at least 4:1. Similarly, through co-operative sportsmen's projects, the WDF reared 1971 brood Samish coho for delayed release in sea-pens off Whidbey Island in 1973, and 1972 brood Minter Creek coho for delayed release in sea-pens in Seattle's Elliot Bay. One group of 4850 marked coho averaging 45 g was released off Whidbey on 29 May, 1973, and another group of 4850 ($\bar{x}$ = 91 g) on 1 August, 1973. The total recovery of the first group was 3·9%, with 18·1% of the catch taken by the Puget Sound sports fishery. The total recovery of the August release was 12·4%, but only 4·6% of the catch was taken by Puget Sound anglers. On 4 August, 1974, 11 035 coho averaging 99 g were released in Elliot Bay, and the total recovery was a spectacular 28·3%. However, only 9·6% of this was taken by the Puget Sound sports fishery (from unpublished WDF data not included in the tables).

Since that time, WDF established a station at Fox Island (Fig. 5) for extended rearing and releasing of coho and chinook salmon. At least 250 000 coho and/or chinook salmon are reared in net-pens each year in Puget Sound for delayed release.

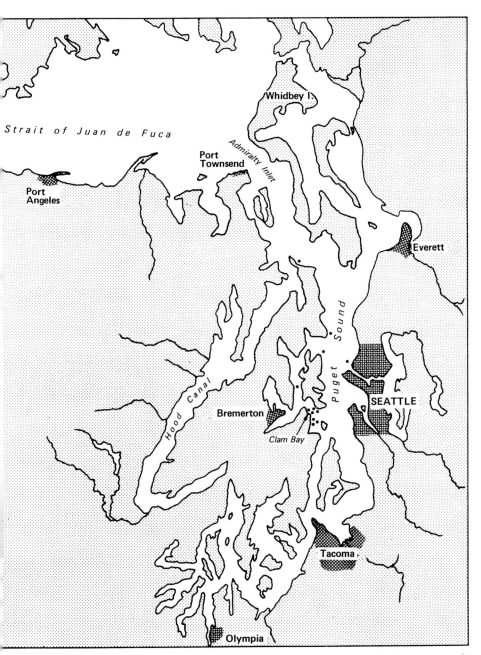

Fig. 4. Sport fishery recoveries (●) of coho salmon of age-group 1 + that were released from sea-pens in Clam Bay.

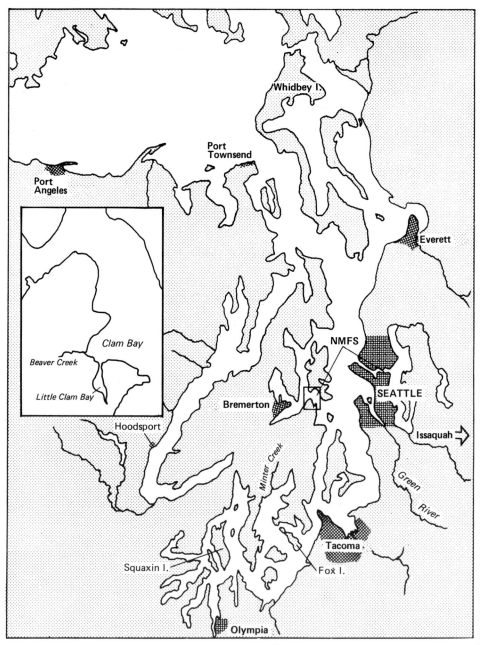

Fig. 5. Locations of the major saltwater delayed release sites in south and central Puget Sound (Squaxin Island, Fox Island, and Clam Bay); the major Washington Department of Fisheries hatcheries that supply production quantities of coho and chinook salmon smolts for transfer to seawater systems (Minter Creek, Hoodsport, Green River, and Issaquah); and, the National Marine Fisheries Service, NOAA, freshwater laboratory in Seattle.

Fig. 6(a). Feeding chinook salmon in floating net-pens near Squaxin Island, southern Puget Sound (Washington). Both coho and chinook salmon were reared in these pens for delayed release by the Squaxin Indians on contract for the Washington State Department of Fisheries.

Fig. 6(b). Aerial view of the Squaxin Island floating net-pens that were used in co-operative programmes of delayed sea release for coho and chinook salmon.

Table VII. Estimated recoveries and distributions of 1971 brood fall chinook salmon reared at Hoodsport Hatchery and Squaxin Island sea-pens (delayed release from net-pens). Data are based on estimates from coded-wire tag recoveries in all fisheries but does not include late data for 5-year old fish from Oregon or Canada.[a] (Data from Washington State Department of Fisheries.)

Group	Release date	Weight at release (g)	Number of tagged fish	Total estimated recovery (%)	Puget Sound sport	Puget Sound net	Washington coastal sport	Washington coastal troll	British Columbia commercial	Escapement
					Distribution of estimated recoveries (%)					
1	5/8/72	16·2	33 467	0·14	19·5	43·5	0	19·6	8·7	8·7
2	18/10/72	54·0	6 048	0·31	0	0	0	0	100·0	0
3[b]	6/4/73	174·6	2 800	4·10	84·5	10·3	0	0	4·3	0·9
4	17/4/73	181·6	4 850	2·80	81·0	1·5	6·6	5·1	2·2	8·7

[a]From Washington State Department of Fisheries data.
[b]Partial use of pelleted dry salmon diets during seawater culture.

The anadromous cutthroat trout *(Salmo clarki)* is another popular game fish in the Pacific Northwest (Washington, 1977), especially in the sheltered waters of Hood Canal. However, in 1972 only 0·1% of the hatchery smolts that were planted in Hood Canal streams were harvested by anglers in marine waters of the canal (Hisata, 1973).

In 1973, several hundred sea-run cutthroat were transported from the Washington State Department of Game (WDG) Shelton Hatchery as yearling spring smolts to net-pens in Clam Bay, cultured in seawater through spring and summer, tagged externally, transported by truck, and released into Hood Canal. The harvest by saltwater anglers was approximately 9%. Research by WDG biologists at NMFS's Manchester facility now includes culturing of thousands of cutthroat trout from a number of genetic strains to examine differential survival in Hood Canal after delayed release (Johnston and Mercer, 1976).

The projects that focused on delayed releases of salmonids from net-pens at the Manchester facility stimulated similar research on delayed releases in other regions, including California. Since 1974, over 28 000 externally tagged (from 2400 to 7600 per group) coho and chinook salmon have been released from net-pens at Tiburon on San Francisco Bay to determine whether they could contribute more heavily to the California sport fishery. The average tag recovery for coho inside San Francisco Bay (including adults returning from the ocean) was 52·0% of the total number recovered and for chinook, only 5·7%. However, the total recovery of five lots of tagged coho in all fisheries was 0·04 to 0·90% (average 0·55%) of the number released, whereas the total recovery of the first group of delayed release fall chinook was an impressive 4·0% of the number released (personal communication, Dan Ralph, National Marine Fisheries Service, Tiburon, California).

In northern Puget Sound, the Lummi Indian aquaculture project cultures coho salmon in net-pens in a 300-hectare shallow, diked tidal pond (Fig. 7). The fish imprint to, and exit through, the dike ꞌoutlet into Lummi Bay, which is a northerly juncture of Puget Sound and the Strait of Georgia (Fig. 2).

Three groups of coded-wire tagged coho, reared at the Lummi's Skookum Creek Hatchery on the tributary to the Nooksack River were released in 1975 (personal communication, Steve Seymour, Manager, Fish Culture Program, Lummi Indian Tribal Enterprise, Marietta, Washington). The treatments were: (1) direct release (control group) from the hatchery; (2) a simultaneous release of a group reared for 45

Fig. 7. Aerial view of the Lummi Indian diked-tidal pond in northern Puget Sound. Its outlet is indicated by the arrow. (Photo courtesy of Lummi Indian Tribal Enterprises.)

days in seawater; and (3) a delayed release after 6 days of seawater rearing (Table VIII). Weights at release for all groups were similar despite a 33-day interval between the first and last releases. In comparison to the control group, rearing for 45 days in seawater reduced the total recoveries by a factor of 3·5, and shifted the contributions toward the Canadian fisheries. The delayed release after only 6 days of seawater rearing approached the high recovery level of the control group and shifted contributions in favour of U.S. fisheries.

At Little Port Walter in southeastern Alaska, NMFS biologists culture salmon in both floating net-pens and unique floating raceways (Northwest Fisheries Center *Monthly Report*, April 1977). Freshwater layers allow the use of varying salinities. In one experiment, pink salmon fry were marked and cultured for serial releases (Northwest Fisheries Center *Monthly Report*, Nov. 1977). Marine survivals, based on the number of marked fry released, suggest a growth and survival pattern for Little Port Walter delayed-release pink salmon (Table IX)

Table VIII. A comparison of the estimated contributions of three groups of coho salmon released from the Lummi aquaculture project (northern Puget Sound) in 1975. The fish were from the 1973 Quilcene Hatchery (northern Hood Canal) brood year and are arranged by chronological release.[a]

Test	Release date	Size at release (g)	Estimated total recovery (%)	Puget Sound sport	Puget Sound net	Washington Coastal sport	Washington Coastal troll	British Columbia commercial	Oregon coastal	Escapement
								Distributions of estimated recoveries (%)		
45 days seawater rearing	30/5/75	25·2	5·3	0·9	22·1	6·8	14·0	46·5	4·4	5·3
Hatchery release	3/6/75	23·9	18·4	1·0	29·2	8·3	14·3	39·8	3·0	4·4
Delayed release with 6 days seawater rearing	3/7/75	25·2	17·0	2·2	31·1	7·0	20·4	31·2	2·5	5·6

[a]Data provided by Steve Seymour, Manager, Fish Culture Program, Lummi Indian Tribal Enterprises, Marietta, Washington.

Table IX. Results of serial releases of marked cultured 1974 brood pink salmon fry (15 000/group) from the National Marine Fisheries Service, NOAA, Little Port Walter, Alaska station.

Culturing time (days)	$\bar{x}$ weight at release (g)	Estimated marine survival (%)	$\bar{x}$ weight of returning males (kg)
0	0·23	2·7	2·36
30	0·27	3·9	2·01
60	0·55	4·6	2·01
90	1·95	3·8	1·65

which is similar to that of delayed-release coho salmon in Puget Sound; i.e., delaying the release frequently increases survival, but returning adults are smaller.

Diked Tidal Lagoons

In 1960, culturing salmon in marine lagoons was proposed as part of a plan to expand the salmon production of Washington State with a minimum of additional capital investment (Moore *et al.*, 1960). The plan included diking many natural saltwater lagoons in the Sound. Young salmon were to be transferred from freshwater hatcheries to the lagoons, where they could forage on natural foods until they migrated or until they were released. Salo (1963) proposed a similar scheme for salmon and steelhead (the anadromous form of rainbow trout) at Big Lagoon in northern California. However, by the mid-1960s, most of the lagoon rearing programmes were abandoned for a variety of reasons, including predation, disease, and lack of natural foods. DeWitt (1969) concluded that natural food production in lagoons had been overestimated and that supplemental feeding was necessary.

In 1974, WDF reactivated the rearing site at Little Clam Bay, an 11-hectare diked, tidal lagoon that discharges directly into the bay (Figs. 5 and 8). Water exchange between the bay and lagoon is regulated by flapper valves in the dike and is dependent on the extremity of the tides (2-5 m). A rotary screen prevents fish from escaping.

Early in February, 1974, yearling coho (14·2 g) at the WDF Green River Hatchery were injected with a *Vibrio anguillarum* vaccine and tagged with the coded-wire tag. A non-vaccinated control group was also tagged, and on February 14th, the two tagged lots plus a large

Fig. 8. Little Clam Bay, a diked-tidal lagoon near Manchester, Washington. *(Upper)* The 11 ha lagoon; *(lower)* the discharge pipe below the dike on a low tide. Note the floating net-pens of a commercial salmon farm in the background.

non-tagged population were trucked to the lagoon at Little Clam Bay and released. The process was repeated in early April, and on April 10th the remaining tagged and untagged yearling coho (18·2 g) were turned loose in the lagoon. A total of 40 000 were released, 10% of which were tagged. Dry pelleted feeds were broadcast by hand from a small powered raft, slowly cruising the perimeter. Early spring salinities in the lagoon ranged from 15 to 26 parts per thousand, top to bottom. The rotary screen was damaged in late April, and some fish may have escaped early. Repairs were made, but further damage caused mortality in coho that became trapped in the rotary screen. The screen was removed on 27th May, and all fish were allowed to escape. They averaged 32·4 g and were in excellent condition.

There was no advantage in vaccinating against vibriosis in either group although the pathogenic bacteria are present in Little Clam Bay (Table X). An April transfer to the lagoon was preferred to February. Most important are the high recoveries from these delayed releases and the geographical distributions. These coho salmon evidently spent very little time in Puget Sound as evidenced by the broad range of coastal recoveries, the lack of recoveries in the Puget Sound angler harvest, and, in contrast, large contributions to the Puget Sound net fishery as returning adults. Comparing the sizes of fish between brood years can be misleading, but the overall mean length of the coho from the lagoon on Little Clam Bay was at least 8 cm larger than normal Minter Creek releases (Table XI, 5-8; 5-9), 19 cm larger than the August delayed-release group (No. 5-10), and 4-5 cm longer than a normal Green River release (5-6). Normal Puyallup Hatchery 1972 brood release (6-4) were 4-5 cm shorter, and the 1972 brood Green River delayed releases (6-6) were 16-17 cm shorter than the same group released from the lagoon on Little Clam Bay (Table XI).

Pumped Seawater

Pumped seawater has been used for experimental culture of Pacific salmon in Puget Sound by WDF at Bowman's Bay, NMFS at Manchester, and Lummi Indian projects in Lummi Bay. Pumped seawater has also been used for large experimental research projects by NMFS in Little Port Walter, Alaska (Northwest Fisheries Center *Monthly Report,* Apr. 1977); for production rearing of totally cultured coho salmon in a diked lagoon in Brittany, France (Harache and Novotny, 1976); and for certain types of Atlantic salmon culture in

Table X. Estimated recoveries and geographical distributions of coded-wire tagged coho salmon released from Little Clam Bay lagoon (central Puget Sound) May 27, 1974.[a]

Date of transfer from Green River Hatchery to Little Clam Bay lagoon	Number tagged at hatchery	Total estimated recovery (%)[b]	Puget Sound sport	Puget Sound net	Washington coastal sport	Washington coastal troll	British Columbia commercial	Oregon coastal	California coastal	Escapement[c]
February 14										
vibrio vaccinated	9 207	7·45	0·6	41·8	8·0	18·1	30·7	0·7	0	0·1
control	9 122	9·41	0·2	54·7	8·2	12·0	24·3	0·7	0	0
April 10										
vibrio vaccinated	9 020	14·75	0·5	38·3	5·9	11·5	33·5	9·1	1·1	0·2
control	9 152	14·55	0·8	41·4	2·8	14·3	32·0	8·5	0	0·2

[a]From Washington State Department of Fisheries data.
[b]Based on the number of fish released into the lagoon.
[c]Adults recovered in the salmon traps in Beaver Creek, Clam Bay.

Table XI. Mean fork lengths (MFL) of 1971 brood normal and delayed release coho salmon from Minter Creek Hatchery and normal Green River Hatchery coho, sampled in the 1974 fisheries, and MFL's of normal 1972 brood Puyallup River Hatchery coho and delayed release coho from Green River Hatchery and Little Clam Bay lagoon, sampled in the 1975 fisheries. Puget Sound sport fishery data are not shown due to insufficient catches of lagoon reared and released fish. (Data from Washington State Department of Fisheries.)

	Mean fork length (cm)			
Year of fishery and test group	Overall (including Puget Sound sport fishery)	Puget Sound net fishery	Washington coast troll fishery	Washington coast sport fishery
1974 FISHERIES (see Table V)				
stock no. 5-6, Green River	63	64	58	59
5-8, Minter Creek	59	62	58	55
5-9, Minter Creek	58	60	57	55
5-10, Minter Creek	48	49	49	—
1975 FISHERIES (see Table X)				
February 14 release group, vaccinated	67	71	64	59
February 14 release group, control	68	71	62	62
April 10 release group, vaccinated	68	63	65	63
April 10 release group, control	67	70	63	61
1975 FISHERIES (see Table VI)				
stock no. 6-4, Puyallup River	63	68	62	60
6-6, Green River	51	58	53	53

Norway. Pumped seawater is the basis of the largest private salmon sea-ranching operations on the coast of Oregon and California (Fig. 9). A total of over 50 million chum, coho, and chinook salmon were cultured for delayed release and imprinting in 1976-78 in pumped seawater raceways; these same firms are licensed to culture 100 million. In Oregon and California, delayed releases from these facilities are so recent that recovery data are still being processed, but data are available from a Lummi Indian Tribal Enterprises (LITE) experiment in 1976 (Table XII).

Four groups of yearling coho salmon were released: two directly from the Skookum Creek hatchery and two after 14 days rearing in concrete circular ponds in seawater pumped from Lummi Bay (Fig. 2). The geographical distribution of the recoveries varied little and unlike the results from other tagging experiments with Puget Sound fish, the

Fig. 9. The pumped seawater release and recovery sites of Oregon Aquafoods Inc. at Newport, Oregon.

Table XII. A comparison of estimated recoveries of coded-wire tagged coho salmon released from a river site and a delayed release from a pumped seawater pond in Lummi Bay. All fish were from the 1974 brood Cascade-Sandy River (Oregon) stock, and all were reared at the Lummi Indian Skookum Creek Hatchery.[a]

Treatment[b]	Number of fish tagged	Average weight (g)	Days reared in seawater	Release date	Total estimated recoveries (%)	Distribution of estimated recoveries (%)				
						Washington (all fisheries)	British Columbia	Oregon	California	Escapement (trap)
I	14 243	33·6	0	7/5/76	2·9	55·0	23·2	11·6	0	10·1
II	10 486	33·6	0	7/5/76	4·7	53·5	20·2	18·7	0	7·5
III	12 677	33·6	14	26/5/76	9·0	59·3	23·0	11·5	0	6·1
IV	14 440	37·2	14	26/5/76	7·5	55·5	25·2	12·1	1·5	5·7

[a] Summarised from data provided by Steve Seymour, Manager, Fish Culture Program, Lummi Indian Tribal Enterprises, Marietta, Washington.
[b] I. Orally vaccinated against vibriosis; released S. fork, Nooksack River.
II. Control for oral vaccine test.
III. Released into Lummi Bay from concrete pumped seawater ponds.
IV. Also released into Lummi Bay from pumped seawater ponds.

Canadian proportion of the catch was low (Table XII). More importantly, the total recovery could be increased by as much as 3:1 with a simple 14-day seawater conditioning. Thus, this technique also appears to be a promising method of enhancing local fisheries.

Extended rearing programmes generally require an increase in available rearing capacity, and in freshwater hatcheries this may be limited (mainly because of water supplies). Therefore, the most likely areas for continued expansion of extended rearing are in salt water, where more areas for diked lagoons, pumped water, and floating pens are available.

IMPRINTING SALMON IN SEAWATER AND ITS IMPLICATIONS

This limited analysis of delayed releases of salmon is focused on changes in survival and geographical distributions of freshwater hatchery releases. Survival includes escapement of the adults to the hatcheries as well as recoveries in the various fisheries. But, when salmon are released into seawater, do they return to their natal stream or imprint to the sea release site? The first substantial salmon returns to a seawater release site (no available freshwater imprinting) were probably at Kennedy's Lagoon in 1962. This lagoon contained 4·5 ha of pure seawater. Biologists of WDF captured 1700 coho and 300 to 400 chum salmon at the tidal dike discharge (WDF Annual Report, 1962).

Scientists at the NMFS Manchester facility on Clam Bay culture some salmon in fresh well-water and water from a small, adjacent stream (Beaver Creek) that terminates at the head of the bay (Fig. 10). Any fish cultured in this hatchery system and released in the bay are expected to return there, eventually entering the small fish ladder at the mouth of Beaver Creek. However, most releases of large numbers of fish in Clam Bay or in other Puget Sound areas such as off Fox and Squaxin Islands (Fig. 5), are trucked from hatcheries that are far from the release site.

The first reported returns from net-pen released salmon were from recoveries in Clam Bay in 1972 from the 1969 brood of Minter Creek coho salmon that were released in 1971 (see p. 341). The fish entered

Fig. 10. An aerial view of the head of Clam Bay near Manchester, Washington. Beaver Creek discharges into the head of the bay (lower left corner).

the bay in September, milled in the net-pen area, and attracted many sports anglers. In early November, approximately 400 mature coho entered the trap in Beaver Creek (Northwest Fisheries *Monthly Report,* Nov. 1972). None of the tagged fish returned to Minter Creek, although it is possible that straying to other streams may have occurred.

In 1971 and 1972, biologists of NMFS found that imprinting Issaquah Hatchery coho salmon for four hours to water from an NMFS hatchery in Seattle was just as effective in establishing a "homing" station as imprinting for 168 hours. All adults returned to the Seattle Hatchery, and none to the Issaquah Hatchery (Fig. 2) (Northwest Fisheries Center *Monthly Report,* Jan. 1974). However, it was not known whether short-term imprinting in seawater would be similarly successful, and a series of experiments were designed to test this. In 1973, four lots of 5000 yearling Issaquah coho were "cold-branded" and treated as follows: (1) trucked from Issaquah Hatchery to Beaver Creek and released in the lowest pond at tide water; (2) reared in net-pens in Clam Bay for 3 weeks and released in the lower Beaver Creek pond; (3) reared in net-pens in Clam Bay for 3 weeks and released; and (4) released directly from the transport truck into seawater in Clam Bay. No marked adults from this group returned to Issaquah Creek in 1974, when recoveries of marked coho (with identifiable brands) in the Beaver Creek trap were as follows: Group one, 2·2%; two, 1·6%; three, 1·4%; four, 0·2% (Northwest Fisheries Center *Monthly Report,* Jan. 1975). This indicated that short-term retention in net-pens before release had good potential for imprinting salmon to sea-release sites.

In 1973, WDF and NMFS released over 600 000 coho in Clam Bay from extended rearing schedules that ranged from 3 weeks to several months. In 1974, returning adults from this release jammed the small fish ladder in the lower Beaver Creek pond after the first November freshet. Moreover, there was also a large return of jack coho (2-year old males) to Little Clam Bay from delayed release there in spring 1974 (Table X). Despite a concentrated and successful sport fishery in Clam Bay from September to mid-November 1974, 8827 salmon entered the Beaver Creek trap (Northwest Fisheries Center *Monthly Report,* Jan. 1974) including 21 large chinook (Fig. 11) from other experimental releases and 2 adult pink salmon from an NMFS experiment with delayed release from a net-pen that was an attempt to develop a run of even-year pink salmon from Alaskan eggs (Northwest Fisheries Center *Monthly Report,* Sept. 1974). A second generation from that pair of

Fig. 11. Adult male chinook salmon that returned to the sea-release site in Clam Bay.

pink salmon returned to Clam Bay in 1976 from delayed releases from net-pens in 1975 (Northwest Fisheries Center *Monthly Report,* Sept. 1976).

The extensive numbers of coho salmon returning to Clam Bay in 1974 created a serious handling problem for our small (NMFS) staff and WDF (Fig. 12). Since a large return of adult fish from this release was expected in 1975, the problem was resolved by establishing a commercial fishing area in the bay for local Indians. Most of the fishing was done by 8 to 10 gill-netters (Fig. 13), using small, outboard powered skiffs (Fig. 14). The fishermen harvested over 6000 coho, catching approximately 20 to 150 fish per boat per night (Fig. 15). Gross revenues were $60 000-70 000, and the coho averaged about 4·8 kg. In spite of this intense fishing effort, many coho attempted to enter the seawater discharge pipe from Little Clam Bay during low tides. Over 400 were diverted into the Beaver Creek trap during the November freshets (Northwest Fisheries Center *Monthly Report,* No. 1975). None of the marked fish returned to the Green River Hatchery.

Similarly, the Squaxin Indians were able to establish a new fishery around their Squaxin Island sea-pens, and many coho returning to the WDF Fox Island net-pen release site entered run-off culverts along the near beaches during heavy rains. Salmon released from pumped seawater ponds and pen enclosures in the Lummi diked tidal pond returned to the seawater trap there. The annual production of 2 million coho smolts from the Lummi Indian's Skookum Creek Hatchery could be acclimatised and imprinted (in 7-day intervals) in the pumped seawater ponds over a 6-week period (personal communication, Steve Seymour, Manager, Fish Culture Program, Lummi Indian Tribal Enterprise, Marietta, Washington).

These tests suggest that imprinting salmon to marine release sites could be an effective management tool. None of the fish released from marine sites returned to the freshwater hatcheries, unless they were close to the delayed sea-release site, such as at NMFS's Little Port Walter facility in Alaska, where 8% of the 1974 delayed release coho smolts returned, first to the net-pen site in the bay and then to the stream used for early rearing. Normally 150-300 wild adult coho returned each year from wild smolt production; in 1975, there were 13 800 adults—survivors of cultured, delayed, sea-release smolts (Northwest Fisheries Center *Monthly Report,* Oct. 1975).

Fig. 12. About 9000 adult coho salmon that had been released as juveniles from floating net-pens in Clam Bay entered the small fish ladder in Beaver Creek.

Fig. 13. A new commercial fishing area was established in Clam Bay as a result of delayed sea releases of juvenile coho salmon from a diked, tidal lagoon. Set gill-nets proved to be the most efficient method of harvesting the adult salmon that returned to the lagoon.

Fig. 14. Fishermen from the Suquamish Indian tribe were able to harvest the adult coho salmon returning to the sheltered waters of Clam Bay with a modest investment in gear.

Fig. 15. National Marine Fisheries Service, NOAA, biologist examining the coho salmon harvested in the terminal fishery in Clam Bay to look for marked ("branded" and fin-clipped) fish.

DISCUSSION

The potential benefits of delaying the releases of salmon have not been limited to the coastal region of the northeastern Pacific Ocean. Sutterlin and Merrill (1978) discussed releases of Atlantic salmon smolts in the early 1960s in Norway after 6-12 months of seawater rearing. The adult returns range from 10-14%; they were probably the stimulus for studies now being conducted in Norway on using early saltwater rearing and delayed releasing to increase oceanic survival and influence migration patterns.

Management research on Pacific salmon and collection of economic data on the production of normal releases of salmon from freshwater hatcheries are extensive. For example, the cost of producing a kilogram of fish for release at any size can be computed; furthermore, data are available for juvenile production strategies for coho salmon that will reveal the weight of fish harvested per weight of fish and time released (Bilton, Chapter 16, pp. 303-322). Firm economic data of this type are not yet available for delayed sea releases, and there are still many variables that must be examined that influence the survival and growth of these salmon and relate to economics. It does seem reasonable to assume, however, that both recreational and commercial fishermen, and even the consumer, will reap an economic benefit from increased survival of fish and establishment of new fishing areas at marine release sites as results of delayed sea releases.

The implications of the additional tools (and problems) given to fisheries management by altering salmon migrations are still being studied. The creation of fishing areas in the sea that salmon return to as adults may only be limited by oceanic capacity to absorb the potential output of cultured fish. In theory, some freshwater hatchery releases could be restricted to provide just enough returning adults for egg production. The remaining hatchery production of smolts could be transported for seawater acclimatisation, imprinting, and delayed release. This theoretical concept of a marine ''terminus'' for cultured salmon may eventually help management by concentrating some harvest activity there. Great care would be needed in planning releases to avoid conflicts with historical allocations of fishing areas, user groups, and most of all, vulnerable wild stocks.

The last and perhaps most important result of delayed-release studies has been the concurrent and fortuitous discovery of imprinting to a sea-release site, without the benefit of a source of "cuing" freshwater. Not only can the coho salmon imprint to a sea-release station and return to it as adults, but they can do this after being transported over land for great distances before being unceremoniously transferred to a marine extended rearing station. How accurately coho salmon (and, presumably other species of salmon) perform this remarkable feat of navigation will probably be the subject of study for some time to come.

ACKNOWLEDGEMENT

It would not have been possible to present most of the data in this chapter without the excellent co-operation of a number of organisations and people. I would like to express my deep appreciation to the Washington State Department of Fisheries and the biologists who provided access to the bulk of this most recent unpublished data: Harry Senn, Earl Finn, Frank Haw, Ray Buckley and, especially Tony Rasch. Also, I extend my thanks to Dan Ralph, NMFS Southwest Fisheries Center, Tiburon, California, and to Steve Seymour, Lummi Indian Tribal Enterprises, Marietta, Washington, for their contributions.

REFERENCES

Buckley, R. M. and Haw, F. (1978). Washington State Department of Fisheries, Olympia, WA. Enhancement of Puget Sound populations of resident coho salmon, *Oncorhynchus kistuch* (Walbaum), p. 93-103. Proceedings of the 1977 Northwest Pacific chinook and soho salmon workshop. Fisheries and Marine Service Technical Report No. 759 (Canada).

DeWitt, J. (1969). The pond, lagoon, bay, estuary and impoundment culture of anadromous and marine fishes, with emphasis on the culture of salmon and trout, along the Pacific coast of the United States. Report to the Technical Assistance Project, Economic Development Administration, U.S. Department of Commerce, by Humboldt State College California. 36 pp. (processed).

Hager, R. C. and Noble, R. E. (1976). *Prog. Fish-Cult.* **38** (3), 144-147.

Haraches, Y. and Novotny, A. J. (1976). *Mar. Fish. Rev.* **38** (8), 1-8.

Haw, F. and Bergman, P. K. (1972). Wash Dep. Fish., Olympia, Inf. Booklet 2, 29p.

Hisata, J. S. Evaluation of stocking hatchery reared sea-run cutthroat trout in streams of Hood Canal. Job completion report AFS 44-1 and 2; May 1970 to June 1973. Washington State Department of Game, 38p. (processed).

Hoar, W. S. (1976). *J. Fish. Res. Board Can.* **33** (5), 1233-1252.

Johnson, A. K. (1970). *Res. Rep. Fish Comm. Oregon.* **2** (1), 64-76.

Johnston, J. M. and Mercer, S. P. (1976). Sea-run cutthroat in saltwater pens: broodstock development and extended juvenile rearing (with a life history compendium). Washington State Department of Game, Fishery Research Report. Olympia, Washington. 92p. (processed).

Lander, R. H. (1970). *Res. Rep. Fish Comm. Oregon.* **2** (1), 28-55.

Mathews, S. B. and Buckley, R. (1974). *J. Fish. Res. Board Can.* **31** (6), 1158-1160.

Mathews, S. B. and Senn, H. G. (1975). Univ. Wash. Seattle, Wash. Sea Grant WSG-TA 75-3, 24p.

Moberly, S. A. and Lium, R. (1977). Japan salmon hatchery review. Alaska Dep. Fish Game, 124 pp.

Moore, M., McLeod, K. and Reed, D. (1960). "Fisheries; Fish Farming; Fisheries Management" (1st ed.). Wash. Dep. Fish., Olympia, 344 pp.

Moring, J. R. (1973). Ph.D. thesis, Univ. Wash. Seattle, 225 pp.

Northwest Fisheries Center *Monthly Report* (November, 1972). Salmon return to Manchester. p. 5. (processed). National Marine Fisheries Service, Seattle.

Northwest Fisheries Center *Monthly Report* (January, 1974). Center scientists continue research on homing of coho salmon to preselected sites. pp. 4-6 (processed). National Marine Fisheries Service, Seattle.

Northwest Fisheries Center *Monthly Report* (September, 1974). Possibility developed for even-year run of pink salmon in Puget Sound. p. 13 (processed). National Marine Fisheries Service, Seattle.

Northwest Fisheries Center *Monthly Report* (January, 1975). Record adult salmon runs in Beaver Creek, Washington. pp. 7-10 (processed). National Marine Fisheries Service, Seattle.

Northwest Fisheries Centre *Monthly Report* (January, 1975). Returning fish show that homing can be manipulated. p. 10 (processed). National Marine Fisheries Service, Seattle.

Northwest Fisheries Center *Monthly Report* (October, 1975). Follow-up report on coho run at Little Port Walter. p. 12-13 (processed). National Marine Fisheries Service, Seattle.

Northwest Fisheries Center *Monthly Report* (November, 1975). Salmon fishery conducted near aquaculture station in Puget Sound. pp. 16-18 (processed). National Marine Fisheries Service, Seattle.

Northwest Fisheries Center *Monthly Report* (July, 1976). Short-term rearing of sockeye salmon fry to increase smolt survival studied. p. 13 (processed). National Marine Fisheries Service, Seattle.

Northwest Fisheries Center *Monthly Report* (September, 1976). Even-year pink salmon return to Manchester. p. 15 (processed). National Marine Fisheries Service, Seattle.

Northwest Fisheries Center *Monthly Report* (April, 1977). Floating raceways developed for freshwater and estuarine culture of juvenile salmon. pp. 7-11 (processed). National Marine Fisheries Service, Seattle.

Novotny, A. J. (1975). *Mar. Fish. Rev.* **37** (1), 36-47.

Novotny, A. J. (1978). *Mar. Fish. Rev.* **40** (3), 52-55.

Salo, E. O. (1963). In report of 2nd governor's conference on Pacific salmon. (Ed. R. S. Croker and D. Reed). Wash. Dep. Fish., Olympia, pp. 123-129.

Sutterlin, A. M. and Merrill, J. P. (1978). Environ. Can., Fish. Mar. Serv., Tech. Rep. 779, 47 pp.

Wahle, R. J. and Vreeland, R. R. (1978). *Fish. Bull., U.S.* **76** (1), 179-208.

Washington, P. (1977). *Mar. Fish. Rev.* **39** (12), 20-22.

Washington State Department of Fisheries (1962). Annual Report, Olympia, Washington. p. 36.

Washington, State Department of Fisheries (1971). Progress Report, Puget Sound Resident Coho Program. July 27, 1971, 3p (processed).

Chapter 18

Intensive Use of Streams

J. H. MUNDIE

*Department of Fisheries and the Environment, Fisheries
and Marine Service, Resource Services Branch, Pacific Biological
Station, Nanaimo, British Columbia, V9R 5K6, Canada*

INTRODUCTION

A conventional North American salmon hatchery (see Bardach *et al.*
(1972) for a review of current practices), with a productive capacity of
one million coho and half a million chinook smolts, might cost $3
million to build and have production costs of about 20 cents per coho
smolt. The fish would be raised entirely on commercial mash and
pellets, and the occurrence of disease in them would give rise to
concern, either occasionally or frequently. In view of this it would be
desirable to reduce capital costs, to offer fish alternative foods, and to
raise smolts of consistently good quality. For these reasons attention
is being directed at the potential of natural streams for rearing
salmonids.

This potential is manifold. Streams already exist and do not have
to be constructed; they offer habitat for both incubation and rearing;
they have metabolic properties so that they can assimilate organic
wastes and pass them to invertebrates; they produce and transport
invertebrates which are eaten by fish; they can benefit from atmospheric aeration; and finally, at a time when many members of the

371

general public are not enamoured of large concrete hatcheries, they are aesthetically appealing.

The limitations to natural production of salmon and trout in streams (reviewed by Mundie, 1974) are numerous, but dominant influences are droughts and spates, available food, and ice. The use of streams to raise smolts in significant numbers for salmon ranching therefore calls for intensive manipulation, especially the control of discharge so that the extremes are eliminated, as well as the provision of food to support high numbers of fish.

The requirements of different species of salmon and trout for specific water velocities and substrate size might suggest that the physical characters of streams be chosen to meet particular species; for example, Atlantic salmon fry enter areas of stronger current and coarser bottom as they grow; coho fry, in contrast, favour pools. Some of these apparent choices are, however, the outcome of competitive interactions between fish species (e.g. Hartman, 1965), for when a species is in isolation, its selection of habitat changes. In addition, high-density rearing, and feeding to satiation, alter the requirements of species, for territorial behaviour is eliminated and aggression reduced. Nevertheless, specific requirements may exist, and these may not be well known.

Irrespective of these distinctions, however, to make the most of streams for high-density rearing both high-velocity and low-velocity water are necessary; the first to produce and release benthic inverte-brates, entrain air, assimilate wastes, transport sand and silt, and offer fish the opportunity to explore a range of velocities; the second to accommodate high numbers of fish and to ensure that they are not expending excessive energy in maintaining position. What *is* difficult to decide for a particular species is the best ratio of riffle area to pool area; but if pools are increased at the expense of riffles, the contri-bution of the riffles to ecological processes is, of course, reduced.

The first questions to be answered in selecting a nursery stream are: is there sufficient water at all times of the year to raise the fish and is the annual temperature regime suitable? The first practical step is the control of discharge. Year-round direct flow control of streams is rarely feasible; discharge in excess of needs would have to be stored or diverted. The simplest way to obtain the required volume is to divert flow into a natural or artificial side-channel and return it in due course to the parent stream.

ILLUSTRATIVE EXAMPLE: REARING COHO IN A CHANNEL WITH RIFFLES AND POOLS

A pilot project is currently in progress on the Big Qualicum River, on the east coast of Vancouver Island, British Columbia, in which coho smolts are raised in a side-channel of the river. The objectives are to reduce the costs of conventional types of rearing and to improve fish quality. The project serves to illustrate, in the present early state of knowledge, the benefits and shortcomings of stream rearing. The theory and some initial research are described by Mundie and Mounce (1978). In this chapter, emphasis is placed on the practical aspects.

The Experimental Rearing Channel is a side-channel 396 m long, excavated with an overall slope of 1:250, and a width of 4·5 m, and provided with 25 riffles, each 6·0 m long and 15 cm deep, alternating with 25 pools, each 10·0 m long and 0·9 m deep (Fig. 1). Stop logs are secured in the gravel at the tail of each riffle to prevent slippage.

Fig. 1. Riffle and pool layout of the channel. Note stop log across tail of riffle.

The gravel has a mean size of 25 mm (Williams and Mundie, 1978) and is 30 cm deep. Boulders are added on the surface to generate turbulence. The intake (Fig. 2) has 18 m² of vertical screen perforated with slots 2·5 mm wide to prevent the passage (in either direction) of small fry. On the river side of this screen is a protective trash rack, and on the channel side is a gate, operated by a screw, to control the discharge. The intake is capable of passing 1·2 m³ sec⁻¹, but the channel is operated at 0·42 m³ sec⁻¹. Piles are driven into the riverbed immediately downstream of the inlet. These accept stop logs at low flows in summer, so that sufficient river water can be diverted to the channel. The outlet consists of two independent inclined screens set in a concrete housing. These can be lowered to let the smolts out.

Fig. 2. Inlet from the channel side. Note wheel of control gate, gabion construction, expanded metal footpath, chain-link fence, floating cover for fry.

An inclined screen is installed in a concrete pad in pool 5 (Fig. 3). This divides the channel into a short (79 m) upstream section used for incubation, and for rearing from April to July, and the remainder of the channel where fish are reared from July until their outmigration in May.

The riffles have a slope of 1:100, and the velocity of water over them is 0·6 m sec⁻¹ at the surface. The pools have a surface velocity of 0·1 m sec⁻¹. With a discharge of 0·4 m³ sec⁻¹ complete exchange of water in the channel takes 23 min.

Incubation has not yet been tried in the channel. Eggs obtained from coho adults returning to the river were incubated in the first two trials by conventional hatchery techniques. In the first trial 105 000 swim-up fry were placed in each of four floating pens in the channel. These

Fig. 3. Screen in pool 5. This separates the short upstream stretch of the channel *(right)* from the remainder. Note footpath, crosswalk and net canopy.

pens, measuring 6 m × 3 m, of marquisette cloth, provided low flows for very small fry and aggregated the fish so that they could be conveniently fed commercial moist mash. In the following year, however, the pens were dispensed with. Suitable velocity was obtained by placing stop logs across the first riffle downstream of the pool screen, so that water was backed up upstream of the screen. Alevins were then ponded directly into the channel. Ensuing mortalities were negligible. The bulk of the alevins disappear initially into the gravel, especially at the margins of the channel. They subsequently reappear and feed both on mash and drifting insects.

After the smolts of the earlier brood have left the channel, a panel in the pool screen is removed, so that fry are given access to the longer section. This panel is replaced in November.

The fry are fed moist pellets by hand. This ensures even distribution of fish throughout the channel and dispersal of wastes; automatic feeders result in dense aggregations of fish in their vicinity and local accumulations of faeces and uneaten food. By midsummer, feeding is reduced to three times per day every second day, so the amounts offered are less than 50% hatchery rations.

Monthly analyses, from June to September, of stomach contents over 24 hours showed that at the upstream end of the channel 79% of fry obtained natural food, and at the downstream end 92%. Many fry had only traces of natural food, but one-third had more than 25% of the stomach volume occupied by insects. The most abundant food items were chironomid pupae and larvae. Pupae are exceptionally available to the fish, a finding supported by detailed studies elsewhere (Mundie, 1971). Terrestrial items made up 5% of the diet.

The benthos of the channel responds to enrichment by a marked increase in naidid oligochaete worms, which drift but are not eaten, and in midge larvae (Williams *et al.*, 1977). Insect diversity is greatest in the riffles.

The smolts, which left in the second half of May, were low in lipid content (1·2% of wet weight, B. W. Ludwig, personal communication) and light in weight relative to length (mean weight 10·4 g, mean fork length 100 mm). They therefore had the appearance of wild rather than of hatchery coho. The adults from the first release were due to return in autumn 1978.

After the exodus of the smolts, the stretch of channel downstream of the screen is washed with a fire hose to dislodge accumulated sand, filamentous algae, and organics. The loss on ignition of the suspended material in the effluent was approximately 6%, most of the material being sand. The channel does not discharge directly into the river but into a broad intervening stretch where most of the sand settles out. In time this may have to be transferred to land.

The channel upstream of the screen must also be cleaned prior to the introduction of eggs, and this is done by hosing in November. An unavoidable consequence is that the fry downstream of the screen are submitted to a substantial increase in suspended organic and inorganic material. No mortalities, however, have been encountered as a result of this practice, but cleaning is done at a cautious rate, one riffle and pool being washed per day. Fry, indeed, respond with interest to the invertebrates released. The first pool, immediately downstream of the inlet, is cleaned with a suction device, so that sand which enters from the river and settles there is removed to land.

Before fry are allowed to pass from the upper section of the channel to the section below the screen, all residual smolts are stunned or driven from the channel with a 110 volt AC fish shocker mounted on a floating aluminium tube which traverses the entire width of the channel. A series of electrodes hangs from this, while the ground electrode is placed further downstream on the substrate. Power is supplied by a portable generator. The shocker is moved down the length of the channel once on 3 successive days. The same procedure is adopted in the upper portion of the channel to remove residual fry prior to incubation. The channel, of course, cannot be drained to facilitate the exodus or removal of fish.

A disadvantage of channel rearing is that fish cannot be readily graded. With coho there is no need for grading, and no evidence was found of cannibalism within a brood. Predation, of course, occurs when fish of the previous brood persist in the channel.

The most negative aspect of the two rearing trials was unaccountable losses. In each year approximately 270 000 smolts were released (120 000 were clipped and tagged with a binary coded nose tag); in the first trial, losses amounted to 37%, and in the second, in which larger numbers of fry were used, to 45%. These losses are attributed, with some evidence, to herons (*Ardea* sp.), mergansers (*Mergus* sp.) and mink (*Mustela vison*). For a third trial the channel was covered with a net canopy to keep out the larger birds, and plywood cover for the fish was provided on each riffle and pool (Fig. 4).

Fig. 4. View of protective net canopy and floating cover for fry.

The holding capacity of the channel is determined by the number and the volume of the pools, i.e. by living space. Throughout the trials the lowest oxygen value found was 8·3 p.p.m. at 16·7°C, and the highest ammonium nitrogen was 97·8 p.p.b. at 15·5°C. In chemical terms, then, more fish could be raised, but the most satisfactory way to do this would be to have a longer channel.

The advantages of this project are simplicity of approach, healthy fish of low lipid content, absence of pumps, feeders and electrical power (the commercial food used could be stored in a propane refrigerator), ease of initial feeding, low food and labour costs, low amounts of waste. The disadvantages are high losses of fry (against which must be set the common practice in hatcheries of ponding twice as many fry as intended smolts), high demand on space, impracticality of grading fish, and difficulties of removing all fish from stretches of the channel.

WIDER APPLICATION

The application of this approach to raising salmonids in a variety of sites, and in different geographical regions, raises many questions.

The chief contribution of the natural stream to channel rearing is the constant provision of drifting invertebrates. This ensures colonisation of the enriched gravel so that there is compensation for the consumption of drift within the channel and for direct loss from it. This compensation operates down the whole length of the channel because sufficient drifting invertebrates escape predation, presumably because most drift takes place in darkness and because of the small size of many of the drifting items.

The capacity of incoming water to provide drift for a channel will vary with the source. Ground water will contibute no drift; surface runoff will contribute in relation to its biological productivity, and to its depth and velocity, extensive areas of shallow fast water being most productive of drift. Lake outflows discharging seston will be highly productive. Side channels incorporating the riffle/pool principle can, of course, only be constructed where there is sufficient slope to the natural terrain. Excessive slope in a channel can be dissipated by shallow drop structures at intervals down the length, and it is therefore better to err in the direction of having too much slope than too little.

Among the difficulties and hazards encountered in making channels are varying river levels, and high silt loads, so the type and location of a channel inlet are of great importance. A widely fluctuating river might require a stepped inlet, so that as levels rise an intake gate can be closed and one directly above it can be opened. The point at which water is diverted from the parent river can also be crucial. It appears, from the limited published results (e.g. Jain, 1969) that the outside, or concave, side of a river bend is the best location, because heavy bed load is transported by helicoidal flow to the inside of the curve where it forms deposits (point bars) in the river. Ground water and lake water are likely to present least silt problems, although shallow peaty or muskeg lakes may discharge much fine organic material.

On the channel side of the inlet, silt which does enter can be settled, to some extent, in the first pool. This may be large and provided with deflectors to ensure meandering flow and assist deposition. The amount of silt passing further downstream will affect survival of incubating eggs. The downstream end of this stretch of the channel should therefore be chosen for incubation. At present it is not known whether incubation would be more successful if the eggs are placed directly in the riffle areas, or if placed on screens in pools in the manner of a shallow matrix incubator (see McNeil and Bailey, 1975).

In northern climates, channel rearing may be impracticable because of ice formation at intakes. At best riparian coniferous trees may give some protection against low air temperatures. Introduction of heat into the flow is probably not feasible.

Temperatures can also impose severe biological limitations in relation to growth rates of salmonids. If surface water from a lake is the source used, midsummer temperatures may be excessive (above 16°C) and winter temperatures too low. Ground water is probably excellent in winter but too cool in summer. Often the climate is such that a species reaches the smolt stage only after 2 ot 3 years of rearing, e.g. Atlantic salmon in Eastern Canada and in Sweden, in which case it would clearly be difficult to make use of single channels containing two broods separated by screens. The procedure would be troublesome and highly risky. Having two or three parallel channels with a common inlet and outlet offers the possibility of holding fish for two years but is costly. More feasible might be accelerated incubation and early rearing at artificially elevated temperatures, followed by ponding into a channel so that the smolt stage is reached in, say, 14 months from the time of first feeding. Yet again, a channel might be used simply to raise fry for the purpose of stocking depleted rivers, where the fish might spend their second year of rearing. Clearly, the numbers of smolts or subsequent adults aimed at would determine the choice of action.

For chinook salmon, at latitudes where only three months are spent in rearing in freshwater, a channel seems highly suitable.

Although the importance of the parent river lies mainly in its contribution of drifting invertebrates, it might possibly also supply, directly, early fry for stocking the channel. Coho, for example, exhibit a very substantial out-migration of swim-up fry in the spring which are usually assumed not to survive on reaching the estuary. These could be trapped in the river and transferred to the channel for rearing, thus obviating the need for collecting and incubating eggs. The genetic implications of the selection would warrant research.

Two other aspects of channel rearing that deserve mention are the potential for adding organics to the gravel to further promote insect production, and the usefulness of shallow weirs for re-aerating the pools.

Perhaps the key issue in channel rearing is the state of health of the fish produced. It is now known (apart from examples of extreme impairment) to what extent the returns of adult salmonids are determined by the condition of the smolts at the time of release. Traditional hatchery experience, however, points to density of fry and fingerlings as a prime determinant of condition, with high density, or crowding, as a factor contributing to disease. One potential of channel rearing is that higher numbers of fish can be raised without increasing density (i.e. numbers per unit of volume or area) by increasing channel length. Long channels are economically feasible because the main costs lie in the inlet and outlet, not in the excavation. If low density, a partly natural diet, the capturing of living food items, and a choice of water velocities are features of rearing that promote smolt excellence, so that adult returns are higher than those attained by conventional rearing strategies, then the intensive use of streams will warrant wide application.

REFERENCES

Bardach, J. E., Ryther, J. H. and McLarney, W. O. (1972). "Aquaculture." Wiley Intersicence, New York.

Hartman, G. F. (1965). *J. Fish. Res. Board Can.* **22**, 1035-1081.

Jain, R. K. (1969). *Water Power*, 338-343.

McNeil, W. J. and Bailey, J. E. (1975). "Salmon Rancher's Manual." Northwest Fisheries Center, Auke Bay Fisheries Laboratory, Alaska.

Mundie, J. H. (1971). *Can. Entomol.* **103**, 289-297.

Mundie, J. H. (1974). *J. Fish. Res. Board Can.* **31**, 1827-1837.

Mundie, J. H. and Mounce, D. E. (1978). *Verh. Int. Ver. Limnol.* **20**, 2013-2018.

Williams, D. D. and Mundie, J. H. (1978). *Limnol. Oceanogr.* **23**, 1030-1033.

Williams, D. D., Mundie, J. H. and Mounce, D. E. (1977). *J. Fish. Res. Board Can.* **34**, 2133-2141.

Chapter 19

Legal Aspects of Salmon Ranching in the Pacific

W. J. McNEIL

Oregon Aquafoods Inc., Springfield, Oregon, U.S.A.

INTRODUCTION

Laws and administrative regulations which establish public policy for ocean ranching of salmon vary greatly among governmental jurisdictions. Some governments have adopted legal frameworks to allow private ownership of salmon; others allow only public ownership. Private ownership is typically restricted to the period during which fish are within waters prescribed for exclusive use of licensed private ocean-ranching facilities, so fish released from private facilities remain a public resource for much of their life while grazing in public waters. They are managed by public agencies and are subject to laws, regulations, and treaties governing harvest by common property recreational and commercial fisheries.

Institutional arrangements for ocean ranching of salmon are changing rapidly. Much of this change is directed toward economic efficiency, and an important question concerning the various institutional arrangements for salmon ranching is whether surplus fish returning from the ocean can repay the cost of artificial propagation.

Salmon released into the ocean by private salmon-ranching firms are a common property resource while in public waters. They contribute to common property commercial and recreational fisheries the same as wild fish and public hatchery fish, because fish from all three sources intermingle freely on ocean fishing grounds.

In such mixed-stock fisheries, it is well known that natural stocks are much more vulnerable to overfishing than hatchery stocks. This is because a spawning pair of adult salmon will produce several times more fish returning to a hatchery than to a natural stream or lake. Where fishery managers attempt to conserve wild stocks, there are typically resultant surpluses of fish returning to hatcheries. Such surpluses force a public hatchery system to enter the salmon market by selling surplus fish or disposing of them by some other means.

Private hatcheries offer an opportunity to utilise surplus hatchery fish in a cost-effective fashion: they relieve government of the necessity of harvesting and marketing surplus hatchery fish; they reduce the necessity for taxpayers to subsidise public hatchery programmes; they free fishery management agencies of the burden of operating costly salmon enhancement facilities; they allow public fishery agencies to concentrate their efforts on managing fisheries rather than on raising fish.

Private hatcheries can range from tax-paying, profit-oriented enterprises to tax-exempt, non-profit corporations. Private hatcheries generate the same benefits to fishermen, processors, and other traditional user groups as tax-consuming public hatcheries. A major advantage of private hatcheries relates to cost efficiency: public hatcheries are typically isolated from discipline imposed by normal market forces; private hatcheries are not. These market forces are described by Orth (1978) as including the following factors:

(1)   Management control over a private hatchery is exercised by a user group with an economic incentive for productive and cost-efficient hatcheries;

(2)   Investors in private hatcheries have an economic incentive to pay close attention to the performance of management and productivity of hatcheries;

(3)   Competition among private hatcheries is a constructive force for high productivity and cost efficiency.

Legal aspects of ocean ranching in the Pacific are considered here from a general viewpoint. Because laws and regulations governing salmon ranching are undergoing continual revision in many countries and states, more detailed information on them should be sought from agencies responsible for administering programmes within specific political jurisdictions. Usually agencies responsible for managing common property fisheries are also responsible for administering laws and regulations pertaining to salmon ranching.

INTERNATIONAL

Salmon ranching is an international undertaking, practised on a large scale in the Pacific Ocean by Japan, U.S.S.R., U.S.A., and Canada and on a smaller scale by the Republic of Korea, Chile, and New Zealand. Statistics on release of juvenile salmon from hatcheries and rates of recapture suggest that fish produced by artificial means contribute 15-20% of the world harvest of salmon. This contribution seems destined to increase in the future through implementation of planned expansion of hatchery production by the principal producing countries.

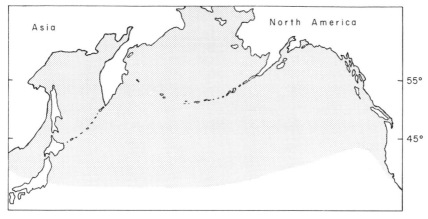

Fig. 1. Salmon are distributed across temperate waters of the north Pacific Ocean, with extensive intermingling of stocks from Asia and North America.

The broader features of oceanic distribution of salmon in the north Pacific and contiguous seas have been described by Friden *et al.*, 1977. Salmon from North America and Asia are broadly distributed in boreal waters, with considerable intermingling of stocks from the two continents (Fig. 1). Ocean migrations of salmon typically cause fish to cross international boundaries. Fish from all salmon-producing countries in the northern hemisphere intermingle in international waters.

Marine waters have historically been considered as "commons" for the use of all nations. The concept of the commons has undergone rapid change in recent times as nations have extended seaward their jurisdiction over marine resources. Salmon within the territorial sea, which extends seaward about 5 km from headlands, have historically been under the jurisdiction of coastal states. A trend emerged among coastal states in the 1960s to establish exclusive fishery zones beyond the territorial sea. In the north Pacific region, these exclusive fishery zones typically extended about 20 km seaward from headlands. By the mid-1970s, major coastal states had adopted fishery conservation zones extending an additional 300 km beyond the exclusive fishery zone. In 1976, the United States declared jurisdiction over salmon and other anadromous species on the high seas beyond the conservation zone so long as the fish remained outside fishery conservation zones of other nations.

NATIONAL

Salmon ranching is highly regulated by governmental agencies throughout the north Pacific rim, and in some political jurisdictions, salmon can be produced artificially only by government. There are also some localities where private enterprise can release and recapture salmon under control of government. Institutional arrangements for salmon ranching within various political jurisdictions, are reviewed below; they are dealt with more fully in several preceding chapters.

Japan (see also Chapter 6)

Of the 225 salmon hatcheries in Japan, 82% are privately owned. The central government operates 37 hatcheries on Hokkaido Island, and there are three prefectural hatcheries on Hokkaido Island. Hatcheries operated by the central government are generally large facilities and collectively produce more juvenile salmon than private hatcheries. The central government exercises control over private hatcheries by retaining ownership of all salmon eggs used for artificial propagation in Japan. Private hatcheries enjoy considerable autonomy for routine operations, but central government is responsible for allocation of eggs among public and private hatcheries, transplantation of stocks, co-ordination of hatchery programmes, and planning.

Many of the private hatcheries in Japan are operated by fishermen's co-operatives. Weirs for recapturing adult salmon in streams are also usually operated by co-operatives. Carcasses of spawned fish and fish surplus to the needs of hatchery brood stock become property of co-operatives and are sold. All fertilised eggs become the property of the central government for restocking public and private hatcheries. The largest concentration of private hatcheries is centred on northern Honshu Island. Prefectural governments on northern Honshu and Hokkaido are encouraging an expansion of private hatcheries, and future growth of salmon ranching in Japan could come mostly in the private sector.

U.S.S.R. (see also Chapter 5)

Salmon ranching in the U.S.S.R. is a government-owned business. There are at least 24 commercial salmon hatcheries located on tributaries to the Amur River, on Sakhalin Island, and in the Kuril Islands. Salmon hatcheries are administered as a branch of Sakhalinrybvod, the Sakhalin Bureau of Fisheries Regulation and Artificial Propagation. About the same number of juvenile salmon are released from Soviet hatcheries as from Japanese hatcheries.

Republic of Korea

Four salmon hatcheries were constructed in the Republic of Korea in the 1960s with assistance from the U.S.A. They are government operated.

Canada

In 1975, the Canadian federal government announced that a salmon enhancement programme would be undertaken to double the harvest of salmon in British Columbia. Planning for this programme has been primarily a federal activity, with assistance from the Province of British Columbia. Operation of spawning channels, hatcheries, and other enhancement facilities is likely to remain primarily a federal activity. Salmon ranching by private firms is not permitted. Production of juvenile salmon will be subsidised by tax revenues, and special taxes are likely to be applied against the fishing industry to repay most of the cost of producing fish through artificial propagation.

United States

Ocean ranching laws and regulations are primarily the responsibility of state governments in the United States. The federal government has jurisdiction where Indian treaty rights are involved and in marine waters which lie beyond the territorial sea. The federal government also regulates importation of live fish and other biological specimens into the U.S.A., use of chemicals for fish husbandry, and discharge of wastewater from aquaculture facilities. However, most laws and regulations which apply to artificial propagation of salmon have their origins within state legislative bodies and regulatory agencies.

Alaska (see also Chapter 2)
The Alaska legislature has taken several precedent-setting actions since 1974 (Robinson, 1977) and authorised:
  Private ownership of salmon by qualified private non-profit hatchery corporations;
  Regional associations of commercial fishermen, processors, sportsmen, personal use fishermen, and other user groups to assist the state with rehabilitation of depressed salmon fisheries;
  State grants to qualified regional associations for planning;
  State fisheries enhancement loan programme to provide low-interest loans to qualified non-profit private hatchery corporations for construction and operation of hatcheries;
  Tax-exempt salmon enhancement authorities as political subdivisions of the State of Alaska.
  None of these initiatives would have been possible before a referendum which amended the Alaska constitution in 1972 to allow limited entry to fisheries and aquaculture. Prior to 1972, the constitution effectively barred private ownership of salmon in Alaska, and initiatives in salmon ranching were limited to programmes undertaken by government.
  By 1978, two regional associations had been organised in south-east Alaska, one in Prince William Sound, and one in Cook Inlet. Several independent private non-profit hatcheries have also been granted licences to produce salmon at sites in south-east Alaska and Prince William Sound. Additional private non-profit hatcheries are expected in future years with financial assistance by means of low-interest loans and grants from the state.

Preference rights to hatchery permits are given to qualified regional associations. The associations also receive more liberal financial assistance in the form of state grants and loans than independent private non-profit hatcheries. Repayment of loans by regional associations is guaranteed to the state by assessments on salmon landed by commercial fishermen. All limited-entry permit holders within an area under a regional association must be given an opportunity to vote on assessments.

The Alaska programme is a unique undertaking designed to encourage commercial fishermen to assume much of the responsibility for artificial propagation of salmon to enhance common property fisheries. The state retains its traditional function of managing fisheries to conserve natural stocks. Surplus hatchery fish returning to private non-profit hatcheries operated by regional associations or by independent firms are sold to repay the costs of artificial propagation, and any income surplus to that for amortising capital costs and paying for annual operations must be reinvested to benefit salmon resources through expansion of hatchery facilities, research and development, fisheries education, or some other programme sanctioned by the state.

Washington (see also Chapter 3)
The Washington legislature passed a law in 1971 which authorised private fish farming. Private operators were initially allowed to release salmon with written approval of the Director of the Washington Department of Fisheries. This policy has been rescinded in more recent years, and salmon must now be retained in captivity by private operators. Legislation to broaden the 1971 law to allow salmon ranching by private firms has consistently failed to pass in the Washington legislature. Salmon ranching in Washington is therefore a governmental activity, with the exception of Indian tribes which have treaty rights with the United States government. Indian treaty rights allow tribes to grow juvenile salmon in reservation waters and release them to emigrate to sea. Several tribes are actively engaged in salmon ranching in Washington State, usually with financial and technical support from the federal government.

Oregon (see also Chapter 4)
Oregon has adopted the most liberal policy of any state in the U.S.A. to encourage private investments in salmon ranching. Oregon law

allows hatcheries to operate for profit, which is a superior incentive for investment of private capital in hatcheries and other salmon ranching facilities than private non-profit hatchery firms authorised by Alaska law. Operation of private hatcheries for profit is conducive to cost efficiency and high productivity (Orth, 1977).

Legislation for private hatcheries was first passed in 1971. The law initially was limited to chum *(Oncorhynchus keta)* salmon, but was broadened in 1973 to include chinook *(O. tschawytscha)* and coho *(O. kisutch)* salmon as well as chum. Oregon law specifies that privately operated release/recapture facilities be located near the ocean. Salmon released from private facilities are public property while free in public waters. Private hatcheries are required to purchase commercial fishing licences to harvest returning fish and must pay poundage taxes to the State of Oregon for all recaptured fish.

California
A law was passed in 1968 to allow a private firm to release salmon for ocean ranching at a specified location. This cumbersome procedure of requiring special legislation for each private firm wishing to engage in salmon ranching had not been changed by mid 1978. Needless to say, progress of salmon ranching has been very slow in California, although it was the first state to legislate for operation of private salmon hatcheries.

Chile (see also Chapter 14)

Pacific salmon are native only to the northern hemisphere, but there have been repeated attempts to transplant salmon to Chile and other southern hemisphere countries (McNeil, 1976). There is currently a renewed interest in possibilities for salmon ranching in the southern hemisphere, and projects supported by Japanese and American interests are attempting to acclimatise salmon to Chilean waters.

There is at present only minimal regulation on salmon ranching in Chile, because the Chilean government treats current initiatives as pilot projects which are allowed to proceed with approval of the central government. Should salmon ranching prove feasible in Chile, it is anticipated that some Chilean ownership in a joint venture would become a necessity. There is presently one Chilean-American joint venture firm producing salmon for ocean release. Japan is also supporting an ocean ranching experiment in Chile.

New Zealand (see also Chapter 15)

Self-perpetuating populations of chinook salmon have existed in southern New Zealand streams for many decades since their introduction from North America. These established stocks reproduce naturally, and there have been only limited attempts to propagate salmon artificially in New Zealand. However, interest in salmon ranching appears to be increasing in New Zealand as elsewhere in temperate waters of the north and south Pacific.

New Zealand has laws prohibiting trout farming, but salmon ranching is not prohibited at present. Only sport fisheries harvest salmon in New Zealand, and private industry is beginning to undertake initiatives for salmon ranching. New Zealand government has been co-operating with pilot salmon ranching projects by providing chinook salmon eggs from natural spawning stocks.

Majority ownership by New Zealand citizens is likely to be a requirement for salmon ranching. Procedures for acquiring salmon ranching permits are expected to remain unclear until government policy becomes formalised. Common property commercial fisheries for salmon in public waters seem unlikely, because of pressures from sportsmen to prevent commercial fisheries. Salmon ranching may be an acceptable alternative to commercial fisheries, since sportsmen would be allowed to harvest ranched fish without competition from commercial fishermen in public waters.

DISCUSSION AND CONCLUSIONS

Artificial propagation of salmon is typically a government activity, but private enterprise is playing an increasingly important role. Hatcheries operated by governmental agencies are typically subsidised by tax revenues and function as "cost" centres. Hatcheries operated by private enterprise or government-owned businesses are typically financed by selling surplus fish for commercial markets and function as "profit" centres. The economic incentives can be quite different between hatcheries operated as cost and profit centres.

The idea of operating salmon hatcheries as profit centres dates back at least to 1877, when the first private salmon hatchery was constructed on the Rogue River, Oregon, by an early pioneer of the salmon industry. A number of additional private hatcheries were constructed around the turn of the century in the United States, Canada, and Japan. These early private hatcheries proved unsuccessful in the United States and Canada and had faded from the scene by the 1930s. In Japan private salmon hatcheries have continued to operate and have developed into an important economic activity.

Rebirth of private salmon ranching in North America began with legislation in California in 1968, Oregon in 1971, and Alaska in 1974. Indian tribes initiated salmon-ranching programmes in Washington State in the early 1970s under privileges granted in treaties with the United States government. Private salmon hatcheries are not permitted in Canada, where salmon ranching remains a tax-subsidised, governmental activity with little likelihood of change in the foreseeable future.

In Asia, salmon ranching receives very strong support from governments in Japan and the U.S.S.R. Private hatcheries in Japan sometimes receive a modest subsidy from government for their contributions to common property ocean fisheries. Tax revenues for this subsidy are derived primarily from commercial ocean fisheries on salmon. Government-owned collective salmon ranches in the U.S.S.R. have economic goals which are parallel to private hatcheries and function as profit centres.

Most salmon hatcheries in the United States are operated by various state and federal agencies and supported entirely by public tax revenues. Renewed interest in private hatcheries is manifested however, by operation of private profit hatcheries in California and Oregon, private non-profit hatcheries in Alaska, and Indian hatcheries in Washington and Alaska. The movement toward private salmon ranching is universal in all states that enjoy access to the salmon-producing waters of the north Pacific Ocean, with the exception of Idaho. Idaho is an inland state lying on the Columbia River watershed. Many salmon populations entering the Columbia spawn in Idaho streams. Nevertheless, because of its distant location from the ocean, economic incentives for private salmon ranching in Idaho are in doubt.

Economic incentives for private salmon ranching undoubtedly exist in Canada, but the institutional barriers against private hatcheries appear to be formidable. The outlook is for Canada to continue with only public facilities subsidised by taxing commercial salmon fisheries.

Oregon has done more to relieve institutional barriers against private salmon ranching than any other political jurisdiction in North

America. By 1978, the State had issued 20 permits to private hatcheries authorising the release of 180 million juvenile salmon. The actual number of juvenile salmon released from private hatcheries in 1978 was about 13 million (public hatcheries 65 million), mainly because there has not been sufficient time for private operators to develop broodstocks. Expansion of public hatcheries in Oregon is being deferred until the economic and social impacts of a rapidly growing private hatchery programme can be assessed more fully. The assumption in Oregon is that enough fish will escape common property ocean commercial and recreational fisheries to pay costs of constructing and operating private hatcheries and provide a satisfactory profit for investors. Several years will be required to evaluate this assumption.

The private non-profit hatchery programme in Alaska is based on the premise that fish escaping common property fisheries will barely cover costs or will fall somewhat short of covering costs of constructing and operating hatcheries. For hatcheries operated by associations of commercial fishermen, deficits would be compensated through modest assessments on salmon caught by commercial fishermen. The assumption is that commercial fishermen will catch enough hatchery fish to more than compensate for the cost of the assessment, which might be 3% or less of the value of the catch.

Although there may be economic advantages to the operation of hatcheries as businesses (i.e. profit centres), there are circumstances in which social benefits from hatcheries may outweigh economic advantages. Preservation of runs of salmon where streams have been dammed or otherwise altered to the detriment of natural reproduction of salmon can make it desirable for government to construct and operate hatcheries as cost centres to provide social benefits. There are also circumstances in which heavy demands for recreational salmon fisheries exceed the capacity of natural recruitment with a resulting need for public hatcheries. These and other examples where social needs are paramount will provide continuing justification for public hatcheries even within political jurisdictions where private hatcheries are encouraged by policy makers.

ACKNOWLEDGEMENTS

Legal frameworks for private salmon ranching are changing rapidly. An attempt has been made in this chapter to provide insights into the legal status of salmon ranching in the Pacific Ocean in the recognition that circumstances are likely to continue to change. The author is grateful to Yoshihiro Aoki, Roger Burrows, Colin Nash, Wally Pereyra, and Keith Sandercock for their counsel on legal status of salmon ranching within various political jurisdictions. Errors in interpretation and reporting are strictly the responsibility of the author.

REFERENCES

Friden, R. A., Major, R. L., Bakkala, R. G. and Tanonaka, G. T. (1977). Northwest and Alaska Fish. Center Processed Rpt. 324 pp.
McNeil, W. J. (1976). FAO Tech. Conf. on Aquaculture, Kyoto, Japan, R. 24, 13 pp.
Orth, F. L. (1977). Univ. of Alaska Sea Grant Rpt. 77-4, 99 pp.
Orth, F. L. and Kerns, C. L. (1978). *Alaska Seas and Coasts* **6,** 8-11.
Robinson, E. T. (1977). Univ. of Alaska Sea Grant Rpt. 77-6, 17 pp.

Chapter 20

Salmon Ranching: Current Situation and Prospects

J. E. THORPE

Department of Agriculture and Fisheries for Scotland,
Freshwater Fisheries Laboratory, Pitlochry, Scotland

It is evident from the foregoing chapters that ranching and augmentation activities are already very extensive, primarily in the highly productive North Pacific area. Altogether 2·8 billion juvenile salmon were released into this region in 1978 (Anon., 1979a), and Konovalov (Chapter 5) has indicated that the U.S.S.R. alone plans to raise their annual release of young salmon to 5 billion by 2000 A.D. The catch from Japanese hatchery production amounts to 8 million salmon per year (Chapter 6), i.e. 28 000 tonnes. Add to this the North American and Russian catches (Chapter 2), and it is evident that 50 000-70 000 tonnes per year are derived from release of hatchery fish, that is, 20-30% of the total world catch of Pacific salmon (Thorpe, 1979). Recent spectacular successes in Alaska (19·5% return from pink salmon (*Oncorhynchus gorbuscha*) released at the Baranof Islands in 1979 (Anon., 1979b)) seems likely to lead to an increase in the scale of releases in that state, and Lannan (Chapter 4) and McNeil (Chapter 19) have noted that the potential output from Oregon ranches is many times higher than their current activity. (A recent estimate (Anon., 1979c) gave the total releases from Oregon ranches as 22 million fish over 7 years, but the potential as 183 million fish per year.)

At these levels it is necessary to question the carrying capacity of the oceans for such quantities of predators, and the likely biological responses among these populations of ranched fishes. Long-period growth-rate and maturation-rate fluctuations are evident among the virtually unaugmented North Atlantic stocks of Atlantic salmon *(Salmo salar)* (Mitchell, personal communication) the causes of which are unknown. Such natural regulations of performance of salmon at sea require thorough study to ensure that augmentation of present stock levels is neither detrimental to the salmon nor to their environment. Evidence that the oceans have surplus capacity to support increased production of salmonids is conflicting. For the North Pacific, Walters *et al.* (1978) have suggested that, historically, salmon stocks were probably twice as abundant as they are at present. McLeod (1977) estimated that the British Columbia salmon fishery had declined from 135×10^6 kg a year 100 years ago to 65×10^6 kg a year currently. However, Ricker and Smith (1975) have noted that increased output of Skeena River sockeye *(O. nerka)* smolts has not been matched by proportionate increases in returns of adults. This could be due to inefficient hatchery practices, to a wild stock declining faster than hatchery production was increasing, or to the achievement of a density asymptote in the ocean. Walters (1977), using these data, showed that adult returns increased as smolt output increased up to 20 million per year; above this level adult returns apparently stabilised at 1-3 million. He also noted that sockeye populations from Bristol Bay and the Skeena River were negatively correlated, and that ocean survival rates decreased with total abundance of fish in the Gulf of Alaska estimated from the catch. Peterman (1978) has documented other instances in which an upper limit on returning adults is apparent, irrespective of the number of smolts entering the sea.

Netboy (1974) has documented the decline of many individual stocks in both the Pacific and Atlantic basins. No precise figure can be placed on the proportionate decline, since stock sizes are inferred from catches and not direct measures of stock, and these catches have been achieved with varying gears, efficiencies, and levels of effort, most of which are now unquantifiable. However, in the Atlantic basin, it is known that the stocks of entire major river systems such as the Rhine and Elbe, and of lesser rivers from wide geographical areas from Spain to Scandinavia have been extinguished. Based on the historical records collected by Netboy (1974), the reduction in catches of Atlantic salmon in Western Europe (Spain, France, Germany and Britain) since the early nineteenth century is at very least two million fish per year. Since this only represents a part of the stock lost from those areas, the reduction in the oceanic stock of salmon is probably at least four million fish per year. Assuming that the survival from smolt to adult was about 10%, then 200 years ago the North Atlantic probably supported 40 million more growing salmon from these nursery areas alone. Thus it is probable that both the Pacific and Atlantic could sustain a greater production of juvenile salmonids.

The determinants of carrying capacity are: (1) productivity of the ocean, (2) availability of food to the salmon, and (3) intensity of predation (or other causes of mortality) on the salmon. Walters (1977), using zooplankton productivity estimates from Parsons and Takahashi (1973), calculated that the population of 10^8 salmon (pink, chum *(O. keta)* and sockeye) growing in the four million km^2 area of the Gulf of Alaska would consume 2·5-10% of the annual zooplankton production there. Since the greater part of this zooplankton production is used in maintenance, or passes to other predators, the proportion currently consumed by salmon may be near the sustainable limit. However, other authors (Le Brasseur, 1972; Rothschild, 1972; Sanger, 1972) have estimated that salmon use only a small fraction of the food available to them. This begs the question as to what food organisms are available to the salmon and when. Calculations of total zooplankton production for a region apply to the whole volume of water. Young salmon are assumed to feed close to the surface (e.g., Straty, 1974; Barraclough and Phillips, 1978), and therefore only an upper fragment of the zooplankton stock is accessible to them. The relevance of measures of productivity of zooplankton to salmon must therefore depend on the rate of replenishment of upper layers of that plankton from below. Total zooplankton also embraces a wide range of particle size. Wankowski (1979) has shown that juvenile Atlantic salmon show a predatory response to only a very narrow size range of particles, and Wankowski and Thorpe (1979) that rapid growth is achieved on an even narrower range. Lasker and Zweifel (1978) showed that density of particles of an appropriate size was critical for survival and growth of young anchovies *(Engraulis mordax)*, and that rapid growth conferred survival advantage. Clearly then, success for salmon at sea depends not simply on a gross quantity of zooplankton food; the zooplankton must be of the correct size, at an adequate density, within the appropriate depth sector for the young fish, and be there at the right time. Walters *et al.* (1978), following several earlier authors, proposed the hypothesis that natural mortality rates decrease with increasing size, and that any mechanisms that produce slower growth will result ultimately in higher mortalities, or in the words of Horwood and Cushing (1978), "an animal in the sea avoids death by growing". The predation element in oceanic carrying capacity for salmon is therefore likely to be most influential on first entry of the salmon into the sea. If the fish are to minimise this influence by growing fast, then it is the zooplankton availability at this time in restricted coastal locations which is likely to be critical, even if the open ocean can support larger numbers of fish (Walters *et al.*, 1978). Support for the hypothesis of high initial mortality of small fishes comes from the pre-feeding and delayed release experiments with pink and chum salmon, especially in Japan (Chapter 6), when return rates of adults have been more than doubled when the fry were fed for one month before release, as opposed to being released at first feeding. Concern about oceanic carrying capacity should therefore focus first on production dynamics of coastal waters at the time of entry of salmon to the sea.

Many data have accumulated on the rhythmicity of hyperosmotic regulation of salt and water balance in salmonids (e.g. Hoar, 1976) and on the physiological anticipation of life at sea. Thus a physiological definition of release time is being attempted, but what of an ecological or behavioural one? What is the nature of the change of response pattern in stream-dwelling fishes moving from a topographically complex and unidirectional environment which provides a highly complicated sensory input, into a topographically simple and multi-directional environment providing a totally new package of sensory experiences with fewer reference points? Supposing adjustment to this radically changed world has also been anticipated behaviourally, and the fishes are evolutionarily equipped to thrive in the new surround-ings, how are their demands met? At what precise season are appropriate food organisms plentifully available, and how does this vary from one release site to another? The model of coastal production developed by Walters *et al.* (1978) suggested that the British Columbia stocks of juvenile salmon avoid certain coastal locations at certain times. Assuming that this conclusion reflects a biological reality and not an artefact of the model, then release of reared stocks at these unfavourable times and places could be a total loss. Empirical methods for timing releases of chum fry have been developed in Japan, based on terrestrial environmental events, but knowledge of the causal relations between food organism qualities and fish growth and survival should improve on these (cf. those established for anchovies by Lasker and Zweifel, 1978).

It has also been shown that delaying release influences migration patterns (see Chapter 17), implying that this practice could be an important tool in regulating the impact of ranched stocks on their environment and in controlling the exploitation of such stocks. Novotny has noted (Chapter 17) that delaying release of coho *(O. kisutch)* and chinook *(O. tschawytscha)* permitted a greater porportion of the harvest of these cultured fish to be taken by the United States rather than the Canadian fishery. Similar manipulations elsewhere might result in a greater return to the rancher by ensuring that the released fish remain within the exclusive economic zone of his country and never become a high-seas common property resource (cf. Chapter 19). This may now be the case in Iceland (Chapter 8), where Mathisen and Gudjonsson (1978) have suggested that oceanic feeding areas for salmon from south western rivers lie wholly within the Icelandic 200-mile economic zone, and now in the N.E. Pacific, where Japan agreed in 1978 not to fish east of 175° 10'E nor in the 200-mile limit around the Aleutian Islands, thus reducing her catch of North American salmonids very considerably (Larkin, 1979).

Such restrictions of movement, and supposed consequent increase in return rate of salmon, can only yield substantial benefits to the rancher if the fishery is controlled on a stock by stock basis at river mouths and release sites (Chapter 1). This requires a change in attitude to salmon exploitation, but as Larkin (1979) has argued wittily and cogently, protection, regulation and enhancement must first serve the interests of the resource in order to serve those of the exploiters, not vice versa. He traced the history of Pacific salmon management and defined its "standard religion" that husbandry of these species required research on biology, regulation of fisheries for maximum sustainable yield, protection of the environment to ensure production of new generations, and enhancement of stocks to augment that natural production and mitigate the effects of imperfect regulation and inadequate protection. With enhancement come potential problems of restriction of gene pools, risk of diseases, and overexploitation. Therefore enhancement needs integration into a total system of management, and he considered that if British Columbia's Salmonid Enhancement Program (McDonald, 1977) "continued as it has been conceived it holds promise of using a wide range of techniques for increasing the abundance of *all* species of salmon and steelhead *(S. gairdneri)* in *all* regions of the coast to the benefit of *all* sectors of the fishery''. However, this is not management of exploitation, and his prognosis for Pacific salmon was ''a long and slow decline in abundance tempered only by the amelioration of some of the effects of environmental attrition and the fisheries by an array of enhancement techniques''.

To avoid this bleak prospect and to keep the resource healthy (Loftus, 1976), management strategies must be viewed from the fishes viewpoint; Larkin (1979) recommended *inter alia* that the permissible harvest of any *race* of salmon should never be exceeded; that regulation, related to fish and not fishermen, should ensure adequate qualitative as well as quantitative escapements; and that the exploitation method should be seen as a ''variable'' and not a ''given'' element in the management sphere. ''Even if the present system of regulation were executed with flawless technique, it is not demonstrably satisfactory as a way of harvesting each race of salmon appropriately.'' The practice of ranching salmon can coexist most satisfactorily with a strategy of management of wild salmon populations based on the stock concept (Simon and Ricker, 1972). This may be illustrated most clearly in the contemporary context by comparing the success of experimental schemes of ranching in Iceland (Chapter 8) and in Ireland (Chapter 10). In Ireland a large gill-netting fishery intercepted the Atlantic salmon adults returning to the release area; in Iceland no high-seas fishing was permitted and fisheries operated on a river basis only. In Ireland 2·4% of the smolts released were recovered as adults in the river trap, in Iceland 9·4%. However, recoveries of Irish hatchery fish in their drift-net fishery offshore amounted to 4·5 times those in their rivers. Hence the potential harvest of ranched fish was 13%, had the fishery been managed on a river-by-river stock basis, rather than by a mixed-stock fishery offshore.

Given a management strategy of this type (still an experimental one in Larkin's North Pacific region), ranching can be made yet more efficient by increasing the precision of homing to a harvest device, through imprinting and genetic selection. Recent developments in Oregon (Chapter 4), Washington (Chapters 3 and 17) and New Brunswick (Saunders, 1977) have shown that imprinting can be achieved at seawater release sites, and thus novel stocks of ranched salmon could be created returning to coastal areas having no local salmon stock. Additionally, artificial imprinting provides a way of segregating ranched from wild salmon as they approach their release points, reduces the likelihood of wandering of ranched stock, and provides a safeguard against genetic pollution of wild by ranched populations.

Transplantations of salmon species into the southern oceans represent a further example of experimental management through ranching. In addition to those in continental South America (Chapter 14) and in New Zealand (Chapter 15), and following successful plantings of brown *(S. trutta)* and brook trout *(Salvelinus fortinalis)* over the past 25 years (Beall and Davaine, 1979), attempts have been made since 1975 to acclimatise Atlantic salmon in the Kerguelen Islands of the Southern Indian Ocean. The objective has been to exploit the vast resources of krill *(Euphasia superba)*, other crustaceans, and possibly squid which occur in this area of the Antarctic (Beall, personal communication). Plantings into fishless lakes and rivers have been preferred to hatcheries in this case. Results of these experiments are eagerly awaited, and much may be learned about the capacity of Atlantic salmon to live in the cold (<2°C) waters south of the Antarctic convergence, where these islands lie. In the Falkland Islands, South Atlantic Ocean, Shackleton's survey team noted (Anon., 1976) that salmon introduced there could be used to harvest the apparently abundant stocks of small pelagic fishes, small crustaceans and squid, and recommended that such an experimental planting should be undertaken. Physical conditions in the sea would appear to be more favourable to salmon here than around Kerguelen. However, successful introduction of brown trout into Falkland Islands rivers about 25 years ago has resulted in their gradual spread, apparently at the expense of indigenous freshwater fish (Stewart, 1973). Ranching salmon, rather than planting them into rivers, would be a more economical means of using them to harvest abundant marine resources and would at the same time avoid further adverse impacts on indigenous freshwater fishes. Since ranching also implies control of the size of the reproducing population, the impact of salmon on the marine environment would be controllable also. Such a scheme of ranching salmon from the Falkland Islands is now under active consideration (Anon., 1979d). Furthermore, success of transplantation, as opposed to ranching, depends on a "protracted and prodigious effort" (Waugh, Chapter 15) and requires sustained plantings of very large numbers of fish, as is evident in the current Soviet programme in the White Sea area (Chapter 13). Ricker (1954) recommended the initial planting of 15-20 million pink salmon in Newfoundland. In the event (Lear, Chapter 12), only ¼ million were planted, and even though a total of 15 million were introduced over 8 years, the species ultimately failed to establish there. It should be noted, however, that the release of 21 000 fingerling pink salmon into a tributary river of Lake Superior in 1956 has resulted in a self-sustaining, increasing population, which has now spread into Lake Huron also (Nunan, 1967; Collins, 1975) and in 1979 was in its eleventh generation.

Elsewhere, France is considering ranching salmon from Brittany, as part of an extensive programme of ocean ranching using other marine fishes and shellfish (Harache, personal communication). The most recent experiments in Chile are proving successful, and returns to a large enterprise in Chiloe began in summer 1979 (Anon., 1979e). Norwegian experiments with releases of Atlantic salmon have shown low percentage returns (Edwards, 1978), but more recent reports have indicated that these rates may be improved by careful choice of release methods (Sutterlin and Merrill, 1978). Jensen (1979) has found significantly increased return rates from smolts released at sea, basing these both on fisheries for adults at sea and within the river of origin. Similar improvements in return rate were found in Sweden when smolts have been floated down-river in a cage and released in estuaries (Johansson, 1979). The implication of both these Scandinavian findings is that high mortality of released smolts takes place in the river mouths (cf. above, and Walters' hypothesis). The Soviet Union has extended its transplantation of Pacific salmon, by releasing batches of pink and chum salmon into the Baltic at Riga (Egglishaw, personal communication). The impact of these fish on the native Baltic salmon is unknown. Recently China has begun to consider ranching salmon, and in 1978 sent a delegation to Hokkaido, Japan, to study the development of the practice there (Anon., 1978).

The rapidly increasing interest in this form of exploitation of marine resources by free-ranging animals implies the need for international agreements on regulatory measures. These already exist in some major fishery areas (Chapters 1 and 19), but advances in practice and in the efficiency of the use of salmonids as food-gatherers at sea will profit from co-operative research at an international level. The International Pacific Salmon Fisheries Commission is an example of a body set up on a co-operative basis between two major exploiters of the North Pacific salmon fishery. But Larkin's (1979) ''standard religion'' of salmon management needs a more general international acceptance, so that the future of salmon stocks may be brighter than he predicts for the Pacific species. A small step in this direction has been proposed, for co-operative studies on the marine phase of Atlantic salmon, among European nations interested in salmon ranching, under the aegis of C.O.S.T. (European Co-operation in Science and Technology).

Besides international co-operation and control of the exploitation of an enlarged salmon fishery generated through ranching, improvements are needed in production practices of the industry. Many indications of incipient improvements have been given in this book. Acceleration of development through both environmental and genetic manipulation is being exploited with most species cultured, and control of growth rate, smolting rate, maturation rate, migration range, and return time all begin to appear feasible. Refinements of husbandry techniques, providing rearing environments tailored more to the needs of the fish than to the convenience of the husbandryman, are gaining acceptance, and ideas such as those of Mundie (Chapter 18) promise to improve both the biological and the economic efficiency of the rearing process for species with a high freshwater requirement. Bilton's experiments (Chapter 16) demonstrate the importance of precision in the matching of rearing methods, release times, and size objectives. But these and the work reviewed by Novotny (Chapter 17) give some idea of the complexity of problems yet to be faced by the salmon rancher.

REFERENCES

Anon. (1976). *Economic Survey of the Falkland Islands.* 2 Vols. 341 + 110 pp. Economist Intelligence Unit, London.
Anon. (1978). Chinese look at salmon ranching. *Fish Farming International* **5** (4), 5.
Anon. (1979a). Statistics on Russian and Japanese salmon farming. *Aquaculture Digest* **4** (6), 86.
Anon. (1979b). Remarkable one-in-five return of salmon. *Fish Farming International* **5** (5), 3.
Anon. (1979c). W. Hublon quoted in *Aquaculture Digest* **4** (7), 28.
Anon. (1979d). Report on a visit by a fisheries team to the Falkland Islands, November 1978. Ministry of Overseas Development, London (Mimeo).

Anon. (1979e). Article in *Mercurio,* May 1979. Santiago, Chile.

Barraclough, W. E. and Phillips, A. C. (1978). Distribution of juvenile salmon in the southern Strait of Georgia during the period April to July 1966-1969. *Fish. Mar. Serv. Can., Tech. Rep.* **826,** 47.

Beall, E. and Davaine, P. (1979). La truite de mer (*Salmo trutta,* L.) aux îles Kerguelen (T.A.A.F.): premiers résultats. *Bull. Centr. Etud. Rech. sci., Biarritz* **12** (3), 531-532.

Collins, J. J. (1975). Occurrence of pink salmon (*Oncorhynchus gorbuscha*) in Lake Huron. *J. Fish. Res. Bd. Can.* **32,** 402-404.

Edwards, D. J. (1978). *Salmon and Trout Farming in Norway.* Fishing News Books, Farnham. 195 pp.

Hoar, W. S. (1976). Smolt transformation: evolution, behaviour and physiology. *J. Fish. Res. Bd Can.* **33,** 1234-1252.

Horwood, J. W. and Cushing, D. H. (1978). Spatial distributions and ecology of pelagic fish. *In* "Spatial Pattern in Plankton Communities" (Ed. J. H. Steele), pp. 355-383. Plenum Press, New York and London.

Jensen, K. W. (1979). Saltwater releases and saltwater adaptation of smolts of Atlantic salmon. ICES CM 1979/M8 10 pp.

Johansson, N. (1979). Sweden. *In* Anadramous and catadramous fish committee report (Ed. C. P. Ruggles). ICES CM 1979/M1. p. 34.

Larkin, P. A. (1979). Maybe you can't get there from here: a foreshortened history of research in relation to management of Pacific salmon. *J. Fish. Res. Bd Can.* **36,** 98-106.

Lasker, R. and Zweifel, J. R. (1978). Growth and survival of first-feeding northern anchovy larvae (*Engraulis mordax*) in patches containing different proportions of large and small prey. pp. 329-354. *In* "Spatial Pattern in Plankton Communities" (Ed. J. H. Steele). Plenum Press, New York and London. 470 pp.

Le Brasseur, R. J. (1972). Utilization of herbivore zooplankton by maturing salmon. pp. 581-588. *In* "Biological Oceanography of the Northern Pacific Ocean" (Ed. A. Y. Takenouti). Idemitsu Shoten, Tokyo. 626 pp.

Loftus, K. H. (1976). Science for Canada's fisheries rehabilitation needs. *J. Fish. Res. Bd Can.* **33,** 1822-1857.

Mathisen, O. A. and Gudjonsson, T. (1978). Salmon management and ocean ranching in Iceland. *J. Agr. Res. Iceland* **10,** 156-174.

McDonald, J. E. (ed.) (1977). *Salmonid Enhancement Program Annual Report 1977.* Fish. Env. Can. Enhancement Serv. Br., Vancouver. 84 pp.

MacLeod, J. R. (1977). Enhancement technology; a positive statement. pp. 137-147. *In* "Pacific Salmon Management for People" (Ed. D. V. Ellis). Western Geogr. Ser. 13, 320 pp. Univ. Brit. Columbia.

Netboy, A. (1974). "The Salmon: Their Fight for Survival." Houghton Mifflin Co., Boston. 613 pp.

Nunan, P. J. (1967). Pink salmon in Lake Superior. *Ont. Fish. Wildl. Rev.* **6,** 9-14.

Parsons, T. R. and Takahashi, M. (1973). "Biological Oceanographic Processes." Pergamon Press, Oxford. 186 pp.

Peterman, R. M. (1978). Testing for density dependent marine survival in Pacific salmonids. *J. Fish. Res. Bd Can.* **35**, 1434-1450.

Ricker, W. E. (1954). Pacific salmon for Atlantic waters. *Can. Fish. Cult.* **16**, 6-14.

Ricker, W. E. and Smith, H. D. (1975). A revised interpretation of the history of the Skeena River sockeye salmon *(Oncorhynchus nerka). J. Fish. Res. Bd Can.* **32**, 1369-1381.

Rothschild, B. J. (1972). Fishery potential from the oceanic regions. *In* "The Biology of the Oceanic Pacific" (Ed. C. B. Miller) pp. 95-106. Oregon State Univ. Press, Corvallis. 157 pp.

Sanger, G. A. (1972). Fishery potentials and estimated biological productivity of the subarctic Pacific region. *In* "Biological Oceanography of the Northern Pacific Ocean" (Ed. A. Y. Takenouti) pp. 561-574. Idemitsu Shoten. Tokyo. 626 pp.

Saunders, R. L. (1977). Sea ranching—a promising way to enhance populations of Atlantic salmon for angling and commercial fisheries. *Int. Atl. Salmon Found, Spec. Publ. 7,* 17-24.

Simon, R. C. and Larkin, P. A. (eds) (1972). *The Stock Concept in Pacific Salmon.* H. R. MacMillan lectures in Fisheries, Univ. Brit. Columbia, Vancouver. 231 pp.

Stewart, L. (1973). *The Fisheries of the Falkland Islands.* Overseas Development Administration, London (Mimeo).

Straty, R. R. (1974). Ecology and behaviour of juvenile sockeye salmon *(Oncorhynchus nerka)* in Bristol Bay and the eastern Bering Sea. pp. 561-574. *In* Hood, D. W. and Kelly, E. J. (Eds): *Oceanography of the Bering Sea.* Univ. of Alaska, Anchorage.

Sutterlin, A. M. and Merrill, S. P. (1978). *Fish. Mar. Serv. Can., Technical Rep.* 779. 47 pp.

Thorpe, J. E. (1979). Ocean Ranching: general considerations. *In* "Atlantic Salmon: its future" (Ed. A. E. J. Went), pp. 152-164. Fishing News Books, Farnham.

Walters, C. J. (1977). Management under uncertainty. *In* "Pacific Salmon Management for People" (Ed. D. V. Ellis) pp. 261-297. Western Geogr. Ser. 13, 320 pp. Univ. Brit. Columbia.

Walters, C. J., Hilborn, R., Peterman, R. M. and Staley, M. J. (1978). Model for examining early ocean limitation of Pacific salmon production. *J. Fish. Res. Bd Can.* **35**, 1303-1315.

Wankowski, J. W. J. (1979). Morphological limitations, prey size selectivity, and growth response of juvenile Atlantic salmon, *Salmo salar. J. Fish. Biol.* **14**, 89-100.

Wankowski, J. W. J. and Thorpe, J. E. (1979). The role of food particle size in the growth of juvenile Atlantic salmon (*Salmo salar* L.). *J. Fish. Biol.* **14**, 351-370.

Index

ABERNATHY DRY PELLET, 40
Abundance of salmon, 69, 85, 87, 127, 132, 134, 142, 224, 225, 250, 254, 256, 263, 286, 293, 396, 400
Access points, boat, 32
Acclimatisation, 78, 245-249, 267, 268, 269, 271, 280, 363, 366, 390, 401
Acclimatisation Societies, New Zealand, 277, 278, 285, 287, 295, 296, 299
Accommodation, 48
Acid precipitation, 165
Activity, levels of, 202
Adaptability, evolutionary, 6, 8, 86
Adaptation
  environmental, 80, 83, 150
  genetic, 25, 59, 73, 78, 79, 216
Admiralty Inlet, 337
Adventure, 261
Advice, technical, 111
Aeration, 116, 380
  atmospheric, 371
Aeration Tower, 116, 117
Aeromonas hydrophila, 117
Aesthetic benefit, 56
Afognak Island, 213
Age
  inverse relationships of, 205
  at maturity, 285-287, 305-323
  sea, 134, 161, 180, 205, 206
  of smolts, 120-121, 134, 146, 160, 205, 206
Age groups, 67, 80, 81, 83
  frequency of, 67
Age regulation, theory of, 80

Age structure, control of, 80
Agencies, public, 15, 47
Aggression, 372
Agreements, international, 6, 166, 402
Ainu, 92
Aisen, 267, 268
Aisen Fjord, 267
Alaska, 4, 6, 13-27, 50, 69, 79, 82, 137, 213, 239, 273, 327, 329, 330, 332, 333, 334, 335, 338, 339, 350, 352, 354, 361, 363, 388-389, 390, 392, 393, 395
Alaska Department of Fish and Game, 23
Alaskan waters, 336
Aleutian Islands, 64, 399
Aleutian Ridge, 67
Alevins, 18, 20, 52, 170, 172, 201, 376
Alewife, *see Alosa pseudoharengus*
Algae, 377
Alosa aestivalis, 114
Alosa pseudoharengus, 114
Alosa sapidissima, 114
Amenity, social, 3
America, 5, 69
  North, 18, 112, 328, 371, 385, 391, 392, 395
  North West, 69, 328
  South, 8, 261-275, 301, 401
Ammodytes spp., 142
Ammonia, 379
Amphipods, 142
Anarchichas denticulatis, 223
Anchovy, *see Engraulis mordax*
Ancud, 268

Anglers, 48, 121, 220, 280, 282, 286, 287, 288, 289, 293, 295, 296, 300, 301, 302, 325, 327, 335, 337, 340, 343, 344, 349, 361
Anguilla anguilla, 154
Anguilla rostrata, 114, 218, 220, 222, 237, 238, 240
Antarctic, 401
Antarctic Convergence, 401
Antibiotics, 117, 193, 198
Antrim, 188, 189
Aquaculture, 27, 61, 63, 127, 131, 388
   Indian, 40-43, 349, 350, 351, 354
   limited entry to, 23
   facilities, 388
Archaeology, 91
Arctic, 258
Arctic char, *see Salvelinus alpinus*
Arctic ocean, 199
Ardea spp. 377
Ardnacrusha, 191
Argentina, 261, 262, 263, 264, 268-269, 274, 275
Arkhangel'sk District, 245, 250, 257
Arnold's Cove, 223
Artificial culture, prospects for, 83-87
Ascorbic acid, 40
Asia, 18, 64, 69, 385, 392
Asiatic coast, 64, 66, 69
Atholl, Duke of, 200
Atkins frames, 72
Atkins troughs, 245
Atlantic
   North, 2, 8, 109-128, 138, 199, 213, 215, 241, 258, 396, 397
   South, 274, 275, 401
Atlantic salmon, *see Salmo salar*
Atlantic tomcod, *see Microgadus tomcod*
Auburn, 34
Augmentation, 6, 7, 111, 201, 207, 287, 295, 395, 396, 399
Avalon Peninsula, 218, 238
Avoidance, 231, 241

BACTERIA, pathogenic, 354

Bag Limits, 295
Baltic coast, 7, 199
Baltic drainage, 157, 158
Baltic salmon, *see also Salmo salar,* 159-162, 205
Baltic Salmon Fisheries Convention, 166, 167
Baltic Sea, 6, 157-182, 402
   Conference 1972, 167
   Main Basin, 160, 163, 181
Bankruptcy, 3
Banks, of lakes, 68
Baranof Island, 22, 395
Barents Sea, 245, 248, 249, 253, 257, 258
Barge, transfer, 344
Barriers
   mechanical, 169
   thermal, 297
Bays, protected saltwater, 23
Beagle, 261
Beagle Channel, 269
Bears, *see Ursus arctos*
Beaver Creek, 355, 359, 360, 361, 363, 364
Bed load, 379
Behaviour
   control of homing, 20
   feeding, 207
   homing, 8, 182
   innate, 207, 216
   intensity of, 202
   leaping, 271, 275
   migratory, 2, 146, 220, 253, 271, 280
   social, 207
   spawning, 231
   territorial, 202, 372
Benefits
   economic, 123, 126, 127, 366, 384, 399, 400
   social, 123, 126, 127, 197, 394, 393
Benthos, 256, 376
Bering Sea, 64, 95
Berufjördur, 152

Big Lagoon, 352
Biological Station, St. Andrews, 124
Biology
of fish, 170
of hatchery stocks, 120-121
of juvenile pink salmon, 252-256
of salmonids, 2, 8, 9, 70, 96
sea, 170
Biotin, 40
Birds, 182, 254
BKD, *see* Disease, BKD
Blooms, plankton, 328
Blueback Herring, *see Alosa aestivalis*
Boats
charter, 32
limited number, 167
Body height index, 79
Bogs, 252
Boldt decision, 31
Bolshaya Basin, 71
Bolshoi Chkhil, 70
Bonds, state, 13, 23
Borgarfjördur, 139, 152
Bornholm, 163
Bowman's Bay, 354
Brachyteuthis spp., 142
Bradan Mhara Teoranta, 193
Brain, fish, 71
Brands, cold, 189, 190, 194, 361, 365
Brazil, 263, 264, 270-271, 274-275
Breeding, selective, 38, 143, 170, 172
Bristol Bay, 273, 396
Britain, 199-208, 250, 396
British Admiralty, 261
British Columbia, 50, 79, 215, 218,
220, 238, 239, 240, 305-323,
329, 330, 333, 334, 336, 338,
339, 340, 348, 351, 355, 358,
373, 387, 396, 399
Brittany, 354, 402
Broodstock, 6, 36, 60, 61, 70, 72, 98,
99, 100, 114, 116, 117, 124,
125, 187, 387, 393
potential, 343
proprietary, 55
Brook trout, *see Salvelinus fontinalis*

Brown Trout, *see Salmo trutta*
Brunswick Peninsula, 265
Budget, hatchery, 49, 105, 106
Burbot, see *Lota lota*

CADDIS FLIES, *see Trichoptera*
Cage-culture, 3, 4, 40, 44-5, 123,
128, 192, 193, 194, 197
Cage, release, 205, 206, 402
California, 17, 50, 264, 270, 271, 274,
280, 332, 336, 338, 339, 349,
352, 357, 358, 390, 392
Canada, 7, 17, 18, 20, 83, 109-128,
136, 283, 301, 330, 333, 334,
338, 339, 340, 348, 385, 387,
392
Atlantic, 118, 380
Maritime Provinces, 109-128
Canadian Federal Government, 110,
114, 127, 305, 387
Canadian waters, 325, 336
Canals, power-plant outlet, 168
Canneries, 16, 17
Cannibalism, 377
Canopy, net, 375, 377, 378
Canterbury, 285, 291
Capacity
carrying, 26, 58, 59, 105, 199, 300,
366, 395, 396, 397, 398
channel holding, 378
drift-carrying, 379
of hatcheries, 18, 54, 71, 72, 74-5,
76, 85, 122, 125, 168, 169, 170,
170, 174, 175, 190, 191, 192,
194, 267, 269, 299, 322, 359, 371
reproductive, 31, 393
Cape Horn, 265
Cape Spear, 220, 239
Capelin, *see Mallotus villosus*
Capital, 52, 54, 154, 352, 371, 389,
390
Capture, 3, 105
Carcasses of spent fish, 97, 98, 387
Carlin, B., 170

Case Inlet, 343
Catch
  quotas, 167, 177, 178
  of salmon, 6, 16, 24, 26, 30, 32,
    48, 49, 50, 51, 53, 57, 69, 85,
    92-95, 99, 106, 107, 113, 121,
    124, 132, 133, 162, 163, 164,
    166, 178, 179, 180, 181, 194,
    195, 196, 199, 220, 249, 255,
    258, 280, 285, 289, 293, 321,
    322, 325, 335, 336, 343, 356,
    389, 393, 395
Cattle, 261
Cavan, 188
Celilo Falls, 29, 30
Census, 199, 289
Channels, 1, 20, 68, 265, 268, 272,
  274, 288
  finishing, 73
  incubation, 20
  migration/effluent, 114, 116
  rearing, 305, 373-378, 379, 380,
    381
  side, 218, 372, 373, 379
  spawning, 2, 20, 26, 218, 387
  unstable, 288, 289
Char, arctic, *see Salvelinus alpinus*
Charter boats, 48
Cheese, cottage, 71
Chemotherapy, 198
Cherry Salmon, *see Oncorhynchus masou*
Chile, 261, 263, 264-268, 272, 273-
  274, 385, 390, 402
  Agriculture Ministry, 267
  Division of Fisheries Protection,
    267, 268
  Instituto de Fomento Pesquero,
    266, 268
  Navy, 268
Chilean Archipelago, 265, 272
Chiloé, 266, 268, 402
China, 402
Chinook Salmon, *see Oncorhynchus
  tschawytscha*
Chironomids, 256, 376
Chromosomes, 159

Chukotka coast, 64, 65
Chum salmon, *see Oncorhynchus keta*
Circulation, surface, 157
Circuli, scale, 239
Clam Bay, 343-346, 349, 355, 359-
  365
Cleaning, 174
Climate, 58, 70, 157, 257, 263, 271,
  335, 380
Climatic analogues, 78
Clupea harengus, 223, 254, 255
Cod, *see also Gadus morhua*
  salt, 215
Coho salmon, *see Oncorhynchus kisutch*
Cold-tolerance, 215
Collembola, 256
Colonisation, 123, 124, 125, 379
Colour, 250
Commission
  International Pacific Salmon
    Fisheries, 402
  permanent, 167
  1890 Washington State Fish, 31
Competition, 215, 231, 237, 372,
  384, 391
Connemara, 193
Conservation, 2, 6, 7, 24, 25, 31, 56,
  63, 70, 96, 98, 167, 198, 201,
  208, 384, 389
Consumers, 4
Continental Shelf, 142
Cook Inlet, 388
Co-operation, international, 154,
  166, 403
Cordova, 17
Coregonus spp., 163, 168
Cork, 188
Corn solubles, dried, 40
Corvus corax, 251
Corynebacterial kidney disease, *see*
  Disease, BKD
C.O.S.T., 403
Cost-benefit analysis, 196
Cost centres, 391
Cost-effectiveness, 122, 126, 384,
  390

Costs, 4, 6, 7, 20, 45, 48, 54, 55, 56, 60, 97, 106-107, 111, 114, 122, 124, 125, 126, 152, 154, 188, 196-197, 267, 283, 301, 302, 371, 373, 378, 380, 381, 383, 389, 393
Cottonseed, 40
Cottus gobio, 256
Courts
  Finnish water, 177
  Swedish, 170
Cover, 202, 205, 223
  floating, 374, 377, 378
  rings, 204, 205
Coves, 102, 223
Coyhaique, 267
Crab, 40
Crossing, 80
Crosswalk, 375
Crustacea, 133, 401
Cues, chemical, 5
Cunner, *see Tautogolabrus adspersus*
Current system, 157, 241
Currents
  Brazil, 263, 273, 275
  Cape Horn, 263, 273, 274
  Falkland, 263, 273, 275
  Humboldt, 263, 273
  Kuroshio, 137
  oceanic, 137, 140, 141, 263, 268, 272, 273, 274, 285, 293-296
  river, 253, 254
  South Equatorial, 273
  surface, 138, 139, 157, 264, 273
  swift, 154, 372
  West Wind Drift, 263, 273
Cutthroat Trout, *see Salmo clarki*
Cycles, pink salmon, 213, 226, 231, 238, 239, 240, 252, 257, 361
Cyclopterus lumpus, 246
Cyprinids, 165

DAMS, 96, 112, 113, 114, 168, 169, 190, 191, 201, 290-293
  Ardnacrusha, 191
  Aviemore, 291, 292
  Beechwood, 113
  Benmore, 290, 291, 292
  Bonneville, 41
  Dalles, 30
  Grand Falls, 113
  Iniscarra, 190, 194
  Mactaquac, 113, 116, 117, 118, 121
  Mayfield, 36
  Mossy Rock, 36
  Parteen, 191, 194
  Roxburgh, 290
  Tinker, 113
  Tobique Narrows, 113
Danish islands, 160
Davis Strait, 137
DDT, 216
Debris, 35
Decoying, 5
Defence, of territory, 202
Deficiencies
  behavioural, 195, 198
  physiological, 195, 198
Deforestation, 60, 70, 97
Degradation, environmental, 1, 96, 110, 112
Demand, 91
Denbigh, 71
Denmark, 157, 163, 166, 169, 177, 179, 181
Density, 86, 91, 165
  of food particles, 397
  rearing, 120, 246, 306, 343, 344, 372, 381
  stocking, 174
Density asymptote, 59, 396
Depth, of spawning grounds, 79
Design, of tanks, 3
Detection, of fish, 3
Development
  economic, 15
  embryonal, 73, 257
  industrial, 110, 112
  larval, 73
  rate of egg, 101, 252

Development *(cont.)*
  rate of smolt, 202
  residential, 60
Developmental stages, 73
Diary schemes, anglers', 289
Diets, 3, 18, 20, 45, 49, 52, 59, 76,
    89, 142, 253, 328
  dry, 117, 170, 344, 348, 354
  high-protein, 45, 241
  nutritional value, 117
Dikes, 352, 353
Dip-nets, 30
Disease, 117, 127, 170, 191, 195, 300,
    301, 322, 328, 352, 371, 381, 399
  bacterial, 60
  bacterial gill, 117, 188
  BKD, 117
  control of, 20, 101, 170, 177, 193,
    198
  diagnosis of, 20
  ERM, 117
  finrot, 117, 122
  fungal, 101, 192
  furunculosis, 170, 188, 191, 192,
    193, 344
  gas bubble, 117
  infections, 56
  introduction of, 60
  IPN, 117
  latent, 193
  parasitic, 60, 258, 301
  prevention of, 20
  risk of spreading, 26, 60
  saddleback, 117
  testing and certification, 26, 60, 61,
    301
  UDN (ulcerative dermal necrosis),
    170
  vibriosis, 344, 354, 358
  viral, 60, 301
  whirling, 300
Disinfection of eggs, 114
Distribution, 48, 66, 67, 91, 94, 95,
    122, 125, 136, 142, 220, 224,
    225, 228-229, 232-235, 240, 241,
    273, 293-296, 329, 330, 333, 334,

    338, 339, 342, 343, 348, 351,
    354, 355, 357, 358, 359, 376, 385
  age, 160, 161, 286
  size, 79, 82, 226, 236, 307
  time, 78, 162, 179
Disturbance, mechanical, 202
Diversity
  genetic, 6
  insect, 376
  specific, 8
Dogfish, 40
Dolly Varden trout, *see Salvelinus
    malma*
Domsea Farms, 45, 268
Donegal, 192
Drain, peripheral, 203, 204
Drainage, 165, 194
Dredging, 96
Drift
  oceanic, 64
  riverine, 256, 379, 380
Dropback, 121
Drought, 372
Drying-up, of redds, 70, 216, 272
Dyke, 153

EARNINGS, 14
Ecology
  behavioural, 102
  regional, 261
Economic data, 366
Economic problems, 325
Economics, 6, 14, 24, 27, 47-48, 50,
    56, 58, 59, 71, 98, 105-107, 123,
    124, 154-155, 196-197, 208, 296,
    301, 381, 392
Economy, Atlantic fishing, 216
Eddies
  Greenland Sea, 141
  Iceland Sea, 141
  Irminger Sea, 137, 139, 141
  Norwegian Sea, 141
  oceanic, 137, 138, 141
Education
  of aquaculturists, 14, 389

Eel, *see Anguilla* spp.
Effectiveness of rearing, 102-107, 111, 121-122, 124, 127, 177
Efficiency
  of artificial culture, 64, 76, 154
  cost, 24, 27, 383, 403
  of fishing, 167, 396
  of hatcheries, 85
  of incubation, 125
  of scale, 20
Effluents, 96, 97, 151, 377
Effort, 396
Eggs, 18, 20, 24, 34, 35, 38, 39, 40, 45, 52, 60, 61, 68, 70, 71, 72, 73, 74-75, 76, 87, 96, 98, 99, 100, 101, 111, 116, 125, 127, 128, 165, 169, 172, 176, 177, 188, 190, 191, 200, 202, 213, 216, 217, 218, 220, 221, 222, 223, 227, 231, 240, 241, 245, 248, 250, 251, 252, 257, 258, 264, 265, 266, 267, 269, 272, 274, 275, 277, 279, 280, 282, 283, 295, 296, 301, 306, 361, 375, 377, 379, 380, 386, 387, 391
  cod, 246
  deposition of, 226, 252
  eyed, 116, 192, 201, 215, 218, 221, 245, 252, 300, 306
  grated, 71
  green, 114
  lumpfish, 246
  supply of, 252
  surplus, 44, 61
  take of, 35, 105, 266
Eidsvatn, 154
Eld Inlet, 329
Electricity Supply Board, 187, 188, 190, 191, 192
Electrodes, 377
Electrofishing, 162, 172
Elliot Bay, 344
Embryos, 73, 252
Employees, 32, 49
Employment, 48, 49
Enclosures, 1, 3, 153

Energy, 3, 4, 47, 122, 178, 301, 372
  efficiency ratio, 4
England, 199, 201, 208
Engraulis mordax, 397, 399
Enhancement, 38, 47, 48, 49, 51, 53, 54, 56, 57, 61, 91, 92, 96, 98, 106, 111, 122, 124, 125, 126, 127, 131, 301, 305, 343, 359, 384, 388, 389, 399
  authorities, 24, 388
  facilities, 387
  potential of, 122
  thermal, 55
Enrichment, 376, 379
Enteric Redmouth Disease, *see* Disease, ERM
Enterprise, private, 15
Entrainment of air, 372
Environment
  riverine, 288-289
  terrestrial, 398
Environmental dependence, 78
Environmental disruption, 96, 164-165, 287, 393, 400
Environmentalists, 296
Environments,
  controlled, 3, 25
  economic, 91
  geographic, 91
Ephemeroptera, 256
Epizootics, 344
Equipment, purchase of, 48
ERM, *see* Disease, ERM
Escapement, 1, 6, 7, 59, 99, 112, 127, 187, 208, 306, 318, 320, 321, 322, 329, 330, 333, 334, 338, 339, 342, 348, 351, 355, 358, 359, 400
Esox lucius, 182, 190, 254, 255
Establishment, 285, 293, 295, 402
Estuaries, 59, 60, 96, 135, 139, 140, 163, 192, 207, 217, 237, 240, 245, 250, 254, 255, 275, 289, 328, 340, 341, 380, 402
Euphausia superba, 401
Euphausids, 142

Europe, Western, 396
Eutrophication, 165
Evolution, 135
Evolutionary history, 77
Exotic species, 8, 124, 261
Expansion
    of extended rearing, 359
    of hatchery programmes, 111, 385,
        389, 393
    of fisheries, 195
    of ranching, 58, 85, 154
Experimental Rearing Council, 373-
    378
Experiments
    controlled growth, 327
    drift bottle, 137
    genetic, 332
    imprinting, 361
    marking, 104, 116, 136, 141, 147,
        151, 160, 161, 171, 179, 200,
        325, 335
    ranching, 143-154, 268, 302, 390,
        400
    rearing, 71, 135, 143, 171, 172,
        200, 201, 207, 252-253
    release, 171, 182, 252-253,
        305-323, 325-367, 398
    release before feeding, 398
    stocking, 266, 267
    transplanting, 150, 213-242, 270,
        271, 275, 401
    transport, 171
Exploitation, 1, 5, 6, 16, 24, 25, 92,
        114, 127, 142, 162, 188, 191,
        192, 193, 194-196, 197, 199,
        208, 226, 231, 295, 296, 342,
        398, 399, 400, 402, 403
    irrational, 70, 76
    rational, 167
Exploitation rates, 59, 208, 321, 325,
        335
Exports, 154

FAECES, 376
Falkland Islands, 401

Falls, 250, 269, 271, 275
Far East, 69, 70, 86
    Soviet, 64, 65, 248
Fares, revenue from, 48
Farmers, 152, 296
Farming
    of salmon, 287, 389
    of trout, 391
Faroe Islands, 136
Fat content, 256, 258
Fauna
    bottom, 73
    invertebrate, 165
Feasibility
    biological, 126
    economic, 124, 126, 128
Fecundity, 73, 127
Feed trials, 117
Feeders, automatic, 117, 176, 306,
    376, 378
Feeding, 3, 4, 18, 20, 29, 38, 39, 40,
    43, 45, 73, 76, 101, 102, 117,
    131, 134, 139, 146, 154, 176,
    177, 200, 220, 237, 253, 256,
    267, 295, 335, 347, 376, 378,
    383, 397
    areas, 257, 268, 327, 399
    coastal areas, 398
    experimental, 101
    extra, 73, 87, 104, 105, 126, 328,
        352
    first, 203, 205, 380, 398
    intensity, 256
    period, 135, 141, 320
    in seawater, 102, 320
Feeding areas, sea, 64, 160
Feeding grounds, 5, 134, 135, 136-
    142
Fence
    chain-link, 374
    counting, 220, 231, 238
Fertilisation
    artificial, 70, 71, 76, 95, 96, 99, 200
    dry, 172
    heterospermic, 73
Fertilising effect, of sewage, 165

Fertility, egg, 127
Feudal lords, 96
Fibres
  natural, 166
  synthetic, 163, 166
Filter-beds, 189
Fin-clipping, 102, 191, 192, 194, 196,
  365, 377
  adipose, 147, 149, 307
Finclips, 114, 200
  ventral, 150
Fingerlings, 18, 34, 39, 111, 112, 116,
  117, 122, 125, 215, 248, 253,
  254, 269, 381, 402
Finland, 157, 162, 163, 164, 165, 166,
  168, 169, 176, 177, 179, 181
Finrot, *see* Disease, Finrot
Fins, condition, 120, 343
Fish
  food, 31, 56
  fresh, 176
  game, 31, 53, 64, 94, 277, 349
  hatchery, 383, 395, 400
  pan-sized, 40, 44, 45
  pelagic, 401
  predatory, 2, 4
  stream, 398
  surplus, 14, 24, 25, 383, 384, 391
  wild, 383
Fish Disease Laboratory, 177
Fish passage, problems, 122, 123
Fisheries, 1, 2, 3, 4, 6, 8, 13, 29, 32,
  48, 49, 57, 102, 112, 118, 119,
  122, 124, 126, 200, 201, 208,
  220, 238, 267, 296, 300, 301,
  305, 306, 328, 329, 333, 334,
  335, 327, 338, 339, 348, 351,
  356, 359, 385, 396, 399, 400
  bag net, 168
  Baltic Salmon, 157-182
  California coastal, 342, 349, 355
  Canadian, 335, 342, 350, 359, 399
  coastal net, 188, 190, 191, 192,
    193, 195, 196, 197, 208, 226,
    228-229, 231, 232-235, 236, 327
  commercial, 6, 7, 27, 32, 47, 53,
    57, 59, 92-95, 98, 111, 116, 117,
    208, 215, 226, 236, 285, 288,
    302, 322, 327, 332, 335, 336,
    342, 363, 364, 366, 383, 388,
    389, 390, 392, 393
  common property, 23, 24, 59, 383,
    384, 389, 391, 392, 393
  depleted salmon, 13, 15-16, 91,
    325, 388
  dip-net, 30
  distant, 118
  drift-net, 195, 208, 337
  estaurine, 6, 92, 208
  foreign ownership, 70
  gillnet, 337, 342, 363, 364, 365,
    400
  growth of, 15-16
  Indian, 30, 31, 32, 41, 118, 122,
    363
  lack of control over, 76
  level of, 166, 208
  mixed-stock, 7, 25, 384, 400
  near-shore, 47, 57, 162, 163, 164,
    167, 178, 180
  North Pacific salmon, 402, 403
  open-sea, 2, 7, 41, 50, 56, 63, 76,
    85, 106, 132, 147, 160, 162,
    163, 164, 167, 178, 180, 181,
    190, 195, 208, 400, 402
  Oregon coastal, 351, 355
  Puget Sound, 325-367
  purse-seine, 337
  put-and-take, 140
  regulation of, 58, 63, 70, 335
  river, 6, 117, 118, 162, 164, 167,
    168, 178, 180, 191, 207, 208,
    322, 400, 402
  rod and line, 208
  selectivity of, 123, 321, 342
  single-day, 163
  sport, 31, 32, 41, 47, 48, 49, 50,
    53, 56, 57, 59, 98, 113, 114,
    116, 118, 122, 131, 139, 147,
    208, 261, 263, 265, 269, 272,
    285, 287-288, 295, 300, 301,
    302, 321, 322, 325, 327, 329,

Fisheries, sport *(cont.)*
    330, 332, 333, 334, 336, 337,
    338, 339, 340, 342, 343, 344,
    345, 348, 349, 351, 354, 355,
    356, 361, 366, 383, 388, 391,
    393
  stock-by-stock, 399
  terminal, 47, 50, 365, 366
  troll, 57, 325, 335, 336, 337, 340,
    348, 351, 355, 356
  U.S.A., 350
  Washington, 54, 337, 342 348,
    351, 355, 356, 358
  winter sport, 335
Fisheries Rehabilitation and Enhance-
  ment Division, *see* FRED
Fisheries Research Board of Canada,
  215
Fishery Agency, Japanese, 98
Fishery areas, 2, 15, 295, 402
Fishery associations, 96, 97, 98, 388,
  389, 393
Fishery authorities, 170
Fishery Boards, District Salmon, 201
Fishery co-operatives, 97, 98, 105,
  386, 387
Fishing, brail, 162
Fishing community, 198
Fishing companies, 76
Fishing grounds, 92, 327, 366, 383
  Canadian Atlantic, 215
Fishing intensity, 154, 167, 178, 180,
  363
Fishing rights
  Indian, 30, 31
  riparian owners, 188
Fish-meal, 3, 101
Fishpasses, 168, 291
Fishways, 2, 167, 168, 169
Fjords, 265, 268
Fleet, fishing, 63, 336
Flesh quality, 56, 300
Flood-control projects, 49
Floods, 72, 139, 272, 293, 325
  flash, 288

Flows
  compensation, 2
  control of, 372
  helicoidal, 379
Flow-meters, 205
Folic acid, 40
Food, 39, 45, 101, 133, 142, 153,
  170, 202, 205, 231, 248, 258,
  266, 272, 309, 371, 378, 381
  availability, 372, 397
  composition of, 39-40, 59, 170
  concentration of, 273
  consumption of, 397
  conversion of, 40
  cost of, 197
  natural, 176, 215, 352, 376, 381
  organisms, 132, 134, 273, 397, 398
  pelletted, 170, 176, 371, 376
  quality, 102
  terrestrial organisms, 376
Food particles, 203
  size-selection of, 202, 272, 397
Footpath, 374, 375
Foraging, 4
Forecast, hydrological, 77
Forestry, 60, 70, 165
Form, of body, 79
Forspata, see Weirs, bank
Fox Island, 344, 346, 359, 363
France, 354, 396, 402
FRED, 23
Fredericton, 113
"Free gap", 187
Freezing, of redds, 70, 250, 272
Freshwater layers of, 4, 350
Freshwater Fisheries Laboratory, 201
Frost, 71
Fry, 6, 17, 18, 34, 38, 39, 40, 43, 71,
  72, 73, 78, 84, 85, 87, 95, 97,
  98, 99, 100, 101, 102, 104, 105,
  106, 111, 117, 122, 123, 125,
  127, 153, 165, 169, 171, 191,
  194, 201, 203, 207, 213, 216,
  217, 218, 219, 220, 221, 222,
  223, 224, 227, 238, 239, 240,

241, 246, 250, 255, 256, 264, 267, 269, 272, 273, 277, 280, 282, 283, 288, 289, 296, 299, 300, 306, 327, 328, 350, 352, 372, 374, 375, 376, 377, 378, 380, 381, 398
Fuerte Bulnes, 261
Funds, 16, 53, 60, 70, 122, 124, 152, 170, 201, 268, 295
Fundy, Bay of, 118
Future of Baltic salmon, 178, 182
Future of ranching, 58, 122-127, 395-403

GABIONS, 374
Gadus morhua, 220, 223, 246, 254
Gaffs, 30
Galaxiid fishes, 293
Galway, 196
Gammarids, 253
Gap, minimum, 166
Gasterosteus aculeatus, 254
Gates, steel, 169
Gear
  drifting, 162
  fishing, 32, 167, 365, 396
  mounting of, 167
  pelagic, 163
Gene pools, 399
Generations, 77, 78, 80, 81, 82, 83, 226, 257, 399
Generator, 377
Genes, 77
Genetic base, 116
Genetic control
  of growth, 308, 403
  of maturation, 202, 207, 308, 403
  of return rate, 205, 216, 308, 403
  of return time, 116
  of smolting rate, 202, 205, 207, 403
Genetic manipulation, 403
Genetics, 127, 134
  population, 77, 78
  research on, 111

Genotypes, 78, 82, 216
Georgia Strait, 238, 239
  Germany, 166, 396
  East (GDR), 157, 177
  West (FRG), 157, 163, 166, 169, 177, 181
Gillnet, 92, 100, 132, 163, 172, 218, 223
  floating, 162, 168
  set, 162
Glacial flow, 288
Glaciation, Pleistocene, 265
Glenariffe, 288, 290, 299
Gobies, *see Cottus gobio*
Golden Bay, 297
Golfo Almirante Montt, 265
Gonads, 250
Goose Creek, 215
Gotland, 163
Grading, 307, 327, 377, 378
Grand Falls, 112
Grants, 388, 389
Gravel, 20, 52, 96, 153, 154, 202, 216, 217, 218, 250, 272, 328, 373, 374, 376, 379, 380
Grayling *see Thymallus thymallus*
Great Lakes, 8
Greenland, 117, 118, 136, 138, 141, 142
Grilse, 109, 116, 118, 120, 121, 132, 134, 136, 140, 141, 142, 145, 160, 193, 195, 196, 197, 200, 205, 206, 207, 231
Grilse: salmon ratios, 120, 121, 132, 135, 147, 207
Grjóteyri, 152
Growth, 2, 17, 18, 29, 102, 127, 131, 165, 177, 201, 267, 269, 273, 277, 285-287, 289, 305-323, 366, 397, 398
  accelerated, 43, 45, 55, 87, 403
  of kelts, 200
  in natural waters, 26
  at sea, 135, 150, 160, 200, 239, 350, 396
Growth rate, 2, 3, 134, 170, 380, 396

Grushetsky, 71
Gulf of Alaska, 95, 137, 396, 397
Gulf of Ancud, 266, 267, 268, 274
Gulf of Bothnia, 157, 160, 163, 179,
    181
Gulf of Finland, 160, 181
Gulf of Riga, 160, 163
Gulf of St. Lawrence, 118
Gulls, *see Larus canus*
Gyres 137, 139

HABITAT, 64, 77, 83, 86, 97, 113,
    122, 124, 154, 201, 249, 266,
    371
  loss of, 110, 165
  spawning, 56, 57, 60
Haddock, *see Melanogrammus aeglefinus*
Hamburg, 264
Handling, 272
Hansen Creek, 79
Harpacticoids, 253
Harvest, 2, 4, 7, 26, 3, 32, 34, 38,
    41, 47, 48, 50, 58, 59, 63, 64,
    69, 76, 83, 85, 87, 92, 95, 98,
    123, 124, 136, 142, 195, 208,
    301, 305, 325, 327, 340, 349,
    363-365, 383-385, 387, 390,
    391, 399-401
  controlled points, 7, 25, 41, 131,
    400
  optimal annual, 31
Hatchability, 127
Hatcheries, 2, 3, 6, 7, 13, 14, 17, 18-
    23, 25, 26, 33, 34, 36, 38, 40,
    48, 49, 59, 66, 71, 73, 76, 77,
    85, 87, 98, 102, 105, 111, 112,
    114-117, 123, 125, 126, 132,
    134, 152, 166, 169, 172, 176,
    177, 179, 182, 192, 201, 207,
    245, 248-252, 255, 262, 265-268,
    280, 282, 296, 305, 322, 325,
    328, 334, 346, 359, 363, 366,
    371, 372, 378, 381, 384, 385,
    387, 393, 401
  Adatymovsky, 71, 72

Ainsky, 75
Aktivny, 75
Almondbank, 206, 207
Älvkarleby, 170, 173, 174, 175
Älrkarleö, 175
Anivsky, 75
Backsport, 97
Bergeforsen, 175
Bidzhansky, 72
Blatjärn, 175
Bollnäs, 175
Brattfors, 175
Breznyakovsky, 74
Bushmills, 188-190, 194
Buyuklinsky, 74
Canadian Government, 111, 112
Carrigadrohid, 188, 190-191, 192,
    196
Chitose Central Salmon, 97
Columbia River, 335, 342
Cong, 188, 194
Construction of, 23, 33, 71, 72, 86,
    97, 111, 388
contribution of, 117-120, 127
Eagle Creek National, 51
Far Eastern, 74-75, 76, 84, 85
Forsmo, 174
Furnace, 188, 192-193
Goltström, 175
George Adams, 338
Green River, 346, 352, 354, 355,
    356, 363
Gursky, 74
Hakataramea, 280, 281, 282, 283
Heden, 174
history, 97-98
Hölle, 175
Hoodsport, 330, 332, 338, 344,
    346, 348
Invergarry, 201
Issaquah, 348, 361
Japanese summer, 71
Kalama River, 332
Kalininsky, 75
Kandalakshsky, 245
Kirillovsky, 75

Knyazhegubsky, 245
Kurilsky, 75
Kvistforsen, 174
Laholm, 175
Lake Ohau, 280, 282, 283
Långhult, 175
Långsele, 174
Laxamyri, 152
Lesnoy, 74
Ljusne, 175
location of, 25
Lower Kalama, 334
Lovetsky, 75
Mactaquac, 112, 113, 114-117, 118, 121, 122
Minter Creek, 327, 329, 336, 337, 343, 344, 346, 354, 356, 359
Munka-Ljungby, 175
Näs, 175
Netarts Bay, 52, 61
Nimbus, 271
non-profit, 23, 24, 27, 388, 389, 392, 393
Nooksack River, 332
Norrfors, 174
Okhotsky, 74
Onezhsky, 245, 251
operation of, 23, 55, 388
Osenny, 75
Pacific Northwest, 336
Parteen, 188, 191-192, 196
Parusny, 75
Pionersky, 75
Pobedinsky, 74
private, 13, 14, 16, 17, 18, 21, 23, 24, 26, 27, 52-58, 60, 97, 98, 105, 384, 386, 387, 389, 390, 391, 392, 393
public, 13, 16, 17, 18, 23, 24, 26, 56-58, 97, 98, 105, 384, 386, 387, 391, 393
Pugachevsky, 74
Puget Sound, 336
Puyallup, 354, 356
Quilcene, 351
reconstruction of, 72, 85, 111, 125

regulation of, 23
Reidovy, 75
research, 14, 38, 43, 55, 61, 70, 71, 85, 143-150
Rio Cautin, 264, 265
Rosewall Creek, 306-323
Sakhalin, 246
Seattle, 361
Shelton, 349
Silverstream, 287, 296, 299
Skagit River, 332, 342
Skookum Creek, 349, 357, 358, 363
Skykomish River, 337, 340
Sokolnikovsky, 75
Sokolovsky, 74
Sopochny, 75
Spring Creek, 41
State, 23, 44, 48-52, 56-58, 60, 61
Taranaisky, 75
Taybolsky, 245, 246, 251
Teplovsky, 71, 72, 73
Toutle River, 332, 337, 342
Udinsky, 74
Umbsky, 245, 246, 250, 251, 254
Uragubsky, 245, 254
Urozhainy, 75
U.S. Federal, 40, 54
Ushkovsky, 71, 72
Ushuaia, 269, 274
Vatutunsky, 75
Virginia, 188, 194
Washington coastal, 335
Yasnomorsky, 75
Hatchery Associations
    regional, 23
Hatchery practice, 202, 396
Hatchery requirements, 72
Hatchery systems, regional, 120
Hatching rooms, 114
Headpond, 116
Health, of fish, 111, 117, 120, 122, 170, 378, 381
Heat, 380
Hemp, 163
Herder's Channel, 218

Herons, *see Ardea* spp.
Herring, 40, 239
  Atlantic, *see Clupea harengus*
  pasteurised, 40
Heterogeneity
  genetic, 77
  of males, 80
Heterozygosity, 77
Hiding, 205, 256
Hokkaido, 91-99, 103-106, 267, 386, 387, 402
  government of, 98
Holding Pools, 114
Hölle, 172
Home pond, 37
Homeostasis, of control, 83
Homing, 1, 5, 6, 63, 83, 95, 102, 109, 131, 135, 151, 154, 182, 213, 216, 257, 290, 400
Homing stations, 327, 361
Honshu, 92, 95-99, 387
Hood Canal, 40, 330, 331, 332, 335, 337, 338, 344, 345, 349, 351
Hooknose Creek, 238
Hooks,
  fixed, 163, 167
  maximum number, 168
  minimum size, 166
Hose, fire, 376
Hudson Bay, 215
Husbandry, 3, 49, 146, 328, 388, 399
Hybridisation, natural, 69
Hydracarina, 256
Hydroelectric installations, 49, 96, 112, 121, 164, 190-192, 290, 293, 297
Hydroelectricity, 6, 166, 201, 290
  North of Scotland Board, 201
Hydrography, 157
Hydrology, 77, 263

ICE, 246, 250, 253, 372, 380
  break-up of, 64
Iceland, 8, 120, 131-155, 250, 399, 400

ICES, 165, 166
Idaho, 392
Ide, *see Leuciscus idus*
Impact
  biological, 54, 62, 124, 398, 401
  economic, 61, 393
  market, 54
  social, 61, 393
Importation, 60, 61, 388
Impoundments, 3, 287, 290-293
Imprinting, 5, 182, 327, 349, 357, 366, 400
  to seawater sites, 5, 56, 359-363, 367
Improvements, environmental, 2
Incentives, financial, 53, 384, 390, 391
Income, 131, 132
Incubation, 18, 29, 38, 39, 52, 70, 72, 73, 95, 96, 99, 101, 111, 116, 169, 172, 176, 217, 218, 245, 246, 265, 266, 272, 306, 371, 375, 377, 379, 380
  accelerated, 380
  temperatures, 74-75, 216
Incubation room, heated, 269
Incubators, 20, 71, 72, 269
  Heath, 38, 306
  shallow matrix, 380
  substrate, 22, 52, 123, 125
Indian Ocean, 401
Indians, 29, 30-31, 388, 389, 392
  Lummi, 42, 43, 349, 350, 351, 354, 358, 363
  Quinault, 42, 43
  Squaxin, 347, 363
  Suquamish, 365
Industrialisation, 60, 70
Industrialists, 72
Industry
  fishing, 91, 92, 387, 403
  private, 391
  ranching, 208, 403
  salt cod, 215-216
  Swedish power, 170
Infection, 101

Infections, fungus, 117
  see also Saprolegnia
Infectious pancreatic necrosis, *see* Disease, IPN
Information, transmission of genetic, 80, 82, 83
Inheritance tendency, 82
Injuries, 114
Inlets, 223, 256
Innovations
  of production strategy, 55
  technological, 20, 23, 56, 91, 127
Inositol, 40
Input, sensory, 398
Insects, 256, 376, 377
Insemination, artificial, 100
Institute of Freshwater Fisheries, Icelandic, 153
Institutional framework, for ranching, 23-24, 27
Institutions, educational, 13
Instituto de Fomento Pesquero, 266, 268
Intake, channel, 374, 377, 379, 380, 381
  control gate, 374, 379
Interactions, biological, 8, 231, 238, 372
Interference, biological, 8, 218, 231, 250, 401
International Council for the Exploration of the Sea, *see* ICES
Introductions, 7, 8, 29, 124, 213-242, 245-258, 261-275, 301, 391, 401, 402
Inundation, 288, 291
Inventories, 343
Invertebrates, 371, 372, 377, 379, 380
  propagation of, 73, 371
Investment, 53, 97, 123-125, 208, 352, 365, 384, 389, 390, 393
IPN, *see* Disease, IPN
Ireland, 187-198, 400
  Dept. of Fisheries, 195, 196
  Northern *see* Northern Ireland
Irminger Sea, 139, 142

Irrigation, 291, 297
Isolates, 67, 77, 79
Isolation, geographic, 135, 159
Iturup Island, 72
Iwate Prefecture, 102

JACKS, 43, 308, 309-312, 361
James Bay, 215
Japan, 6, 7, 17, 18, 19, 26, 63, 64, 69, 72, 91-107, 137, 267, 273, 301, 328, 342, 385, 386-387, 390, 392, 395, 398, 399, 402
  Fisheries Association, 267
  International Co-operation Agency, 267
Juan de Fuca Strait, 330, 331, 332, 335, 337, 338
Jumping, 36
Juneau, 22

KAIKOURA, 295
Kamchatka, 64, 65, 67, 68, 69, 71, 77, 82, 84, 85, 86, 95, 137, 245
Kandalakshsky Gulf, 245
Karafuto masu, *see Oncorhynchus gorbuscha*
Karelia, 250
Kelp, 40
Kelt reconditioning, 126-127
Kelts, 126, 127, 139, 140, 141, 200
Kennedy's Lagoon, 359
Kerguelen Islands, 401
Ketchikan, 17
Khaborovsk province, 84, 85, 86
Kodiak Island, 14, 16, 17
Kokanee salmon, 49
Kola peninsula, 8, 245-258
Kollafjördur, 131, 132, 135, 136, 139, 140, 143-150
Komandorskie Islands, 67
Korea, 385, 387
Krill, 401
Kuriles, 64, 65, 69, 84, 85, 86, 95, 387

LABORATORIES, research, 13, 170, 201, 346

Labour, 52, 71, 99
    cost of, 197, 378

Labrador, 226, 273

Ladders, 37, 292, 359, 361, 364

Lagoons, 143, 146, 148, 149, 352, 354, 359, 364
    diked tidal, *see also* Ponds, diked tidal
    352-354, 359, 364

Lakes, 17, 25, 49, 68, 69, 73, 78, 124, 126, 143, 153, 154, 207, 208, 215, 252, 253, 264, 265, 268, 272, 280, 283
    Alecnaguik, 79
    Auke, 327
    Azabachye, 64, 67, 68, 77, 79, 80, 81, 82
    Blizhny, 68
    Capitol, 329
    Dalny, 68
    fertilisation of, 126
    fishless, 401
    Huron, 402
    Kurilsky, 67
    Lago Yehuin, 269
    Manapouri, 279
    man-made, 126, 291
    muskeg, 379
    Nahuel Huapi, 269
    Nerka (Wood River), 79, 82
    Nerpichy, 71
    Ohau, 283, 284
    outflow of, 379
    peaty, 379
    Quinault, 42, 43
    rearing in, 126, 207-208
    Rotorua, 278
    storage, 291
    Superior, 402
    Taupo, 278
    Te Anau, 279
    Tekapa, 279
    Teploe, 73
    Vänern, 159

Lamutka Creek, 68

Lancetfish *see Paralepsis* spp.

Landings, *see* Catch

Landowers, 287

Lárós, 143, 153

Larus canus, 251

Larvae
    deformed, 252
    salmon, 70, 72, 73, 87, 245, 251, 252, 253

Lautaro, 264, 265, 266

Law, 23, 24, 52, 53, 56, 57, 132, 208, 287, 295, 383-393

Legislation, 7, 23, 24, 52, 70, 98, 110, 167, 187, 188, 197, 208, 287, 390
    environmental, 168

Legislature, Washington State, 44

Lengths, of body, 73, 79, 82, 202, 223, 226-231, 253, 286, 307, 342, 356, 376
    minimum, 167

Leuciscus idus, 246

Levies, 6

Licences, 6, 52, 54, 70, 195, 285, 295, 388, 390

Life-cycles, complex, 80

Life-history, patterns, 135, 200

Lifespan, 64, 226

Light, 202, 216
    artificial, 146
    intensity, 254
    preferences, 205
    red, 203

Limited entry, 7, 23, 388, 389

Lines, long, 163, 167

Lipid content, 376, 378

Little Clam Bay, 352-356, 361, 363

Little Port Walter, 350, 352, 354, 363

Liver, 176
    cod, 246

Living space, 378

Loans
    low-interest, 13, 388, 389
    state, 23, 24, 388, 389

Loch Kinardochy, 207
Locomotion, 201
Logging, 85, 165
Lota lota, 182
Lough Corrib, 188
Lough Feeagh, 192
Lough Furnace, 192
Lummi Bay, 349, 354, 357, 358
Lummi Indian Tribal Enterprises (LITE) *see also* Indians, Lummi 357, 363
Lumpfish *see Cyclopterus lumpus*
Lutra canadensis, 126

MACKEREL, 239, 240
Mackerel, Atlantic, *see Scomber scombrus*
Mactaquac, *see also* Dams, Hatcheries, 114, 116-121
Magadan province, 84, 85, 86, 245
Magallanes, 268, 274
Magellan, 261
 Strait of, 261, 264, 265
Maine, 97, 112, 113, 213, 252, 257
Maintenance, of body tissue, 397
 costs of, 196
Malachite Green, 101, 172
Males
 precocious, 141, 286
 predominance of, 83
 sea-run, 202
Mallotus villosus, 133, 142, 220, 223, 231, 237, 246
Management, 2, 6, 27, 29, 31, 32, 56, 59, 98, 105, 110, 112, 114, 122, 127, 165-169, 170, 178, 179, 199, 208, 268, 272, 277, 287, 291, 295, 296, 322, 366, 383, 384, 389, 399, 400, 403
 experimental, 401
 research on, 366
Management agencies, governmental, 262, 383, 384, 386
Management plans, long-term, 122, 123, 127
Management practices, 327, 363

Manchester, 44, 343, 349, 349, 353, 354, 359, 360
Manpower, 58
Mariculture, 6
Marietta, 349, 363
Mark-recapture, Bailey's method, 218
Market evaluation, 300
Market forces, 384
Market quality, 56
Marketing, 143, 154, 197, 287, 384
Markets
 international, 58, 300
 salmon, 54, 132, 195, 300, 384, 391
Marking, 102, 131, 200
Mash, 371, 376
Masu salmon, *see Oncorhynchus masou*
Mating, assortative, 79
Matings, 116
Maturation, 1, 77, 78, 80, 85, 116, 127, 134, 135, 141, 202, 207, 257, 280, 300, 396
 regulation of, 258
Maturity, 34, 70, 100, 121, 123, 172, 200, 216, 250, 275
 early, 286
 late, 287
Mayflies, *see* Ephemeroptera
Mayo, 188
Meal, moist, 40
Meiji Restoration, 92
Melanogrammus aeglefinus, 223, 254
Mergansers, *see Mergus* spp.
Mergus spp., 377
Mesh, minimum size, 166, 335
Metals, heavy, 165, 168
Methods, acclimatisation, 245-249
 conservation, 2, 170
 enhancement, 400
 exploitation, 5, 7, 400
 fishing, 2, 167, 295
 harvesting, 25
 husbandry, 403
 microtagging, 147
 rearing, 4, 49, 52, 102, 111, 143, 146, 170, 172, 182, 201, 246, 342, 375, 403

Methods *(cont.)*
  release, 102, 143, 146, 150, 152, 154, 182, 201, 205, 327-359, 402
  spawning, 34-35
  tagging, 146, 147
  transportation, 246
Microgadus tomcod, 223
Microtag, *see* Tags, micro-
Microtag reading, 150
Migrants, 2, 114, 117, 121, 134, 220, 256
  downstream, 169, 190, 218, 221, 231, 237, 251, 252, 253, 257, 290, 291, 299, 327, 328
  spawning, 160, 161, 164, 172, 179
  upstream, 190, 192
Migration, 5, 38, 39, 43, 56, 57, 58, 58, 60, 68, 76, 92-95, 114, 116, 123, 131, 132, 140, 160, 182, 213, 216, 240, 336, 337-342, 366
  contranatant, 140, 141
  control of range, 403
  current-guided, 137
  delayed, 135
  denatant, 139, 141
  distant, 147
  downstream, 102, 109, 113, 126, 134-135, 139, 200, 202, 205, 215, 251, 253, 254, 255, 256, 258, 380
  feeding, 63, 137
  motivation for, 205
  passive, 137, 202
  patterns, 58, 241, 332, 335, 337, 366, 399
  period, 256
  routes, 58, 95, 138, 140, 141, 264, 325, 327
  at sea, 136-137, 139, 196, 264, 268, 295, 332, 385
  seaward, 102, 150, 153, 195, 200, 271, 273, 274, 275, 279, 325, 389
  smolt, 137, 143, 146, 255, 328, 352, 375
  spawning, 29, 63, 77, 95, 97, 139,
    162, 178, 249-252, 257, 258, 283
  timing of, 134-135, 250, 255
  upstream, 113, 288, 293
  wintering, 63
Migration theories, 137-142
Migratory Fish Committee, 166, 170
Migratory species, 83
Milk, 4
Milt, *see* Sperm
Minerals, 101
Mink, *see Mustela vison*
Miyagi Prefecture, 102
Moncton, 269
Moorings, cost of, 197
Morphological groups, 83
Mortality, 3, 6, 70, 71, 72, 76, 77, 83, 85, 101, 102, 114, 117, 165, 170, 172, 177, 178, 179, 191, 216, 217, 238, 239, 240, 245, 248, 251, 252, 253, 271, 272, 273, 275, 336, 344, 354, 376, 377, 378, 397, 398, 402
Motovsky Gulf, 245
Mouldings, corrugated plastic, 203
Mt. Esja, 150, 152
Mouth, subterminal, 73
Movements, 79, 140, 253, 343
  prohibition of, 301
  restriction of, 399
Mud, 250
Murmansk District, 246
Mustela vison, 126, 251, 377
Myoxocephalus scorpius, 223

NAIDID WORMS, 376
Nanaimo, 306
National Marine Fisheries Service (NMFS), 44, 327, 342, 343, 344, 346, 349, 350, 352, 354, 359, 361, 363, 365
Natural selection, 216, 241
Navigation, 137, 139, 216, 367
  celestial, 137
Netpens, 22, 42, 43, 44, 45, 87, 102, 126, 182, 307, 308, 342-352,

353, 359, 361, 363, 364
fry, 375, 376
Nets, 131, 194
  bag, 163, 196
  coastal set, 92, 95, 250, 265
  drift, 163, 164, 166, 167, 195
  estuarine, 191
  fibre, 30
  fyke, 163, 215
  gill, *see* Gillnets
  illegal, 192, 195
  pound, 163
  seine, *see* Seine
  set in rivers, 250
  trammel, 162
New Brunswick, 109-128, 269, 400
  Electric Power Commission, 113, 114
Newfoundland, 117, 118, 213-242, 252, 257, 402
  Wildlife Branch, 215
Newport, Ireland, 188
Newport, Oregon, 357
New Zealand, 7, 8, 264, 277-302, 385, 391, 401
  Department of External Affairs, 278
  Department of Internal Affairs, 287
  Government of, 277, 302
  Marine Department, 285
  Ministry of Agriculture and Fisheries, 287, 288, 290, 296, 297
  North Island, 280, 285
  Salmon Anglers Association, 287
  South Island, 279, 280, 282, 285, 286, 287, 288, 290, 297
  South Island Council, 295, 296
  West Coast, 285, 288, 293
Niacin, 40
Niches, ecological, 265
Nitrogen, *see also* Disease, gas bubble supersaturation, 116, 117
Nizhne-Kamchatsk region, 68
Nobility, 91
Nordic Council, 152

North Harbour Arm, 218, 219, 220, 223
North Harbour Pond, 218, 220, 240
Northern Ireland, 187, 188, 189, 190, 197
  Dept. of Agriculture & Fisheries, 188
Northern Wolffish, *see Anarchicas denticulatus*
Northwest Fisheries Center, 44
Norway, 8, 165, 250, 342, 357, 366, 402
Norwegian Sea, 136, 141, 249, 258
Nova Scotia, 109-128, 226
Numbers, population, 2
Nurseries, 70, 268, 274
  heated, 71
Nursery ground, 2, 207, 266, 397
Nutritional requirements, 20, 117, 127
Nutritionists, 111

Obstacles to migration, 254, 266, 288
Obstructions, natural, 168
Ocean Areas, for ranching, 133-142
Ocean masses, 139
Ocean range, 58
Oceans, 2, 5, 26, 57, 58, 63, 67, 78, 91, 216, 272
Okhotsk, *see* Sea of Okhotsk
Okhotsk-Penzhinsk region, 65
Olezhkin pond, 82
Oligochaetes, 376
Oncorhynchus gorbuscha, 6, 7, 8, 14, 18, 19, 20, 22, 29, 32, 34, 35, 38, 49, 64, 65, 66, 67, 68, 69, 72, 73, 74, 75, 76, 77, 79, 84, 85, 91, 92, 94, 95, 96, 101, 213-242, 245-258, 328, 350, 352, 361, 363, 395, 397, 398, 402
Oncorhynchus keta, 18, 19, 20, 26, 29, 32, 34, 35, 38, 40, 41, 42, 47, 49, 52, 54, 55, 57, 61, 64, 65, 66, 67, 68, 69, 71, 72, 73, 74, 75,

Oncorhynchus keta (cont.)
    76, 77, 84, 85, 91, 92, 93, 94,
    95, 96, 99, 100, 101, 103, 104,
    105, 106, 215, 217, 245, 246,
    248, 252, 253, 254, 255, 262,
    267, 268, 274, 328, 357, 359,
    390, 397, 398, 402
Oncorhynchus kisutch, 1, 5, 7, 14, 17,
    18, 20, 29, 32, 34, 35, 37, 38, 39,
    40, 42, 43, 44, 45, 47, 49, 50, 52,
    54, 55, 57, 60-61, 64, 65, 66,
    67, 68, 69, 71, 74, 84, 85, 121,
    262, 264, 265, 266, 267, 268,
    274, 305-323, 325, 327, 332,
    336-342, 343, 344, 345, 346,
    347, 349, 352, 354, 355, 356,
    357, 358, 359, 361, 363, 364,
    365, 366, 367, 371, 372, 373,
    375, 376, 377, 380, 390, 399
Oncorhynchus masou, 64, 65, 66, 67,
    68, 69, 84, 85, 91, 92, 94, 95,
    96, 101, 267
Oncorhynchus nerka, 17, 18, 20, 29, 32,
    42, 43, 49, 63, 64, 65, 66, 67,
    68, 69, 71, 74, 77, 79, 80, 81,
    82, 84, 85, 215, 239, 241, 264,
    265, 269, 273, 283-285, 327,
    396, 397
Oncorhynchus spp., 7, 48, 58, 60, 64,
    65, 66, 67, 68, 69, 77, 78, 80,
    83, 85, 87, 91, 92, 124, 126,
    137, 139, 154, 203, 215, 216,
    267, 305, 327, 342, 354, 395,
    399, 400, 402, 403
Oncorhynchus tschawytscha, 1, 7, 18, 20,
    29, 32, 34, 35, 36, 37, 38, 40,
    41, 42, 47, 49, 50, 52, 54, 55,
    57, 61, 64, 65, 66, 67, 68, 69,
    84, 85, 264, 265, 268, 270, 271,
    274, 275, 280-283, 285-302, 305,
    325, 328-336, 343, 344, 346,
    347, 348, 349, 357, 361, 362,
    371, 380, 390, 391, 399
Opercula, marks, 200
Oregon State, 17, 21, 27, 47-61, 266,
    340, 342, 348, 358, 389-390,
        391, 392, 393, 395, 400
    Department of Fish and Wildlife,
        48, 52, 56, 60, 327
    Fish Commission, 48, 61
    Wildlife Commission, 48, 61
Oregon Aquafoods, Inc., 21, 357
Oregon coast, 329, 330, 333, 334,
    335, 338, 339, 357
Oregon Moist Pellet (OMP), 40, 49,
    52, 306, 344
Oregon-Washington Propagation
    Company, 52
Orientation, mechanisms of, 5, 8, 9,
    137, 141, 295
Osmerus mordax, 218, 222, 223
Otag, 277, 291, 300
Otters, *see Lutra canadensis*
Ovaries
    capelin, 246
    redfish, 246
Overfishing, 1, 2, 7, 24-25, 59, 70,
    85, 110, 123, 178, 384, 399
Overstocking, 26, 58
Ownership of ranched fish, 7, 383,
    388
Oxygen, 73, 116, 253, 332, 378
Oxytetracycline, 117

PACIFIC OCEAN, 2, 6, 8, 16, 26, 29,
    50, 63-87, 91-107, 137, 216,
    238, 241, 250, 252, 255, 256,
    257, 273, 295, 300, 328, 366,
    383-393, 395, 396, 397, 399, 400
Pacific, South, 295, 391
Pacific Biological Station, 306
Pacific Northwest, 18, 20, 230, 333,
    334, 338, 339, 349
Paint, antifouling, 174
Pantothenic acid, 40
Paper mills, 96, 165
Paralepsis spp., 133, 142
Parasites, *see* Disease, parasitic
Paratunka basin, 68
Parr, 102, 112, 118, 153, 165, 170,
    171, 177, 188, 191, 193, 194,
    196, 197, 202

precocious male, 202
Particles of food, *see* Food particles
Passage facilities, 113
Passengers, 48
Patagonia, 261
Patagonian Shelf, 273, 275
Pathogens, 60, 117, 301
Pathologists, 60, 111
Pathology, 170
PCBs, 165, 172
Pebbles, 252
Pens, 3
Periodicity of catch, 92
Permits, 53, 54, 288, 388, 391, 393
Perturbations, environmental, 49
Peru, 273
Peter the Great Bay, 87
pH, 165
Pheromones, 152, 231
Photoperiod
  declining, 337
  increasing, 337
  natural, 146, 148, 149
Physiologists, 111
Physiology, 73, 127, 170
Pick Creek, 79, 82
Pike, *see Esox lucius*
Pilot farm study, 343
Pilot ranching projects, 390
Pilot stream channel, 373-378
Pink salmon, *see Oncorhynchus gorbuscha*
Pitlochry, 201
Placentia Bay, 223, 239
Plan, Alaska salmon fisheries, 26
Planning, co-operative, 23, 27
  regional, 25, 386, 388
Planning teams, regional 24
Planting, 153, 170, 171, 213, 216,
  217, 218, 220, 223, 240, 241,
  264, 265, 266, 267, 269, 272,
  273, 274, 280, 328, 349, 401,
  402
Poland, 157, 162, 164, 165, 167, 168,
  169, 172, 177, 181
Polar day, 254, 256
Polcura, 266

Policy
  fiscal, 60
  public, 383
Policy decisions, 15, 27, 54, 59, 128
Political force, 54
Pollachius virens, 254
Pollution, 96, 112, 123, 165, 168,
  189, 248, 287, 301
  genetic, 401
  thermal, 168
Polymorphism
  biochemical, 77
  chromosomic, 77
  genetic, 77
Ponds, 1, 20, 35, 36, 37, 52, 55, 111,
  126, 174, 191, 283
  Burrows, 306
  circular, 174, 175, 357
  concrete, 116, 357
  diked tidal, 349, 350, 351, 363
  earthen, 175, 176
  freshwater, 172
  indoor, 143
  natural, 175
  outdoor, 143, 146
  release, 143, 144, 146, 152, 307, 358
  salt-water, 42, 56, 358, 363
  self-cleaning, Swedish, 116
  semi-natural, 123, 125-126
  spring-fed, 332
Pools, 372, 373, 375, 376, 377, 378,
  379, 380
Population analyses, virtual, 239
Population biology, 83
Populations
  age structure, 80, 257
  artificial, 77, 80, 86, 87
  of Baltic salmon, 170
  biological structure, 77
  breeding, 272
  fluctuation of, 239, 396
  genetic structures, 77
  homeostasis, 77, 86
  models of, 178
  panmictic, 86
  of ranched fishes, 395

Populations *(cont.)*
  reproducing, 401
  research on, 76-83
  self-sustaining, 240
  sex-age structure, 80, 81, 83
  sibling, 205
  size structure, 79
  sockeye, 396
  spatial structure, 77, 83
  spawning, 110, 216
  structure of, 257
  studies of, 77
  temporary, 252, 257
  wild, 85, 87, 400
Port Severn, 215
Postsmolts, 160
Power
  companies, 6
  generation, 7, 291
Power plants, 169, 201, 285, 291
Predators, 1, 43, 56, 73, 79, 86, 126,
    179, 182, 190, 208, 217, 218,
    220, 222, 223, 239, 240, 241,
    251, 253, 254, 255, 266, 267,
    272, 273, 274, 352, 371, 377,
    379, 395, 397, 398
Prehistory, 91
Price, first sale, 106, 196
Primorsky district, 85
Primorye, 64, 65, 84, 86
Prince Edward Island, 109-128
Prince William Sound, 14, 23, 388
Processing, 48
Processors, 32, 39, 384, 388
Producers, 4, 53, 58, 61
Production
  annual, 2, 3, 92, 117, 169, 191,
    192
  area, 91
  coastal, 398
  costs of, 106-107, 371
  decline of, 59, 168
  dynamics of, 398
  of eggs, 366
  expansion of, 60
  facilities, 53, 54

  food, 27, 301, 352
  of insects, 380
  of jacks, 322
  levels of, 25, 58, 60
  loss of, 114
  multi-species, 58
  natural, 50, 58, 169, 207, 399
  of plants, 165
  potential, 110, 124, 125
  practices, 403
  of protein, 4
  of salmon, 9, 16, 24, 26, 40, 41,
    54, 59, 98, 99, 112, 122, 123,
    125, 133, 215, 265, 268, 305,
    320, 322, 352, 372, 396
  seasonal 58
  seed, 128
  single species, 58
  of smolts, 6, 7, 19, 20, 41, 42, 47,
    49, 60, 117, 124, 126, 146, 154,
    167, 169-177, 188, 192, 196,
    197, 207, 208, 295, 305, 325,
    363, 366, 387, 395, 396, 397
  staging of, 58
  of trout, 111
  of zooplankton, 397
Production trends, ocean, 58
Productivity, 24, 27, 59, 60, 105,
    132, 150, 152, 153, 154, 208,
    216, 301, 379, 384, 390, 397
  decreasing, 59
  low (oligotrophic), 109
Products
  salmon, 32, 47
Profit, 56, 97, 154, 196, 197, 305,
    384, 390, 393
Profit centres, 391, 392, 393
Programmes
  artificial propagation, 97-102, 106
  augmentation, 199
  breeding, 3, 116
  delayed release, 326, 359
  enhancement, 34, 91, 96, 99, 100,
    104, 387
  extended rearing, 359
  hatchery, 3, 16, 18, 20, 23, 24, 26,

34, 40, 43, 48-56, 111, 117, 120,
122, 328, 386, 393
lagoon rearing, 352
loan, 388
management, 29, 47, 56, 57
ranching, 13, 14, 15, 27, 34, 124,
142, 147, 154, 257
restoration, 192
stocking, 119
Progress, economic, 293
Propagation, artificial, 15, 16-17, 18,
23, 24, 25, 26, 27, 33, 57, 58,
59, 63, 64, 70-71, 76, 77, 80, 83,
85, 86, 91, 95-107, 116, 127,
164, 166, 199, 200, 201, 262,
383, 386, 387, 388, 389, 391
Protection
of environment, 399
of fisheries, 288, 399
of natural populations, 24-25, 31,
96, 166, 167
from predators, 223
in space, 257
of spawning streams, 96, 98
in time, 257
Protein, 4, 170
animal, 91
high quality, 301
producing systems, 4
single-cell, 170
Pseudopleuronectes americanus, 223
Public opinion, 53, 58
Public relations, 3, 218
Puerto Bories, 265
Puerto Montt, 265, 266
Puget Sound, 29, 40, 44, 45, 213,
325-359
Pumps, 378
Punta Arenas, 261, 264
Pu Pu Springs, 297, 298, 299, 300

QUARANTINE, 60
Quebec, 112, 118
Quinnat salmon, *see Oncorhynchus
tschawytscha*

Quotas, catch, 2, 7

RACE, 400
Raceways, 20, 21, 23, 298, 300, 357
cement, 269
floating, 22, 23, 350
gravel-lined, 18, 52
Racks,
river, 100
trash, 374
Raft, powered, 354
Rain, 257
Rainbow trout, *see Salmo gairdneri*
Raja radiata, 223
Ranchers, commercial, 263
Ranching
feasibility, 296
pilot schemes, 208, 217
private operations, 357, 383
Ranching potential, 142, 154, 155,
208, 268, 395
Range, 285
Rapids, 250
Ration, daily, 102, 205, 376
Raven, *see Corvus corax*
Reafforestation, 85
Rearing
areas, 153-154
extended fry, 327-328
facilities, 33, 298, 305, 352
period, 325, 344
in seawater, 366
facilities, 34, 41, 208, 357, 390, 400
Recaptures, 152, 161, 171, 177, 179,
193, 195, 200, 205, 208, 215,
332, 337, 340, 345, 354, 357
distant, 136
Reciprocal crossing, 78
Recirculation, of water, 87
Recovery
freshwater facilities, 114-117
seawater facilities, 5, 56, 357
Recreation, 56, 300, 301, 302
Recreationalist, 301
Recruitment, 7, 26, 56, 57, 59, 60,
111, 116, 169, 337

Redds, 70, 71, 101, 202, 250, 251, 252, 258, 288
Redfish, *see Sebastes marinus*
Re-entrapment rate, 121
Reflectiveness, 202
Reflexes, defence, 73
Refrigerator, propane, 378
Regulation, of fisheries, 399, 400
Regulations
  administrative, 383, 393
  international fishery, 7, 63, 167, 402
  local, 168
Release, 3, 7, 14, 16, 18, 26, 33, 34, 38, 39, 40, 41, 42, 43, 47, 49, 50, 51, 52, 53, 54, 55, 57, 58, 59, 60, 71, 72, 77, 84, 85, 95, 98, 99, 100, 101, 102, 104, 105, 106, 111, 112, 114, 126, 117, 118, 119, 120, 121, 127, 131, 136, 140, 143, 144, 145, 147, 149, 150, 152, 153, 166, 169, 170, 171, 172, 177, 178, 179, 182, 188, 189, 192, 193, 194, 195, 196, 205, 208, 213, 227, 246, 248, 249, 252, 253, 254, 257, 264, 267, 268, 274, 277, 279, 280, 282, 283, 293, 295, 296, 297, 300, 305-323, 376, 381, 383, 385, 386 389, 390, 393, 395, 398, 402
  conditions at, 170, 182, 205, 305-323
  delayed, 9, 126, 305-323, 325-367, 399
  direct, 150, 182, 205, 349
  early, 140, 305-323
  freshwater, 327-342
  from seawater, 56, 102, 182, 342-359, 361, 400
  seawater facilities, 5, 357
  size at, 305-323, 327, 329, 330, 333, 334, 337, 338, 339, 348, 351, 352, 354, 358
  timing of, 102, 146, 148, 149, 205, 248, 305-323, 325-367, 398, 403

upstream, 114, 117, 118, 121, 169, 187
Release cage, *see* Cage, release
Release sites, 34, 40, 56, 102, 131, 144, 148, 149, 152, 154, 208, 250, 295, 297, 328, 329, 330, 331, 333, 334, 338, 339, 346, 347, 357, 358, 359, 361, 362, 366, 398, 399, 400, 401
Religion, 91
Reloncaví Sound, 266, 267
Reports, annual, 33
Reproduction, 6, 7, 24, 33, 59, 63, 65, 69, 77, 78, 80, 83, 86, 100, 103, 104, 112, 164, 165, 170, 190, 213, 252, 257, 258, 393
  Ricker's formula, 104
Requirements, biological, 17, 52, 217, 285, 302, 372, 398, 403
Research, 32, 64, 71, 73, 111, 131, 170, 295, 389, 399
  co-operative, 402
  population, 76-83, 86
Research Center, North American Salmon, 111, 124
Research Institutes, 167
Reservations, Indian, 31
Reservoirs
  finishing, 73
  hydroelectric, 190
  rearing in, 208
Residency, 335, 342, 344
Resources
  biological, 70, 399, 400
  common property, 47, 53, 56, 383, 399
  natural, 29, 47, 54, 98, 167, 178, 208
Restoration
  environmental, 8, 165
  of fisheries, 24, 56, 301, 388
  of populations, 78, 83, 85, 96, 125
Retailing, 48
Return rates, 6, 33, 55, 59, 98, 99, 101, 102-105, 112, 119, 123, 126, 131, 132, 142, 143, 145,

146, 148, 149, 150, 152, 154,
179, 189, 190, 191, 193, 194,
195, 196, 197, 205, 207, 216,
223, 239, 249, 305-323, 328,
329, 330, 333, 334, 335, 336,
338, 339, 344, 348, 349, 350,
351, 355, 358, 366, 385, 398,
399, 402
adult, 114, 116, 119, 120, 121,
132, 136, 143, 146, 147, 150,
152, 153, 154, 189, 190, 194,
195, 201, 213, 218, 220, 222,
223, 226, 227, 228-229, 230,
231, 232-235, 236, 238, 239,
240, 241, 246, 248, 249, 252,
253, 256, 257, 265, 266, 267,
268, 271, 274, 275, 277, 279,
282, 283, 285, 286, 288, 291,
293, 295, 296, 297, 300, 312-
318
commercial, 301, 399
timing of, 116
Reykjanes Peninsula, 139, 140
Reykjavík, 150
Rheotaxis, positive, 139, 202
Rhythmicity, 398
Riboflavin, 40
Riffle: pool area, 372
Riffles, 201, 372, 373, 375, 376, 377,
380
Riga, 402
Ringold ponds, 332, 334
Río Grande do Sul, State of, 271, 274
Río Negro, Territory of, 269
Ripeness, 35
Risks
disease, 26
genetic, 25
Rivers
"Abbey", 191
Abernathy, 333
Alsea, 51
American, 271
Amur, 64, 65, 68, 70, 71, 84, 86,
387
Anadyr, 64

Ångermanälven, 161, 172
Ártúnsá, 150, 151, 152
Baker, 338, 339
Baltic, 166, 172
Beckford's, 240
Big Barasway, 240
Big Qualicum, 306, 373
Blackwater, 187
Boyne, 187, 188, 189, 194
Branch, 240
Burrishoole, 187, 188, 192
Bush, 187, 188, 189, 190, 194,
195, 197
Bushinka, 68
Clackamas, 52
Clady, 192
Clutha, 277, 282, 285, 288, 290,
295, 297
Columbia, 29, 30, 33, 36, 40, 41,
50, 51, 57, 329, 330, 332, 333,
334, 337, 339, 392
Connecticut, 112
Conon, 201
Cook Creek, 333
Corrib, 187, 194
Cowlitz, 36, 333
Crolly, 192
Currane, 187
Dalälven, 161, 162, 169, 172
Dangava, 164
Dennys, 213
Deschutes, 329
Drawa, 164
Drowse, 187
Dungeness, 330
Elbe, 396
Ellidaár, 150, 151, 152
Elwha, 330
Emån, 165
Erne, 192
Finch Creek, 330
Fraser, 29, 238, 239
Glenariffe Stream, 279
Glendale, 221
Green, 33, 34, 329, 338, 339
Gulf of St. Lawrence, 118

Rivers *(cont.)*
Hakataramea, 279, 282, 283
Halladale, 201
Hoko, 330
Indal, 160, 161, 172
Indian, 221
Ishikari, 97
Issaquah Creek, 361
Kaiapoi, 297
Kakanui, 280
Kalama, 33, 332, 334
Karluk, 16
Keret, 252
Koeye, 217
Kola, 245, 248, 253
Lakelse, 215, 217
Larch Stream, 283, 284
Laxá, 152
Lee, 188, 190, 192, 194, 196
Lennon, 187
Little Barasway, 240
Ljungan, 172
Ljusnan, 161, 172
Lule, 161, 172
Makarewa, 279, 280
McCloud, 16
Mena, 267
Minter Creek, 329, 338, 361
modifications to, 302
Molyneux, 277
Mörrumsån, 160, 162, 165, 168
Moy, 187
Nemah, 332, 333, 339
Nestucca, 51
Nooksack, 329, 349, 358
Nore, 187
North Harbour, 215, 218, 219,
    220, 221, 222, 226, 227, 228-
    229, 230, 231, 232-235, 236,
    237, 238, 239, 240
Odra, 164
Ölfusá, 139, 140
Onega, 248
Oreti, 279, 280
Oyster, 217
Pelorous, 279

Ponoy, 250, 256
Porya, 250, 255, 256
Praure, 71
Puyallup, 338, 339
Pysht, 330
Quilcene, 40
Quillayute, 333
Quinault, 40
Raduga, 68
Rakaia, 282, 285, 288, 289, 290
Rangitata, 280, 282
Red Head, 240
research, 166
Rhine, 396
Rickleån, 160, 165
Río dos Antos, 271
Río Blanco, 266
Río Caí, 271
Río Cautin, 264
Río Claro, 267
Río Jaquarí, 271, 274, 275
Río Olivia, 269
Río de la Plata, 275
Río Serrano, 265
Río Simpson, 267
Río Uruguay, 271, 275
Rogue, 17, 52, 391
Rosewall Creek, 306
Sacramento, 295
Saint John, 112-122
Saint Lawrence, 112
Sakhalin, 245
Salatsa, 160, 164
Samish, 344
Satsop, 329
Shannon, 187, 188, 191, 192, 194
Siletz, 51
Skagit, 213, 329, 338, 339
Skeena, 215, 396
Skellefte, 172
Skykomish, 338
Soleduck, 333
Soyana, 256
Spey, 201
Sydorovka, 255
Tainhos, 271

Takaka, 297, 298
Tanya, 250
Tay, 200, 207
Thjorsa, 139
Tokachi, 267
Torne, 162, 164
Toutle, 334, 339
Tsolum, 217
Tumnin, 68
Umba, 245, 252, 253, 254, 255
Ume, 161, 162, 168, 172
Umpqua, 333
Upukerora, 279
Ura, 245
Waiau, 279, 283, 285, 295
Waikato, 280
Waimakariri, 280, 296, 297
Waipahi, 279, 280
Wairau, 300
Waitaki, 281, 282, 283 285, 290, 291, 297
Wilson, 51
Wood, 79
Yenisei, 250
River-bed, 68, 250, 374
  structure, 165, 252, 288
River bends, 379
River discharge, 135
River levels, 379
River mouths, 5, 182, 255, 288, 293, 399, 402
Road construction, 60
Rockefeller Foundation, 268
Rocks, 30
Rods, 131, 168, 194
Roof, transparent, 146
Rotorua/Taupo Conservancy, 287
Rügen, 163
Run-off
  culverts, 363
  surface, 252
Runs, 17, 38, 43, 51, 143, 150, 152, 158, 160, 164, 168, 188, 191, 197, 219, 238, 239, 250, 251, 255, 257, 287, 288, 289, 393
  decline of, 153, 238

new, 216, 282, 296
  timing of, 116, 123
Russia, *see* U.S.S.R.

SAC-FRY, 153, 215
St. Andrews, 111
St. John's, 238
St. John's Biological Station, 218
St. Mary's Bay, 214, 215, 218, 220, 224, 225, 226, 227, 230, 239, 240
Saithe, *see Pollachius virens*
Sake, *see Oncorhynchus keta*
Sakhalin Island, 18, 64, 65, 69, 71, 72, 73, 77, 84, 85, 86, 87, 137, 245, 246, 387
Sakhalinrybvod, 387
Sakura masu, *see Oncorhynchus masou*
Salinity, 17, 127, 134, 157, 159, 217, 238, 251, 253, 273, 274, 350, 354
Salmo clarki, 29, 31, 349
Salmo gairdneri, 5, 29, 31, 36, 42, 47, 48, 50, 51, 53, 57, 264, 265, 269, 271, 285, 342, 352, 400
Salmo salar, 6, 8, 29, 109-128, 131-155, 159-182, 187-198, 199-208, 218, 220, 222, 223, 231, 237, 246, 249, 250, 254, 255, 256, 262, 264, 265, 266, 269, 277-280, 285, 286, 295, 342, 354, 366, 372, 380, 396, 397, 400, 402, 403
Salmo spp., 327
Salmo trutta, 8, 29, 163, 166, 170, 171, 187, 188, 190, 201, 218, 222, 223, 237, 238, 254, 255, 257, 264, 265, 267, 269, 271, 277, 285, 401
Salmon, Atlantic, *see Salmo salar*
  Baltic, *see Salmo salar*
  canned, 92, 300
  Cherry, *see Oncorhynchus masou*
  Chinook, *see Oncorhynchus tschawytscha*
  Chum, *see Oncorhynchus keta*

Salmon *(cont.)*
  Coho, *see Oncorhynchus kisutch*
  dried, 30
  frozen, 92
  green, 35
  Kokanee, *see* Kokanee salmon
  landlocked, 159, 262, 269, 271,
    272, 274, 280
  Masu, *see Oncohynchus masou*
  pan size, 300
  Pink, *see Oncorhynchus gorbuscha*
  Quinnat, *see Oncorhynchus tschawytscha*
  salted, 92
  Sebago, 269
  Silver, *see Oncorhynchus kisutch*
  smoked, 30, 92
  Sockeye, *see Oncorhynchus nerka*
Salmon Committee, 295, 296, 299
Salmon Research Institute, 166, 170-
  177
Salmon Research Trust, 187, 188,
  192-193, 194, 195, 197
Salmon viscera, pasteurised, 40
Salmonid Enchancement Pro-
  gramme, 399
Salmonidae, 29, 261
Salt balance, regulation of, 398
Salto, 271
Salvelinus alpinus, 8, 153, 154, 246
Salvelinus fontinalis, 29, 218, 220, 222,
  223, 237, 240, 264, 269, 401
Salvelinus malma, 29, 31
Salvelinus spp., 257
Samlets, 200
Sampling, 60
San Carlos de Bariloche, 269
Sand, 250, 252, 272, 376, 377
Sand bars, 293
Sandeels, *see Ammodytes* spp.
San Francisco Bay, 349
Santa Cruz, Territory of, 268, 274
Santiago, 266
Saprolegnia, 101, 117, 172
Scale analysis, 161, 166, 286
Scale growth, 239
Scales, 160

Scandinavia, 396
Schools, 254, 255, 256, 336
Scientists, 167
Scomber scombrus, 223
Scotland, 8, 199, 200, 201, 206, 207,
  208, 280
Scouring, 216
Screens, 52, 290, 291, 375, 376
  electric, 169
  inclined, 374, 375
  light, 169
  rotary, 352, 354
  vertical, 374
Sculpin, Shorthorn, *see Myoxocephalus*
  scorpius
Sea of Okhotsk, 64, 65, 104
Sea, territorial, 386, 388
Sea-absence, 134-135
Sea Trout, see *Salmo trutta*
Seasons
  closed, 163, 166, 167, 168, 208,
    300
  fishing, 2, 7, 32, 163, 191, 208,
    301
Seattle, 344, 346, 361
Seawater, pumped, 330, 354-359
Seaweed, 223
Sebastes marinus, 246
Sector
  private, 23, 24, 27, 47, 52, 54,
    122-123, 124, 126, 127, 196,
    197, 387
  public, 23, 27, 124, 126, 127, 196,
    197, 198
Sediments, loose, 165
Seeding, 123
Seine, 162, 172, 220
  beach, 92, 100, 152, 207, 208, 218
Selection
  of broodstock, 73, 79, 86, 287
  coefficient of, 86
  genetic, 20, 77, 79, 85, 286, 380,
    400
  trends, 79
Services, 48
Seno Otway, 265

Seno Skyring, 265
Seston, 379
Sewage, 97, 165
Seward, 17
Sex, 83
Sex-linkage, 80
Sea Ratio, 73, 77, 80, 82, 120, 121, 160, 308, 312-318
Sex structure,
  control of, 80
Shad, 31, *see aslo Alosa sapidissima*
Sheep, 261
Sheldon Jackson College, 14
Shellfish, 31, 402
Shipping, 217
Ships, 3, 4
Shoals, *see* Schools
Shocker, 377
Shoreline, 154
Shrimp, 40
Siberian coast, 137
Silt, 165, 220, 272, 288, 325, 372, 379
Silver Rings, 200
Silver salmon, *see Oncorhynchus kisutch*
Silvering, 200
Sitka, 14
Size
  of adults, 312-318
  body, 85, 86, 117, 120, 121, 160, 202, 241, 250, 283, 285, 295, 305, 335
  fry, 220, 241
  grilse, 135
  of jacks, 309-312
  at maturity, 336
  smolt, 134, 135, 147, 149, 150, 153, 190, 256, 305-323
Size groups, 83
Size limits, 166, 167, 336, 337
Skagafjördur, 152
Skiffs, 363
Smell, 139, 151, 152
Smelt, 31, *see also Osmerus mordax.*
Smoltification, control of, 20, 170
Smolting rate, 202, 205, 207

Smolt-rearing, 157-182, 188, 296, 372
Smolts, 5, 6, 7, 40, 41, 42, 44, 45, 55, 56, 58, 77, 102, 109, 111, 112, 113, 114, 116, 118, 119, 120, 121, 122, 123, 124, 125, 126, 128, 131, 132, 135, 136, 139, 140, 141, 142, 143, 145, 148, 149, 150, 151, 152, 153, 160, 169, 170, 171, 177, 188, 189, 190, 191, 196, 200, 205, 237, 249, 253, 254, 255, 266, 267, 268, 274, 275, 277, 280, 289, 290, 291, 296, 297, 305-323, 346, 363, 371, 373, 374, 376, 377, 378, 381, 396, 397, 400, 402
  hatchery, 166, 171, 172, 178, 179, 182, 188, 191, 192, 193, 194-195, 196, 198, 205, 293, 349
  indoor, 146, 148
  outdoor, 146, 148, 149
  quality of, 59, 112, 117, 120, 143, 150, 151, 152, 154, 170, 176, 190, 371, 373, 381
  residual, 377
  transformation to, 202
  wild, 166, 194-195, 205, 231, 251, 256
  one-year, 120-121, 122, 125, 143, 145, 146, 147, 148, 149, 152, 172, 177, 188, 189, 190, 191, 192, 193, 194, 196, 205, 206, 207
  two-year, 120-121, 122, 125, 126, 131, 143, 145, 146, 147, 148, 149, 152, 170, 176, 177, 189, 193, 196, 206, 207
Snaefellsnes, 143
Snout, 147, 150
Snow, 257
Sockeye salmon, *see Oncorhynchus nerka*
Solar heating units, 269
Solids, suspended, 377
Soos Creek, 33
Sounds, 265, 268, 294

Southern Alps, 288, 290, 291
Southern Lakes Conservancy, 287
Southern Ocean, 295, 301, 401
Spain, 396
Spates, 372
Spawners, 2, 6, 59, 69, 104, 160, 168, 182, 216
  ascending, 162, 164, 168
  previous, 110, 118
Spawning, 6, 35, 43, 63, 64, 67, 68, 69, 70, 72, 78, 92, 95, 96, 101, 109, 114, 117, 121, 131, 139, 164, 165, 200, 208, 220, 221, 231, 241, 249-252, 265, 279, 280, 283, 286, 287, 293, 300, 392
  area, 257, 288, 302
  grounds, 2, 64, 67, 68, 70, 71, 72, 79, 85, 86, 165, 167, 169, 218, 250, 255, 265, 271, 285, 293
  period, 241
  race, 291, 292
  repeat, 257
  runs, 29, 67, 68, 73, 258, 288, 296
  sites, 79, 288
Spears, 30
Species memory, constant, 82-83
  operational, 82-83
Species-mix, 58
Sperm, 35, 100
Spillway, 153
Spitsbergen, 250
Spray, 36
Spread, of species, 265, 285, 401, 402
Springfield, 21
Springtails, *see* Collembola
Squaxin Island, 344, 346, 347, 348, 359, 363
Squid, 133, 401
Stamina, population, 79
Station-holding, 201, 202, 205, 372
Statutes, 7, 53, 56
Steelhead trout, *see Salmo gairdneri*
Sterna paradisea, 254, 255
Stickleback, *see Gasterosteus aculeatus*
Sticks, 30

Stock concept, 400
Stockholm, 167
Stocking, 111, 120, 125, 167, 168, 170, 191, 194, 197, 207, 264, 280, 285
  optimum level, 59
  supplemental, 123, 168, 192
Stocks
  Afognak, 213
  Amur, 70
  artificial, 6, 106, 112, 116
  Asiatic, 63, 76
  Atlantic, 159, 396, 397
  Baker River, 268
  Baltic, 159, 166, 167, 280
  British Columbia, 398
  Canadian, 274
  Cascade-Sandy River, 358
  decline of, 15-16, 25, 26, 57, 70, 76, 94, 164, 166, 190, 191, 192, 194, 199, 238-240, 280, 396, 400
  delayed-release, 325-367
  depressed state of, 110, 111, 199, 380
  disease-free, 301
  donor, 59, 78, 79, 216
  East Pacific, 216
  European, 261, 268
  exotic, 332
  experimental, 306
  exterminated, 199
  genetic discreteness, 5, 25, 328, 349
  Gulf of Finland, 163
  hatchery, 32, 117, 118, 124, 125, 187, 188, 189, 194-196, 197, 286, 336, 384, 398
  Icelandic northern, 133, 135, 139, 141, 152
  Icelandic southern, 133, 135, 136, 137, 139, 147, 152
  identification of, 76
  landlocked, 266
  local, 77, 152, 168, 248, 327, 400
  Lower Columbia River, 332

mixed, 5, 7, 25, 136, 335
New Zealand, 296
North American, 261, 268
novel, 400
offshore, 57
Oregon coastal, 332
of Pacific salmon, 70, 76, 396
proprietary, 60
ranched, 208, 398, 400
recipient, 59, 78
sea-trout, 170
river, 6, 208
seed, 123, 125
self-sustaining, 217, 271, 302, 391, 402
Shannon, 192
sibling, 202
sizes of, 238, 240, 287-296
Skagit, 213
Southern Hemisphere, 293
Southern Kamchatka, 216
spawning, 154, 391
structure of, 85
trout, 272
viable, 122
wild, 1, 2, 3, 5, 6, 7, 8, 24, 32, 53, 57, 58, 59, 63, 64, 91, 92, 94, 96, 100, 104, 110, 116, 117, 118, 120, 122, 123, 124, 131, 132, 154, 162, 188, 192, 199, 201, 217, 238, 241, 286, 287, 289, 300, 301, 325, 328, 336, 366, 384, 389, 396, 400
of zooplankton, 397
Stock-units, 208, 399
Stomach, fullness index, 253, 256
Stop-logs, 373, 374, 376
Storage, of gametes, 20
Stormontfield, ponds, 200
Storms, oceanic, 335
Strains, seasonal, 64, 67, 77, 95
Strait of Georgia, 349
Strategies,
  management, 400
  production, 57, 76, 124-127, 366, 381

stock-enhancement, 122, 123-124
stocking, 124
Straying, 136, 139, 147, 150, 151, 152, 182, 226, 238, 275, 282, 285, 361, 401
Streams
  donor, 217, 221
  gradients, 216, 217, 266
  home, 5, 92
  improvement, 302
  intensive use of, 371-381
  natal, 4, 5, 116, 150, 152, 265, 289, 295, 359
  nursery, 372
  rearing potential of, 371
  regulation of, 165, 372
  spawning, 68, 99, 289, 291, 293
  underchannel, 68
Stream bed
  conditions of, 271, 292
  porosity, 266
  texture, 266
Stress, 188, 193, 309
Stripping, 35, 97, 99, 100, 162, 164, 172, 200, 282, 287, 296, 299
Stump Channel, 218, 220, 221
Sturgeon, 31
Subisolates, 77, 79-83, 86
  biological structure, 83, 86
Subsidies
  government, 27, 98, 384, 387, 391, 392
Substrates
  artificial media for, 20
  incubation, 18
  size, 372
  spawning, 2, 250, 252
  stream, 201, 217
Súgandafjördur, 143, 152
Support, physical, 202
Surfaces, rough, 202, 203
Survival, 5, 6, 25, 38, 72, 78, 102, 105, 109, 111, 112, 116, 117, 118, 120, 122, 125, 126, 127, 132, 133, 143, 146, 147, 149, 150, 151, 152, 153, 154, 170,

Survival *(cont.)*
    176, 182, 188, 189, 190, 191,
    192, 193, 195, 197, 200, 201,
    205, 207, 216, 217, 218, 220,
    238, 239, 240, 241, 249, 251,
    252, 253, 257, 267, 269, 275,
    277, 286, 289, 295, 302, 305-
    323, 327, 328, 329, 330, 333,
    334, 337, 338, 339, 344, 349,
    350, 352, 359, 363, 366, 379,
    396, 397
Survival value, 202
Sveinhúsavatn, 143, 154
Swamp, 275
Sweden, 6, 120, 157-182, 380, 402
Swimming, 202, 246, 272
    performance, 241

TACOMA, 36
Tag attachment
    polyethylene, 147, 149, 150
    steel, 147, 149, 150
Tagging, 20, 166, 307, 308, 309,
    343, 344, 349, 377
    double, 149
Tag loss, 149, 150, 189, 190, 307
Tag retention, *see* Tag loss
Tag returns, 118, 146, 148, 149, 150,
    189, 190, 194, 195, 205, 207,
    321, 344
Tags, 114, 150, 344
    Carlin, 136, 147, 148, 149, 150,
    343
    micro-, 147, 148, 149, 150, 152,
    287, 307, 308, 328, 329, 330,
    332, 333, 334, 337, 338, 339,
    344, 348, 349, 352, 355, 358,
    377
    modified Carlin, 120, 148, 149
Tanegawa No Seido, 96, 98
Tank, floor of, 203, 204, 205
Tanks, 3, 203, 269
    concrete, 174, 175
    fibreglass, 174, 175
    radial flow, 203-205

    steel, 174, 175
    types of, 172
    wooden, 175
Tasmania, 283
Tautogolabrus adspersus, 223
Tax incentives, 17
Taxes, 6, 54, 196, 384, 387, 388,
    390, 391, 392
Taybola, 245
Technology, hatchery, 17, 18-23, 26,
    76, 85, 96, 105, 122, 124, 128,
    375
Temperature, 73, 77, 109, 116, 134,
    192, 202, 217, 245, 246, 253,
    255, 273, 285, 297, 306, 309,
    322, 325, 380, 401
    air, 380
    constant, 101, 116
    cumulative, 101, 252
    estuarine, 328
    gradients, 135
    regimes, 257, 306, 372
    sea, 135, 226, 231, 238, 239, 253,
    295
    stream, 328
    surface water, 219, 226, 231, 238,
    239, 332
Temperature stability, 72
Tendipedids, 253
Terminus, 366
Terns, *see Sterna paradisea*
Territorial Board of Road Com-
    missioners, 17
Territoriality, *see* Behaviour territorial
Territories, 201, 203
Thiamin, 40
Thomond Weir, 187, 191, 194
Thorny skate, *see Raja radiata*
Thymallus thymallus, 256
Tiburon, 349
Tide
    ebb, 254, 352, 363
    flood, 251
Tide flat, 42, 153
Tide movements, 157
Tides, 352

Tierra del Fuego, 261, 265, 266, 269, 274
Tinker Foundation, 268
Tolerance, physiological, 253, 401
Topography, 271, 398
Toxicants, 168
Toxicity, 165
Trade
  hotel, 300
  salmon, 30
  tourist, 300
Transfer, fresh to sea-water, 253, 346, 352
Transplant sites, 218
Transplanting, 7, 25-26, 59, 112, 116, 135, 150, 217, 220, 231, 238, 240, 241, 275, 386, 390, 401, 402
Transport
  of adult fish, 114, 140, 169
  of gametes, 20, 60, 78, 218, 245
  of juvenile fish, 20, 56, 60, 143, 152, 154, 332, 334, 344, 349, 354, 359, 361, 366
  of silt, 372
  of timber, 165
Trap-nets, 256
Traps, 114, 118, 120, 131, 143, 144, 145, 147, 152, 153, 162, 172, 188, 189, 190, 193, 194, 195, 196, 197, 218, 220, 231, 288, 290, 297, 299, 344, 355, 361, 363, 400
  Basketry, 30
  floating fry, 299
  river, 100, 187, 208, 400
  seawater, 363
  Urai, 100
Trash racks, 35
Travel, 48
Trawling, pelagic, 167
Trays, 35, 101, 203
  Washington, 300
Treaties, 30, 31, 383, 392
Treaty Rights, Indian, 388, 389
Trees, 380

Tribal enterprises, 32
Trichoptera, 256
Troughs, 35, 38, 116, 174, 176, 203
  Atkins concrete, 245
Trout, Brook, *see Salvelinus fontinalis*
  Brown, *Salmo trutta*
  cutthroat, *see Salmo clarki*
  Dolly Varden, *see Salvelinus malma*
  rainbow, *see Salmo gairdneri*
  red-fleshed, 265
  sea, *see Salmo trutta*
  sea-run, 265, 271, 277
  steelhead, *see Salmo gairdneri*
  Vistula Sea-, 177
Tsarist Government, 70
Tulalip Ponds, 338
Tuna viscera, 40
Turbidity, 165
Turbines, 114, 169
Turbot, 40
Turbulence, 374
Turf, artificial, 172

ÚLTIMA ESPERANZA, 265, 274
Umba, 245
Union Carbide Corporation, 268
United Nations Development Programme, 270
United States, *see* U.S.A.
University
  Oregon State, 52, 55, 61
  of Washington, 37, 38, 43, 328, 343
  of Wisconsin, 1
Uraguba, 245
Uragubinsky Gulf, 254
Urbanisation, 70
Ursus arctos, 251
Uruguay, 270-271
U.S.A., 7, 9, 16, 153, 264, 286, 301, 305, 385, 386, 387, 388-390, 392, 399
  Agency for International Development, 270
  Bureau of Sport Fisheries, 40

U.S.A. *(cont.)*
  Congress, 17
  Federal Government, 30, 41, 48, 389
  Fish Commission, 16, 17
  Fish and Wildlife Service, 41
U.S.S.R, 6, 7, 16, 18-20, 63-87, 157, 160, 162, 163, 164, 166, 167, 168, 169, 177, 181, 301, 385, 387, 392, 395, 401, 402
Ushuaia, 269

VACCINATION, 354, 355, 356, 358
Vaccines, 198, 352
Valley, Saint John River, 112
Valparaíso, 265
Value, economic, 26, 32, 47-48, 92, 107, 178, 180, 215, 216, 288, 300, 301, 393
Valves, flapper, 352
Vancouver Island, 306, 325, 340, 342, 373
Variability
  genetic, 25
  intrapopulational, 76
  phenotypic, 73
Variability tendency, 82
Variation
  genetic, 170, 241
  morphological, 159
Variety, 83
  maintenance of, 80
Vascular system, 73
Vessels, fishing, 167
Veterinary Research Station, 177
Viability
  commercial, 188, 197, 302
  of smolts, 188, 193, 194-195, 197, 198
Vibert boxes, 271
Vibrio anguillarum, 352
Vistula Sea-trout, *see* Trout, Vistula sea-
Visual range, 203

Vitamins, 40, 101, 176
  B_{12}, 40
  E, 40

WALES, 199, 201
War
  First World, 166
  Second World, 166, 201
Warm-up, rate of, 135
Washington coast, 30, 40, 329, 330, 332, 333, 334, 335, 338, 339, 348, 355, 356
Washington, State of, 29-45, 50, 54, 266, 325, 326, 328, 329, 332, 335, 336, 352, 389, 392, 400
  Department of Fisheries (WDF), 31, 32, 33, 34, 35, 38, 39, 40, 427, 328, 329, 330, 333, 334, 337, 338, 339, 342, 343, 344, 346, 347, 348, 352, 354, 355, 356, 359, 361, 363, 389
  Department of Game (WDG), 31, 38, 349
Wastes
  assimilation of, 372
  organic, 371, 376, 377, 378, 380
  water, 97, 388
Water
  abstraction, 285, 287, 290-293
  Arctic, 135, 137, 142
  Atlantic, 135, 137
  balance, 398
  brackish, 127
  chemistry, 151, 152, 154, 168, 378
  column, 201
  contamination, 97
  deep well, 55
  depth, 174, 207, 217, 379
  diversion of, 201
  estuarine, 94
  exchange, 352, 375
  flow, 68, 96, 101, 126, 165, 174, 203, 205, 217, 218, 250, 288, 293, 297, 374, 375, 376, 380

ground, 72, 116, 257, 306, 379, 380
hot, 55
hypolimnetic, 116
Japanese, 91
lake, 379
level, 86, 379
near-shore, 56, 57, 94
organic content, 168
permeation, 101
quality, 177, 188, 189, 266, 272
quantity, 72, 96, 131, 297, 372
range of velocities, 372
silt-free, 72
source, 379
spring, 55, 68, 72, 101, 266, 297, 298
static, 207
surface, 72, 101, 116, 306, 379, 380
temperature of, 70, 101, 177, 220, 252, 266, 269, 275
transparent, 256
treatment of, 35
usage, 296
velocity, 135, 202, 205, 250, 372, 375, 379, 381
warmed, 43, 45, 55, 122, 172, 192, 205
well, 359
Water Authorities, Regional, 201
Water mites, *see* Hydracarina
Water quality, management of, 20, 35, 117
Water source, hatchery, 25
Water supply, 116, 188, 205, 257, 359
gravity fed, 72
mixed, 72, 257, 306
subsurface, 257
surface, 257
Weight
body, 64, 73, 79, 106, 122, 150, 160, 170, 190, 196, 197, 253, 255, 286, 308, 344, 350, 363, 376

increase, 2, 200
without viscera, 82
Weirs, 162, 191, 380, 386
bank, 162
brush, 30
Wells, 116
Western civilisation, 261
Weyerhaeuser Corporation, 154
Wheat germ, 40
Wheels, fish, 100
Whidbey Island, 344
Whitebait, New Zealand, 293
Whitefish, *see Coregonus* spp.
White Sea, 245, 248, 249, 250, 253, 254, 257, 258, 401
Wholesaling, 48
Winter flounder, *see Pseudopleuronectes americanus*
Wintering areas, 67

YAMAL PENINSULA, 250
Yearlings, 39, 177
Yeast, 176
Yield, 1, 6, 162, 166, 195, 197, 305, 322, 323
maximum sustainable, 399
Yolk, 52, 73, 101, 201
Yolk-sac, 64, 101, 246, 255, 267, 268

ZONES
economic, 178, 399
exclusive fishing, 386
fishery conservation, 386
GDR Fishing, 179
Polish fishing, 179
protection, 168
Swedish fishing, 167, 177, 179
U.S.S.R. fishing, 179
200-mile, 63, 83, 142, 399
Zoning, 7
Zooplankton, 253, 265, 272, 274
availability, 398